Stars *and* Ribbons

Stars *and* Ribbons

Winter Wassailing in Wales

RHIANNON IFANS

UNIVERSITY OF WALES PRESS

2022

www.uwp.co.uk

British Library CIP Data
A catalogue record for this book is available from the British Library
ISBN   978-1-78683-824-7
eISBN   978-1-78683-825-4

Published with the financial support of Cymdeithas Alawon Gwerin Cymru/Welsh Folk-Song Society.

Designed and typeset by Chris Bell, cbdesign
Printed by the CPI Antony Rowe, Melksham, United Kingdom

$\mathcal{A}$cknowledgements

I TOOK AN INTEREST in Welsh wassail songs for the first time during my years as a teenager in Anglesey. Later, I embarked on a PhD thesis on this subject at Aberystwyth University under the supervision of the late Dr John Rowlands, for whose friendship and guidance I am deeply grateful. I also wish to thank D. Roy Saer, who was an Assistant Keeper at St Fagans National Museum of History (St Fagans Museum of Folk Life, as it was then known) for acting as Joint Supervisor. I am deeply indebted to Roy for his friendship over many decades, and for sharing with me much relevant material that he had collected on his travels around Wales, including the tune 'Deffiwch! Benteulu' published here.

I am grateful too for the assistance of the following family members and friends while I was preparing this volume: Dafydd Ifans for his help in procuring images, and in particular for compiling the General Index; Dr Rhidian Griffiths for many valued comments and for assistance regarding the music; Ric Lloyd of Cleftec for the preparation of the music for publication; Olwen Fowler for a magnificent cover design, yet again; and Dr Allan James, Professor Christine James and Professor E. Wyn James for important suggestions and advice. I am also deeply indebted to the following: the staff of the National Library of Wales; the staff of St Fagans National Museum of History (Cardiff); the staff of Ceredigion Library (Aberystwyth); Teresa Davies, North

East Wales Archives (Hawarden); Andrew Hawke, Managing Editor of *Geiriadur Prifysgol Cymru*, the University of Wales Dictionary of the Welsh Language; Elen Wyn Simpson, Archives and Special Collections Manager, Bangor University; Simon Golding (Treorchy Library) and Hywel W. Matthews (Aberdare Library), Reference and Local History Librarians, Rhondda Cynon Taf County Library Services. Thanks too to Bill Bradshaw, Isobel Brown, Anna Burnside (Bonhams) and Charles Goring. I am very grateful to the staff of the University of Wales Press for their unstinting support throughout the publishing process. I am particularly indebted to the Welsh Folk-Song Society for their generous financial assistance in the production of this book.

I dedicate this book to my mother and to
the cherished memory of my late father.

Contents

Acknowledgements   v

List of illustrations   xi

List of abbreviations   xiii

An Introduction to *Winter Wassailing in Wales*   1

Christmas Wassailing   15

Wassailing at the New Year   45

Hunting the Wren   77

Stars and Ribbons: The Mari Lwyd Ritual   105

Gŵyl Fair y Canhwyllau (Candlemas)   143

Tunes   173

    Beth sy mor feinion?   173

    Calennig (1)   173

    Calennig (2)   174

    Cân Hela'r Dryw   174

    Cân y Dryw   174

    Cân y Fari Lwyd   175

Cerdd Dydd Calan 175

Consêt Prince Rupert *or* Prince Rupert's Conceit 175

The Cutty Wren 176

Cyfri'r Geifr (1) 176

Cyfri'r Geifr (2) 177

Y cyntaf dydd o'r Gwyliau *or* The first day
of Christmas 177

Deffrwch! Benteulu 178

Dibyn a Dobyn 178

Y Fedle Fawr 179

Ffarwel Gwŷr Aberffraw 179

Hyd yma bu'n cerdded 179

Joan's Placket 180

Leave Land *or* Gadael Tir 180

May Day 180

Y Mochyn Du 181

Peg O'Ramsey 181

Pilgrim 181

Sosban Fach 182

Susannah 182

Tri Thrawiad Gwynedd 183

Y Washael (Wel, dyma enw'r feinwen) 183

Ymdaith Gwŷr Harlech *or* The March of the
Men of Harlech 183

Winter Wassailing Songs and Poems	185
Christmas Wassail Songs	186
New Year Wassail Songs	222
Wren Hunt Wassail Songs	252
Mari Lwyd Wassail Songs	264
Gŵyl Fair Wassail Songs	304
Appendix: Verse Forms	341
Bibliography	347
Indexes	367
Index to first lines	367
Index to poets	369
Index to tunes	369
General index	371

$\mathcal{L}$ist of illustrations

Figure 1: Wassailing the apple trees at the Gaymers wassail in Stewley Orchard, central Somerset, 2010/2011: the new wassail queen drinks a draught of cider; a piece of toast dipped in cider hangs in the tree in the background; image © Bill Bradshaw.

Figure 2: A rare Ewenny wassail bowl and cover, dated 1832–3; image courtesy of Bonhams.

Figure 3: Ewenny wassail bowl cover, dated 1832; image courtesy of Bonhams.

Figure 4: Ewenny wassail bowl inscribed 'William James Tonyrevil January 12th 1832'; image courtesy of Bonhams.

Figure 5: Two boys holding a *rhodd galennig*, Llangynwyd *c.*1905; image © National Museum of Wales.

Figure 6: Children singing and collecting *Calennig* (New Year's gifts) in Cwm Gwaun, January 1961; pictured (left to right) are Rita Davies, Ionwy Thomas, Ifor Davies (almost out of sight), Sally Vaughan, Menna James, Eirian Vaughan (Sally's sister), John Morris, and Gwyn Davies (Ifor's brother). The photograph was taken by Geoff Charles (1909–2002) for the Welsh-language newspaper *Y Cymro* outside Tŷ Bach, Cwm Gwaun, where Ionwy Thome's (née Thomas) grandfather lived; image © National Library of Wales.

Figure 7: The Bidder's visit; image © National Library of Wales.

Figure 8: Two examples of 'Halsing y Dryw' (The wren carol) from 'Melus geingciau Deheubarth Cymru', f. 27ᵛ; image © National Library of Wales.

Figure 9: Wren-house, Marloes, Pembrokeshire; image © National Museum of Wales.

Figure 10: Mari Lwyd and Sianco'r Castell, Llangynwyd; image © National Museum of Wales.

Figure 11: Mari Lwyd, Llangynwyd, *c.*1910–14; image © National Library of Wales.

Figure 12: Sharper, the Swansea Mari Lwyd; image courtesy of Isobel Brown.

Figure 13: A cut by J. Blight (possibly J. Slight) from a drawing by Talbot Bury of a cup owned by the antiquary Angharad Llwyd; image *Archaeologia Cambrensis* (1872).

$\mathcal{L}$ist of abbreviations

Bangor Arch. Selden   Manuscript held at the Bodleian Library, Oxford.

AWC   Amgueddfa Werin Cymru/St Fagans National Museum of History (Cardiff).

Bangor   Manuscript held in Archives and Special Collections, Bangor University, Bangor.

BL Add   Additional manuscript, held at the British Library, London.

Bodley Welsh   Manuscript held at the Bodleian Library, Oxford.

Cardiff   The Cardiff Central Library Manuscripts, Cardiff.

Cwrtmawr   The Cwrtmawr Manuscripts collection, held at the National Library of Wales, Aberystwyth.

Jesus   Jesus College MSS held in the Bodleian Library, Oxford.

Llanstephan   The Llanstephan Manuscripts collection, held at the National Library of Wales, Aberystwyth.

Mostyn   The Mostyn Manuscripts collection, held at the National Library of Wales, Aberystwyth.

NLW   The National Library of Wales Manuscripts collection, held at the National Library of Wales, Aberystwyth.

Peniarth   The Peniarth Manuscripts collection, held at the National Library of Wales, Aberystwyth.

J. Lloyd Williams Papers   Dr J. Lloyd Williams Music MSS and Papers, held at the National Library of Wales, Aberystwyth.

*A*n Introduction to
Winter Wassailing in Wales

WASSAIL SONGS are part of Welsh folk culture, but what exactly are they? When are they sung? Why? Where do stars and pretty ribbons fit in? This study addresses these questions, identifying and discussing the various forms of winter wassailing found in Wales in times past and present. It focuses specifically on the Welsh poetry written over the centuries at the celebration of several rituals held most particularly at Christmas, the turn of the year and Twelfth Night. This poetry served a distinct purpose, aspiring to improve the quality of the earth's fertility in three particular spheres: the productivity of the land, the animal kingdom and the human race.

The Welsh *gwasael* is a cognate of the English word *wassail*, from the Anglo-Saxon greeting *Wæs þu hæl*, meaning 'be thou hale' or in good health. In his *Historia Regum Britanniae*, an account of the history of the kings of Britain written between 1135 and 1139 (much of it fictional), Geoffrey of Monmouth (*c*.1100–*c*.1154) describes how Rhonwen (Rowena) the daughter of Hengist knelt before the king, Gwrtheyrn (Vortigern) and presented him with a cup of wine saying 'Lauerd king wæs hæil', the Middle English greeting from the Old Norse *ves heill*.[1] Gwrtheyrn responded with the words 'Drinc hæl' meaning 'drink and be healthy'. Geoffrey's Latin text was translated into Welsh as 'Brut y Brenhinedd' (History of the Kings):

A gwedy daruot udunt vwyta o vrenhinawl anregyon. nachaf y
uorwyn yndyuot or ystauell a gorulwch eur yny llaw yn llawn
owin. Ac yndyuot hyt rac bron y brenhin. A gwedy adoli idaw
ar dal y deulin adywedut wrthaw val hyn Lofyrt kig wassail. A
phan welas y brenhin pryt y uorwyn. Anryfedu aoruc yn uawr
ytheckct. ac yny lle ymlenwi oe charyat. Agofyn yr ieithyd beth
a ddywedassei y vorwyn. A phy beth adylyei ynteu y dywedut
yn atteb idi hitheu. Ac yna y dywawt yieithyd wrthaw. Arg-
lwyd heb ef hi athelwis di yn arglwyd ac yn urenhin yny ieith
hi. Ac uelly ythanrydedwys. Yr hyn adyly ditheu y wrtheb idi
yw hyn. Sef yw hynny drinc heil. Ac yna y dywawt gwrtheyrn
wrthi drinc heil. Ac erchi yr uorwyn yfet y gwin. Ac yr hyny
hyt hediw ymae y deuot honno wedy hynny ymplith y kyfed-
achwyr ynynys prydein.[2]

[After he had been refreshed by a royal banquet, the girl came
out of her chamber, carrying a golden goblet full of wine. Going
up to the king, she curtseyed and said: 'Lauerd king, wassail.'

At the sight of the girl's face he was amazed by her beauty
and inflamed with desire. He asked his interpreter what the girl
had said and what he should reply. He answered: 'She called
you lord king and honoured you with a word of greeting. You
should reply "drincheil."'

Then Vortigern, giving the reply 'drincheil', told the girl
to drink, took the goblet from her hand with a kiss and drank.
From that day forward it has been the custom in Britain that at
feasts a drinker says to his neighbour 'wasseil' and the one who
receives the drink after him replies 'drincheil'.][3]

Two modes of wassailing prevailed, the wassailing of trees and
the wassailing of homes, both observed in Wales at some point,
although the latter was much more popularly participated in, more
records of it have survived, and more examples of the ritual have
remained to this day. The wassailing of apple trees – a sacred tree,
its fruit symbolising health and sexuality – was observed in Wales
at Christmastide and at the welcoming in of the New Year, a ritual
also practised (perhaps more widely) in England during the early
nineteenth century in areas such as Somerset, Sussex and the West
Country, to induce bountiful crops.[4] Even today wassailers encircle

the apple trees, pour cider over their roots, the new queen drinks a draught of cider, and toasted bread soaked in cider is placed in the tree branches (see figure 1) before they sing their wassail song and fire shotguns into the bare boughs, shouting and banging trays and drums to frighten away evil spirits.

In Wales the more popular custom was that a large drinking cup referred to as a wassail bowl be escorted from house to house and passed from hand to hand for all to drink from. The accompanying greeting was just as important as the drink. Householders were greeted in song or verse, the constant emphasis being laid firmly on requesting a blessing on people and homes, on nurturing strong children, and on the increase in quality and quantity of animals and crops.

The earliest wassail bowl held by the National Museum of History in St Fagans, Cardiff, is made of *lignum vitae*, Latin for the 'wood of life', the tree's resin used at one time to treat numerous medical conditions. Made of hard, durable wood this bowl is less decorative than the three Ewenny[5] pieces also held at the Museum, and it might possibly represent 'the traditional wooden vessel taken around during the wassailing season',[6] as one Gower wassail song notes that 'Our bowl it is made of an elbury bough.'[7] Most wassail bowls used in Glamorgan, however, were made in the pottery at Ewenny, near Bridgend.[8] Extant examples bear dates in the range 1825–41. Iorwerth C. Peate (1901–82), in 1948 appointed Keeper-in-Charge (later Curator) of the new Folk Museum created in the grounds of St Fagans Castle, provides a detailed description in his study from 1935 of one of the three Ewenny bowls held in the Museum:

> It is 21.5 cms. in height (42.0 cms. with the lid); diameter at lip 26.5 cms. The bowl is of reddish earthenware covered with white slip and glazed. It had originally eighteen loop handles, three of which have been broken off. The bowl is decorated with scratch decoration, zig-zags and circles on the handles, zig-zags, leaf-designs, circles and intersecting circles on the bowl itself.[9]

The bowl is inscribed 'Thomas Arthyr/De ber 30 Maker 1834'. This is followed by an *englyn*, a quatrain composed (not altogether successfully) in the Welsh strict metre by a person who wished to depict the maker Thomas Arthyr as a diligent worker of great renown, one who used the best clay for his bowls to produce blemish-free vessels. Peate describes the bowl's lid as being of still greater interest than the bowl itself:

> The flat top is inscribed *Spring* and *Langan* (*i.e.*, Llangan, Glamorgan). From this a figure, obviously that of Spring, has been broken off. The lid originally had a series of nine rows of loops, three loops in each row. Many of these have now been broken off. On each and in between each loop, as well as in between each row of loops, the potter placed a variety of figures: oakleaves with human faces at their base, berries, birds of various descriptions, dogs and other animals, with two human figures, the less mutilated of which has its arms outstretched over the flat top on which was placed the figure of Spring. All these figures, representative of the life of the countryside, are shown groping towards the central and dominating figure of Spring surmounting the bowl.

St Fagans's other two examples of Ewenny ware also have looped handles and decorative lids with motifs such as birds and berries. Trefor Owen suggests it seems likely that the Ewenny wassail bowls incorporate 'ornamental features which had earlier been separately displayed in the *perllan*'[10] (orchard), a decorated object probably used to wassail apple trees.[11]

A closely related example of a wassail bowl (see figures 2–4) was sold at Bonhams on 9 October 2010 and sold by Bonhams for the second time on 31 January 2019. The catalogue description reads as follows:

> A RARE EWENNY WASSAIL BOWL AND COVER, DATED 1832–33 Glazed in yellow over a white slip and with sgraffito decoration, the eighteen plain strap handles with zig-zags and circles, a border of interlocking circles below the rim, a leafy stem and the inscription 'WIM Clay pits/1833' below the handles, the high domed cover with a figure of a man kneeling before a round table surrounded by birds and two foxes, one with a mouse in its mouth, inscribed 'William/James/Tonyrevil/Jany 12th/1832', *39cm high*

In a description of the wassail bowl's function, it is noted that groups of celebrants would carry the bowl from house to house and that the communal nature of the custom 'is emphasized by the multiple handles which may have been entwined with decorative ribbons'. It is also noted that the bowls may have been made for parish use 'so that the inscription refers to the donor of the bowl rather than the owner'. In the 1820s a potter at Claypits, William Williams, made wassail bowls for other parishes at a cost of one guinea each.[12]

The origins of wassailing customs have long been debated. Life's hardships induced people to find ways of persuading the earth to bear fruit, animals to breed, and women to be with child. Those who lived under the harshest conditions devised the most customs to aid the increase of their raw materials. During the Palaeolithic Period animal husbandry was imperfectly understood, and hunting for food was the order of the day. Life was fragile and the food supply uncertain and intermittent. Seemingly supernatural techniques were adopted to ensure the increase and continuation of the hunt. Palaeolithic artwork in Lascaux, France, depicts animals such as bison, aurochs and mammoth painted on cave walls. These are enormous, strikingly beautiful images. Similarly decorated caves have been discovered worldwide, the latest in Croatia in April 2019. It is believed that ritual dances were performed before these images, to musical accompaniment and possibly with the aid of songs.

The magico-religious interpretation of this beautiful cave art is that the images were there to magically attract the animals depicted, so that the prey would be drawn towards the hunters and fall easily into their nets. Dancers made themselves as similar as possible to the animal to be communicated with, in appearance and movement, for example wearing deerskin and horns to increase the number of deer to be hunted, and imitating the animal's movements. The ritualist would effectively lose his own identity and become the animal he represented. Having hunted and caught a good catch, it was believed that it was the detailed dramatisation of events that caused that success, and if such a system was successful one year it would be foolish to discontinue the pattern.

Following the invention of the plough it was recognised that there were two opposite poles to the creative, fertile energy, one female-receptive, the other male-originative. The most detailed description of ritual ploughing comes from the *Iliad*, in the description of Achilles' shield. The term *Τρίπολος* used to describe the shield, usually translated 'thrice-ploughed' or a synonym, would be more correctly rendered 'triple-furrowed'.[13] The number *three* symbolises sanctity, perfection, or the whole. It is highly likely that the scene on the shield, in which three sacred furrows are opened by the ruler or his deputy, represents ritual ploughing, and he is depicted on the shield supervising the work, thereby performing his function of promoting the fertilisation of the land.[14] It is likely that the Plough Monday rituals[15] observed at places such as Haxey (in north Lincolnshire) and Maldon (in Essex), where wassailers form a procession and take a plough from house to house performing rituals relating to amplitude and to sacrifice, correspond to the earlier Dionysian practices in Greece.

In his study of various aspects of the life of Native Americans living in the neighbourhood of the rivers Issá and Japurá in South America, T. W. Whiffen records that it is through dance that they approached the gods. He focuses on a specific dance performed for securing a supply of manioc, a woody, nutty-flavoured shrub native to South America from which cassava flour and tapioca are prepared. Women are the agriculturalists, and it is they who plant the manioc slips. At the Boro Manioc-gathering Dance the men 'form up into an outer circle, the women in the centre or behind the men of their choice, dancing with steps complementary to, and not identical with'[16] those of the men. The Chief opens with a question:

> I am old and weak and my belly craves food,
> Who has sown the *pika* [manioc slips] in the *emiye* [plantation]?

His wife answers:

> I have sown the *pika*, long, long ago;
> The *maika* [manioc] is sown with young shoots.

A chorus of women repeat the answer in the plural. The Chief then asks, following the same introductory line, 'Who has cut the *pika* in the *emiye*?' and is answered in like manner. The song continues until the whole process of growing manioc is described, 'and the meaning will gradually shift from the birth and growth of the plant to the birth of a human being'. The song will only be concluded when the Chief pronounces:

Imine [it is good], *imine,*
The women are good women,
Imine.

The Celtic new year began on the first day of November. At this transitional stage between one year and the next it was believed that the spirits of the dead roamed freely. To keep them at bay, bonfires were lit and noises made to safeguard the community from evil influences. In Wales it was Hwch Ddu Gwta, the spirit of a tail-less black sow who roamed north Wales at Halloween, and 'Ladi Wen heb ddim pen' (the headless White Lady) equally feared in south Wales, who posed the greatest threat. After All Hallows' Eve the most portentous period of the year was midwinter on 21 December. This date denoted the zenith of the powers of darkness and the lowest ebb of summer. The most popular custom observed at this time was the celebration of the Saturnalia, held originally on 17 December but later lasting over a period of seven days around the winter solstice on 21 December, the birth date of the Invincible Sun, the *Dies Natalis Invicti Solis*. The name is associated by many with King Saturnus, who was believed to have had a Golden Age of rule over Latium, and who first introduced the country to agricultural techniques; others doubt the efficacy of these methods of cultivation, and the very existence of Saturnus.

At the Saturnalia lamps were lit to protect humanity from evil spirits, schools were closed, prisoners were pardoned, and masters ate with their servants to represent the harmony of the country during the alleged reign of Saturnus. However, 'his altars are said to have been stained with the blood of human victims.'[17] A mock king was appointed to govern the kingdom over the short period of the Saturnalia. He was then sacrificed at the close of his reign as a symbol that a good ruler had given his life for the prosperity and reawakening of nature. Reviving and reinvigorating the sterile earth often meant a sacrificial ritual. It was so indispensably important among the Khonds in Bengal that it was only with the arrival of the British government there around the second quarter of the eighteenth century that the practice was stopped. The sacrifices were considered necessary in the cultivation of turmeric, 'the Khonds arguing that the turmeric could not have a deep red colour without the shedding of blood'.[18]

In due course the Church arranged for the celebration of the Christian Christmas to coincide with the Saturnalia, on the principle that it was easier to change the meaning of the Saturnalia than to delete it from the calendar. The Church pressed down hard on some of the early beliefs and practices even to the point of their destruction, but wherever possible adapted established traditions to conform to Christian ends.

Five occasions provided opportunities for singing winter wassail songs in Wales: Christmas itself, the New Year, the Mari Lwyd ritual, the Wren Hunt, and Candlemas on 2 February, since Christmastide in its greater sense extends until this feast day commemorating the presentation of Jesus Christ at the Temple and the Purification of the Blessed Virgin Mary.

Outside the winter period there would be wassailing again on May Day, the first day of the summer season and the beginning of the second half of the year, an opportune time to renew contact with nature. The chief attractions of May Day were the setting up of the maypole and the singing of May carols. Wassailers sang of the hardships of winter, and of their joy that the season of abundance had finally arrived. Carols often proclaimed that lovers felt revived in May after the coldness of winter; they were urged to be warm-hearted towards each other in the warmth of the summer sun. Since there is such a close connection between men and women and the earth on which they live, it was a commonly held belief that engaging in carnal love would encourage the earth's growth. May Eve, more than any other night, was the most suitable for love.

Much can be learned from May carols regarding the political and social climate of the day. War was one of the main influences on the poems. During years of strife, strength and wisdom were required of the king to lead his country, soldiers were encouraged to be valiant, and those left behind were comforted with the knowledge that God would uphold them. Having given thanks to God for his goodness in providing sustenance for humankind, prayers were offered for the Anglican Church and for the monarchy. Every king was honoured and upheld as a symbol of the country: if one prospered, so did the other. Before taking leave, it was essential to confer blessings upon the house and its occupants, goods, livestock, crops and garden produce. In exchange for good wishes, a generous gift was accepted.

In many of the southern counties of Wales wassailers also appeared at weddings[19] to gain access to a house when a woman was about to marry. Her fiancé (or his representatives) would have to gain his way into her home on the morning of the proposed marriage to claim his bride and take her to church to be married. Access was only allowed by winning the *pwnco*, a question-and-answer ritual in verse, the bridal party reciting rather than singing their stanzas.[20] A company of the bridegroom's friends would dispute from outside the door with the bride's father (who waited inside the house) for his daughter's hand. Only once the bridegroom's worth and that he was fully able to maintain a wife were proved, was she allowed to go to church to be married. Various tests of mettle appear throughout the world. A. H. Krappe notes that the indigenous Amerindian people living in Venezuela's Orinoco Delta region demanded a special standard of behaviour and strength before giving permission for their men to take a wife. The test placed on them was to lie completely still for a day or two in a sack full of fire ants.[21] In Russian folklore, once the wedding had been held, the bed for the newly married couple was often made in the cattle shed 'in the belief that the first sexual act of the young woman would exert a magical influence on the fertility of the cattle'.[22]

Both May Day wassailing and wassailing at weddings fall outside the scope of this study of winter wassailing in Wales, which discusses the five winter wassailing occasions in turn. It provides selected Welsh wassail songs and stanzas in modern Welsh orthography, a translation of those pieces into English, with musical notation, and provides a comprehensive analysis of the poems and of the society in which they were sung.

Christmas

Wassail songs sung at Christmas were published under various titles, principally *carol tan bared* (a carol [to be sung] beneath the wall), *carol gwirod* (a wassail song/a drinking song) and *carol yn drws* (a carol [to be sung] at the door). Several wassail song subtypes are discussed here, including the carol requesting entrance into a home (which might discuss the world's fall from grace and might offer some philosophical commentary), the householder's reply, the *pwnco* (the contest in song to gain access to the home), cumulative songs, riddle songs and the farewell carol that often revelled in the abundance of '[g]waed Bregyn fab Heidden' (the blood of Ale son of Barley) better known as John Barleycorn, a personification of the malt liquor provided during the evening's festivities.

The New Year

Going about the neighbourhood at the New Year distributing kind wishes and collecting monetary gifts in exchange was a lucrative business. With their golden knives, the ancient Druids collected mistletoe twigs in forests devoted to the gods and distributed them as gifts on New Year's Day to resurrect and strengthen the powers of nature following the death of the old year and the birth of the new. The calends were celebrated by the kings of England and by other eminent community leaders. King Henry III, 'shamelessly exceeding the limits of royal authority', *demanded* gifts from the upper echelons of London society in 1249.[23] During the eighteenth century in Wales, the New Year was regarded by some as an opportunity to sing religious carols similar to those sung at Christmas; a carol composed by Jonathan Hughes of Llangollen speaks of the sinner's need to submit to Christ's authority. There were two dates of celebration, attributable to the two different calendars in use in Europe for a number of years. As the purpose of the custom became less familiar it eventually deteriorated into child's play, but still retains a cherished place in many Welsh communities.

Hunting the Wren

Discussed in a Welsh context, the tradition of Hunting the Wren was thought to be confined to Pembrokeshire in south-west Wales, since it is there that the fullest records of this tradition have been kept. Remnants of the practice, however, have survived in north Wales, and instances of wren hunt songs from Llanrhaeadr-ym-Mochnant (north Powys), Denbigh, Amlwch (Anglesey), Llŷn, and Llwyngwril (a coastal village south of Dolgellau in Gwynedd) were noted by Lewis Davies Jones 'Llew Tegid' (1851–1928).[24] The custom was observed in two parts: the hunt, and the procession around the parish. A captured wren was placed in a wren-house or bier decorated with colourful ribbons, and carried around the neighbourhood. The wren was hunted because of its sovereignty over the other birds, and on the understanding that the sacrifice of a king would secure fertility. Examples abound throughout the world of sacrificing someone or something considered sacred as a means of redress on the one hand and of reinvigorating creation on the other.

Mari Lwyd

Of all the Welsh wassailing practices, the Mari Lwyd mask custom probably creates the most splendid spectacle. The three earliest animal masks were those of the deer, the horse and the calf. As far back as the fourth century, St Augustine decreed: 'Si adhuc agnoscatis aliquos illam sordissimam turpitudinem de hinnicula vel cervula exercere, ita durissime castigate' (if you ever hear of anyone pursuing that extremely filthy practice of dressing like a horse or deer, punish him most severely). The custom entails the use of a horse's skull placed on a pole and covered in a white sheet. Adorned with knots of pretty ribbons, Mari would be taken on her journey around the parish to bless the householders. The period 1850–1920 was the liveliest period for Mari, and there was a close connection between the south Wales mining areas and Mari Lwyd. In her study of the Sword Dance, Violet Alford identifies a similarity and connection between the hilt-and-point European Sword Dance and areas rich in minerals and having historical and prehistoric mines.[25]

Candlemas

Throughout the Middle Ages, Mary the mother of Jesus was highly venerated in Wales. Many holidays were consecrated in Mary's honour, among them *Gŵyl Fair y Canhwyllau* or Candlemas on 2 February. In addition to the praise poetry sung in her honour a number of wassail carols were also sung on this day. The fullest extant manuscript of Candlemas songs belongs to Anglesey, in the form of a collection of poems in the hand of Richard Morris (1703–79).[26] Conundrums and puzzles formed part of the rite to enter the house. Once inside, the wassailers carried a lighted wassail bowl around a chair where a young child representing Mary sat; the 'chair carol' was sung while the wassail bowl was handed around. This celebration was held at the beginning of spring when nature's forces were thought to require support. It possibly evolved from an ancient rite to welcome the spring, but was latterly linked to one of the Church's festivals to make it more acceptable: instead of drinking to spring the revellers drink to the Virgin.

Today only a small number of wassailing rituals are known to the public, and a still decreasing number of people observe them. Some of these customs have disappeared altogether, others have not survived their original purpose and are now regarded as children's games. Mari Lwyd, however, continues to roam some Welsh streets and valleys, her merriment and vitality still loved and treasured.

Notes

1. *Oxford English Dictionary*, available online at: *https://www.oed.com/ view/Entry/226012?rskey=IVlTrh&result=1&isAdvanced=false#eid* (accessed 7 November 2020).
2. John Rhŷs and J. Gwenogvryn Evans (eds), *The Text of the Bruts from the Red Book of Hergest* (Oxford: J. G. Evans, 1890), 135.11–27.
3. Loosely translated in Michael D. Reeve (ed.), Neil Wright (trans.), *The History of the Kings of Britain: An Edition and Translation of* De gestis Britonum [Historia regum Britanniae]/*Geoffrey of Monmouth* (Woodbridge: The Boydell Press, 2007), p. 128.
4. See further A. R. Wright and T. E. Lones, *British Calendar Customs: England* (London: W. Glaisher for The Folk-Lore Society, 1936–40), pp. 235–7; K. Palmer and R. W. Patten, 'Some Notes on Wassailing and Ashen Faggots in South and West Somerset', *Folklore*, 82 (1971), 281–91.
5. J. M. Lewis, *The Ewenny Potteries* (Cardiff: National Museum of Wales, 1982); Ann Gruffydd Rhys, 'Gwell crefft na golud: Caitlin Jenkins a phridd-lestri Ewenni' [Better a craft than riches: Caitlin Jenkins and Ewenny pottery], *Barn* [Opinion] (July/August 2012), 66–8; Gwyneth Evans and Ieuan R. Evans, *Ewenny – Potteries, Potters and Pots* (Abertillery: Old Bakehouse Publications, 2001); John Cockell and Ann Holmes, *Ewenny Pottery: The Cockell collection* (no imprint, 2007).
6. Trefor M. Owen, *Welsh Folk Customs* (Cardiff: National Museum of Wales/Welsh Folk Museum, 1974), p. 61.
7. J. D. Davies, *A History of West Gower, Glamorganshire*, 2 (Swansea: H. W. Williams at 'The Cambrian' office, 1879), p. 87; elder wood is particularly suitable for whittling and carving.

8.   Iorwerth C. Peate, 'A Welsh Wassail-Bowl: with a Note on the Mari Lwyd', *Man*, 35 (1935), 82.
9.   Peate, 'A Welsh Wassail-Bowl: with a Note on the Mari Lwyd', 82.
10. Owen, *Welsh Folk Customs*, p. 61.
11. See the chapter entitled 'Wassailing at the New Year'.
12. Lewis, *The Ewenny Potteries*, p. 73.
13. E. A. Armstrong, 'The Triple-Furrowed Field', *The Classical Review*, 57 (1943), 5.
14. Armstrong, 'The Triple-Furrowed Field', 4.
15. Thomas Davidson, 'Plough Rituals in England and Scotland', *The Agricultural History Review*, 7 (1959), 27–37.
16. T. W. Whiffen, 'A Short Account of the Indians of the Issá-Japurá District (South America)', *Folklore*, 24 (1913), 51–2.
17. J. G. Frazer, *The Golden Bough: A Study in Magic and Religion* (London: Macmillan and Co., 1922), p. 583.
18. Frazer, *The Golden Bough: A Study in Comparative Religion* (London: Macmillan and Co., 1890; Edinburgh: Canongate Books Ltd, 2004), pp. 330–1.
19. For the contests forming part of Welsh marriage traditions see T. Gwynn Jones, *Welsh Folklore and Folk-Customs* (London: Methuen & Co. Ltd., 1930), pp. 182–94.
20. Roy Saer, 'Canu at iws' ['Song for use'], in *'Canu at Iws' ac Ysgrifau Eraill* ['Song for use' and other articles] (Talybont: Cymdeithas Alawon Gwerin Cymru [Welsh Folk Song Society], 2013), p. 34.
21. Alexander Haggerty Krappe, *The Science of Folklore* (London: Methuen and Co., 1930), pp. 218–19. A 2015 film by Mario Crespo, the Cuban-Venezuelan film director, entitled *Dauna. Lo que lleva el río* (Gone with the River) spoken in the Warao language, tells the story of Dauna, a young indigenous woman who faced the ancestral practices of her culture and paid the price.
22. Y. M. Sokolov, *Russian Folklore*, translated by Catherine Ruth Smith (New York: Macmillan, 1950), p. 206.
23. Richard Vaughan (ed.), *The Illustrated Chronicles of Matthew Paris* (Stroud: Alan Sutton Publishing, 1993), p. 86.
24. [Lewis Davies Jones] Llew Tegid, 'Hunting the Wren', *Cylchgrawn Cymdeithas Alawon Gwerin Cymru/Journal of the Welsh Folk-Song Society*, 1 (1909–12), 106–8.
25. Violet Alford, *Sword Dance and Drama* (London: Merlin Press, 1962), p. 15.
26. BL Add MS 14992, copied and edited by T. H. Parry-Williams, *Llawysgrif Richard Morris o Gerddi* [Richard Morris's Manuscript of Poems] (Cardiff: University of Wales Press, 1931).

Christmas Wassailing

CHRISTMAS CAROLLING is observed worldwide. What would the Welsh Christmas be without its *plygain* carols? Each church held its own *plygain* service, initially on the *plygain* hour, the *pulli cantus*, at the crowing of the cockerel sometime between three and six o'clock in the morning. During this service of prayer, carols, possibly a short address and Holy Communion, parishioners professed their Christian faith and affirmed their allegiance to God.[1]

At Christmastide too, a second group of celebrants sang their own carols – wassail carols. Or was it the same company of people? It cannot be claimed that *plygain* singing gave rise to wassail singing or vice versa. There was, however, a tendency in Wales to Christianise wassail carols sung during the Christmas period. Extant religious wassail carols date from around the end of the seventeenth and beginning of the eighteenth century.[2]

Wassail songs appear under various titles, including *canu tan bared* (singing beneath the wall), *canu gwirod* (wassail songs or drinking songs), *canu yn drws* (singing at the door), *pricsiwn* (prick song), and in one instance the song title refers to the author's occupation: *Carol ysglater neu benillion gwirod* (The slater's carol or wassail stanzas). More than one type of song is associated with the wassailing customs observed over the Christmas season: the carol requesting entrance into a home, the householder's reply, the *pwnco*, cumulative songs, riddle songs, and the farewell carol.

Having assembled a company of men, the leader of the wassailers began the structured journey around the neighbourhood determined to gain admittance into as many houses as possible. To do so, wassailers entered into an exchange of verses with the householder in which challenges and insults were traded. The *pwnco* – the contest in song to gain access to the home – would continue until the established verses (together with some witty improvisations) came to an end and a victor was declared. The expression 'i ganu mesura' (to sing metres) indicates the potential complexity of the challenge the wassailers set the householder. Should the challengers sing their carol in more than one metre, the challenged should answer in those exact same metres.

> A chwithe y glân gantorion, dymunwn arnoch hyn,
> Gael carol o dri mesur on'd e na chanoch ddim,
> A'r rhain o'r un mesure ag ydyw 'ngharol i,
> Ac onid e gwllysiwn agoryd drws eich tŷ.³

> [And from you, honest singers, we wish this, | That you give us a carol on three metres, or else do not sing at all, | And these the same metres as my carol, | Otherwise we insist you open the door to your house.]

Early *pwnco* stanzas might discuss the world's fall from grace and might offer some philosophical commentary. Eighteenth-century carols are more secular and involve the community drinking from a shared wassail bowl carried from door to door in anticipation of the beer, food and female company that awaited them at various houses in the community, and to receive good luck wishes and blessings for the year ahead.

Wassailers faced many hindrances and obstructions as they made their way in the darkness, as John Edwards of Cae-môr explains in his 'Pricsiwn i'w ganu dan bared Wyliau Nadolig'⁴ (Pricksong to be sung beneath the wall at Christmastide), to the tune 'Cyntri Boncyn'⁵ ('Country Bumpkin') as mentioned in the final stanza, in which the poet also refers to himself by name. His first difficulty is an unfortunate encounter with the miller, followed by a lucky escape from hostile ghosts; he then falls into a pond, later into a dark pit, and again into a deep dingle where he almost loses his senses. From one calamity to the next he stumbles his way in the dark over the mountain and along the valley:

> Rholio a threiglo fel rhyw bren,
> Ael olwyn men, neu garreg wen,
> Weithie ar 'y nhin, weithie ar 'y mhen
> Ac weithie a'm llen yn ucha.

[Reeling and tumbling like a piece of wood, | A wheel of a cart, or a white stone, | Sometimes on my backside, sometimes standing on my head | And sometimes with my cloak uppermost.]

Geographically, his journey took him from his home in Cae-Môr towards Corwen (formerly in Merionethshire), onwards in the direction of Tir y Glyn, Tŷ yn y Bryn, Allt y Saint, on towards Llidiart Fawr, and finally to Nant y Fallog. He boasts that he cares little about the dangerous 'Wits o'r Sbaen' (Spanish Witch) or the spectres that bothered travellers in the area, but is faintly concerned that his last fall had resulted in a nosebleed. At this point he reaches his destination and requests admittance.

Should the wassailers arrive late at night and ask the householder for assistance in their distress, convention demanded that he should refuse. The travellers might emphasise their lengthy journey through wind and rain, ice and snow, along muddy tracks and mountainsides, and voice their expectation of being welcomed and provided for:

> Yr ŷm ni ymron rhynnu yn aros agori,
> Mwy gweddus na chanu oedd gweiddi ar ein gwedd;
> Mae'n hôl ni o'r eglura yn rolio yn yr eira,
> Mae rhan o bob lluchfa yn eich llechwedd.

> Ein dannedd sy'n clecio a'n gwynt ni ar ffaelio,
> Y tafod yn stytio, ar drigo rŷm ni.[6]

[Stanza 1: We are almost frozen to death as we wait for admittance, | It would be more fitting for us to bellow than to sing; | Our trail can be seen clearly, rolling in the snow, | Part of every buffeting [is to be seen] on your hillside.

Stanza 2: Our teeth are chattering and our breath is about to
fail, | Tongues stuttering, we are about to perish.]

To dispel any doubts, Siôn Prys (d. 1640), heir of Caerddinen and Llwyn
Ynn in the Vale of Clwyd (as if his status might reassure the prospective
host), guarantees that there are no more than six or seven in his party of
carollers and that they are good men, not in search of a drunken evening
of carousing but in search of good company and a quiet evening by the
fire with a jug of strong dark beer, 'y ddiod ddu'[7] (the black drink).

Many stanzas refer to specific foods requested of the host to
accompany the strong drink: 'bara can' (white bread), broth, bacon,
goat meat, brawn, 'adar gwylltion' (wild birds), mustard, and white
sugar are all requested of the householder in one anonymous carol
from Anglesey.[8] Another anonymous poet requests white bread,
boiled and roast meat, capon, geese, venison, pasties, followed by
custard, cracknel and cheese; and last of all he asks that a 'pitl pot
llydan' (a wide piddle pot) be filled to the brim and that not a drop
of it should be left over.[9] Tobacco is requested by one member of a
party of three (the first requests beer, the third wants to kiss a young
woman), but his plea is ridiculed by the other two members of his
party: they claim that if he were given a roll of rope tobacco he would
choke to death on it.[10] Yet another wassailer specifically seeks 'dau
afal melyn', the two yellow apples (open to interpretation) he knows
are kept in the maid's coffer; the said apples, he demands, should be
roasted and shared out 'yn dwymwyn'[11] (at white heat).

Hard times and high prices cause societal restlessness that leads
ultimately to jealousies and disturbances. To avoid such disharmony
the wassailers remind their potential benefactors of the peace and
generosity that characterised the lives of their forefathers:

Roedd hawddfyd dewisol yn nyddie'r hen bobol
Yn cyrredd pob maenol a mynydd;
C'redigrwydd yn wastad yn rasol ei riwliad,
A chariad a gluded i'n gwledydd.

A heddiw'n holl Fryden mae llid a chenfigen
Yn llenwi daearen dda iredd ei modd;
Na fyddwn yn unnedd yn hoffi'r un fuchedd,
Na barieth diburedd a'i parodd.[12]

[Stanza 1: In the days of our forefathers a pleasant prosperity | Extended to every vale and mountain; | There was a constant kindness that was gracious in its rulings, | And love was carried abroad in our lands.

Stanza 2: And in the whole of Britain today there is anger and jealousy | Filling the earth that is so verdant and goodly in its means; | Let us not be of the same mind, delighting in the same way of life, | Or in the corrupt wickedness that caused it.]

Wassail carols place great importance on ancestry, and on men observing the ritual in the same manner as the previous generation:

Pan oedd ein hen deidiau yn ifanc fel ninnau
Nhwy fydden trwy'r Gwyliau 'n ymganlyn yn llon,
A ninnau sydd eto gyd oll wedi ymrwymo:
Ni fedrwn ni fario eu harferion.[13]

[When our forefathers were young as we are [now] | They would follow [the observance] merrily throughout Christmastide | And all of us have again committed to it: | We cannot put a stop to their customs.]

Great emphasis is placed on continuity, on the annual observance of the ritual, the 'hen gostwm' (old custom), and there is a strong sense that what had been passed down over many generations should be continued:

Heno rwyf finna, yn ôl yr hen deidia,
Yn dŵad, drwy eich cennad chwi, i ganu mesura.[14]

[Tonight, I, in accordance with [the customs] of the forefathers, | Come, with your permission, to sing metres.]

One of the criteria in deciding whether the ritual had been observed in the honourable manner of their generous forefathers was whether the householder had been magnanimous enough in his provisions for the visiting company. Full permission was given to defame those who kept their wealth and resources to themselves. Wassailers believed they had a right to their neighbours' means, and should they be refused, vindictive, defamatory stanzas were composed in retribution. In 1729 John Maurice warned that he would not carry news, stories or song to the house of a miser, 'y cibddall di-gwd'[15] (the ignorant one without a scrip) even though he had fought in battalions in Asia, India and the countries of Europe and could tell numerous tales of wonder. Nor would some wassailers visit the home of Quakers, 'Sy yn breferad hyd ein bro | Gan rodio i dwyllo deillion'[16] (Who bleat around our neighbourhood | And walk about to deceive the blind).

Morgan Llwyd (1729), not the prominent Quaker of the same name, attempts to reason a miser's thoughts:

> Ni roir ond yn rhywle am ganu carole
> Fawr ddiod i lancie, yn ddiau, pan ddon':
> Mae bagad mewn alaeth yn ofni drudaniaeth,
> Gwan ydyw crediniaeth rhai dynion (...)

> Mae'r cybydd digroeso, ŵr cynnil, yn cwyno
> Mai'r bwyd sy'n ei ysbeilio, gan ruo yn ddi-rôl;
> Ni rydd y gŵr hwnnw, mae'n gerlyn blin, garw,
> Un dernyn o gwrw i ni am garol.[17]

[Stanza 1: In some places, for singing carols, | It is certain that young men are given very little drink when they arrive: | A troop [of householders] are in a state of sorrow, fearing scarcity and high prices, | The faith of some men is weak (...)

Stanza 2: The inhospitable miser, parsimonious man, complains | That it is the [price of] food that is ravaging him, as he roars uncontrollably; | That man, he is a rough quarrelsome churl, will not give | Us one small sip of beer for a carol.]

Miserliness is the chief of sins, and whoever falls into it is contemptible, and shunned by the wassailing party. An anonymous poem dated 1741 warns that the wassailers refuse to visit crass, angry churls to offer high-principled music; they visit only generous, open-handed people who extend them a gracious welcome. They poured scorn on the names of those, a minority, who kept their doors locked. House-holders were occasionally threatened with physical violence if the door remained secured:

Nid oes na chlo haearn na dôr dderw gadarn
Na chlicied fawr lydan na hoelion
Na gorddrws na bacha na mehiniog yn unlla
Na thynnwn ni oddi yma yn olwythion.

Os rhaid i ni wrth gryfdwr i ennill eich parlwr
Ni chewch chi fawr swcwr pan ddelom i'ch tŷ;
Ni a'ch gyrrwn oddi yma fel llygod i'w gwalfa
Am ein dal ni cyd allan i rynnu.[18]

[Stanza 1: There is no iron lock or strong oak door | Or large wide latch or nails | Or wicket or hooks or doorpost anywhere | That we shall not take out of here in pieces.

Stanza 2: If we must display strength before we gain admittance to your parlour | You will receive little succour when we enter your house; | We shall send you away from here like mice to their burrows | For keeping us out for such a long time to perish with cold.]

Followers of the wassail in Carmarthenshire had three degrees of response to the varying generosity of householders:

Os cawn ni lawer ni bynciwn yn llawen,
Os cawn ni 'chydig ni ddawnsiwn heb fiwsig,
Os ewch chwi'n draws, ni gachwn wrth y drws.[19]

[If we receive much we shall sing merrily, | If we receive little we shall dance without music, | If you become violent we shall shit on your doorstep.]

There was, however, another side to Christmastide wassail carols, many emphasising that it is not beer the carollers are after, but a worthy celebration of the true meaning of the Nativity. In the words of Lewis Morris of Anglesey:

Nid awydd i'ch seigie a chwrw, na chware
A'n gyrrodd ni i'ch dryse, na'ch trysor di-drai,
Ond er moli'r un meddyg, y Duw bendigedig.[20]

[It is not a desire for your food and beer or play | That has directed us to your doors, or your inexhaustible treasures, | But [we are here] in order to praise the one physician, the glorious God.]

The sixteenth and seventeenth centuries saw the rise of a strong tradition of religious free-verse poetry in Wales. The Roman Catholic martyr, Richard Gwyn (c.1537–84), wrote five poems in defence of Roman Catholicism;[21] and a great many Glamorgan poets composed religious *cwndidau*, a word that derives from the Latin *conductus*, 'a sort of motet, sung while the priest was proceeding to the altar'[22] but which later became a generic term for Latin poems on various topics religious and secular. In 1603, the metrical psalms of the cleric Edward Kyffin (c.1558–1603)[23] were published (possibly not extensively); in 1621 Edmwnd Prys (1542/3–1623) published his own *Salmau Cân* (Metrical Psalms) in a metre that could be set to music far more easily than the metres of previous adaptations published, and he had also included tunes for their performance; and Rhys Prichard 'Yr Hen Ficer' (The Old Vicar) (1579?–1644) published the popular *Canwyll y Cymry*[24] (The Welshman's Candle), verses of moral guidance.

This activity had paved the way for the writing of religious songs to be sung during wassailing ceremonies, partly for evangelising purposes. The main message is that God's son came to this earth, a Messiah to save sinners from falling 'i ddamnedigaeth aflan'[25] (into foul damnation). No request is made to enter the house or to secure gifts of food and drink. The opening line of an anonymous carol, 'Carol i'r Gwylie'[26] (A carol to Christmastide), echoes the sentiments of the opening line of several wassailing carols, 'Gyda'ch cennad rŷm ni'n dowad' (We come, with your permission), but the remainder of 'Carol i'r Gwylie' bears no other similarities to the secular wassailing tradition. The carol desires sprriritual knowledge and blessings, that singers and audience should love one another as brothers, put away evil thoughts and actions, and welcome God's Word into their hearts. The poem is based on the Scriptures:

Pob rhodd weddus, berffaith, rymus
O'r nef uchod y mae'n dyfod. (lines 25–6)

[Every good, perfect, mighty gift | Comes from heaven above.]

The lines reflect the Epistle of James 1:17, 'Every good and perfect gift is from above, coming down from the Father of the heavenly lights, who does not change like shifting shadows.' And again:

Pawb sy'n gwrando'r Gair heb gofio
I ŵr yn wir y'i cyfflybir
A fai'n edrych ryw dro mewn drych
Yn gweld tegwch a hawddgarwch.

Mae'r gŵr ffel, call, ynte'n deall
Drych a chyfreth Duw yn hel'eth:
Trwy weithred dda fe bwrcasa
Y nef eilchw'eth yn 'tifeddieth. (lines 45–52)

[Stanza 1: Anyone who listens to the Word and [then] forgets it | Is indeed like a man | Who at some time looks in a mirror | And sees handsomeness and amiability.]

Stanza 2: The sagacious, wise man himself understands | Extensively the mirror and law of God: | Through good works he will purchase at the cost of [Christ's] suffering | Heaven as his inheritance once more]

The lines reflect the message of the Epistle of James 1:23–5,

Anyone who listens to the word but does not do what it says is like someone who looks at his face in a mirror and, after looking at himself, goes away and immediately forgets what he looks like. But whoever looks intently into the perfect law that gives freedom, and continues in it – not forgetting what they have heard, but doing it – they will be blessed in what they do.

Another 'Carol i'r Gwylie' (A carol to Christmastide), this time by William Phylip of Ardudwy (1579/80–1669/70), narrates the story of the Nativity, the virgin birth of Jesus, and the visits of the shepherds and Magi. In particular it records the events leading up to, together with the actual, crucifixion of Jesus and explains the significance of his redemptive death:

Iachawdwr eneidie a brenin a bryne,
Er maint oedd ein beie, inni'n bywyd.

Mab Duw a fu fodlon i ddiodde rhwng lladron
A gollwng gwaed gwirion o'i galon heb gêl,
A hyn yn ddiarswyd er safio inni'n bywyd
Pan oeddem mewn caethrwydd i'r Cythrel.[27]

[Stanza 1: Saviour of souls and king who redeems, | However great our transgressions, our life.

Stanza 2: The Son of God was willing to suffer between thieves | And to shed innocent blood from his heart, in public, | And [he did] this without fear in order to save our lives | At a time when we had been taken captive by the Devil.]

A recurrent theme in the religious wassail carols is the attribution of man's corruption to the Fall, and man's redemption under the covenant of grace to Christ, as exemplified by William Humphrey[28] in two carols, one written in 1690, 'Carol Gwyliau i'w ganu dan bared, ar ôl rhyfel' (A carol to be sung beneath the wall at Christmastide, following war), the other in 1691, 'Carol i'w ganu yn hwyr dan bared (ar hin rewllyd) Wyliau'r Nadolig' (A carol to be sung under the wall at a late hour (in icy weather) at Christmastide). In a similar vein William Gruffydd emphasises the same theological points, but having praised Jesus for granting sinners free salvation and for his wondrous miracles, Gruffydd unexpectedly demands of the householder:

Danfonwch riain feingan, gu,
Yn rhwydd i egori o gariad.[29]

[Send a young woman, slender and fair of complexion, amiable, | Quickly to open [the door] in affection.]

Examples abound of various wassailing parties wishing to avail themselves of spiritual gifts (salvation, faith, hope, grace) as well as temporal gifts (beer, women and song). Humphrey Owen in 1723 desires both, for himself and for the host family:

Haelion ydych, cawsoch glod
Am rannu diod Wylie;
Mae'n cyflawn obeth yn ddi-feth
Y rhowch chwi beth i [ni]nne (...)

Trugarog ydyw Brenin Ne
A llawn o wrthie nerthol
Am roddi i ni ei un Mab rhad
I'n dwyn i'r wlad dragwyddol.

Ac i dragwyddol wlad y saint
Yr elo'ch braint at Iesu,
Ac na bo un gronyn gwaeth eich byd
Er ichwi agoryd inni.[30]

[Stanza 1: You are generous people, you have gained praise | For sharing Christmastide liquor; | We have every hope that you will without fail | Give a little to us (...)

Stanza 2: The King of Heaven is merciful | And full of mighty miracles | For he has given us his one gracious Son | To deliver us into the eternal land.

Stanza 3: And into the eternal land of the saints | May it be your privilege to go to Jesus, | And may you not be the least bit worse off | Even though you have opened [the door] to us.]

One intriguing 'Carol gwirod'[31] (Wassail carol) that dates from the early years of the eighteenth century is the anonymous carol composed in two parts and in two metres, the first part on *tôn deuair* and the second in Psalm metre, in which there is a dialogue between a penitent sinner and God. The poem records a man's plea that God may forgive him and not count his sin against him as he seeks to find a way to heaven. The discussion between God and man continues, culminating in the promise that God will be merciful if man puts all his confidence in Him, prays to Him morning and evening, and lives in harmony with his fellow men.

There is evidence that performers sang to musical accompaniment, most often to harp accompaniment as the following title attests: 'Carol Natalic, i'w ganu (gyda thannau) tan bared'[32] (A Christmas carol, to be sung (with harp accompaniment) beneath the wall). The harper in the closing two stanzas of William Phylip's carol complains that his hands are freezing cold:

Nid ydym ni'n medru dan bared mo'r canu,
Mae'n cerddor ni ar rynnu, wych deulu da,
Agorwch yn fwynedd eich dôr yn ddiomedd
Neu 'winedd a bysedd a basia.

Os allan y'n deliwch ar ganu drwy degwch
A'n hoeri ni a fynnwch, anfwynedd yw hyn:
Ni ymrown ichwi heno, er dim a'r a fyddo,
Tra gellir dal dwylo ar delyn.[33]

[Stanza 1: We can do no more singing beneath the wall, | Our musician is about to freeze to death, excellent good family, | Open your door in an obliging manner, without refusal, | Or nails and fingers will pass away.

Stanza 2: If through flattery you keep us outside to sing | And you insist on causing us to grow cold, this is unkind: | We shall dedicate ourselves to you this evening, no matter what, | For as long as we are able to continue playing the harp.]

The performers were very pleased with themselves, calling out to the householder to listen well to the beauty and musicality of their voice-and-harp recital:

Gwrandawed pawb o'r teulu pêr
Ar fwynder tyner tannau
Sy'n seinio'n llwyr yn un â'n llais
I glymu adlais odlau.[34]

[Let each one of the agreeable family listen | To the gentle melodiousness of [harp]strings | That sound out in total accord with our voices | In order to bind together the sounds of song.]

There is further evidence that wassailers (less frequently) sang to the accompaniment of a *crwth*, or crowd, a six-stringed instrument enjoying a great resurgence in popularity in Wales at present, having been consigned for generations to various public libraries and museums.

Atebwch am hynny neu agorwch eich llety,
[Fe] ddarfu inni ganu, rwy'n gweinio fy nghrwth.[35]

[Answer these [questions] or open up your lodgings, | We have finished singing, I sheathe my crowd.]

The householder's answer is not an encouraging one:

I mewn yma, coeliwch fi,
Ni ddaw y chwi na'ch crythod.[36]

[In here, believe me, | Will neither you nor your crowds enter.]

Named in the Laws of Hywel Dda, the crowd was a popular musical instrument in Wales but by the end of the eighteenth century had to all intent outlived its purpose and been overtaken in popularity by the more versatile, more melodic fiddle.

Towards the close of the wassail carol sung beneath the wall (and/or the farewell carol), there would often be a stanza noting the poem's date of composition – 1741 in the following example:

Mil saith gant a deugain mlwydd
Ac un i'w gwiwlwydd ganu
Oedd oed ein t'wysog, enwog ŵr,
Ein Prynwr, oeswr, Iesu.[37]

[One thousand seven hundred and forty years | And one, of successful song, | That was the age of our prince, illustrious one, | Our Redeemer, one who gives life, Jesus.]

Another type of carol sung during the wassail ritual is the house-holder's reply to the carol requesting admittance. Property owners insist that they will sing to the fullest extent of their ability, win the *pwnco* contest at the door, and prevent the songsters from entering the house. There are threats of setting the dogs on them if they refuse to return home immediately. One householder in the Trawsfynydd area is particularly adamant that the wassailers should stop singing instantly for fear his grey mare should abort on hearing such unme-lodic sounds.[38] Another complains that the wassailers squeal like pigs, or emit strange hooting sounds like owls on a perilously cold night:

Yr y'ch fel twlc yn llawn o foch,
Dy ich, dy och, â'i gilydd,
Ne dylluanod fwy na rhi
Pan fai hi'n rhewi'r ceyrydd.[39]

[You are like a pigsty full of pigs, | Oink oink, snort snort, one to another, | Or owls without number | [On a night] when it is cold enough to freeze fortresses.]

The singing is variously compared to a peacock's scream on a raw winter morning, unruly children clattering about a kitchen, and greedy ducks quacking at a barn door. Robert Evan of Rhedyn Cochion, Trawsfynydd in Gwynedd, orders the singers outside his door: 'cau dy ddannedd'[40] (put your teeth together) to stop their insufferable noise.

The occasion provides an ideal opportunity for householders to reproach the wassailers for their absenteeism at harvest time, sheep shearing time, at the peat cutting season and other busy periods in the agricultural calendar. Householders plead extreme poverty and lack of provisions as their reasons for refusing them food and drink. Some had intended to receive guests and had remained at home to welcome them; they had even made lengthy preparations to see to their best interests:

Mi leddis fuwch oedd hŷn na'm nain
A honno oedd fain ei 'senna:
Chwi gewch ran o gig ei phen
I gadw i chwi lawen Wylia (...)

Y mae yma ar y tân,
O barch i'r glân gwmpeini,
Gi yn rhostio er hanner dydd
A'i berfedd sydd yn berwi.

Fel bai yr arfer ar ôl bwyd
Gael cosyn llwyd go dene
Ac ynddo o gynrhon fwy na rhi,
Mi a'i gwelis i nhw yn chware.[41]

[Stanza 1: I have slaughtered a cow that was older than my grandmother | And it had sharp ribs: | You can have a little meat from its head | To celebrate a merry Christmas (...)

Stanza 2: There is on the fire here, | Out of respect for the good company, | A dog roasting since noon | And its entrails are on the boil.

Stanza 3: As is the custom after a meal | We shall eat a slim piece of mouldy cheese | That has maggots without number in it, | I have seen them at play.]

Jesting added to the attraction of the *pwnco*.

Another attractive feature of Christmas wassailing was the singing of cumulative songs outside the door, songs such as 'Y cyntaf dydd o'r Gwyliau' (The first day of Christmas) known also as 'Y Perot ar y Pren Pêr' (The Parrot in the Pear Tree) and its many Welsh versions.[42] D. Roy Saer considers the song to be a type of 'memory and forfeits game' that would have been sung 'either during the Christmas holiday in general or perhaps on Twelfth Day/Night specifically'.[43] It challenged singers to list twelve unfamiliar objects, such as 'petrisen/perot ar y pren pêr' (a partridge/parrot in the pear tree), a pear being an emblem of fertility ('I suspect that "pear-tree" is really *perdrix* (O. F. *pertriz*) carried into England'),[44] in their correct order and without memory lapses. A version collected by John Thomas of Abercastell near Mathri in Pembrokeshire lists the gifts thus:

Deuddeg pâr o sgidiau (...)
Un ar ddeg o dwmplins (...)
Deg swllt ar hugain (...)

Naw ceffyl halio (...)
Wyth ceffyl (yn) cicio (...)
Saith cusan melys (...)
Chwe ceffylgyn (...)
Pum deryn pert (...)
Pedair gŵydd dew (...)
Tair giâr Ffrainc (...)
Dwy golomen ddof (...)
Y Perot ar y Pren Pêr (...)[45]

[Twelve pairs of shoes (...) | Eleven dumplings (...) | Thirty shillings (...) | Nine horses hauling | Eight horses kicking (…) | Seven sweet kisses (...) | Six woodcocks (...) | Five pretty birds (...) | Four fat geese (...) | Three French hens (...) | Two tame doves (...) | The Parrot in the Pear Tree.]

This list of luxuries (the first five are gifts of fine food fit for a feast, the remainder luxuries of general attraction) may have varied in content over the years but might possibly pertain to the feast held inside the house.

Conundrums and riddles formed part of the contest at the door. It is likely that there existed a wide stock of versified questions, plus ready answers for each one. 'Carol ysglater neu benillion gwirod'[46] (The slater's carol or wassail stanzas) tests the biblical knowledge of those within the house. It asks, for example, which did God create first, the hand or the foot? Mr Sames, the author, replies that God created both in one moment.

In the humorous poem entitled 'Ar y mesur – "Yn tŷ"' (in the metre – 'Yn tŷ'), a tune now lost, the householder declares his wish to welcome the wassailers into his home but is unable as yet to do so as he must first brew his own liquor. The song forms part of a tradition of gathering together a list of items that are impossible to collect, reminiscent of the performing of impossible 'anoethau' (wondrous tasks) in the medieval Welsh tale 'Culhwch ac Olwen'.[47] In this poem all the materials necessary for the brewing are scattered the length and breadth of Wales and beyond, but the wassailers are invited to return at some point in the future when all has been gathered, the brewing is done, and the householder is straining the beer for consumption. Note that the word *pinslab* (stanza 14) does not appear in the University of Wales *Dictionary of the Welsh Language* and that this is the only extant example of its use.

1. Mae gen i ddeunydd cwrw newydd
2. O ddwy heidden a thair ceirchen.
3. Mi af i grasu rheini fory.
4. Y mae'r odyn yn Rhoscolyn.
5. Y mae'r marchbren yn Llanhaearn.
6. Y mac'r llymbrenni yn Llangefni.
7. Y mae'r gwasarn yn Llandrygarn.
8. Y mae'r ffagal ym Modeinial.
9. Y mae'r felin yn Llansilin.
10. Y mae'r melinydd yn Drenewydd.
11. Y mae'r drybedd yn Nhreberfedd.
12. Y mae'r badell yn Nhrecastell.
13. Y mae'r cerwyn yn y Dyffryn.
14. Y mae'r pinslab ym Mhresaddfed.
15. Y mae'r draen yn Ysbaen.
16. Y mae'r barilau yn ganghennau.
17. Y mae'r burum yn nhre Ddulyn.
18. Y mae'r seiri heb eu geni,
19. A heb siglo eto i'w ccisio.
20. Os dowch chwi ar dro pan fwy yn hidlo,
21. Fe fydd parod i chwi wirod.[48]

[1. I have the materials for new beer | 2. Made of two grains of barley and three grains of oatmeal. | 3. Tomorrow I shall go and fire them in a kiln. | 4. The kiln is in Rhoscolyn. | 5. The main beam is in Llanhaearn. | 6. The kiln sticks are in Llangefni. | 7. The straw to be placed on the kiln [under the grain that is to be dried] is in Llandrygarn. | 8. The firebrand is in Bodeinial. | 9. The mill is in Llansilin. | 10. The miller is in Newtown. | 11. The trivet is in Treberfedd. | 12. The pan is in Trecastell. | 13. The mash tun is in Dyffryn. | 14. The *pin-slab* is in Presaddfed. | 15. The strainer is in Spain. | 16. The barrels are still branches. | 17. The yeast is in Dublin town. | 18. The carpenters are yet to be born, | 19. And no rocking has yet been done to conceive them. | 20. If you visit when I am straining [the beer], | 21. The drink will be ready for you.]

The names of two characters, Holin (Holly) and Ifin (Ivy), make an occasional appearance in wassail songs sung at the door. In a different capacity Brinley Rees[49] refers to the two in the context of four types of dream song and the Latin *conflictus*, a contention between two contrasting characters. The earliest examples of contention date back to the reign of Charlemagne, for example the 'conflictus Veris et Hiemis' attributed to Alcuin of York (b. *c*.735), the genre reaching its peak at the end of the twelfth and beginning of the thirteenth century. The form was popularised and disputes were held, for instance, between Water and Wine, Body and Soul, and the sixteenth-century 'debate and stryfe betwene Somer and Wynter'.[50]

In English literature the contention between Holly and Ivy is seen as a rivalry between man, represented by Holly, and woman, represented by Ivy. Their argument centres on the question of ascendancy and which is the stronger of the two. The fifteenth-century carol 'Holvyr and Heyvy Made a Grete Party' to decide 'who should have the mastery in lands where they go',[51] curiously, declares no victor. In another fifteenth-century carol Holly and his merry men stand 'in the hall, fair to behold' while 'Ivy stands without the door; she is full sore a cold'[52] and concerns the matter of who shall have mastery of the household during the coming year. Ivy is kept outside the hall: must she win a disputation in verse before being admitted? Or is it simply that '*holly* was used only to deck the inside of houses at Christmas: while ivy was used not only as a vintner's sign, but also among the evergreens at funerals', that is, outside?[53] Holly was used to decorate churches at Christmas, as two thick folios of early churchwardens' accounts from the church of St Mary-on-the-Hill, Chester, suggest. A special decoration made of holly referred to as 'the holyn' was exhibited in the church. The accounts also make occasional references to:

> a sort of scenic arrangement in which the moon and stars figured prominently. Thus, in 1540, 'paide for nayles and tymber to make the mone [moon] under the holyn,' and 'paide for hanging the rope in the pulle [pulley] for the holyn,' and 'for making a skaffolde to take down the mone.' Again, in 1544, 'paid for candles to ye sterr and to ye hollyn.'[54]

A fifteenth-century macaronic (English and Latin) carol of five verses on the Nativity, prefaced and followed by the words 'Holy' and 'yffy', has been preserved in a Radnorshire deed of 1471 at Bridgwater, Somerset.[55] The carol opens 'Now well may we myrthys make', followed by the refrain 'Letabundus exultet fidelys chorus, Alleluia' (Let the faithful choir gleefully rejoice, Alleluia). It is one of two carols found on the reverse of a Latin indenture (Bridgwater Corporation Muniments, 123), and may have been sung 'at St Davids Cathedral soon after 1471'.[56] The manuscript was later held at Llangunllo near Knighton in central Powys. The carol also survives in the fifteenth-century part of a manuscript held at the Bodleian Library in Oxford, MS Arch. Selden B. 26, and in the sixteenth-century BL Add MS 5665.[57] It has been suggested that the words 'Holy' and 'yffy' are 'perhaps a reference to another associated melody' and 'may even suggest something of a Welsh seasonal repertory'.[58]

In Welsh literature Holly and Ivy's counterparts Holin and Ifin are depicted in a slightly different manner from the English tradition, Holin being the dominant male and Ifin a male hunchback. Holin 'ydoedd iôr o ras'[59] (was a gracious lord), Ifin not so:

Mae fo'n feingam ac yn druan
A'i din sy ar ei arre;
Cwlwm gwythi sy ar ei hyd
Ne glefyd cryd cymale.[60]

[He is thin and hunchbacked, and is wretched, | And is at rock bottom; | Spasms spread through him, | Or else the disease of muscular rheumatism.]

Holin, at times, appears in drinking songs not in contention with Ifin but in contention with a company of wassailers. They request Holin to open the door so that they may enter his home:

Mae alarch ar lyn, mae hwyaid gwyn gwyn,
Mae mwy na hyn yn ymganlyn, Holin.

Holin, weithan agor yn llydan
Y drws imi, 'rwi ymron rhynnu yn canu.[61]

[Stanza 1: There is a swan on a lake, there are white white ducks, | More than this number keep company, Holin.

Stanza 2: Holin, open wide now | The door to me, I am almost frozen to death as I sing.]

Ifin does not feature in the song and no mention is made of him. Nor is he part of yet another drinking song that mentions Holin as being the householder:

Olin, Olin, weithan
Agor ddrws yn llydan;
Ni ddown i fewn i fynnu ein llwyn
Fel gollwng ŵyn o'r gorlan.[62]

[Holin, Holin, now | Open the door wide; | We shall come inside to demand our meat | In the manner of one letting lambs out of the fold.]

It is intriguing that a reference to both holly and ivy appears in a wren hunt song sung on St Stephen's Day in the south of Ireland during the ritual of hunting the Wren:

Sing holly, sing ivy, – sing ivy, sing holly,
A drop just to drink, it would drown melancholy.[63]

Farewell songs sung in gratitude for the welcome received from the host family make no mention of theological topics such as the Fall from grace, or atonement for sin. They do, however, call down God's blessing on the house, its inhabitants and their possessions, desiring that God should call them home to himself at life's end. Wassailers express gratitude for the wassail drink, emphasising how much it had contributed to the success of the evening. A farewell carol by J. J. Ystrad Alun dating from 1676 revels in the abundance of '[g]waed Bregyn fab Heidden'[64] (the blood of Ale son of Barley) or John Barleycorn, a personification of malt liquor.

At evening's end the celebrants were all rather the worse for wear, Huw Morys (1622–1709) admitting that if they drank any more beer they would be unable to distinguish between 'brân ac ysgubor'[65] (a crow and a barn). One anonymous carol reports that the woman of the house had been in the cellar all evening discharging her duties as sharer of a strong home brew, and compares its quantity and force to the flow of many rivers. They were all as drunk as a young calf. Furthermore:

> Rwyf i yn dychmygu bydd un cyn yfory
> Mewn pwll wedi glynu 'mron rhynnu yn y rhos,
> A'r lleill yn ei ymyl a'u [hiaith] yn ansuful,
> Fel tynnu hen geffyl o geuffos.[66]

[I imagine before tomorrow there will be one [person] | Stuck in a ditch, almost frozen to death out on the moor, | And the others close by using uncivil language, | Like dragging an old horse out of a deep pit.]

R. T. describes his wassailing adventures in a similar manner: strong beer, weak legs, and eyes shining like stars by the close of the evening. It would be a long and winding road home, if ever the company reached that destination:

> Mae ohonom ŵr difrad mewn ystum anwastad
> A gymer ei gennad ar doriad y dydd;
> Cychwynned pan fynno, bydd rhaid cael ei gario
> Ne' ei ado i orffwyso yn y ffosydd.
>
> Dyw'r rest ohonom ninne fawr sobrach nag ynte,
> Ni 'dwaenom ffordd adre na llwybre un lle;
> Ni phcidiwn ni â meddwi olynol eleni,
> Ein diwedd ni yw ein claddu'n y cloddie.[67]

[Stanza 1: There is in our midst a guileless man in an unsteady posture | Who will take his leave at daybreak; | Let him start off whenever he chooses, he will have to be carried | Or be left to rest in the ditches.

Stanza 2: The rest of us are hardly more sober than he is, | We do not know our way home or any of the paths anywhere; | This year we have not stopped getting drunk time and again, | Our end is that we shall be buried in the hedges.]

Before leaving they demand a kiss from every young woman in the house, in accordance with the warranty received.[68] As they take leave of their neighbours, thanking them for all their provisions, the revellers bless the house and family, wishing them fertile crops and an increase in their livestock. Singing at various doors, and drinking to the health of the neighbourhood families from a communal cup, encouraged fertility and increased the number of strong, healthy children conceived; produced good harvests, vital for prosperity; and secured the proficient raising of animals for meat, milk, hides, and for draught purposes – 'yn filoedd bo'ch 'nifeiliaid'[69] (may your animals be numbered in their thousands). R. T. sings:[70]

> Duw a ranno'i fendithion i'ch da ac i'ch dynion
> A gado'ch gelynion awch tynion o'ch tŷ;
> Mewn gras, clod a rhinwedd, ymerod a mawredd
> Y byddo 'ch etifedd chwi'n tyfu.
>
> Cynhaea da cynnar i'ch ŷd sy'n y ddaear,
> Pob cwysiad a thalar heb gymar yn gry',
> A thegwch da eglur i hau haidd yn bybyr,
> A thywydd di-fudr i'w fedi.

> [Stanza 1: May God share his blessings among your animals and your people | And keep your enemies and their perverse sharpness from your house; | In grace, praise and virtue, grandeur and greatness | May your offspring grow up.

> Stanza 2: May there be a good, early harvest for your corn that is [now] in the earth, | May every furrow and headland of ploughed field be matchlessly strong, | And may you have good clear sunshine to sow barley with eagerness, | And good weather to harvest it.]

The revellers wish the family (husband, wife and children, in order) happy days, health and long life. Richard Abram 'Dic y Dawns' (fl. 1673–1700), possibly from Anglesey, desires that the family may be blessed with 'iach wythoes'[71] (eight ages of health), an exceptionally long period of wellbeing. When all the troubles and joys of daily life are over:

Duw'ch gwnelo'n edifeiriol i ddŵad yn dduwiol
I'r nefol, wiw, radol ardd Eden.[72]

[May God bring you to repentance, that you may come in a
godly manner | To the heavenly, excellent, blessed garden of
Eden [fig. for paradise/heaven]].

Having reached that blessed abode they expected to meet their friends
and all the faithful deceased:

Cyfarfod da inni yn nheyrnas ne
Ymysg seintie a gwylic golau;
Mewn modd di-wawd, Ddydd Brawd mewn bri,
Amen i chwi a minnau.[73]

[Let us meet happily in the kingdom of heaven | In the pres-
ence of saints and at bright festivities; | In a delightful manner,
in favour on Judgement Day, | Amen to you and me.]

And with that final 'Amen' the observance is at an end for another
year.

Having customs in common with previous generations, holding
on to a previous era, preserving it in the present and extending it into
the future would afford the wassailers much pleasure,[74] strengthen
community ties and uphold Welsh identity: 'Na fariwch hen arferion'[75]
(Do not prevent [the observance of] old customs). By the last quarter
of the eighteenth century, Jonathan Hughes (1721–1805) of Llangollen
mourns the loss of 'canu Gwylie'[76] (singing at Christmastide), claiming
that it was widely done at one time but 'mae hynny nawr yn oeri'
([the enthusiasm for] that is now cooling) and is being replaced by
pride, iniquity, violence and jealousy. In another of his carols, 'Carol
Wyliau, 1769'[77] (A Christmastide carol), he discloses his intention to
travel with his friends from house to house in a conscious attempt to
halt the slowing down, as he describes it, of the custom of wassailing
at Christmastide. He also calls attention to the increasing habit on
the part of diverse sections of the community to 'cau'n glosiach eu
drysau' (close their doors more tightly) and to discourage wassailing
parties. All such people are concerned about, he says, is gossip and
news; they only become excited when they hear of an increase in

market prices, or of war breaking out in some part of the world giving them an advantage in the fluctuating economy. Yet there were still some honest people who would share their feast with wassailers. He rejoices in the opportunity to visit them, even though he has to do that on foot rather than on horseback because of the necessity and expense of having to buy 'darn o diced' (a scrap of ticket) before he and his friends can move any distance at all. 'Cloi'r ffordd heb ddim rhyddid' (Putting a lock on the road to prohibit freedom) refers to the setting up of turnpike roads and setting a locked gate across the road to prevent travel until a toll was paid, the first of which appeared in Wales (between Shrewsbury and Wrexham) in 1752 and had a detrimental effect on wassail observances in Wales.

A narrative poem, not considered to be part of the observance itself, was published in 1924 by William Williams 'Crwys' (1875–1968). Brought up in Craig-cefn-parc, Clydach in Glamorganshire, he describes with great humour the adventures of a wassailing party of three (Moc, Rhys and the poet himself) making their difficult journey around the neighbourhood carrying a horn lantern and a tallow candle and for various reasons their efforts not being appreciated. Even so:

(...) pe bawn i'n awr
Ond llanc yn Llangyfelach,

Goleuwn eto'r lantern gorn,
Gan gychwyn rhwng dau olau
I 'ganu wasail' hyd y plwy,
Moc a Rhys a minnau.[78]

[(...) if I were now | But a lad in Llangyfelach, | I would once more light the horn lantern, | And start off at dusk | To 'sing wassail' all over the parish, | Moc and Rhys and I.]

The poem suggests that the custom was still observed at the end of the nineteenth century in Llangyfelach, a small village situated four miles north of Swansea city centre. There is no evidence that the custom continued into the twentieth century and it is no longer observed in Wales.

Notes

1. See further Gwynfryn Richards 'Y Plygain', *Journal of the Historical Society of the Church in Wales*, 1 (1947), 53–71; Enid P. Roberts, 'Hen Garolau Plygain' [Old *plygain* carols], *Transactions of the Honourable Society of Cymmrodorion* (1952), 51–70; D. Roy Saer, 'The Christmas Carol-Singing Tradition in the Tanad Valley', *Folk Life*, 7 (1969), 15–42; D. Roy Saer, 'A Midnight *Plygain* at Llanymawddwy Church', in *'Canu at Iws' ac Ysgrifau Eraill* ['Song for use' and other articles] (Talybont: Cymdeithas Alawon Gwerin Cymru [Welsh Folk Song Society], 2013), pp. 81–9.

2. For examples see Thomas Jones, *Llyfr Carolau a Dyrïau Duwiol* [A book of carols and devout songs] (Amwythig [Shrewsbury]: Thomas Jones, 1696).

3. Untitled, NLW 11991A, 139.

4. Cwrtmawr 171D, 87–90.

5. For 'Country Bumpkin' see John Walsh, *Caledonian Country Dances* (London: J . Walsh, *c*.1745), p. 85.

6. 'Carol i fynd i dŷ' [A carol for admittance to a house], NLW 5261A, 99.

7. Untitled, NLW 6499B, 431.

8. 'Carol Tan Bared' [A carol [to be sung] beneath the wall], J. H. Davies, *A Bibliography of Welsh Ballads Printed in the Eighteenth Century*, 4 (London: The Honourable Society of Cymmrodorion, 1911), p. xx; T. H. Parry-Williams, *Llawysgrif Richard Morris o Gerddi* [Richard Morris's Manuscript of Poems] (Cardiff: University of Wales Press, 1931), pp. 132–3.

9. Parry-Williams, *Llawysgrif Richard Morris o Gerddi*, pp. 192–3.

10. 'Untitled', NLW 9168A, ff. 28ᵛ–29ʳ.

11. 'Untitled', NLW 19163A, f. 10ʳ; 'Triban', Cwrtmawr 225B, 59.

12. Untitled, NLW 434B, 47.

13. 'Un arall ar yr un mesur' [Another in the same metre], NLW 9168A, f. 55ʳ.

14. 'Carol gwirod yn drws [A wassail song [to be sung] outside the door], Parry-Williams, *Llawysgrif Richard Morris*, p. 8.

15. 'Tw ganu dan bared' [To be sung beneath the wall], Cwrtmawr 228A, 430.

16. Untitled, Cardiff 2.137, 61, a poem attributed to Edward Morris of Cerrigydrudion in Denbighshire; Gwenllian Jones argues against the attribution in 'Bywyd a Gwaith Edward Morris Perthi Llwydion' [The life and works of Edward Morris Perthi Llwydion] (unpublished MA thesis, University of Wales [Aberystwyth], 1941), 141–2.

17. 'Carol i'w ganu tan bared Wyliau'r Nadolig' [A carol to be sung beneath the wall at Christmastide], Cwrtmawr 171D, 97–8.

18. '[Carol w]irod a mesur yn drws' [A wassail carol and metre at the door], Parry-Williams, *Llawysgrif Richard Morris*, p. 7.
19. 'Canu Gwaseila sir Gaer' (possibly the work of Edward Williams 'Iolo Morganwg'), NLW 13148A, 82.
20. 'Carol wirod yn drws ar dri chwarter tôn' [A wassail carol at the door in *tri chwarter tôn*], Parry-Williams, *Llawysgrif Richard Morris*, pp. 153–4.
21. T. H. Parry-Williams (ed.), *Carolau Richard White* [The carols of Richard White] (Cardiff: University of Wales Press, 1931).
22. Ifor Williams, 'Lexicographical Notes', *Bulletin of the Board of Celtic Studies*, 3 (1926), 127. See further L. J. Hopkin-James 'Hopcyn' and T. C. Evans 'Cadrawd', *Hen Gwndidau, Carolau a Chywyddau, Being Sermons in Song in the Gwentian Dialect* (Bangor: Jarvis & Foster, 1910); Ceri W. Lewis, 'The Literary History of Glamorgan from 1550 to 1770', in Glanmor Williams (ed.), *Glamorgan County History*, 4 (Cardiff: University of Wales Press, 1974), 535–639.
23. Edward Kyffin, *Rhann o Psalmae Dafydd Brophwyd* [Some of the Psalms of David the Prophet] (London: Simon Stafford for T[homas] S[alisbury], 1603); it contains the first twelve psalms and some verses of Psalm 13.
24. Rhys Prichard, *Canwyll y Cymry* [The Welshman's Candle] (London: printed in Shrewsbury by Thomas Durston, 1696); Nesta Lloyd (ed.), *Cerddi'r Ficer* [The Poems of The Vicar] ([Swansea]: Cyhoeddiadau Barddas, 1994), an annotated selection from the 1672 edition of the didactic religious verses of Rhys Prichard (*c.*1579–1644), vicar of Llandovery in Carmarthenshire.
25. 'Arall' [Another], Cwrtmawr 128A, 86.
26. 'Carol i'r Gwylie' [A carol to Christmastide], Bodley Welsh f 6 (i), 50–3.
27. 'Carol i'r Gwylie' [A carol to Christmastide], NLW 434B, 3.
28. Jones, *Llyfr Carolau a Dyriau Duwiol*, pp. 339–41, 341–2.
29. 'Carol i'w ganu tan bared' [A carol to be sung beneath the wall], Jones, *Llyfr Carolau a Dyriau Duwiol*, p. 166.
30. 'Un arall ar yr un testun' [Another on the same theme], NLW 788B, 41.
31. Parry-Williams, *Llawysgrif Richard Morris*, pp. 187–8.
32. Jones, *Llyfr Carolau a Dyriau Duwiol*, p. 118.
33. 'Carol i'r Gwylie' [A carol to Christmastide], NLW 434B, 4; although not the same poem, the stanza 'Nid ydym (...)' is a variant of poem 4.29–32.
34. 'Arall' [Another], Cwrtmawr 128A, 86.
35. 'Carol ysglater neu benillion gwirod' [The slater's carol or wassail stanzas], Parry-Williams, *Llawysgrif Richard Morris*, pp. 12–14.
36. 'Ateb i'r garol ddiwaetha, o waith Mr. Sames' [Reply to the preceding carol, by Mr Sames], Parry-Williams, *Llawysgrif Richard Morris*, pp. 15–16.
37. Poem 5.25–8.

38. 'Carol ateb o'r tŷ' [A reply carol from the house], Cwrtmawr 128A, 95.
39. 'Carol i rwystro rhai i'r tŷ' [A carol [sung] to prevent some from coming into the house], Cwrtmawr 128A, 92.
40. 'Sosi garol yn tŷ' [A saucy carol [sung] inside the house], Cwrtmawr 128A, 96.
41. Poem 8.5–8, 25–32.
42. For the tune 'Y cyntaf dydd o'r Gwyliau' see p. 177 for further examples and variants see Cylchgrawn Cymdeithas Alawon Gwerin Cymru/ Journal of the Welsh Folk-Song Society, 1 (1909–12), 175–6; Cylchgrawn Cymdeithas Alawon Gwerin Cymru/Journal of the Welsh Folk-Song Society, 2 (1914–25), 283–4.
43. D. Roy Saer (ed.), Caneuon Llafar Gwlad (Songs From Oral Tradition), 1 (Cardiff: National Museum of Wales/Welsh Folk Museum, 1974), p. 63.
44. Cecil J. Sharp, A. G. Gilchrist and Lucy E. Broadwood, 'Forfeit Songs; Cumulative Songs; Songs of Marvels and of Magical Animals', Journal of the Folk-Song Society, 5 (1916), 280.
45. Saer, Caneuon Llafar Gwlad, p. 39.
46. Parry-Williams, Llawysgrif Richard Morris, pp. 12–14; the answer, 'Ateb i'r garol ddiwaetha, o waith Mr. Sames' [Reply to the preceding carol, by Mr Sames], pp. 15–16.
47. Rachel Bromwich and D. Simon Evans (eds), Culhwch and Olwen: An Edition and Study of the Oldest Arthurian Tale (Cardiff: University of Wales Press, 1992).
48. Parry-Williams, Llawysgrif Richard Morris, pp. 88–9; for a twelve-line variant see NLW 9168A, f. 33ʳ.
49. Brinley Rees, Dulliau'r Canu Rhydd 1500–1650 [The Forms of Free-verse Poems] (Cardiff: University of Wales Press, 1952), p. 76.
50. J. O. Halliwell-Phillipps (ed.), The Debate and Stryfe Betwene Somer and Wynter: A Poetical Dialogue (London: printed for the editor by Whittingham & Wilkins, 1860).
51. William Henry Husk, Songs of the Nativity (London: John Camden Hotten, 1868), p. 128.
52. Husk, Songs of the Nativity, p. 131.
53. John Brand, Observations on the Popular Antiquities of Great Britain (London: Henry G. Bohn, 1849; first edition 1777), p. 523.
54. J. P. Earwaker, 'The Ancient Parish Books of the Church of St. Mary-on-the-Hill, Chester', Journal of the Chester Archaeological and Historic Society (1888), 140.
55. Andrew Breeze, 'Two English Carols in a Radnorshire Deed of 1471 at Bridgwater, Somerset', National Library of Wales Journal, 31 (Winter 1999), 118.
56. Breeze, 'Two English Carols', p. 118.

57. Anastasia S. Pilato, 'The carols of the Ritson Manuscript, BL Add. 5665, at Exeter Cathedral: repertory and context' (Senior Honors Thesis, University of Connecticut, 2013) [Online]. Available at *https://opencommons. uconn.edu/cgi/viewcontent.cgi?article=1506&context=srhonors_theses* (accessed 29 October 2020).

58. Sally Harper, *Music in Welsh Culture Before 1650: A Study of the Principal Sources* (Abingdon: Routledge, 2007), p. 281.

59. Poem 9.7.

60. Poem 9.13–16.

61. 'Carol Gwirod yn Drws' [A wassail song [to be sung] outside the door], Parry-Williams, *Llawysgrif Richard Morris*, p. 185.

62. Parry-Williams, *Llawysgrif Richard Morris*, p. 133.

63. Quoted in [Lewis Davies Jones] Llew Tegid, 'Hunting the Wren', *Cylchgrawn Cymdeithas Alawon Gwerin Cymru/Journal of the Welsh Folk-Song Society*, 1 (1909–12), 110.

64. 'Diolch am groeso'r Gwyliau' [Gratitude for the welcome received at Christmastide], NLW 7191B, f. 226ʳ.

65. 'Pedwar pennill i'w canu wrth fyned allan o dŷ ar amser Gwyliau'r Nadolig, ac i ddiolch am y croeso gan y tylwyth' [Four stanzas to be sung on departure from a house at Christmastide, and to give thanks for the welcome received from the family], Cwrtmawr 398B, 8.

66. 'Carol i'w ganu wrth fynd allan o dŷ' [A carol to be sung on departing from a house], Cwrtmawr 171D, 39.

67. 'Carol i fyned allan o dŷ' [A carol [to be sung] on departing from a house], NLW 5261A, 101–2.

68. 'Carol wrth ymadel' [A carol [to be sung] on departure], NLW 527A, 97.

69. 'Dechrau Carol diolch yn llys yr un gŵr ar yr un dôn 1767' [The beginning of a carol of gratitude sung at the hall of the same man to the same tune 1767], NLW 6740B, 80–2. A postscript states that the carol was sung at the home of the Revd William Jones, Tŷ Fry; the carol was composed by 'Dafydd Jones o'r Penrhyn' on 31 December 1767.

70. 'Carol i fyned allan o dŷ' [A carol on departing from a house], LlGC 5261A, 101–2.

71. 'Carol wrth ymadael â Thŷ, Wyliau'r Nadolig' [A carol on departing from a house, at Christmastide], Dafydd Jones, *Blodeu-Gerdd Cymry* [An Anthology of Welsh Poems] (Amwythig [Shrewsbury]: Stafford Prys, 1779; first edition 1759), p. 131.

72. 'Carol i fyned allan o dŷ' [A carol on departing from a house], NLW 5261A, 102.

73. Poem 11.45–8.

74. 'Defod ac arfer sy lawer o bleser' [Custom and habit afford much pleasure], Parry-Williams, *Llawysgrif Richard Morris*, p. 8.

75. An anonymous carol entitled 'Ei Dechre' [Its beginning] from the Traws-fynydd area, Cwrtmawr 128A, 93.
76. 'Carol tan bared, yn dangos allan ddieithred yw cariad brawdol; ar "Ffar-wel Ned Puw"' [A carol [to be sung] beneath the wall, setting forth how unfamiliar brotherly love has become, to 'Ffarwel Ned Puw'], in Jonathan Hughes, *Bardd, a Byrddau* [Bard, and Board] (Amwythig [Shrewsbury]: Stafford Prys, 1778; facsimile reprint Whitefish (Montana): Kessinger Publishing, 2010), pp. 243–7.
77. Siwan M. Rosser (ed.), *Bardd Pengwern* [The poet of Pengwern] ([Swansea]: Cyhoeddiadau Barddas, 2007), pp. 120–4.
78. 'Canu Wasail (Yr arferiad o ganu Carolau o gylch y Nadolig.)' [Wassailing (The custom of singing carols at Christmastide)], in W. Crwys Williams, *Cerddi Newydd Crwys* (Wrecsam: Hughes a'i Fab, 1924), pp. 64–5.

Wassailing at the New Year

THERE WAS A TIME when Andreas Huws[1] would knock on our front door early in the morning to greet us with New Year's Day songs and blessings, and the voices of his friends would carry over from the nearby farms as they sang their good wishes to our neighbours. Present-day custom often dictates that children visit village homes and farms ferried in their parents' cars and accompanied to the door by an adult at all times.

It is a lucrative business to go about the neighbourhood distributing kind wishes and collecting monetary gifts in exchange, and for that reason it is problematic for practitioners to know when to set aside its observance. Local custom might suggest that it is nowadays primarily practised by children of primary school age and into the low teens. This is confirmed by a stanza from Pren-gwyn near Llandysul in Ceredigion, sung in the early years of the twentieth century:

> Mi godais heddiw'n fore o bentre bach Pren-gwyn
> I ofyn am galennig cael towlu'r flwyddyn hyn,
> Rwy'n mynd i wasanaethu pan ddelo dechrau haf,
> Cewch lonydd ar ôl 'leni, O rhowch galennig braf.
> Blwyddyn Newydd Dda![2]

> [I was up early this morning [and have come] from the little village of Pren-gwyn | To request a New Year's gift to cast

out this year, | I shall go into service in early summer, | [And]
I shall leave you in peace after this year, O give a substantial
New Year's gift. | A Good New Year!]

The young boys of Laugharne who were to be apprenticed to a trade
took advantage of New Year's Day to collect money to help them
establish their new start in life, particularly those who were to be
masons or carpenters. 'They carried square money boxes, with a slit
in the middle for the money, ornamented with crosses and hearts,
with the words, "The apprentices of Laugharne" inscribed.'[3]

New Year's Day lent itself to the distribution of charitable dona-
tions from those highly placed in society, particularly so in days of
economic depression. Bryn Myrddin mansion near Abergwili, Car-
marthen, contributed in such a way:

> On New Year's Day the *calenig* was given to every man, woman
> or child who cared to come and fetch it – threepence to a man,
> twopence to a woman and a penny to each child. Once my
> brother and I thought ourselves very clever by dressing up in
> dishevelled garments and snatching a *calenig* from the crusty old
> gardener, Davy Evan, who acted as almoner on these occasions.[4]

No rhymes were sung, however, and it was more a matter of distribut-
ing money to the deserving poor than observing a wassailing custom.

It is widely accepted that New Year was established as a Christ-
ian holiday in AD 487. In more recent centuries it was regarded by
some as an opportunity to sing religious carols similar to those sung at
Christmas, for example 'Cywydd ar Epistol ddydd Calan: Rhûfei.4:8'[5]
(A *cywydd* on the Epistle for New Year's Day: Romans 4:8) by James
Dwnn (c.1570–c.1660) from Montgomeryshire, and 'Carol ar yr un
mesur i'w ganu'r Calan'[6] (A carol in the same metre to be sung on
New Year's Day) by Jonathan Hughes (1721–1805), Llangollen. Jon-
athan Hughes speaks of the sinner's need to surrender to Christ's
authority, that the 'pethau cynta' (the old order of things) has passed
away[7] and that the law of the Mosaic dispensation has been fulfilled
by the Messiah. The opening line states of New Year's Day, 'dyma
nodol ddydd enwaediad' (this is the specified day of circumcision),
but Jonathan Hughes emphasises that to gain true circumcision one
must accept the Word of God.

Many of the religious carols sung at the New Year are linked to the Feast of the Circumcision of Christ, now celebrated as The Solemnity of Mary, the Holy Mother of God. The birth of Christ was celebrated on 25 December. Jewish boys were circumcised and named on the eighth day and consequently (according to certain calculations of the intervals of days) the Feast of the Circumcision of Christ fell on 1 January, the eighth day after Christmas,[8] as noted by Dafydd Jones of Penrhyndeudraeth in 1767:

> Ar gyfer hyn enwaedwyd Iesu
> Yn ôl y ffasiwn i'w chyffesu;
> Rhown ninna chwedyn fawl barchedig
> Lawn galonnau, lân galennig.[9]

> [It was on this day that Jesus was circumcised | As was the custom, it must be acknowledged; | Subsequently, let us all give reverential praise | [From] full hearts, a fine New Year's gift.]

A tradition more closely associated with the wassail ritual was that known as 'Y Berllan' (The Orchard). Similar to the wassailing practised in the cider orchards of England, it is an inventive means of securing a good harvest. In his discussion of the origin and meaning of apple cults J. Rendel Harris emphasises the associated fertility rituals, and that 'the female has the right of way against the male' because the woman is the fertile element in humanity, and that 'the tree itself, considered as fruit-bearing, is commonly regarded as feminine'.[10] The *Berllan* custom was observed in Kidwelly in Carmarthenshire during the first half of the nineteenth century and is described in the following report:

> A small rectangular board with a circle marked in the centre and ribs of wood running from the centre to each of the four angles. At each corner of the board an apple was fixed, and within the circle a tree with a miniature bird thereon. One of the group of young men who approached the house 'honoured' by their visit, carried the Perllan, and another bore a large cup full of beer. The *rhigwm* was best remembered by Mr. Francis Randell, aged 82 years. It ran thus:

CAN Y BERLLAN

1. Dyma lân gyfeillion
Yn dyfod i'ch danfon
A chwrw a digon i'ch gweled,
Afalau pur hefyd,
Y gore'n y gwledydd,
I gynnal llawenydd y Gwyle.

2. A chyda ni mae perllan
A dryw bach ynddi'n hedfan,
Rheolwr pob adar yw hwnnw;
A chanddo mae ffiol
Aiff naw cwart i'w chanol
A wnaiff eich holl bobl chi'n feddw.

3. Ni ddaethom ni ddim yma
Fel *spongers* fai'n hela,
Ar hyder eich difa na'ch torri;
Mae'n jiwgs ni'n go lawned,
Pe bae'ch ond eu gweled
Chwenychech gael yfed oddeutu.

4. O ddiod a llyse,
Sweet peraidd arogle
Sy'n blino'n garddyrne wrth gerdded;
Agorwch heb rwgnach,
On'de awn ymhellach
I weled a gawn rai i yfed.

5. Gŵr y tŷ yn gyntaf,
A'r wraig dda yn nesaf,
Duw'ch cadwo'ch mewn iechyd i reoli,
Fe gawsom ni'n parchu,
Do'n siŵr, a'n croesawu,
O ffarwel, dyma ni'n ymado.[11]

[Song of the Orchard
Stanza 1: Here are true friends | Coming to attend to you |
[Bringing] beer and plenty for you to behold, | Pure apples

too, | The best in all the lands, | To celebrate the joy of
Christmastide.

Stanza 2: And we have an orchard | With a little wren flying
about in it, | He is the ruler of all birds; | And he has a cup
| That takes nine quarts | That will make all your people
drunk.

Stanza 3: We did not come here | As spongers on the hunt, |
In expectation of destroying or breaking you; | Our jugs are
quite full, | If you could only see them | You would want to
drink from them.

Stanza 4: Of drink and spices, | [The] sweet aromatic fragrances
| Are tiring our wrists as we walk; | Open up without com-
plaint, | If not we shall go further | To see whether we can find
anyone to drink with.

Stanza 5: First the gentleman of the house, | And next the good
wife, | God keep you in good health to rule, | We have been
esteemed, | Yes indeed, and welcomed, | O farewell, we now
take our leave.]

The Orchard was evidently perceived as a symbol of fruitfulness and
fecundity, and it was believed that visiting houses with the orchard
of apples in tow would encourage an abundance of new growth and
a multiplicity of offspring, and in fact the increase would be a hun-
dredfold. The Glamorgan bardic entrepreneur Edward Williams 'Iolo
Morganwg' (1747–1826) speaks of the custom of '[t]awlu afalau at a
font briod flwyddyn heb blant' (throwing apples at married couples
who had been childless for a year) to increase their fertility.[12] The
wren, perched in the Orchard branches, is referred to as the ruler
of the bird kingdom, a title the wren had fought for and in many
countries won.[13]

Those who took part in the Orchard ritual would bring their own
provisions rather than accept supplies from householders. They are
not beggars, as they are quick to point out. The large cup full of beer
to which they refer is the wassail bowl, that carried so much drink
their wrists ached at its weight. The image is one of abundance, the

seed having reached full maturity during the previous year causing the cup to overflow during this. There is hope too for the future, as a result of the visitation with the Orchard. The custom was still celebrated in Wales at the end of the nineteenth century and into the first quarter of the twentieth.

The Revd Thomas Rees (1815–85), when he was a child in Llangathen near Llandeilo in Carmarthenshire, used to sell orchard boards to farmers in return for food and a little money:

Yn adeg y Nadolig a'r Calan arferai [Thomas Rees] fyned oddiamgylch amaethwyr y wlad i werthu perllanau, fel eu gelwid, neu yn hytrach i'w rhoddi yn gyfnewid am galenig (...) Darn o astell ysgwar ydoedd, o faint llyfr deuddeg-plyg. Yr oedd pedair olwyn fechan dani, ac yr oedd ei harwyneb yn llawn tyllau bychain. Yn y tyllau hyn rhoddid pinau pren, ac ar flaen y pin canol gosodid afal coch, os gellid ei gael, ac ar flaen y pinau eraill griafol (*berries*) cochion, a rhyw bethau eraill i amrywio y lliwiau. Yr oedd golwg brydferth iawn ar y berllan, a chadwai am fisoedd. Gwaith y taid a'r ewythr ydoedd, y rhai oeddynt gelfydd mewn pethau o'r fath. Rhoddid weithiau ryw gymaint o arian am y berllan, heblaw y blawd gwenith, a cheirch, a sucan, a chaws, a nwyddau bwytadwy eraill. Ceid fel hyn ddigon o fodd i gynal y teulu am wythnosau.[14]

[At Christmastide and on New Year's Day [Thomas Rees] would visit the farmers in the area to sell orchards, as they were called, or rather to give them in exchange for a New Year's gift (...) It was a square plank, the size of a twelvefold book. There were four small wheels under it, and its surface was covered with little holes. Wooden pins were placed in these holes, and at the tip of the central pin, a red apple was placed, if one could be found, and at the tip of the other pins red rowan berries, and other such things to vary the colours. The orchard looked very beautiful, and kept for months. It was the work of the grandfather and the uncle, who were skilled in such things. Sometimes a little money was given for the orchard, besides the wheat flour, and oats, and sowens, and cheese, and other edible goods. In this way enough means [of living] was obtained to support the family for weeks.]

Several New Year's Day traditions were celebrated that had little bearing on the wassailing ritual but because of the money collected, and because they claimed to determine the success or otherwise of the coming year, they require attention. The first person sighted on New Year's Day could determine one's fate for the year. In Carmarthenshire, if the coming year was to be a successful one, 'rhaid i fachgen weled merch ac i ferch weled bachgen yn gyntaf'[15] (a boy must first see a girl and a girl must first see a boy). Catching sight of a woman, however, could bring bad luck and misfortune:

> A farmer, lately deceased, who lived less than ten miles from Caermarthen, in the Eastern Division of the county, was troubled some years ago at seeing a certain female neighbour entering his yard on New Year's morning. Soon afterwards a cow died and a few other misfortunes happened. It chanced that the very same woman approached his house before anyone else was astir on the next New Year's morning, whereupon the old man rushed out with a pitchfork and chased her for her life.[16]

For a girl, or even a married woman, seen out on the morning of New Year's Day, it could be dangerous: the boys would set upon her with holly twigs and thrash her 'nes fo'r gwâd yn dod'[17] (until the blood came). Should one encounter a man, particularly a man named Dafydd, Ifan, Siôn or Siencyn, all would be well. Meeting a man with red hair was unlucky, and the people of Cardigan would groan if they saw a man named Twm first thing in the morning:

> Blwyddyn drwm
> Wrth weled Twm.[18]

[The year will be heavy | From seeing Tommie.]

This belief persisted in Llanddewibrefi in the Tregaron area of Ceredigion certainly until 1911. If a male person visited a household on New Year's morning he would be enthusiastically ushered upstairs so that even those who were still in bed could benefit from this piece of good luck. As a rule the boy would be given a sixpenny coin on his departure, 'but in former times he got a loaf of bread instead'.[19] Bread was a symbol of sustenance for the approaching year, as was any money received. In Pembrokeshire, similar rules applied. When visitors knocked on a door, the inmates would ask the names of those outside. If it was a woman, or if the name began with an unlucky letter, the door remained locked. 'H, J, R, were fortunate [letters], for they denoted Happiness, or Health, Joy, Riches. The letters T, W, S, foretold Trouble, Worry, Sorrow.'[20]

Other traditions suggest a link between New Year's Day customs and wells. Under the title 'dŵr newy' (new water) the tradition was upheld, for example, in Llanfyrnach, near Crymych in Pembrokeshire. Mistletoe, holly or other evergreen sprigs or leaves were floated on the water as a symbol of the permanence of the well water's beneficial influence. In south Pembrokeshire, on New Year's morning 'boys and girls went round from house to house with the "New Year's Water" and an evergreen sprinkler, with which they sprinkled all who received them.'[21] The following rhyme from Capel Cynon in Ceredigion suggests a similar concept, adding the intention of using the new water to make the first cup of tea:

> Mi godes yn fore, mi ginnes y tân,
> Mi redes i'r ffynnon i mofyn dŵr glân;
> Mi dacles y tegyl a'r tebot yn fuan
> Er meddwl cael brecwast ar fore dydd Calan.[22]

> [I rose up early, I lit the fire, | I ran to the well to draw fresh water; | I quickly tackled the kettle and the teapot | With the intention of having breakfast on New Year's Day morning.]

When boys carrying well water visited, they sprinkled it throughout the home and over the face and hands of whomever they met, singing or reciting the following stanza as they sprinkled:

> Here we bring new water from the well so clear,
> For to worship God with, this happy new year;
> Sing levy dew, sing levy dew, the water and the wine,
> With seven bright gold wires,[23] and bugles that do shine;
> Sing reign of fair maid, with gold upon her toe,
> Open you the west door, and turn the old year go;
> Sing reign of fair maid, with gold upon her chin,
> Open you the east door, and let the new year in.[24]

The same stanza was sung in Tenby on New Year's morning; the singers always received half a crown, even a crown, for their trouble.[25] In Carmarthenshire it was a girl who would give new water to a boy, and a boy to a girl.[26] The custom of sprinkling New Year's water continued to be observed in Pendine in Carmarthenshire 'on old New Year's day, which occurs on 12th January'[27] at least until 1880; the same source states that in Laugharne on 1 January 1873 'it was discontinued for the first time, and I have not heard of it since'. Sprinkling New Year's water is recorded as late as 1913 in Kidwelly: 'Mothers still sprinkle fresh water with a spray of boxwood on the faces of their sleeping children. It was done in Lady Street, on New Year's Day, 1913.'[28]

It was believed that water from a well could heal, bring about good fortune, and safeguard the community against any malicious forces rampant in the countryside. Natural springs were often consecrated and became revered holy wells endowed with healing qualities. The pioneering work of Francis Jones[29] makes reference to over a thousand wells, from St Seiriol's well at Penmon in Anglesey to St Sannan's well in Bedwellty, Monmouthshire.

Well water might bring luck, but it could also bring ill fortune, especially when sprinkled over doors that had not granted admittance to well-wishers. 'New water', the first water drawn from a well on New Year's morning, was particularly powerful in affecting human affairs. This gave rise to competitiveness: who would be first to draw water and first to wish the neighbourhood a prosperous New Year? It is recorded that the Revd T. A. Davies, Llanishen in north Cardiff, c.1910:

> had seen an old well, near a small larch wood not far from 'The Cross,' Llanishen, dressed with sprigs of box by an old man of 80 years of age. This was on new year's eve and, at 12 midnight, the old man and another old neighbour used to race to the well to see who would be first in getting what they called the 'crop of the well,' with which to make tea.[30]

The New Year had held a special significance for centuries prior to the Middle Ages. With their golden knives, the Druids[31] (a high-ranking class of priests in Welsh society) as a sacrificial act used to cut mistletoe in forests devoted to the gods and distribute it as gifts on New Year's Day. Mistletoe was a symbol of fertility; distributing sprigs of mistletoe throughout the community to heal its inhabitants was hailed as an opportunity to strengthen nature's rejuvenating powers following the death of the old year and the birth of the new.

The wassailing custom held at the New Year is the *calennig* tour, making a calends journey of the neighbourhood in order to maintain the community's vigour and strength. In its early form the tradition was upheld by men, as Huw ab Ifan, singing at the *Gŵyl Fair* (Candlemas) celebrations, suggests:

> Ar ddechrau'r mis, rai dilys, da,
> Bûm yn eich noddfa anheddfawr
> Â chân i chwi, down ni un wedd
> Ar ddiwedd iawnwedd Ionawr.[32]

> [At the beginning of the month [of January], sincere good people, | I visited your spacious refuge | With a song for you, we come in the same manner, | Fittingly, at the end of January.]

Traditionally, the men visited neighbourhood houses and farms carrying with them a bag (often hanging from a long piece of twine placed around the neck) and a cudgel:

> Mi godes heddiw mas o'm tŷ,
> A'm cwd a'm pastwn gyda mi.[33] (Llandysul, Ceredigion)

> [I set out from my house today | Taking with me my bag and my cudgel.]

In addition to the bag and cudgel, they carried with them a calends gift (see figure 5), particularly in the counties of Carmarthen, Glamorgan and Monmouth – an apple or orange supported on three willow skewers, sometimes carved, forming a tripod. The apple was pierced with a thin piece of wood to form a handle, and was studded all over with raisins and dried oats or barley husks; a sprig of holly, mistletoe, box or rosemary housing cracked hazelnuts was placed on top of the fruit and the whole decoration would be covered in white flour. Writing in 1959 Trefor M. Owen remarks: 'Latterly the carrying round of the apple has been discontinued.'[34]

This *calennig* gift would be displayed in each home to ensure prosperity in the coming year. The apple (possibly representing the sun as the ultimate source of life) was tantamount to fertility; the nuts, berries, oats and raisins represented an abundance of the fruits of the earth; rosemary symbolized longevity and perpetuity (as did mistletoe, holly and box, three evergreen plants), and would be thrown into graves to signify faith in the resurrection and the immortality of the soul.

Gentry and common people observed the New Year celebrations. Noblemen, lords and princes gifted the royal family with very expensive gemstones or vast sums of money; the less affluent tended to send books, gloves, capons, beautifully decorated eggs, cakes, apples and oranges studded with cloves as New Year's Day gifts. Henry VIII, Edward VI and Elizabeth I observed this custom; Matthew Paris reports that Henry III in 1249 ordered the upper echelons of London society to provide him with gifts.[35]

In Wales, eighteenth-century wassailers at times visited by invitation, as Dafydd Jones, a Penrhyndeudraeth bookbinder, testifies in the opening stanza of his 'Carol i'w chanu ar nos Galan wrth fynd i'r tŷ a'r ddawns'[36] (A carol to be sung on New Year's Eve on entering the house and the dance) composed in 1767. He states that he and his friends are singing outside the house, praising in song the home and its inhabitants, in response to an invitation to the celebrations held at the house to welcome in the New Year. The following nine stanzas praise the Lord God for sending a glorious Saviour on Christmas Day. This Saviour, Jesus Christ, was (line 9) circumcised 'ar gyfer hyn' (against this day), and they praise him as their Redeemer and blessed mediator. In Adam, mankind had been placed under condemnation; in Moses, placed under the law and the commandments; but in Christ, made a justified and blessed people. Joy and merriment abound and in the closing stanza a musician is called upon to make music so that they can dance 'fesul cwpwl' (in couples/one couplet at a time). This is a rare example of reference being made by a wassailing party to receiving a specific invitation to an eighteenth-century New Year's Eve dance.

Caleniga, visiting neighbourhood homes collecting New Year's gifts on New Year's Day, was observed very early in the morning as gifts were not distributed after mid-day: 'The proper time to sing was from 12 o'clock midnight until daylight.'[37] D. Roy Saer records:

Obviously some of these rhymes were at one period sung during
sleeping-hours: they call upon people to rise from bed. Custom
was for young men (and *men* only) to sing at the doors after
midnight on New Year's Eve and for children to do likewise later
that morning, from rising-time through until mid-day.[38]

The opening lines of a rhyme from Llanerfyl in Montgomeryshire con-
firms the men's timetable:

> Gwrandewch ar fy nhestun
> pan ddechreuodd y flwyddyn
> pan darodd hi ddeuddeg o'r gloch.[39]

[Listen to my message, | At the turn of the year, | When it
struck twelve o'clock.]

Groups of about six or seven young men in Penegoes, Montgomery-
shire, would 'hel yn ystod y nos' (collect [gifts] during the night); in
Ffair-rhos in Ceredigion and in Ystradfellte in south Powys c.1920,
young men would visit farms at night and the householders would
throw down their coins from bedroom windows.[40] A party of four
wassailers, Gwennan Evans and her brother Ifan Evans of Fferm Parc-
y-mynydd, and another brother and sister, Manon Jones and Gwion
Jones of Fferm y Lan, all in their early twenties, still visit homes on 1
January, starting off just as the clock strikes midnight. They visit family
members and friends in the villages of Bryn Iwan, Hermon, Blaen-y-
coed and Tre-lech near Cynwyl Elfed (Carmarthenshire) until about
2.00 a.m. collecting New Year's gifts. As a rule, they sing the old Welsh
plygain carol 'Ar gyfer heddiw'r bore'. Younger children start out at
about 9.00 a.m.[41]

For early morning visitors the first task was to get the house-
holders out of bed. One group of singers have a specific request: 'A
wnewch chwi godi lawr i roi te?'[42] (Will you come down to give [us]
tea?)' possibly made using new water to make the first cup of tea of
the year. Other singers desire a stronger drink:

> Codwch lawr o'r gwely,
> Agorwch eich seleri.[43] (Cross Hands, Carmarthen)

[Come down from your bed, | Open up your cellars.]

The poets requested gifts of monies, bread and cheese, or small cakes and drinks. A stanza from Tregaron in Ceredigion refers to Trecefel farm:

> Rhowch i mi docyn diogel
> Fel gallo Mam ei arddel,
> Neu chwech gael cwart,
> Dwi'n hidio fawr,
> Waeth fi yw gwas mawr Trecefel.[44]

[Give me a big slice of bread | That Mother would approve of, | Or a sixpence for a quart, | I don't much care [which], | For I am the head manservant at Trecefel.]

Not all request poems were sung at farmsteads or private dwellings; one extant stanza was sung at the village stores and has a specific New Year's gift in view:

> Atoch chwi, y siopwr mwyn:
> Rhowch hyd eich trwyn o 'sbani'.[45]

[To you, genial shopkeeper: | Give a stick of liquorice the length of your nose.]

Request poems were also composed in strict metre, taking advantage of New Year's Day to petition for gifts, for example 'Englyn i ofyn Calennig' (An *englyn* requesting a calends gift) composed by Robert Hughes 'Robin Ddu yr Ail o Fôn' (Robin Ddu II of Anglesey) (1744–85):

> Mi dybiais coeliais mai Calan—Ionawr
> Sydd inni'n Ŵyl weithian;
> Rhoddwch, wŷr rhwydd, o'ch arian
> Ddernig o Galennig lân.[46]

[I have judged [and] believed it to be New Year's Day | That is now our high festival; | Give, generous men, from your wealth | A small sum as a fine New Year's gift.]

In addition to food and money the wassailers requested beer or spirits:

Diod! diod! lond siwg geinog:
Yfed honno (hy)d at y gweilod.
Diod! diod! lond siwg ddime:
Sarnu honno am ein sodle![47]

[Drink! drink! a penny jug full: | Drink that to the bottom. |
Drink! drink! a halfpenny jug full: | Spill that about our heels!]

This rhyme was recorded by D. Roy Saer on 12 September 1963 from
the singing of Phillip Owen, a farmer born in 1879 who recalls that
the children of St Davids in Pembrokeshire used to sing this stanza
outside the doors of various homes and farmsteads on Christmas Day
morning as well as on New Year's Day morning.

A similar *quête* (begging) rhyme was recorded by Roy Saer from
a female informant, Miss Selina Griffiths (b. 1880) of Garn, y Dinas
near Fishguard in Pembrokeshire, a rhyme she had learnt as a child
during the years 1885–90 when she lived in the Caersalem area, near
Newport in the upper reaches of the Gwaun Valley in Pembrokeshire,
and which she sang on New Year's morning only:

Deffrwch! benteulu,
Tyma bore'r Flwyddyn Newy'
Wedi dod adre
O fewn y drwse.
Drwse yng nghloion,
Wedi eu paro
Drost y nos:
O mistres fach fwyn,
Gwrandewch ar ein cwyn;
Plant ifenc ŷn ni,
Gyllyngwch ni i'r tŷ;
Gyllyngwch ni'n glou
Ynte tyma ni'n ffoi.
Rhowch galennig yn galonnog
I blant bach sy heb un ceinog;
Ceinog neu ddime,
P'un a fynnoch chwithe:
Ceinog sy ore.[48]

[Awake! head of the family, | Here is New Year's morning | Come home | Within the doors. | Locked doors, | Bolted | Overnight: | O dear gentle mistress, | Listen to our plea; | We are young children, | Let us into the house; | Let us in quickly | Or we run away. | Give a New Year's gift heartily | To little children who haven't a penny; | A penny or a halfpenny, | Whichever you prefer: | A penny is best.]

The Gwaun Valley in Pembrokeshire is notable for celebrating the Old New Year's Day on 13 January (see figure 6). The difference in the two dates of celebration can be attributed to the two different calendars in use in Europe for a number of years. The Gregorian Calendar used today was adopted in the United Kingdom in September 1752 to replace the historic Julian Calendar.[49] George II's Parliament in 1751 introduced an Act to make the British calendar conform to the one in use throughout most of the world. The new dates were eleven days ahead of the traditional way of counting. But in Wales the old dates were observed, especially in regard to agricultural matters, for instance when renting land. The Church and other anglicised elements in society followed the new system. In Wales, New Year celebrations followed the old calculation of dates. In Carmarthenshire the harvest-feast was held on New Year's Day, a supper for all who had assisted in bringing in the harvest:

> but this was done more often on Old New Year's Day than on the present New Year's Day (...) Feasting of a similar kind took place on Old New Year's Day in the Gwaun Valley (Pembrokeshire).[50]

The wassailers wished to be afforded the comforts of hearth and home: a light in their darkness, 'Ac hefyd cynnwch dân'[51] (And also kindle a fire). The harshness of the weather contributed to the earnestness with which they begged for sanctuary:

> Calennig rwyf yn mofyn
> Dydd Calan cynta'r flwyddyn,
> Nid yw'n hen fritsh werth dim grot:
> Mae godre 'nghot i'n gregyn.[52] (Peterwell, Lampeter, Ceredigion)

[My request is for a New Year's gift | On New Year's Day the first of the year, | My breeches aren't worth a groat: | The hems of my coat are in tatters.]

Mae boreu calennig yn foreu calonnog,
Plant bach yn dŵad a'u dillad yn dyllog
A'r windrew arswydus ar flaenau eu bysedd
A'r gwinedd bron codi wrth gydio'n y cydau.[52]

(Llanwenog, Ceredigion)

[New Year's Day morning is a cheerful morning, | Little children coming along, their clothes full of holes | And with terrible frostbite on their fingertips | And their nails almost hanging as they hold the bags.]

The long, arduous journey along valleys, dales and upland moors was challenging. Muddy roads, filthy byways, bushes and brambles caused the revellers much pain and grief:

Trwy'r baw a'r llaca
Daethom ni yma,
Drwy'r eithin weithiau
Gan bricio'n coesau.[54] (Solva, Pembrokeshire)

[Through the dirt and the mud | We came here, | Sometimes through the gorse | And stinging our legs.]

Most rhymes plead the poverty of the wassailing party and request a gift 'I ddyn gwan sy heb un geiniog'[55] (For a frail man who is without a penny [to his name]):

A chofiwch chwithau wrth rodd[i]
I ddiolch am eich ffawd,
Na fuasech wedi'ch geni
Fel finne'n blentyn tlawd.[56] (Llandysul, Ceredigion)

[And just you remember as you give [gifts] | To give thanks for your good fortune | That you were not born | Into poverty as I was.]

Gyda chwi mae'r helmi mawrion,
Gyda chwi mae'r gwartheg brithion,
O's 'da Mam ddim un o'r rheini
Ond lot o blant yn cael eu magu.[57] (Adpar, Ceredigion)

[You own large barns, | You own speckled cows, | Mother has
none of those | Just a lot of children being raised.]

Another songster, one of four young children all needing to be raised,
asks for compassion, and is grateful that 'Tad yr Amddifaid'[58] ([the
Father of the Orphaned/Destitute] cares for them yet).

Householders are cautioned against sharing their wealth with
town children, or with children from certain villages:

Dydd Calan yw hi heddi, ontê, ontê?
Peidiwch rhoi dim i blant y dre,
Na phlant Cwm-cou na phlant Dre-wen
Ond plant Johnnie Bach o'r Stafell-wen.[59]

(Adpar, Ceredigion)

[Today is New Year's Day, is it not, is it not? | Don't give any-
thing to town children, | Or to the children of Cwm-cou or to
the children of Dre-wen | Only to the children of Johnnie Bach
from Stafell-wen.]

In answer to the above:

Dydd Calan yw heddi, onid e?
Na rowch chwi ddim i blant y dre,
Ond rhowch galennig pert dros ben
I blant Cwm-cou a phlant Dre-wen.[60] (Ceredigion)

[Today is New Year's Day, is it not? | Don't give anything to
town children, | But do give an exceedingly pretty New Year's
Day gift | To the children of Cwm-cou and the children of
Dre-wen.]

Miserliness is frowned upon, and householders are encouraged to
contribute generously:

Yr hwn sydd â chyfoeth ac a'i ceidw,
Nid oes lwyddiant i'r dyn hwnnw;
Y neb a gadwo bob rhyw geiniog
Sydd yn casglu i'r god dyllog.[61] (Tal-y-bont, Ceredigion)

[He who has riches and retains his hold on them, | There is no
prosperity for that man; | The one who retains possession of
every penny | Gathers into a bag full of holes.]

Hynny rowch, O rhowch yn ddiddig,
Peidiwch grwgnach am ryw ychydig.[62] (Llanwenog, Ceredigion)

[Whatever you give, O give it contentedly, | Don't begrudge a
little something.]

A share of the profits was requested on behalf of party members,
sometimes named at the point indicated by the star:

Dydd da chwi bawb o'r teulu,
Mae Anna fach* yn pori.[63] (Llandysul, Ceredigion)

[Good day to you, all the family, | Little Anna* is grazing.]

Occasionally the householder's name might be disclosed:

Mi godais yn fore, mi redais yn ffyrnig
I dŷ Mr Morris i mofyn Calennig.[64] (Llanwenog, Ceredigion)

[I rose up early, I ran furiously | To Mr Morris's house to
request a New Year's gift.]

Various names could be fitted into the stanza as necessary:

Blwyddyn newydd dda i chwi,
Meistr Jones a Meistres Jones,
A'r rest o'r teulu i gyd.[65] (Llandybïe, Carmarthenshire)

[A good new year to you, | Mr Jones and Mrs Jones, | And all
the rest of the family.]

If no name is mentioned, a reference to their profession might answer the purpose equally well. From rural Pontsian in Ceredigion where agriculture is the main industry:

Mi godes yn fore,
Mi redes yn ffyrnig
Ar draws y tai *farmers* i mofyn Calennig,
A'r caws yn yr ysgubor
A'r bara yn y tŷ,
A'r arian yn eich poced yn swno drwy'r dydd.[66]

[I rose up early, | I ran furiously | Across to the farmers' houses to request a New Year's gift, | And the cheese in the barn | And the bread in the house, | And the coins in your pocket jangling all day long.]

Using their collection of gifts, the singers were mindful to provide for the needs of their parents and even for auntie 'Am bod hi mor gam'[67] (Because she is so crooked). A share is commonly requested for the '*gŵr* bonheddig'[68] (gentleman) and for the stick. The stick is referred to in stanzas recorded in Newport (Pembrokeshire), Tre-lech, Llanybydder and Llanelli (Carmarthenshire), Llandysul parish (Ceredigion), and even further afield, and often appears in the opening line 'Calennig i mi, calennig i'r ffon' (A New Year's gift for me, a New Year's gift for the stick). The following stanza recorded in the parish of Trefeglwys in Montgomeryshire differs slightly:

'Nghlennig i'n gyfan ar fore Dydd Calan,
Unwaith, dwywaith, tair;
Clennig i mi, clennig i'r ffon, a chlennig i minnau i fynd adre,
Gŵr y tŷ a'r teulu da, a welwch chwi'n dda ga i glennig?[69]

[My New Year's Day gift in full on New Year's morning, | Once, twice, thrice; | A New Year's gift for me, a New Year's gift for the stick, and a New Year's gift for me to take home, | The gentleman of the house and the good family, please may I have a New Year's gift?]

The significance of the line 'Unwaith, dwywaith, tair' (Once, twice, thrice) is uncertain, and whether it refers to the stick is also unclear. If so, the line might refer to the 'pastwn draenen'[70] (blackthorn cudgel) being used three times to beat back the thorn bushes and briars that impeded the progress of the wassailing party, or it might assist the drunken singers to keep upright to their journey's end, or again it might refer to the cudgel being used to beat the door three times in an appeal for entry. There may be a similarity between this shout and that of the Bidder, whose task it was in the eighteenth and nineteenth centuries to travel around the neighbourhood distributing bidding letters inviting friends to the wedding of a couple about to be married.[71] As he travelled the neighbourhood the Bidder would strike the floor with his stick to call for silence as he prepared to deliver his verbal invitation (see figure 7).

The stick, however, was not universally appreciated. From Llandyfaelog in Carmarthenshire:

Rhanna, rhanna yn ddwbwl ddyrneidiau,
Rhan i 'Nhad am gwyro sgidiau,
Rhan i Mam am gwyro 'sanau,
A rhan i'r ffon am aros gartre.[72]

[Share, share in double fistfuls, | A share for Father for repairing boots, | A share for Mother for darning socks, | And a share for the stick for staying at home.]

The stanza has been noted as a 'Diwarnod Rhana' (Sharing Day) rhyme, which took place at or about 'Dygwyl eneidiau' (All Souls' Day). In Kidwelly, the evening before 'Diwarnod Rhana':

the good wife of the farm busied herself with the baking of large flat cakes. Early next day both women and children of the labouring class came to the kitchen door reciting in monotone –

"Rhana! Rhana! Dwgwl aneide,
Rhan i nhad am gywiro scidie,
Rhan i mam am gywiro sane,
Rhan i'r plant sy'n aros gartre."

The good wife then asked "Faint ych chi?" and distributed the cakes according to the number in the family. Only those who had helped, or the children of those who had helped, at the harvest got the *Pice Rhana* [Rhana cakes] (...) and thus in course of time the custom became bound up with the harvest.[73]

The stanza's opening line has been variously converted to 'dwbwl dameide' (double portion) and 'dwbwl ddyrneidiau' (double fistfuls).

Wassailers promised greater gifts than they received. What is a little beer and cheese compared with health and longevity, luck and prosperity?

O byddwch mor garedig
Ag agor drws eich tŷ
Mae'r flwyddyn fwyaf lwcus
Yn dŵad gyda ni.[74] (Resolven, Vale of Neath)

[If you would be so kind | As to open the door of your house | The luckiest year [ever] | Is coming [in] with us.]

Having gained admittance into the home, the wassailers would receive their reward, give praise, and give thanks for every contribution received:

Fe gawsom lath enwyn a bobo sgadenyn,
Orenjes, fale a reis,
Plwm pwdin a *whisky* a phob math o jelis,
A lot o bethe neis, neis.[75]

[We have received buttermilk and a herring each, | Oranges, apples and rice, | Plum pudding and whisky and all sorts of jellies, | And lots of nice, nice things.]

In three *englynion* dated 6 January 1832 John Roberts greets the Revd Ll. Lloyd, Nannerch in Flintshire, delighting in the opportunity to offer him a New Year's gift. The poet is persuaded that some of his lines will gladden the minister's heart, thereby restoring his health. He wishes Revd Lloyd the attention of 'ffyddlon feddygon'[76] (loyal doctors), supremely magnificent men who will heal him. This echoes

the common wish for longevity and good health that are the order of
the day at the turning of the year.

A successful harvest was essential:

Calennig yn galonnog
Gan obeithio cewch gynhaeaf toreithiog,
Ceirch a barlys, rhyg a gwenith,
Shiprys ddigon, tato gwynion,
Diolch yn fawr am eich rhoddion.[77] (Cribyn, Ceredigion)

[[Give] a New Year's gift cheerfully | In the hope that you
reap an abundant harvest, | Oats and barley, rye and wheat, |
A mixed crop of oats and barley in profusion, white potatoes,
| Thank you very much for your gifts.]

O dewch â chalennig, gyfeillion caredig,
Rhowch chwi galennig yn g'lonnog;
Does gyda ni gartre ddim cwrw Gwylie,
Rhowch siâr o'ch barilau ddiwrnod.
Gobeithio cewch gynhaeaf temprus
Ar geirch ac ar farlys, haidd a siprys ddigon.
Diolch byth ichwi am eich rhoddion.[78] (Llanwenog, Ceredigion)

[O bring a New Year's gift, generous friends, | Give a New Year's
gift ungrudgingly: | We have at home no Christmastide beer, |
Give a share of your barrels today. | We hope that you have a
temperate harvest | Of oats and barley, barleycorn and plenty
of mixed-crop grain. | Eternal gratitude to you for your gifts.]

Not all wassailing parties were lucky in their gifts. The disap-
pointed sought revenge by wishing evil on the householders, as the
following stanzas reveal:

Blwyddyn Newydd ddrwg
A llond y tŷ o fwg
Ac ysbryd drwg yn y simne.[79] (Lampeter, Ceredigion)

[A bad New Year | And a house full of smoke | And an evil
spirit in the chimney stack.]

Blwyddyn Newydd ddrwg
A llond y tŷ o fwg,
Pen 'r hen geliog o dan y drws,
Pen 'r hen wraig yn sitrws.[80] (Montgomeryshire)

[A bad New Year | And a house full of smoke, | The head of
the old cockerel under the door, | The head of the old woman
in smithereens.]

Blwyddyn Newydd gas
Llond tŷ o gachu.[81] (Blaenau Ffestiniog, Gwynedd)

[A nasty New Year | A house full of shit.]

Mae'r hen gorgi yn y gwely,
A'r hen sopen wrth ei gefn;
Cwthwm tro a ddelo heibio
Eto a'r tŷ a'r cwbl ganddo.[82] (south Pembrokeshire)

[The old corgi is in bed, | And the old sop at his back; | May a
whirlwind pass over them | Even now and take the house and
everything else with it.]

Calennig i fi, Calennig i hon,
Os na cha i galennig, mi'ch bwra i chi â ffon.[83]
(Capel Cynon, Ceredigion)

[A New Year's gift for me, a New Year's gift for her, | If I don't
receive a New Year's gift, I'll beat you with a stick.]

Lyric poetry of a slightly sentimental nature was also composed
at the New Year, much of it melancholic and referring to the host
of departed loved ones sorely missed at the turn of another year.
Sung to the popular tune 'Sosban Fach' (see p. 182), the following
is typical:

Gyfeillion rhowch glust o wrandawiad,
Mae'n destun llawenydd drwy'r lle
Fod blwyddyn ychwaneg wedi'i geni

I ni rai annheilwng dan y nef.
Rhown ein llef i ddiolch iddo Ef,
Rhown ein llef i ddiolch iddo Ef,
Am weld blwyddyn eto cyn ein bedd.

Y rhai oeddynt hoff gan ein calon
Oedd fyw ddechrau'r flwyddyn a fu,
A'u henaid sydd wedi ffarwelio
A'u cyrff ym mhriddellau'r dyffryn du.
O na chawn ni rodio'r flwyddyn hon
Yn fwy tebyg i'r Gŵr fu'n rhodio'r don
Fel y cawn gyfarfod yn y nef.[84]

[Stanza 1: Friends, give ear, listen, | It is a subject of joy
throughout the land | That another year has been born | To
us, unworthy ones under the heavens. | Let us raise our cry to
thank Him, | Let us raise our cry to thank Him, | For seeing
another year before [going to] our grave.

Stanza 2: Those whom we were fond of | Were alive at the
beginning of last year, | And their souls have now departed |
And their bodies are in the soil of the graves of the black val-
ley. | O that we may walk this year | More like the Man who
walked on water | So that we can meet in heaven.]

And again:

Mae'r hen flwyddyn wedi mynd,
Ac ni ddaw hi fyth yn ôl;
Mae wedi mynd â llawer ffrind
Ac wedi 'ngadel i ar ôl.[85] (Llandybïe, Carmarthenshire)

[The old year has departed, | And it will never return; | It has
taken numerous friends | And it has left me behind.]

Those nervous about their longevity in this world turned to God for
strength to face the journey into eternity:

Llawer leni raid mynd heibio
I breswylio'r eilfyd maith,
Falle finne wedi eu rhifo,
Arglwydd, dyro fodd i'r daith.[86]

(Brynberian, north Pembrokeshire)

[This year many must pass away | To reside in the eternal
world to come, | I myself might well be counted in their midst,
| Lord, grant succour to make the journey.]

Traditional New Year's Day customs are now in decline. Most
present-day rhymes request a gift and wish the giver a prosperous
New Year, but any ritualistic significance is largely absent. In many
neighbourhoods the custom in its entirety has fallen by the wayside.
Even during the closing years of the nineteenth century (c.1896), one
songster admits that the New Year's Day observance had gone clean
out of his mind:

Calennig yn gyfan
Drannoeth i'r Calan;
Y Calan aeth heibio
Pan nad own yn cofio.[87] (Llandysul, Ceredigion)

[A New Year's gift in full | On the day after New Year's Day; |
New Year's Day passed by | Unremembered by me.]

Slowly the custom loosened its traditional grip on society, particularly
when its importance was surpassed by the importance of Christmas
and its expensive gifts. But New Year's Day still resonated with the
public in many areas of Wales into the 1920s:

1922 sydd wedi mynd,
Nis gwelwn mwy ein hannwyl ffrind,
1923 a ddaeth i'w lle
Croesawn hon â hipwrê.

Chorus:
Roedd hon yn flwyddyn lawen (x3)
I bawb sydd yn y tŷ.[88] (Pontsian, Ceredigion)

[1922 has departed, | We shall no longer see our dear friend, | 1923 has taken its place | Let us welcome it with a hip-hooray. | *Chorus:* This was a joyful year (x3) | For everyone in the house.]

Over twenty years later the tradition was still observed, as a stanza written in 1944, during the Second World War, establishes:

Gobeithio yn *nineteen forty-four*
Bydd heddwch dros y tir a'r môr,
Ac elo'r byd i gyd mewn trefn
Ac na foed rhyfel byth drachefn.[89] (Llandysul, Ceredigion)

[Let us hope that in nineteen forty-four | There will be peace over land and sea, | And that the whole world should be in order | And that there is never war again.]

The tradition is still observed in many parts of twenty-first-century Wales, mostly led by the child's hope of monetary gain and by the eagerness of parents and grandparents to uphold a folk custom that reminds them of their childhood; a nod to a distant past, it still retains its charm in many Welsh communities. New Year's Day 2021 celebrations, however, were hampered by the restrictions on movement enforced by the Welsh Government during the coronavirus (Covid-19) pandemic. It was illegal in Wales to roam the locale wishing residents a 'Happy New Year'. Not willing to disengage entirely with the custom, the following stanza was e-mailed during the lockdown in early January 2021:

Myfi yw'r flwyddyn newydd
Sy'n dod ar ysgafn droed,
Yr wyf yn hen ac eto
Mor ifanc ag erioed.
Yr wyf yn dwyn bendithion
I bawb yn ddiwahân,
Agorwch chithau'r drysau
A dof i mewn â chân!

[I am the new year | That comes with a light foot, | I am old and yet | As young as ever. | I bring blessings | For everyone indiscriminately, | Open the doors | And I will come in with a song!]

It must be stressed that no examples of entering homes with a song were noted in 2021.

Notes

1. Born and brought up in Penrhyn-coch, Aberystwyth, Ceredigion, Andreas Huws greeted householders on New Year's morning during the late 1970s and early 1980s.

2. Tegwyn Jones, *Ar Dafod Gwerin: Penillion Bob Dydd* [Oral Folk Poetry: Everyday Stanzas] (Aberystwyth: Cymdeithas Lyfrau Ceredigion Gyf., 2004), p. 257.

3. Mary Curtis, *The Antiquities of Laugharne, Pendine, and their Neighbourhoods: Carmarthenshire, Amroth, Saundersfoot, Cilgetty, Pembrokeshire, South Wales* (London: printed for the author by R. Clay, Sons & Taylor, 1880; facsimile reprint Carmarthen: Dyfed County Council, Cultural Services Department, 1991), p. 203.

4. Herbert M. Vaughan, *The South Wales Squires* (Carmarthen: The Golden Grove Book Company Ltd, 1988; first published in 1926 by Methuen & Co. Ltd), p. 34.

5. NLW 7191B, f. 264^r–^{v}.

6. Cwrtmawr 294B, ff. 39^r–40^v.

7. The Book of Revelation 21:4.

8. The Gospel according to St Luke 2:21: 'On the eighth day, when it was time to circumcise the child, he was named Jesus, the name the angel had given him before he was conceived.'

9. Poem 12.9–12.

10. J. Rendel Harris, 'Origin and Meaning of Apple Cults', *Bulletin of the John Rylands Library*, 5 (Manchester, 1918–20), p. 51.

11. Gruffydd Evans, 'Carmarthenshire Gleanings (Kidwelly)', *Y Cymmrodor, the Magazine of the Honourable Society of Cymmrodorion*, 25 (1915), 114–15.

12. G. J. Williams, *Iolo Morganwg, 1747–1826* (Cardiff: University of Wales Press, 1956), p. 39.

13. See the chapter 'Hunting the Wren'.

14. J. Thomas, *Cofiant y Parch. T. Rees, D.D. Abertawy* [A biography of the Revd T. Rees, DD Swansea] (Dolgellau: William Hughes, 1888), pp. 15–16.

15. D. G. Williams, 'Casgliad o Len-Gwerin Sir Gaerfyrddin' [An Anthology of the Folklore of Carmarthenshire], in *Transactions of the National Eisteddfod of Wales Llanelly, 1895* (London: National Eisteddfod Association, 1898; Caerfyrddin [Carmarthen]: Cyngor Sir Caerfyrddin [Carmarthen County Council], 1996), p. 20.

16. Arthur Mee (ed.), 'New Year's Customs in South-West Wales', *The Caermarthenshire Miscellany*, 1 (London: Elliot Stock, 1892), p. 2.

17. A reference to the tradition known as 'Whipo'r Celyn' [Whipping with Holly]; see Evans, 'Carmarthenshire Gleanings (Kidwelly)', p. 115.

18. John Rhys, 'Folk-lore Miscellanea', *Folklore*, 3 (1892), 381.

19. Jonathan Ceredig Davies, *Folk-lore of West and Mid-Wales* (Aberystwyth: Welsh Gazette offices, 1911; facsimile reprint Felinfach: Llanerch, 1992), p. 64, available online at *http://www.gutenberg.org/files/53915/53915-h/53915-h htm#ch4* (accessed 25 June 2020).

20. Curtis, *The Antiquities of Laugharne*, p. 202.

21. Mary Beatrice Mirehouse, *South Pembrokeshire: Some of its History and Records* (London: David Nutt, 1910), p. 73.

22. David Thomas, OBE, Aberystwyth, Papers (NLW): 'Cardiganshire Schools Folklore Collection', 1918–c.1926, B15 Capel Cynon School, unpaged.

23. The meaning of 'seven bright gold wires' is unclear; 'my parents [Rosemary and Jeremy Goring] wondered if the "seven bright gold wires" were a corruption of *vials* and, together with the "bugles that do shine", were imagery from the Book of Revelation', personal e-mail from Charles Goring, 25 February 2020.

24. Davies, *Folk-lore of West and Mid-Wales*, p. 65; Edward Laws, *A History of Little England beyond Wales, and the Non-Kymric Colony Settled in Pembrokeshire* (London: George Bell and Sons, 1888; British Library Historical Print Edition), p. 407.

25. Curtis, *The Antiquities of Laugharne*, p. 202.

26. Williams, 'Casgliad o Len-Gwerin Sir Gaerfyrddin', p. 20.

27. Curtis, *The Antiquities of Laugharne*, p. 202.

28. Evans, 'Carmarthenshire Gleanings (Kidwelly)', 114n4.

29. Francis Jones, *The Holy Wells of Wales* (Cardiff: University of Wales Press, 1992; first published 1954); see also Eirlys and Ken Lloyd Gruffydd, *Ffynhonnau Cymru* [The Wells of Wales], 2 vols (Llanrwst: Gwasg Carreg Gwalch, 1999); James Rattue, *The Living Stream: Holy Wells in Historical Context* (Woodbridge: The Boydell Press, 1995); S. Baring-Gould and J. Fisher, *The Lives of the British Saints*, 4 vols (London: The Honourable Society of Cymmrodorion, 1907–13).

30. A. R. Wright and T. E. Lones, *British Calendar Customs: England* (London: W. Glaisher for The Folk-Lore Society, 1936–40), p. 21.

31. W. Stukeley, '"Much Greater, than Commonly Imagined": Celtic Druids and the Universal Religion', in David Boyd Haycock, *William Stukeley: Science, Religion and Archaeology in Eighteenth-Century England* (Woodbridge: Boydell, 2002), pp. 160–88; Prys Morgan, 'Jonathan Williams (1752–1829) a derwyddon Sir Faesyfed' [Jonathan Williams (1752–1829) and the druids of Radnorshire], *Taliesin*, 82 (1993), 89–94.

32. Cwrtmawr 128A, 87.

33. W. J. Davies, *Hanes Plwyf Llandyssul* [The History of Llandysul Parish] (Llandyssul: J. D. Lewis, 1896; facsimile reprint Llandysul: Gomer, 1992), p. 258.

34. Trefor M. Owen, *Welsh Folk Customs* (Cardiff: National Museum of Wales/Welsh Folk Museum, 1974), p. 45.

35. Richard Vaughan (ed.), *The Illustrated Chronicles of Matthew Paris* (Stroud: Alan Sutton Publishing, 1993), p. 86.

36. Poem 12.

37. A letter dated 13 January 1896 written by H. W. Evans of Solva, published in H. W. Williams, *Pembrokeshire Antiquities: Reprints from 'Amsang ein tadau', the Antiquaries' Column in the 'Pembroke County Guardian'* (Solva: H. W. Williams, 1897), p. 45.

38. D. Roy Saer (ed.), *Caneuon Llafar Gwlad (Songs From Oral Tradition)*, 1 (Cardiff: National Museum of Wales/Welsh Folk Museum, 1974), pp. 59–60.

39. Heledd Maldwyn Jones (ed.), *Blas ar Fwynder Maldwyn* [A Taste of Montgomeryshire Geniality] (Llanrwst: Gwasg Carreg Gwalch, 2003), p. 78.

40. Tecwyn Vaughan Jones, '"Calennig a Chalennig a Blwyddyn Newydd Dda": Y Plentyn ar Ddydd Calan yng Nghymru' [A New Year's gift and a New Year's gift and a Good New Year: the child in Wales on New Year's Day], in Robert M. Morris (ed.), *Ar Lafar ei Wlad: Cyfrol Deyrnged John Owen Huws* [His Country's Oral Tradition: A *Festschrift* in Honour of John Owen Huws] (Llanrwst: Gwasg Carreg Gwalch, 2002), p. 231.

41. Gwennan Evans, *Geraint Lloyd*, BBC Radio Cymru, 18 November 2021.

42. D. Roy Saer, personal file.

43. Williams, 'Casgliad o Len-Gwerin Sir Gaerfyrddin', p. 21.

44. Davies, *Folk-lore of West and Mid-Wales*, p. 63.

45. D. Roy Saer, personal file.

46. NLW 4550B, 109; BL Add MS 14968, f. 63ᵛ; BL Add MS 14993, f. 11ᵛ.

47. The closing lines of a rhyme sung in St Davids c.1886, see Saer, *Caneuon Llafar Gwlad*, p. 37.

48. Ibid., p. 29.

49. See further B. Blackburn and I. Holford-Strevens, *The Oxford Companion to the Year* (Oxford: Oxford University Press, 2003, repr. with

corrections); D. Feeney, *Caesar's Calendar: Ancient Time and the Beginnings of History* (Berkeley and London: University of California Press, c.2007); S. Stern, *Calendars in Antiquity: Empires, States and Societies* (Oxford: Oxford University Press, 2012).

50. Owen, *Welsh Folk Customs*, p. 46.

51. Davies, *Hanes Plwyf Llandyssul*, p. 257.

52. Thomas, 'Cardiganshire Schools Folklore Collection', 1918–c.1926, B61 Peterwell School, unpaged.

53. NLW 10551B, Exercise Book 3, stanza 76 from Llanwenog; stanza 77 is similarly worded; see also J. Islan Jones, *Yr Hen Amser Gynt* [Times Past] (Aberystwyth: Cymdeithas Lyfrau Ceredigion, 1958), p. 10.

54. Williams, *Pembrokeshire Antiquities*, p. 44.

55. NLW 10551B, Exercise Book 3, stanza 72.

56. Davies, *Hanes Plwyf Llandyssul*, p. 259.

57. Thomas, 'Cardiganshire Schools Folklore Collection', 1918–c.1926, B3 Adpar School, Newcastle Emlyn, unpaged.

58. NLW 10551B, Exercise Book 3, stanza 81.

59. Thomas, 'Cardiganshire Schools Folklore Collection', 1918–c.1926, B3 Adpar School, Newcastle Emlyn, unpaged.

60. Nansi Hayes, 'Hen Benillion Calan' [Old Verses for New Year's Day], *Y Tincer* [The Tinker] (January 1979), unpaged.

61. Poem 19.13–16.

62. NLW 10551B, Exercise Book 3, stanza 72.

63. Davies, *Hanes Plwyf Llandyssul*, p. 257.

64. NLW 10551B, Exercise Book 3, stanza 71.

65. Gomer M. Roberts, *Hanes Plwyf Llandybïe* [The History of the Parish of Llandybïe] (Cardiff: University of Wales Press, 1939), p. 277.

66. Thomas, 'Cardiganshire Schools Folklore Collection', 1918–c.1926, B64 Pontsian School, unpaged.

67. Jones, *Ar Dafod Gwerin*, p. 248.

68. From Llandysul see Williams, 'Casgliad o Len-Gwerin Sir Gaerfyrddin', p. 21.

69. Charles Ashton, 'Bywyd Gwledig yng Nghymru' [Rural life in Wales], *Transactions of the National Eisteddfod of Wales Bangor, 1890* ([Liverpool], I. Foulkes, 1892), p. 67.

70. Thomas, 'Cardiganshire Schools Folklore Collection', 1918–c.1926, B15 Capel Cynon School, unpaged.

71. E. Emrys Williams, 'Arferion Priodasol yn yr Hen Ddyddiau' [Wedding Customs in Former Days], *Y Casglwr* [The Collector] (August 1983), 18; Dafydd Ifans, 'Lewis Morris ac Arferion Priodi yng Ngheredigion' [Lewis Morris and Wedding Customs in Ceredigion], *Ceredigion: Journal of the Cardiganshire Antiquarian Society*, 8 (1977), 193–203; Trefor M. Owen,

'Some Aspects of the Bidding in Cardiganshire', *Ceredigion: Journal of the Cardiganshire Antiquarian Society*, 4 (1960), 36–46.

72. Cardi, 'Cardiganshire Customs and Superstitions', *Bye-gones: relating to Wales and the Border Counties* (29 September 1897), 207.

73. Evans, 'Carmarthenshire Gleanings (Kidwelly)', pp. 112–14.

74. Allan James, 'Astudiaeth o'r geiriau a genir ar alawon Gwent a Morgan- nwg' [A study of the words sung to the tunes of Gwent and Glamorgan] (unpublished MA thesis, University of Wales [Swansea], 1968), 295.

75. D. Roy Saer, personal file.

76. NLW 1578B, 20.

77. AWC MS 1737/8.

78. NLW 10551B, Exercise Book 3, stanza 78.

79. AWC Tape Archive 3396/3.

80. R. W. Jones, *Bywyd Cymdeithasol Cymru yn y Ddeunawfed Ganrif* [The social life of Wales during the eighteenth century] (Llundain: Gwasg Gymraeg Foyle [an imprint of Foyle's bookshop in London], 1931), p. 122.

81. Jones, 'Calennig a Chalennig', p. 232.

82. Williams, *Pembrokeshire Antiquities*, p. 45.

83. Thomas, 'Cardiganshire Schools Folklore Collection', 1918–*c*.1926, B15 Capel Cynon School, unpaged.

84. D. Roy Saer, personal file.

85. Roberts, *Hanes Plwyf Llandybïe*, p. 277.

86. AWC MS 2186/4, ex inf. H. Glyn Bowen, Brynberian in Pembrokeshire, a member of staff working at Esgair Moel Woollen Mill at St Fagans National History Museum (1965).

87. Davies, *Hanes Plwyf Llandyssul*, p. 257.

88. Thomas, 'Cardiganshire Schools Folklore Collection', 1918–*c*.1926, B64 Pontsian School, unpaged.

89. Jones, *Ar Dafod Gwerin*, p. 247.

Hunting the Wren

THE CUSTOM OF HUNTING the wren, placing it in a decorated box and parading it ceremonially around the neighbourhood during the Christmas season, is yet another form of winter wassailing observed in Wales at one time. The earliest evidence for the custom dates to the latter part of the fourteenth century, in the form of three references found in the satirical poems preserved in Llyfr Coch Hergest[1] (The Red Book of Hergest), compiled c.1375–1425.

Two of those references appear in a satirical poem written by Trahaearn Brydydd Mawr to his fellow poet Casnodyn entitled 'Dychan i Gasnodyn'.[2] The first reference alludes to the hunted wren's cry (line 33), 'Begr golwyn gwadd drwyn gwaedd dryw—ar helcud' ([Casnodyn,] the son of a beggar [with] the snout of a mole [and] the cry of a hunted wren). The second reference to a wren (line 48) 'Dwy ysgwydd dryw blwydd drwy'r blwch' compares Casnodyn's two shoulders to the shoulders of a wren but does not allude to a wren hunt. N. G. Costigan (Bosco) in her notes on this poem mentions the poet's extensive references to locations in Glamorgan, suggesting that he spent a long period of time in that area; the poem also mentions that Trahaearn spent some time in the Teifi Valley: he may have observed this custom on his journeys in these two areas.

A further reference to the custom of hunting the wren appears in the only surviving poem written by Iocyn Ddu ab Ithel Grach (fl. c.1380), 'Helyntion bardd crwydrol'[3] (Troubles of an itinerant poet).

Iocyn Ddu recalls his travel adventures during the time he spent on circuit as a bard (or minstrel) in north-east Wales and Chester in search of patronage. He refers to the Vale of Clwyd, Marchwiel near Wrexham, Llanferres in Denbighshire, Berriew and Cemmaes in historical Montgomeryshire, and Caerffawydd (Hereford) on the Welsh border; other possible place names (that could also be common nouns) are Y Gwreiddiau (possibly in Llanwddyn, Montgomeryshire), Y Nugarth and Y Fferi (two unknown locations). During this journey Iocyn Ddu took part in a wren hunt and struck a wren:

> Goruwch Clawdd Offa da y digonais,
> Goris Aberryw dryw a drewais,
> Dyrnod graen â maen, y mae yn glais—a chlwyf,
> Ni wn nas lladdwyf neu a'i lleddais.[4]

[Above Offa's Dyke I laboured well, | Below Berriew I struck a wren, | A nasty blow with a stone, it is a bruise and a wound, | I am not sure whether I have killed it or not].[5]

Whether Iocyn Ddu attacked the wren on Offa's Dyke itself or whether the attack took place nearer to the village of Berriew is unclear. He does specify, however, that the hunt took place (line 32) on 'diw Ystwyll' (Twelfth Night), evidence that the custom was observed in north-east Wales on 6 January during the last quarter of the fourteenth century. Huw M. Edwards notes[6] that this date coincides with the date of the Life of the Irish Saint Moling,[7] compiled towards the end of the fourteenth century or the beginning of the fifteenth. In it the saint curses the wren for hopping on a fly and killing it, and his wish is that the wren be destroyed by children and young people,[8] and 'we may suppose that the curse put into the mouth of St. Moling (...) was an indication of some such practice [i.e. hunting the wren] being current in medieval times'.[9]

In the seventeenth century, the practice was noted and briefly described in north Pembrokeshire by Edward Lhuyd (1660–1709) in his *Parochialia*, compiled when he was keeper of the Ashmolean Museum in Oxford:

> Arverant yn swydh Benfro &c. dhwyn driw mewn elor nos ystwylh; odhiwrth gwr Ivank at i Gariad, sef day neu dri ai dygant mewn elor a ribane; ag a ganant gorolion.

Ant hevyd i day ereilh lhe ni bo kariadon a bydh kwrw v. &c.
A elor o'r wlad ai galwant Kwlli [*sic* Kwtti][10] wran.[11]

[It was customary in Pembrokeshire &c. to carry a wren in a
bier on Twelfth Night; from a young man to his sweetheart,
that is two or three carry him on a bier with ribbons; and sing
carols.

They also go to other houses where there are no sweet-
hearts and there will be beer &c. And a bier from the country
they call Cutty Wran.]

One anonymous writer assures his readers that this custom was
not confined to Pembrokeshire; he had heard 'from the lips of several
old inhabitants in the rural parts of Carmarthenshire, that "the wren"
flourished at one time in that county also'.[12] The cleric and antiquary
John Jenkins 'Ifor Ceri' (1770–1829), originally from Llangoedmor
near Cardigan in Ceredigion and writing *c*.1815, describes a custom
'probably of Druidical origin' observed in the vicinity of Cardigan on
5 January:

a certain Number of Young men, generally four, take a Wren
which is considered a Sacred Bird, and confine him in a cage
(which they call his (elor) Bier) decked with all the Ribbons
they can procure from the Girls of the neighbourhood. With
the Wren thus gaudily housed they visit the Families of the
District, singing alternate Stanzas in his praise as King of the
Birds and as procuring for them many Blessings during the
ensuing Year, on account of his being made a Captive and a
Victim.[13]

Ifor Ceri's note follows two tunes (see figure 8), each entitled 'Halsing
y Dryw' (The wren carol), the first to be sung 'moderately', the second
'more lively'; he adds, 'To these two short airs the praises of the Wren
are sung.'[14] No song text appears with either tune.

No detailed description of the custom has survived in north Wales.
Remnants of the practice, however, have persisted. Instances of wren-
hunt songs from Llanrhaeadr-ym-Mochnant (north Powys), Denbigh,
Amlwch (Anglesey), Llŷn, and Llwyngwril (a coastal village south of
Dolgellau in Gwynedd) have been noted by Lewis Davies Jones 'Llew

Tegid' (1851–1928).[15] The existence of the Llanrhaeadr-ym-Mochnant
wren song was noted in the 1840s following a rendition by an illiter-
ate farm hand in the Cwm-du area. It was noted as being more of an
intriguing chant than a melodic song. His friends would congregate in
the stable loft to listen to him and to watch him act the parts, evidence
of the farm hand's dramatic originality, or possibly that the custom as
well as the songs existed across north Wales at one time. This chant
was collected in Llanrhaeadr c.1876. It is intriguing that when a shep-
herd in Adderbury West in Oxfordshire, a certain Mr Hawkins, acted
and sang an old wren song, his wife (well over ninety years old in
1907) tried to stop him:

> when the old shepherd sang 'everyone' he stamped violently,
> so much so that his wife bade him be quiet, but he refused,
> saying that to stamp was the right way and reminded him of old
> times (...) the tune went with emphasis and swing, the old man
> banging the floor with his stick at the accented notes, bringing
> out all his words very clearly and swinging his body in time to
> the tune.[16]

W. Walter Gill records that on the Isle of Man it is 'customary to gab-
ble [the song] at top speed (...) so that the words would be difficult to
follow by one not previously familiar with them'.[17]

There were wren hunts in many parts of England. English emi-
grants from County Durham took the custom with them to America;
versions exist for example in Nebraska, Texas and South Carolina.
The Nebraska version cites a wren; the Texan versions substitute a
rat or various small game such as coons, possum and rabbits. The
Nebraska wren is feminine, as is the South Carolina wren.[18] T. H.
Thomas of Cardiff asks the question: 'why is the wren sometimes
called "King" and sometimes "Queen" without any regard to the sex
of the particular custom? There seems to have been no Salic Law in
the wren kingdom.'[19]

John Aubrey recorded the custom of hunting the wren in Ireland
in 1696:

> the wild Irish mortally hate these birds, to this day, calling them
> the Devil's servants, and killing them wherever they can catch
> them; they teach their children to thrust them full of thorns; you

will see sometimes on holidays, a whole parish running like mad men from hedge to hedge a wren-hunting.[20]

George Waldron (1687–1728) in 1726 (published in 1731 after his death) described the wren hunt on the Isle of Man on 24 December,[21] although Joseph Train reports that the custom was observed there on St Stephen's Day.[22] Little information exists regarding Scotland, but the PEARL server at the University of Edinburgh's School of Scottish Studies Archives includes a wren-hunt song recorded from John Dass, Burray, Orkney, by Alan Bruford on 17 September 1971:

> Mr Dass heard the song from William Sinclair (Billy o Stane) as a boy in South Ronaldsay. The custom of 'hunting the wren' about Christmastime, known in Ireland, Northern England and the Isle of Man, seems to have been almost unknown in Scotland, but the associated song has survived as a nonsense song for children in several regions including the Northern Isles: other versions have been recorded recently from Flotta and Shetland. The end with the wren's bones causing shipwrecks seems to be a local addition. The tune is a variant of 'Kenmure's on and awa'.[23]

The wren song begins with the stanza:

> 'Come to the wood,' says Tozie Mozie,
> 'Come to the wood,' says Johnnie Red-hosie,
> 'Come to the wood,' says brithers and three,
> 'Come to the wood,' says Wise Willee.

Accounts from the south of France vary, but the ritual retains the themes of kingship and sacrifice. The wren used to be hunted in La Ciotat near Marseille 'at the beginning of *Nivose*', late in December, by a 'numerous body of men, armed with swords and pistols'. When a wren was found – they always had one at the ready – they suspended it on a long pole 'which two men carry on their shoulders, as if it were a heavy burden. This whimsical procession parades round the town; the bird is weighed in a great pair of scales, and the company then sits down to table and makes merry.'[24]

The custom was observed on various dates. Following the pres-
entation of the new calendar in Britain in 1752, it may be tempting to
believe that customs held on Epiphany during the nineteenth century
may have previously been celebrated at Christmas. However, Iocyn
Ddu in the fourteenth century hunted the wren in north-east Wales
on 6 January. Edward Lhuyd writing in the seventeenth century states
that the custom was observed on 5 January in Pembrokeshire. Ifor
Ceri writing early in the nineteenth century describes a wren hunt
held on 5 January in the Cardigan area. A report written in Pembroke-
shire at a later point in the nineteenth century however, c.1897, states:
'At New Year all was altered. Work ceased and the villagers came
round for the usual present of "Cwkau" and the children with the
wren in its cage decked with ribbons.'[25]

Dorothy and Elizabeth Phillips, two retired schoolteachers,
remember the wren custom from the 1920s and how it would be
observed on Twelfth-tide, between 6 and 12 January. The wren-house
was made of wood 'and dressed with ribbons – really crêpe paper –
and the wren was inside and when they entered the house of course
they all looked in and wanted to see the king'.[26]

A collection of four wren hunt stanzas compiled by the Revd
J. S. Jones, St Davids, Pembrokeshire, includes a couplet that sug-
gests that the custom was observed on the Feast of Saint Stephen on
26 December:

Ti gei ginio falau a chan,
Ddaeth o'r berllan boreu dy'gŵyl Stephan.[27]

[You will have a meal of apples and white flour, | Collected
from the orchard on the morning of Saint Stephen's Day.]

The reference to a 'perllan' (orchard) is reminiscent of a custom
observed, for example, at Christmas and the New Year in Kidwelly,
Carmarthenshire, during the first half of the nineteenth century,[28]
'Y Berllan', and it is possible that Revd Jones had that in mind as he
listed his texts.

In Ireland, the ritual was held on 26 December. In a letter dated
21 June 1929, Sir W. Goscombe John recalls seeing in the 1860s
'groups of young roughs – they were generally Irish, I think' wander-
ing the Canton area of Cardiff on St Stephen's Day carrying a holly

tree decorated with ribbons, and a dead wren 'with a bottle of spirits attached'.[29] They sang the following song:

> Mister Jones is a worthy man,
> And to his house I brought my wran
> I brought my wran to visit him here
> To wish him a Merry Christmas and a Happy New Year.
> The Wran, the Wran that you may see
> Here guarded on our Holly Tree,
> A bunch of ribbons by his side,
> And a bottle of whiskey to be his guide,
> (...)
> St. Stephen's Day was caught in the furze.
> We hunted him up and we hunted him down
> Till one of our brave boys knocked him down.

One intriguing but unsubstantiated piece of evidence states: 'Suffolk. The Wren Hunt took place on St. Valentine's Day.'[30] Karl P. Wentersdorf makes a case for the existence, at least during the medieval and Renaissance periods,

> of a literary tradition in which the wren figured as a symbol of eros. The tradition certainly supports the theory that the wren-hunts and wren-songs of West European folklore derive from ancient fertility ceremonies, and may well have had their origins in that folklore.[31]

In Wales in general, the wren ritual was observed at around Twelfth Night. Wrens were hunted from thatched roofs, deciduous woodland, farmland, heathland, and from shady, overgrown hedges and bushes. Constantly on the move, darting from bush to bush, they were difficult to catch. In parts of Wales it was preferable to catch a live wren, in other parts to kill it. Either way, the hunted wren was scarcely still alive: 'it was next to impossible to secure the little thing until it had been thoroughly exhausted, and then the act of pouncing upon it would itself put an end to its existence.'[32] Although wrens were in plentiful supply in nineteenth-century Wales, should the wassailing party be unlucky and fail to capture a wren, seizing a house sparrow as a substitute was permitted:

Dyma'r dryw
Os yw e'n fyw,
Neu 'dderyn to
I gael ei rostio.

[Here is the wren | If it is [still] alive, | Or a sparrow | To be
roasted.]

The captured bird was placed in a wren-house (see figure 9) or
bier decorated with colourful ribbons and carried around the houses
of the locality. 'The wren's visit was a source of much amusement to
children and servants. Sometimes two or three wrens would be caged
together and their little house always had at least one window,'[33]
often a glazed window at each of the two gable ends. All eyes would
be keen to take a peek inside. Some wren-houses were crafted from
wood, others from a cardboard box or paper; one intriguing example
of a Pembrokeshire wren-house is made from glass. 'Pieces of ribbon
of various colours are fixed to the ridge of the roof outside.'[34] Mrs
Eliza Thomas remembers tying a red ribbon around the wren's neck
as well as on the wren-house roof:[35] 'Rubanau pob lliw sy'n clymu y
dryw' (Ribbons of every colour tie the wren). Ribbons were an indis-
pensable part of the ritual: 'every young lady, and even old ladies,
used to compete in presenting the grandest ribbon to the "wren".'[36] A
wooden handle was placed at each corner of the house to allow four
people to carry it.

The wren was sometimes exhibited in a lantern, possibly a stable
lantern. T. H. Thomas of Cardiff suggests in a letter to the *Pembroke
County Guardian and Cardigan Reporter* that the lantern in which the
wren was carried perhaps represents the shape of the original wren-
house and that the square model was a modern version. He bases his
theory on the fact that the homes of the 'hen dadau' (old fathers) were
round rather than square.[37] In County Louth on the north-east coast
of Ireland, the wren-boys carried a thorn bush decked in streamers of
coloured paper, with a wren tied to one of its bushes. An alternative
was 'to carry the wren in a little coffin carved out of a turnip and
covered with coloured paper.'[38]

Wassailers carried the wren from door to door, four strong men
'groaning under the weight of their burden, and looking as if they
had just relieved Atlas of his shoulder-piece'.[39] They approached the

principal homes of the neighbourhood where, 'accompanying themselves with some musical instrument, they announce their arrival by singing the "Song of the Wren"'.[40] Certain stanzas were used both in the wren-hunt context and as part of the New Year celebrations:

O feistres fach fwyn,
Gwrandewch ar ein cŵyn;
Plant ifenc ŷm ni,
Gadewch ni i'r tŷ;
O dewch, dewch yn gloi,
'Nte dyma ni'n ffoi.[41]

[O dear gentle mistress, | Listen to our plea; | We are young children, | Let us into the house; | O come, come quickly, | Or we run away.]

In Pembrokeshire the wren hunters sprinkled water over the householders first thing in the morning before they were out of bed, as did the New Year's Day wassailers. There is possibly a merging here of two customs, their forgotten purpose becoming of less and less relevance to modern-day practitioners. A further example of the possible merging of two customs is the report from County Kerry that highlights a similarity between the wren hunt and the Mari Lwyd custom in Wales. In West Kerry:

the focal point of the Wrenboys parade is a hobby horse. A pantomime-type horse with a wooden head, snapping jaws and a body made from cloth stretched across a timber frame, it is worn on the shoulders of one of the members of the Wren – who whirls and capers at the head of the parade.[42]

Edward A. Armstrong states that in County Roscommon in north-central Ireland, the wren-boys' leader was dressed in straw and one of his followers wore women's clothes, much like Siwan of the Mari Lwyd custom.[43]

The Welsh wren hunters' pause on the doorstep to request admission was at times a mere convention, as visitors were often invited to the home beforehand, particularly by farmers' wives. Scott records, however, that in Tenby while the men accompanied the wren,

Another custom prevailed on the same day, in the country rather than in the town, called 'tooling,' which consisted in calling at the different farm-houses, or wherever Sir John Barleycorn held his court, and under the pretext of searching for one's tools behind the 'beer cask,' giving an unmistakable hint of the occasion for the visit.[44]

The women from poorer backgrounds went 'souling',[45] a custom more generally observed on All Souls' Eve on 1 November. It included visiting homes and requesting gifts of soul cake, and any food that could accompany bread, for example cheese or meat, in exchange for which the women sang a souling song wishing all good things on the master of the house, the mistress, their children and their livestock.

Having gained admittance, the wren company receive 'a draught from the cellar and a present in money. The "Song of the Wren" is generally *encored*.'[46] While some wren hunters received money, Eliza Thomas (1834–1920) of Casnewydd-bach (Little Newcastle) between Fishguard and Haverfordwest in Pembrokeshire received a *calennig* (a gift), 'ddim cash'[47] (not cash). Many received 'cwkau', flat cakes with pinched edges and a centre the size of a saucer, made with flour, butter, caster sugar and currants, and decorated with more currants on top. One observer records that the head of the household would open the door, admit the wassailers, and 'regale them with plenty of Christmas ale, the obtaining of which being the principal object of the whole performance. The company then departed in a merry mood.'[48] J. Tombs recalls that 'the proprietors very commonly commence high life below stairs, dancing with the maid-servants, and saluting them under the kissing-bush – where there is one'.[49]

Should the wren party not be admitted into the home, they expressed their anger and disappointment:

Gwynt ffralwm
Ddelo'n hwthwm
I droi'r tŷ
A'i wyneb fyny.

Which may be rendered:

Come, raging wind, in fury frown,
And turn this house all upside down.[50]

On subsequent nights the wren party would visit other local households until 'distyll y Gwyliau' (the ebb of Christmastide), the Epiphany observed on 6 January, at which time most Christmas festivities came to an end.

Many song texts and several reports concerning the observance of the custom refer to the wren as king, hunted because of its sovereignty over the other birds on the understanding that the ritual sacrifice of a king would procure benefits for his people. The Latin name for the wren is *Regulus*, in French *Roi des oiseaux* (king of the birds), in Italian *Re di siepe* (king of the hedge) and in German *Zaunkönig* (king of the hedge). The king's strength and virility were intimately linked to the strength and fertility of the locality. Carrying the royal wren and displaying it throughout the community would ensure that the profit emanating from its sacrificial death would benefit the neighbourhood, its crops and livestock, that the locality would be redeemed by the sacrifice, and the seasonal cycle regenerated. It has been suggested that 'the Classical story of the wren becoming king of the birds had entered those cultures'[51] where the wren was hunted, rather than being evidence of an indigenously created observance of the ritual.

Both Aristotle (Historia Animalium 9.11) and Pliny (Natural History 10.95) were familiar with the legend about a quarrel between the eagle and the wren concerning who should be king of all birds. The birds had decided that their ruler would be the bird that could fly highest. When the eagle had spread its wings and soared to the highest heights and become so exhausted it could fly no more, the wren appeared from the warmth of the eagle's feathers, soared higher, and defeated its closest rival for the title. Variants of this legend exist worldwide. Many countries have been influenced by the concept of a sacrificial death, but it is not the wren that is perceived to be king in all cultures. The quest to be king assumes multiple forms, 'and is made to refer to other creatures, but the main lines of the legend are well marked throughout all the different variants'.[52]

In Wales, the wren was honoured as a sacred king that was hunted on one day of the year for sacrificial purposes. On all other days it enjoyed protected status as many traditional rhymes indicate:

Dryw bach yn dedwi pedwar ar ddeg
A rheiny'n lân ac yn deg,
A chrechi dim ond doi
A rheiny'n llawn crach a lloi.

[The little wren laying fourteen [eggs] | And those clean and
pretty, | And the heron only two | And those full of scabs and
parasites.]

Sawl a dorro nyth y dryw,
Chaiff c byth o ffafr Duw.

[Whoever robs the wren's nest | Will never secure God's
favour.]

Sawl dorro nyth y dryw
Cyll ei iechyd tra bo byw.[53]

[Whoever robs the wren's nest | Will lose his health for the
rest of his life.]

In his seventeenth-century *Parochialia* Edward Lhuyd states that
the wren was sent from a young man to his sweetheart, but that the
wassailers also visited other houses where there were no sweethearts.
D. Silvan Evans (1818–1903) states that young men carrying wrens, at
night-time, visited homes where there were couples who had been
married within the year and that they did so throughout the Christmas
season until 6 January. Both accounts imply that the visit is a charm,
probably related to fertility. The accompanying ribbons were indeed
simple tokens of gaiety and colour, but were also a visible and tan-
gible representation of supplication and receipt conferred in private
between a young man and his sweetheart.

In a more general sense, the wren visitation signified prosperity
for the community at large. During a visit, the wren's feathers and
body parts were shared and distributed to householders in exchange
for money and gifts, in order to keep the community from evil and
misfortune, and to arouse and strengthen regeneration and an excel-
lent quality of life. On the Isle of Man this was particularly relevant to
the herring industry, the mainstay of island life:[54]

It was the belief that it [the wren] would bring good luck that
made old men and young boys run after it, over hedges and
ditches, until it would be caught. The man who caught it was
the great man of the day at that time, and it brought him good

luck the whole year. The little bird was carefully kept, and brought on board the boat to the herrings (herring fishing) for good luck.

Some of the feathers were given to other people, and some kept a feather in their purse.

> The little wren was placed on a stick between two boys, on a piece of fir tree tied with ribbons, for a sign of their good going (success), and in remembrance of the good luck it had brought in days long ago. There was a third boy, and he was covered with a net, and his face made black, and a bunch of leeks tied together to make a tail behind his back. He carried a long pole for a stick, and he kept time with the tune.[55]

Eliza Thomas does not mention that the wren hunters dressed up for the hunt, or that they blacked their faces. Hugh James Byrne's record of the custom as observed in Connacht in the west of Ireland, however, states that the wren-boys met in the early hours on the morning of St Stephen's Day to dress up for the occasion. The leader was tied around with straw and had his face blacked, another dressed in women's clothes, and the remainder had scarves and ribbons tied to their sleeves, and wore 'every sort of fanciful headgear'. Two 'sergeants' collected the money, and there was also a musician, perhaps two. They walked miles, calling at all the big houses. 'The leader goes first, and cuts all manner of capers, and jumps about; the rest dance – jigs or any kind of dance.'[56] Edward A. Armstrong in his description of the custom in southern Ireland states that those taking part in the hunt 'attire themselves grotesquely in such garments as pyjamas and women's blouses', and although the wren-boys may sing unaccompanied, 'there are frequently musicians in the party who play the tin whistle, mouth organ, or accordion or, in a few localities, thump a peculiar flat drum known as the bodhrán.'[57]

There were two parts to the custom of hunting the wren. The first part comprises the hunt itself, the second the wren-house procession. The ritual opens with a dialogue song held between two or more parties concerning the hunt, its location and its outcome, in readiness for the procession held on Twelfth Day.[58] The dialogue follows a question-and-response pattern, such as that recorded in

Tenby in Pembrokeshire in an English-language wren-hunt song (see poem 26). In such a song 'the verses are composed on a uniform plan of questions by the young, and a negative and affirmative answer'.[59] Another (similar) English-language wren song from Pembrokeshire was noted by L. P. Barnaschone, together with 'The Cutty Wren', the popular tune to which it was sung (see p. 176):

O where are you going? says Milder to Melder,
O where are you going? says the younger to the elder;
O I cannot tell, says Festel to Fose;
We're going to the woods, said John the Red Nose,
We're going to the woods, said John the Red Nose.

O what will you do there? says Milder to Melder,
O what will you do there? says the younger to the elder;
O I do not know, says Festel to Fose;
To shoot the cutty wren, said John the Red Nose. (x2)

O what will you shoot her with? says Milder to Melder,
O what will you shoot her with? says the younger to the
    elder;
O I cannot tell, says Festel to Fose;
With bows and arrows, said John the Red Nose. (x2)

O that will not do! says Milder to Melder,
O that will not do! says the younger to the elder;
O what will you do then? says Festel to Fose;
With great guns and cannons, says John the Red Nose. (x2)

O what will you bring her home in? says Milder to Melder,
O what will you bring her home in? says the younger to the
    elder;
O I cannot tell, says Festel to Fose;
On four strong men's shoulders, said John the Red Nose. (x2)

O that will not do, says Milder to Melder,
O that will not do, says the younger to the elder;
O what will you do then? says Fester to Fose;
On big carts and wagons, said John the Red Nose. (x2)

What will you cut her up with? says Milder to Melder,
What will you cut her up with? says the younger to the elder;
O I do not know, says Festel to Fose;
With knives and with forks, said John the Red Nose. (x2)

O that will not do, says Melder [*sic*] to Milder, [*sic*]
O that will not do, says the younger to the elder;
O what will do then? says Festel to Fose;
With hatchets and cleavers, said John the Red Nose. (x2)

What will you boil her in? says Milder to Melder,
What will you boil her in? says the younger to the elder;
O I cannot tell thee, says Festel to Fose;
In pots and in kettles, said John the Red Nose.[60] (x2)

W. Walter Gill[61] adds another stanza, and notes that the song was sung in Tenby:

O that will not do, says Milder to Melder,
O that will not do, says the younger to the elder,
O what will do then? says Festel to Fose;
In brass pans and cauldrons, says John the Red Nose.

Furthermore, Gill mentions an 'inferior version' of the Tenby song found in Rhydberth (Redberth), four miles from Tenby, a version that includes all the above stanzas plus the following four that follow immediately after the 'brass pans and cauldrons':

Who is to eat her? says Milder to Melder,
Who is to eat her? says the younger to the elder;
I cannot tell, says Fiddledefoze;
The Poor of the Parish, says John the Red Nose.

That won't do, says Milder to Melder,
That won't do, says the younger to the elder;
I cannot tell, says Fiddledefoze;
Then we'll have the whole Kingdom, says John the Red Nose.

That is well said, says Milder to Melder,
That is well said, says the younger to the elder;
I cannot tell, says Fiddledefoze;
That is well said, says John the Red Nose.

What's to be done with the spare meat? says Milder to Melder,
What's to be done with the spare meat? says the younger to
    the elder;
I cannot tell, says Fiddledefoze;
We'll give it to the Poor of the Parish, says John the Red Nose.

Walter Gill notes that the date 1849 is appended to this wren song
from Rhydberth, and that:

> Though corrupt, it has several additional stanzas, besides differ-
> ing in another. Where Tenby says, 'O what will you cut her up
> with?' Rhydberth asks, 'How shall we feather her? says Milder to
> Melder,' etc., and continues, 'Seven women of the parish, says
> John the Red Nose.'

That won't do, says Milder to Melder,
That won't do, says the younger to the elder;
I cannot tell, says Fiddledefoze;
Then we'll have the whole Parish, says John the Red Nose.

Five named characters take part in the above wren hunt: one lead
character, John the Red Nose, who provides the answers; and two sets
of inquirers, Milder and Melder, and Festel and Fose, who provide
John the Red Nose with an opportunity to come to their rescue with
an informed plan of action.

It is similar to Welsh-language wren songs sung in various parts
of north Wales, such as the following from Amlwch in Anglesey
c.1909, which features the question-and-answer pattern, but not the
leadership of a single person:

1. 'Ddoi di i'r coed?' meddai Risiart wrth Robin,
'Ddoi di i'r coed?' meddai Dibin wrth Dobin,
'Ddoi di i'r coed?' meddai Abram ei hun,
'Ddoi di i'r coed?' medda' nhw bod ac un.

2. 'Beth wnawn ni yno?' meddai Risiart wrth Robin (...)

3. 'Hela'r Dryw Bach,' meddai Risiart wrth Robin (...)

4. 'Sut cawn ni o adref?' meddai Risiart wrth Robin (...)

5. 'Ceffyl a throl,' meddai Risiart wrth Robin (...)

6. 'Sut gwnawn ei fwyta?' meddai Risiart wrth Robin (...)

7. 'Cyllell a fforc,' meddai Risiart wrth Robin (...)[62]

[Stanza 1: 'Will you come to the woods?' says Risiart to Robin, | 'Will you come to the woods?' says Dibin to Dobin, | 'Will you come to the woods?' says Abram himself, | 'Will you come to the woods?' they say, one and all.

Stanza 2: 'What shall we do there?' says Risiart to Robin (...)

Stanza 3: 'Hunt the Little Wren,' says Risiart to Robin (...)

Stanza 4: 'How shall we get him home?' says Risiart to Robin (...)

Stanza 5: 'A horse and cart,' says Risiart to Robin (...)

Stanza 6: 'How shall we eat him?' says Risiart to Robin (...)

Stanza 7: 'A knife and fork,' says Risiart to Robin (...)]

In all contexts, the emphasis is on exaggeration and burlesque. The enormity of the task in hand is highlighted, the immense size and weight of the hunted prey commented on, as is the inadequacy of the weapons used for the kill. Then there is:

a conference about how to bring the body home, and after a cart has been obtained, the lowland Scots ask, 'What way will ye get her in?' They needs must 'drive down the door cheeks' (1776). The dinner that the little bird's carcass will provide is such that the Manx would invite 'King and Queen' and yet have enough over to give 'eyes to the blind, legs to the lame, and pluck to the poor'; while in some versions of the rhyme methods of disposing of the bones also engage discussion (...) The rhyme was chanted in the ceremonial procession after the kill had been made.[63]

The Llŷn version of the wren song maintains a similar metrical pattern to the Amlwch version, but differs in that the hunters find their prey in the vineyard of the local manor house. Its final stanza, however, is metrically different, and in content is a description of the purpose of the wren cult rites. The song appears to have changed from being a hunt song into being a processional song that takes in all the local houses, and that reflects the sacrificial nature of the custom and the dissemination of the wren's powers and virtues among all members of society. Feathers, legs, wings and head are all shared throughout the community:

> Hegal i Dibyn, a hegal i Dobyn,
> Aden i Risiart ac aden i Robyn,
> Hanner y pen i Siôn pen y stryd,
> A'r hanner arall i'r cwbwl i gyd.

[A leg for Dibyn, and a leg for Dobyn, | A wing for Risiart and a wing for Robyn, | Half the head for Siôn at the top of the street, | And the other half for one and all.]

On the Isle of Man the wren bearers 'sang certain lines in which reference was made to boiling and eating the bird'[64] to secure its protection for the coming year. W. Walter Gill records that in north Wales, after the indication 'We will hunt the wren', further action lies ahead:

> 'We will boil it for broth!' says Owen to Hugh,
> 'We will boil it for broth!' says Morgan to Pugh,
> 'We will boil it for broth!' say John Jones and Son. –
> And they did. And the broth drowned every one![65]

Gill quotes here a (loose) translation of a Welsh stanza rather than the original. As regards tunes, 'Most of the north Wales wren songs are lively medium compass tunes in the major, but a rare minor key example collected in 1976 is in a narrow 5-tone compass with a chant-like rhythm.'[66]

No women ever planned the hunt; it is always men or young boys who are mentioned in the reports. The same is true of Ireland: even though 'the Wrenboys wore skirts, there was never a girl among them, but their heavy nailed boots never looked strange to us, because all the girls we saw wore the self-same boots on Sundays'.[67] In the Llŷn version of the wren hunt, five men are mentioned by name: Dibyn, Dobyn, Risiart, Robin and Siôn, but at the wren procession in Marloes, Pembrokeshire, the participators were only four in number, probably those who carried the wren-house by its four corners:

> In his coach he does ride with a great deal of pride;
> And with four footmen to wait upon him.
>
> We were four at watch and all nigh of a match.[68]

J. Tombs suggests these lines imply 'that the wren at one time used to occupy a coach, or that her house was placed upon wheels'.[69]

Reports of Welsh wren hunts do not mention more than one company at work on the same night, but on the Isle of Man in 1842 'no fewer than four companies were seen in Douglas alone'.[70] In parts of Ireland every street had its own wren company; each one 'would do the round of the town several times during the day – dancing all the time, knocking at doors and collecting money' before joining forces in the evening when 'all the wrans would join together for one big parade around the town'.[71]

Wren hunters were armed with two sticks, one to beat the bushes or roofs where the wren was hiding, the other at the ready to strike him. In Llwyngwril, a coastal village in Gwynedd, the hunter's tools were 'twca a mynawyd' (cleaver and awl). In answer to the question, 'Beth wnawn a geddo?' (What shall we do with him?), the hunters want to eat the wren with a knife and fork (Amlwch), or 'Fe wnawn ag ef botes'[72] (We'll use him to make a stew); the Llanrhaeadr-ym-Mochnant hunters do not want to sacrifice the wren at all, but to sell him for a shilling to buy beer; in this instance the purpose of the ritual seems to have changed, and the primitive power of the hunt lost.

The second type of wren-hunt song was sung during the procession, on the doorstep or under a bedroom window, and shows clearly how the procession was conducted. From Solva in Pembrokeshire:

> Dryw bach ydyw'r gŵr, amdano mae stŵr,
> Mae cwest arno fe nos heno 'mhob lle.
>
> Fe ddaliwyd y gwalch oedd neithiwr yn falch
> Mewn stafell wen deg, a'i dri brawd ar ddeg.

Fe dorrwyd i'r tŵr a daliwyd y gŵr,
Fe'i rhoddwyd dan len ar elor fraith wen.

Rhubanau bob lliw sy o gwmpas y dryw,
Rhubanau'n dri thro sy arno'n lle to.

Mae'r drywod yn sgant, hedasant i bant,
Ond deuant yn ôl trwy lwybrau'r hen ddôl.

O meistres fach fwyn, gwrandewch ar ein cŵyn,
Plant ieuainc ym ni, gadewch ni i'r tŷ.
Agorwch yn glou, 'n te dyma ni'n ffoi.[73]

[Stanza 1: The fellow is a little wren, there is a commotion con-
cerning him, | The hunt for him is everywhere tonight.

Stanza 2: The rogue who was proud last night is captured |
In a fair white room, together with his thirteen brothers.

Stanza 3: The tower was broken into and the fellow caught,
| He was placed under a shroud on a blessed bier of many
colours.

Stanza 4: Ribbons of all colours encompass the wren, |
Ribbons in three turns enclose him instead of a roof.

Stanza 5: The wrens are scarce, they have flown away, | But
they will return along the old meadow paths.

Stanza 6: O dear kind mistress, listen to our plea, | We are
young children, let us into the house. | Open quickly or we
flee.]

The reference to the thirteen brothers in the second stanza alludes
to the rhyme 'Dryw bach yn dedwi pedwar ar ddeg' (The little wren
laying fourteen [eggs]); the wrens are scarce (stanza 5) for the simple
reason that they have fled the hunt.

Few records of the fate of the wren at the close of the cere-
mony have survived in Wales. Llew Tegid states that 'the men of

Pembrokeshire (...) bury the body in a corner of the churchyard'.[74] On the Isle of Man (1731), at the end of the evening they bring the wren to the parish church for a mock funeral, 'burying her with a whimsical kind of Solemnity, singing Dirges over her in the *Manks* Language, which they call her Knell; after which *Christmas* begins.'[75] A folklore survey of County Clare in western Ireland recorded the following couplet (1909), suggesting that the burial of the wren was an integral part of the custom and that it held great significance:

> Put your hand in your pocket and take out your purse
> And give us some money to bury the wren.[76]

Several theories have been put forward regarding the origins of the custom of hunting the wren. James Frazer argued that the wren cult is steeped in pagan influences concerning sacrifice and renewal, and that '[r]eligious processions of this sort must have had a great place in the ritual of European peoples in prehistoric times'.[77] E. A. Armstrong also suggests it has its origins in prehistoric times, and that the wren ritual came to the United Kingdom 'by the prehistoric route from the Gulf of Lion up the west coast of France – a route by which Mycenaean influences reached Britain'. Armstrong further suggests that, although the wren hunt was only observed in western Europe, 'it is possible that in Greek swallow ritual and the Portuguese cuckoo procession (...) we have vestiges of rites derived from a common ancient source'.[78] In conclusion, Armstrong proposes:

> that the Wren Cult reached the British Isles during the Bronze Age and was carried by megalith builders whose cultural inspiration came from the Mediterranean region. Probably these folk cherished mainly solar magico-religious beliefs. The Wren Hunt represents New Year ceremonial having as its purpose the defeat of the dark earth-powers and identification with the hoped-for triumph of light and life.[79]

Karl P. Wentersdorf believes that what had 'degenerated into an ugly practice of random and pointless killing had undoubtedly had its beginnings in some purposeful and probably elaborate pagan ritual in which the victim was originally the representative of a divinity'.[80] In Wales, however, no known record of the custom exists prior to *c*.1380.

It has been suggested that since Welsh wren hunts are located in close proximity to the coast the custom is an importation, possibly from Scandinavia as there was a close conceptual association between the Celts and the Scandinavians.[81] Not all are in agreement. Based on the theory that the wren cult 'extends from the Gulf of Lyons in the Mediterranean, up western France to Brittany, then into southern England, Wales, the Isle of Man and southern Ireland', E. A. Armstrong argues that 'its distribution lies along the ancient trade route to this country from the Mediterranean (...) and led through France to ports from which ships sailed to Britain'.[82]

Niall Mac Coitir believes that the wren hunt in Britain and Ireland corresponds to areas of Anglo-Norman control,[83] is strongest in areas of Norman influence in the south, with no direct evidence of the custom in Celtic Cornwall or in Ulster, and only a few instances in Scotland.[84] Concerning Pembrokeshire, an anonymous writer argues that 'the custom obtained in the Welsh speaking districts rather than in the English part of the county',[85] but Mac Coitir argues that the Welsh evidence was strongest 'around Tenby, in an outpost of Anglo-Norman control known as "the little England beyond Wales"'; north Wales was 'also an area of early Anglo-Norman settlement, around the ring of castles and fortified "bastide" towns built by Edward I of England in the thirteenth century', and that there is little evidence of the wren hunt where the Welsh culture 'remained strong'.[86] He makes a similar case for the Isle of Man, which was 'under the control of the Earls of Derby, the Stanley family, on behalf of the English Crown from 1405 to 1627'. Mac Coitir argues that the custom has its origins 'in Medieval France in the wider context of the Feast of Fools, and involves a search for alms through a humorous parody of St John the Evangelist'[87] whose festival is on 27 December and whose symbol, interestingly, is the eagle.

Whatever its origins, from the 1860s onwards it seems that the wren ritual lost much of its popularity in Wales and eventually became confined to Pembrokeshire. In conversation with Bertram Lloyd in 1927, H. W. Evans of Solva in Pembrokeshire remarked that some fifty years earlier, c.1877, wren hunting was still much practised in that area. At that time Evans was a boy living at Lower Clegyr farm near St Davids, and he had 'assisted in capturing Wrens in holes in ricks at night, and in the actual "wren-bearing" procession'.[88] In 1891 Arthur Mee remarks that 'the custom of Bearing the Wren has by no means died out in Pembrokeshire; but Moody and Sankey's hymns and the like are taking the place of the quaint old songs'.[89] Twenty years later, writing in 1910 about south Pembrokeshire, Mary Beatrice Mirehouse states that the wren ritual 'has now entirely died out'.[90] Bertram Lloyd in 1927 remarks that 'T. R. Davis (Newport) tells me that the custom is now (1927) utterly dead in the county'.[91] D. Roy Saer, however, records that the custom continued in Pembrokeshire into the twentieth century, and that boys in the town of Haverfordwest carried a wren up High Street during the years 1926–9 singing the wren song.[92]

The wren hunt and its savage killings were a cause for concern. One informant, whose mother observed the wren hunt as a child in Wales in the 1880s, remembered 'how upset she was about the wren'.[93] Because of this, in many instances a replica wren was used. In Ireland wren-boys, where 'the killing of the wren is disapproved the Boys carry a potato with feathers stuck into it (...) or some other object, such as a celluloid budgerigar'.[94] Wren songs also underwent a change, moving from the domain of wren hunters to being part of the repertoire of children. Primary schools in Anglesey still taught the Amlwch wren-hunt song as a nursery rhyme as late as 1960, and it was included in a collection of folk songs for children in 1981, a publication that has seen several reprints.[95]

Notes

1.   The Red Book of Hergest is held at the Bodleian Library, Oxford, reference no. Jesus College MS 111, possibly compiled for Hopcyn ap Tomas of Ynysforgan, Swansea, and named after the colour of its leather binding and its association with Hergest Court in Herefordshire.

2.   J. Gwenogvryn Evans (ed.), *The Poetry in the Red Book of Hergest* (Llanbedrog: the author, 1911), 1340.39–1342.28; N. G. Costigan (Bosco), R. Iestyn Daniel and Dafydd Johnston (eds), *Gwaith Gruffudd ap Dafydd ap Tudur, Gwilym Ddu o Arfon, Trahaearn Brydydd Mawr ac Iorwerth Beli* [The works of Gruffudd ap Dafydd ap Tudur (...)] (Aberystwyth: Centre for Advanced Welsh and Celtic Studies, University of Wales, 1995), pp. 110–17, 132–7.

3.   Gwenogvryn Evans, *Red Book of Hergest*, 1358.26–1359.24; Barry J. Lewis (ed.), *Gwaith Madog Benfras ac eraill o feirdd y bedwaredd ganrif ar ddeg* [The works of Madog Benfras and other fourteenth-century Welsh poets] (Aberystwyth: Centre for Advanced Welsh and Celtic Studies, University of Wales, 2007), pp. 289–307.

4. Lewis, *Gwaith Madog Benfras*, p. 295, lines 17–20.

5. For a translation of the poem into English see Dafydd Johnston (ed.), *Canu Maswedd yr Oesoedd Canol/Medieval Welsh Erotic Poetry* (Cardiff: Tafol, 1991), pp. 87–9; note Johnston's contrasting translation of line 20.

6. Huw M. Edwards, 'Rhodiwr fydd clerwr': sylwadau ar gerdd ymffrost o'r bedwaredd ganrif ar ddeg' [A bard will be an itinerant: comments on a fourteenth-century boasting poem], *Y Traethodydd* [The Essayist], 149 (1994), 50–5.

7. Brussels, Bibliothèque Royale de Belgique, MSS. 4190–4200, ff. 43ʳ–65ᵛ.

8. Whitley Stokes (ed.), 'The Birth and Life of St. Moling', *Revue Celtique*, 27 (1906), 302.

9. Brian Ó Cuív, 'Some Gaelic Traditions about the Wren', *Éigse: A Journal of Irish Studies*, 18 (1980–1), 53.

10 For 'Kwtti' see T. H. Parry-Williams, *The English Element in Welsh: A Study of English Loan-Words in Welsh* (London: The Honourable Society of Cymmrodorion, 1923), s.v. 'Cwta', p. 94.

11. Edward Lhuyd, *Parochialia: being a summary of answers to 'Parochial queries in order to a geographical dictionary, etc., of Wales'* (1696), ed. Rupert H. Morris (London: Cambrian Archaeological Association, 1909–11), Part 2 (South Wales), p. 82; translation by Iorwerth C. Peate, 'The Wren in Welsh Folklore', *Man* (January 1936), 2–3, although 'countryside' might be more appropriate than 'country'. See also Brynley F. Roberts, 'Edward Lhwyd (*c.*1660–1709): Folklorist', *Folklore*, 120 (2009), 36–56.

12. [Anonymous], 'County Notes', *The Pembroke County Guardian and Cardigan Reporter*, 11 January 1907, 4.

13. Dr J. Lloyd Williams Music MSS and Papers AH1/34 (NLW) 'Melus geingciau Deheubarth Cymru' [The Sweet Melodies of South Wales], *c.*1815, f. 28ʳ.

14. Ibid., f. 27ᵛ; see figure 8 for the two tunes.

15. [Lewis Davies Jones] Llew Tegid, 'Hunting the Wren', *Cylchgrawn Cymdeithas Alawon Gwerin Cymru/Journal of the Welsh Folk-Song Society*, 1 (1909–12), 106–8.

16. Cecil J. Sharp, Ralph Vaughan Williams, Frank Kidson, Lucy E. Broadwood and A. G. Gilchrist, 'Ballads and Songs', *Journal of the Folk-Song Society*, 5 (1914), 78; cf. references to the use of a stick in New Year wassail songs.

17. W. Walter Gill, *A Second Manx Scrapbook* (London: Arrowsmith, 1932), p. 383.

18. Alisoun Gardner-Medwin, 'The Wren Hunt Song', *Folklore*, 81 (1970), 215–18.

19. T. H. Thomas, in H. W. Williams, *Pembrokeshire Antiquities: Reprints from 'Yn Amsang ein tadau', the Antiquaries' Column in the 'Pembroke County Guardian'* (Solva: H. W. Williams, 1897), p. 51.

20. John Aubrey, *Miscellanies upon Various Subjects* (London: printed for Edward Castle, 1696; London: Reeves and Turner, 1890), pp. 47–8.

21. George Waldron, *The History and Description of the Isle of Man* (Dublin: printed for E. Rider in George's-Lane, and J. Torbuck at the Bear in Skinner-Row, [1742?]; Gale ECCO, Print Editions, 2010), p. 64; see further A. W. Moore, *The Folk-Lore of the Isle of Man* (London: D. Nutt, 1891; facsimile reprint Felinfach: Llanerch Publishers, 1994), pp. 133–40.

22. Joseph Train, *Historical and Statistical Account of the Isle of Man*, 2 (Douglas: Mary Quiggin, North Quay, 1845), p. 124, available online at: *http://www.isle-of-man.com/manxnotebook/fulltext/tr1844/index.htm* (accessed 22 June 2020).

23. John Dass, 'Hunting the Wren' (SA 1971/265/A1) available online at the School of Scottish Studies Archives, The University of Edinburgh, PEARL server: *http://www.pearl.celtscot.ed.ac.uk/Samples/08-233/08-233.html* (accessed 23 July 2020).

24. C. S. Sonnini de Manoncourt (translation by Henry Hunter), *Travels in Upper and Lower Egypt* (London: printed for J. Debrett, 1800), pp. 11–12.

25. Williams, *Pembrokeshire Antiquities*, p. 39.

26. Phyllis Kinney, *Welsh Traditional Music* (Cardiff: University of Wales Press in association with Cymdeithas Alawon Gwerin Cymru [Welsh Folk Song Society], 2011), p. 80.

27. J. S. Jones, quoted in Williams, *Pembrokeshire Antiquities*, p. 46.

28. Discussed in the chapter 'Wassailing at the New Year'.

29. Peate, 'The Wren in Welsh Folklore', 3.

30. Edward A. Armstrong, *The Folklore of Birds: An Enquiry into the Origin and Distribution of some Magico-Religious Traditions* (London: Collins, 1958), p. 142.

31. Karl P. Wentersdorf, 'The Folkloristic Significance of the Wren', *The Journal of American Folklore*, 90 (April–June 1977), 198.

32. D. Silvan Evans, 'Hunting of the Wren', *Bye-Gones: relating to Wales and the Border Counties* (April 1885), 206.

33. [Anonymous], 'A Quaint Pembrokeshire Custom', *The Pembroke County Guardian and Cardigan Reporter*, 4 January 1907, 4.

34. J. Tombs, 'Twelfth-Day', *Notes and Queries*, Series 3, 5 (1864), 109.

35. From a conversation recorded by D. Roy Saer, St Fagans National Museum of History (Cardiff), 6 September 1963.

36. Quoted in Jonathan Ceredig Davies, *Folk-Lore of West and Mid-Wales* (Aberystwyth: Welsh Gazette offices, 1911; facsimile reprint Felinfach: Llanerch, 1992), p. 65, available online at: *http://www.gutenberg.org/files/53915/53915-h/53915-h.htm#ch4* (accessed 25 June 2020).

37. T. H. Thomas, quoted in Williams, *Pembrokeshire Antiquities*, p. 51.

38. Bryan J. Jones, 'Wren Boys', *Folklore*, 19 (1908), 235.

39. Gill, *A Second Manx Scrapbook*, pp. 375–6.

40. Tombs, 'Twelfth-Day', 109.

41. Williams, *Pembrokeshire Antiquities*, p. 46; cf. poem 17.9–10.

42. [Anonymous], 'Hunting the Wren' [Online]. Available at *https://dingle-peninsula.ie/wren-s-day.html* (accessed 29 October 2020).

43. Armstrong, *The Folklore of Birds*, p. 157.

44. G. P. W. Scott, *Tales and Traditions of Tenby* (Tenby: R. Mason, 1858), pp. 16–17.

45. Scott, *Tales and Traditions of Tenby*, p. 17.

46. Tombs, 'Twelfth-Day', 109.

47. Information gathered by D. Roy Saer (6 September 1963) from James Symonds (b. 1887), Eliza Thomas's grandson. Adults in Casnewydd-bach (Little Newcastle) rounded the neighbourhood at the New Year or the Old New Year.

48. Silvan Evans, 'Hunting of the Wren', 206.

49. Tombs, 'Twelfth-Day', 109.

50. Silvan Evans, 'Hunting of the Wren', 206.

51. Niall Mac Coitir, *Ireland's Birds: Myths, Legends and Folklore* (Cork: The Collins Press, 2015), p. 37.

52. Llew Tegid, 'Hunting the Wren', 101.

53. Elfyn Scourfield, 'Astudiaeth o Ddiwylliant Lleol a Thraddodiadau Llafar Ardal Tre-lech' [A study of local culture and oral tradition undertaken in the Tre-lech area] (unpublished MA thesis, University of Wales [Swansea], 1969), 145.

54. Cecil J. Sharp, A. G. Gilchrist and Lucy E. Broadwood, 'Forfeit Songs; Cumulative Songs; Songs of Marvels and of Magical Animals', *Journal of the Folk-Song Society*, 5 (1916), 283–6: Lucy E. Broadwood notes that 'the herring like the wren is popularly designated as "King," so that the apportioning of their members would seem to represent the distribution of a charm', p. 286.

55. John Clague, *Cooinaghtyn Manninagh/Manx Reminiscences* (Castletown: M. J. Backwell, 1911), pp. 13–15, available online at: *http://www.isle-of-man.com/manxnotebook/fulltext/mr1911/index.htm* (accessed 17 June 2020).

56. Hugh James Byrne, 'All Hallows Eve and other festivals in Connaught', *Folklore*, 18 (1907), 437–9.

57. Edward A. Armstrong, 'The Wren-Boys Ritual', *Country Life*, 122 (26 December 1957), 1417.

58. Peate, 'The Wren in Welsh Folklore', 2.

59. Llew Tegid, 'Hunting the Wren', 105.

60. L. P. Barnaschone, 'Manners and Customs of the People of Tenby in the Eighteenth Century', *The Cambrian Journal*, 4 (1857), 183–4.

61. Gill, *A Second Manx Scrapbook*, pp. 387–8.
62. Llew Tegid, 'Hunting the Wren', 107. For the tune 'Dibyn a Dobyn' see p. 178; the only variant in a minor key (see 'Cân Hela'r Dryw', p. 174) 'was noted from the singing of Mostyn Lewis in 1976; he had learned it from his father's cousin who lived at Ruthin in Denbighshire and sang it often in the early years of the 20th century. There is a strong Welsh flavour about the tune; it has a narrow 5-note compass'; see Phyllis Kinney and Meredydd Evans, *Canu'r Cymry 1 a 2* ([Aberystwyth]: Cymdeithas Alawon Gwerin Cymru [Welsh Folk Song Society], 2014), pp. 112–13.
63. Iona and Peter Opie, *The Oxford Dictionary of Nursery Rhymes* (Oxford: Clarendon Press, 1951), p. 369.
64. J. G. Frazer, *The Golden Bough: A Study in Comparative Religion* (London: Macmillan and Co., 1890; Edinburgh: Canongate Books Ltd, 2004), p. 473.
65. Jennett Humphreys, *Old Welsh Knee Songs, lullabies, frolic rhymes, and other pastime verse: now first collected and issued in English form/the English by Jennett Humphreys* (Caernarvon: Welsh National Press Company, 1894), p. 12.
66. Kinney, *Welsh Traditional Music*, p. 81; in total, Kinney notes and discusses eight wren-hunt tunes.
67. Seán C. O'Leary, *Christmas Wonder* (Dublin: O'Brien Press, 1988), p. 88.
68. Poem 27.5–7.
69. Tombs, 'Twelfth-Day', 109
70. Llew Tegid, 'Hunting the Wren', 103.
71. O'Leary, *Christmas Wonder*, p. 86.
72. John Ceiriog Hughes, *Oriau'r Haf* [Summer Hours] (Wrecsam: R. Hughes and Son, 1870), p. 32.
73. Williams, *Pembrokeshire Antiquities*, pp. 48–9; for the tune 'Cân y Dryw' see p. 174.
74. Llew Tegid, 'Hunting the Wren', 112.
75. Waldron, *The History and Description of the Isle of Man*, p. 65.
76. Thomas J. Westropp, 'Collectanea: A Folklore Survey of County Clare', *Folklore*, 22 (1911), 207.
77. Frazer, *The Golden Bough*, p. 475.
78. Armstrong, *The Folklore of Birds*, p. 164.
79. Armstrong, *The Folklore of Birds*, p. 166.
80. Wentersdorf, 'The Folkloristic Significance of the Wren', 192.
81. Williams, *Pembrokeshire Antiquities*, p. 50.
82. Armstrong, 'The Wren-Boys Ritual', 1418.
83. Mac Coitir, *Ireland's Birds*, p. 38.
84. David Herd, *Ancient and Modern Scottish Songs, Heroic Ballads, etc.*, 2 (Edinburgh: John Wotherspoon, 1776), pp. 210–11; Alan Bruford,

'Festivities and Customs, Seasonal', in David Daiches (ed.), *A Companion to Scottish Culture* (London: Edward Arnold, 1981), pp. 118–25.

85. [Anonymous], 'County Notes', *The Pembroke County Guardian and Cardigan Reporter*, 11 January 1907, 4.
86. Mac Coitir, *Ireland's Birds*, p. 39.
87. Mac Coitir, *Ireland's Birds*, p. 41.
88. Bertram Lloyd, 'Notes on Pembrokeshire Folk-Lore, Superstitions, Dialect Words, etc.', *Folklore*, 56 (1945), 309.
89. Arthur Mee, Editor's note, *The Carmarthenshire Miscellany* (May–June 1892), 48.
90. Mary Beatrice Mirehouse, *South Pembrokeshire: Some of its History and Records* (London: David Nutt, 1910), p. 73.
91. Lloyd, 'Notes on Pembrokeshire Folk-Lore, Superstitions, Dialect Words, etc.', 309.
92. Information recorded by D. Roy Saer, St Fagans National Museum of History (Cardiff), 14 May 1965.
93. Mary Corbett Harris, *Crafts, Customs, and Legends of Wales* (London: David & Charles, 1980), p. 76.
94. Armstrong, *The Folklore of Birds*, p. 155.
95. Phyllis Kinney and Meredydd Evans (eds), *Caneuon Gwerin i Blant* [Folk Songs for Children] (Aberystwyth: Cymdeithas Alawon Gwerin Cymru [Welsh Folk Song Society], 1981), p. 36; Opie, *The Oxford Dictionary of Nursery Rhymes*, pp. 367–9, offers a composite set of thirteen verses based on early printed sources.

Stars and Ribbons: The Mari Lwyd Ritual

OF ALL THE WINTER wassailing rites observed in Wales, the Mari Lwyd custom is possibly the strangest and most exciting. Mari Lwyd, a cavorting mare, was fearful to behold, and there followed after her a carnival of traditional characters. Frequently observed in Gwent, Glamorgan and Carmarthenshire, the custom of accompanying Mari on a dark midwinter evening, the procession 'accompanied by men holding burning brands',[1] was at its most popular in the south Wales mining areas. Violet Alford made a similar connection between the hilt-and-point Sword Dance and mineral-rich areas related with mining activities in historical and prehistoric mines.[2]

In 1943 Iorwerth C. Peate claimed that the Mari Lwyd custom 'was formerly found in varying forms throughout Wales'.[3] No records of a Mari Lwyd custom prior to 1943 have survived from north Wales, however. The earliest example was noted in Barmouth in December 1950, staged to mark Barmouth town's special effort to celebrate the Festival of Britain held in the summer of 1951. The collection taken during the Mari Lwyd event was transferred to the local Festival of Britain fund.[4] In the twenty-first century the custom has been observed in Mallwyd and Dinas Mawddwy, Gwynedd.[5]

Mid-Wales, an area with no collieries, is represented by a significant example of a horse's head from Defynnog (Powys) in the Brecon Beacons National Park. Dating to 1798, it is the earliest surviving record of the tradition:

byddent yn cario dyn (...) wedi ei wisgo mewn dillad taclus, a'i
addurno â phob math o ribanau amryliw, a phen hen geffyl ar
ei ben, yn cael ei gario ar hyd yr heolydd gan dri neu bedwar
o ddynion cryfion a phenwan, a galw wrth bob drws trwy y
pentref am elusen ac ewyllys da pawb.[6]

[they would carry a man (...) dressed in presentable clothes,
and adorned with all manner of multicoloured ribbons, and an
old horse's skull on his head, being carried along the roads by
three or four strong and senseless men, calling at every door in
the village for charity and for everyone's goodwill.]

On Twelfth Night, the diarist Francis Kilvert (1840–79) witnessed the
custom at Clyro, close to Hay-on-Wye in the historic county of Rad-
norshire, now Powys. He wrote the following undated account some
time after the event itself had taken place:

It was between the Christmasses, and at eight o'clock I was sit-
ting with some other people around the fire, when we heard
tramping outside, and a loud knocking on the door, which was
locked. There was the sound of a flute a moment later, and a
man began singing – I could not distinguish the words – then a
few minutes later another man, inside the room, went to the door
and sang what was apparently an answer to the song without.
Then the door was thrown open, and in walked about a dozen
people, headed by a most extraordinary apparition, an animal
covered with a flowing sheet, and surmounted by a horse's skull,
to which a bridle was attached. This apparation [sic], I saw a
moment later was really a man covered with a sheet; his head
was bowed down, and a skull had been fastened on to it. The
people sang, collected some money, and then went off. They
ought by rights, apparently, to have had an ass's skull, but then,
dead donkeys, are proverbially hard to come by![7]

In the twenty-first century, Mari Lwyd appeared in Tal-y-bont near
Aberystwyth in Ceredigion.[8]
    The custom was held on various dates. In Llandybïe (Carmarthen-
shire) Mari Lwyd participators started singing the wassail immediately
after All Hallows' Day (1 November) and continued until the New

Year – particularly during Christmas week.[9] Frances Hoggan mentions the last day of November as a starting date,[10] John Davies of Pentyrch on the western outskirts of Cardiff records that the Mari Lwyd custom was observed for about a fortnight before Christmas and a fortnight into the New Year, the highlight being the week between Christmas and the New Year.[11] In Barmouth (Gwynedd) Mari appeared at Christmas;[12] William Roberts 'Nefydd' (1813–72), reporting on Glamorgan and Gwent gives Christmas night as the date of Mari's first appearance, continuing for a fortnight, three weeks or a month.[13] T. C. Evans 'Cadrawd' describes it as a New Year custom;[14] a manuscript dated 1818 states 'on the Eve of the Epiphany';[15] David Jones in 1888 writes that it was a Twelfth Night custom.[16] The recently established Mallwyd and Dinas Mawddwy Mari celebrates on the Saturday evening following the Mallwyd *plygain* (a service of traditional Welsh carols) on 13 January, to coincide as closely as possible with Old New Year's Day celebrated on 13 January.

The custom is referred to by several titles: 'Y Feri Lwyd' in the Vale of Glamorgan and the Glamorgan uplands,[17] 'Y Fari Lwyd Lawen' (The Merry Mari Lwyd) in the Rhymney area,[18] 'Pen Ceffyl' (Horse's Head) in the Vale of Neath, 'Y Warsel' (the Wassail) in Llandybïe and other parts of Carmarthenshire, and 'cwnseila' or 'cwrseila' in Blackmill near Bridgend.[19] The custom was at its most popular during the period 1850–1920, when the greatest number of horse's heads made an appearance, and is still observed in parts of Wales today.

Characters

Historically only men took the roles of Mari Lwyd and her entourage. She was a noisy, restless creature, monstrous in appearance, her yards of white canvas swirling in the winter winds, her skull gleaming in the moonlight. Coming down into Merthyr Tydfil from the direction of Penydarren Ironworks she threw herself into all manner of contortions:

> Daeth *Mary* Lwyd lawen
> I lawr o Bendarren
> Gan branco a neidio a thawlu ei thin
> A Sol Nant-y-ffin yn ei harwain.[20]

[Merry Mary Lwyd came | Down from Penydarren | Prancing and jumping and wiggling her backside | And Sol Nant-y-ffin leading her.]

The success of the custom took many long evenings of preparation. A local lad would hide under a white sheet to work Mari's jaws – the jaws of a horse's skull (or as noted by William Roberts, the skull of a donkey,[21] and by Thomas Evans the head of a horse or cow[22] in the absence of a horse's skull) – using two sticks fastened to the lower jaw, with a spring for snapping and biting anyone who ventured near. The skull was buried in the ground[23] from one year to the next to prevent theft and to prevent it from yellowing. In the Vale of Neath it was buried in lime for the same purpose.[24] Should no skulls be available, one would be carved from a wooden block,[25] or formed from straw and rags.[26] The Oystermouth Mari Lwyd, formed from the skull of the deceased horse Sharper (see figure 12) who 'used to come up from Gower with vegetables every week and the boys used to mind the horse while the man got on with his rounds', looked particularly splendid 'for he still had all his teeth'.[27]

The youth would place a pole of approximately five feet in height inside the skull, and cover himself from head to foot in a white sheet, or in the Vale of Neath a mottled cloak or shawl.[28] Mari's head was dressed with horsehair or rope for a mane, and decorated with knots of colourful ribbons obtained from sisters and girlfriends. She had eyes of shining coal, or made from the base of milk bottles or 'out of the bottoms of broken beer-bottles carefully chipped round';[29] her ears were made of bright cloth, black leather or felt. The jingle of bridle bells added to the excitement. Stock Mari Lwyd stanzas used in Blackmill near Bridgend and in other parts of Glamorgan describes her thus:

Ma'r Feri Lwyd yma
'N llawn sers a rybana,
Ma' i'n werth i roi gola (x3)
'R nos heno.

Ei chefan a'i chynffon
A'i dou lygad gleision
A'i thrimins yn gochion (x3)
Nos heno.[30]

[Stanza 1: Mari Lwyd is here | Full of stars and ribbons, | It is worth bringing light | Tonight.

Stanza 2: Her back and her tail | And her two bright eyes | And her red trimmings | Tonight.]

A special guard escorted Mari from door to door. The retinue was dressed in Sunday best, and 'in great bravery of ribbons of many colours (cheerfully lent them by the women) superadded to coats and hats. If ribbons were not abundant enough, the want would be supplied by a sort of frilling of coloured paper.'[31]

Ostler Smart, the Leader, was responsible for Mari and for maintaining control over her movements. As his name implies he was a smart, well-turned-out character. He conducted the party around the neighbourhood in as seemly a manner as possible, leading Mari 'by a long rein of wide scarlet braid'[32] held in one hand, and carrying a stick or whip in the other to knock on doors, and to restrain Mari and prevent her from injuring onlookers and damaging property as she kicked and curvetted. The guard numbered about six members, a total usually decided by the number of available men. The main strengths of the guard members were the ability to help form skilful rhymes, be entertaining, and to drink large quantities of beer. According to Charles Ashton, 'y llebanod mwyaf meddw a digymeriad yn y fro sydd yn chwareu "Mari Lwyd"'[33] (it is the most drunken and disreputable louts of the area who play 'Mari Lwyd').

Other Company members were the Sergeant, the Corporal and the Merryman if there were six players in total. Should Mari be counted as one of the six then the Sergeant and the Corporal could be one and the same person, or one of the other characters might lose his place in the ensemble. Occasionally the Merryman played a fiddle, or there was often a crowther accompanying the group of six players,[34] or (infrequently) a flute,[35] but the Pen-coed guard in Glamorgan played no musical instruments.[36] All three characters were dressed in attractive clothes decorated with ribbons or rosettes and wore a wide belt about the waist. Some might carry a stick, others might carry a bucket or bag to collect money and gifts, and various accounts mention a hat: 'after a due exhibition of this horse's various antics, a hat is put into his mouth, and a collection is levied upon the spectators.'[37] Gifts were generally shared among the party, or donated to a local cause. Mrs Bowden of Oystermouth (in the district of Mumbles, Swansea) who stabled Mari Lwyd recalls the Christmas of 1970 when her sons 'made enough money to give the OAPs a night out'.[38]

Pwnsh and Siwan (corresponding to Punch and Judy), two characters sometimes counted among the six members, may be considered an independent element in the drama, or sometimes did not appear at all. They professed to be husband and wife, and were different from the other characters, their faces blacked, their dress ragged and filthy, Siwan carrying a broom, Pwnsh carrying a formidable club.

All the characters apart from Siwan have English names even though they sing in Welsh. It is possible that the labels were imported from corresponding English rituals. Unlike their role in the mumming plays, Pwnsh and Siwan did not play a verbal part in the Mari Lwyd custom. Their function was to assist and support Mari by dancing and creating a commotion, bustling about, shouting and clapping. Tom Jones of Trealaw in the Rhondda Valley notes that the Mari Lwyd dancers were called 'hoen ddawnswyr' or merry dancers.[39] He adds that Pwnsh and Siwan had their own dance, different from the one danced by the Mari Lwyd followers:

> Nid oedd gan y ddeuddyn direidus ond ffon a sgubell, ac ni chaffent ychwaith gymorth na thelyn na chrwth. Cadwai Pwnsh yr amser drwy fwrw ei daplath ar y llawr, neu efallai ar gefn Shiwan. Yng nghrog wrth wisg Pwnsh yr oedd cloch yn canu (...) Diweddai Pwnsh a Shiwan eu dawns drwy afaelyd yn nwylo neu arddynau y naill y llall, a dwytroed y naill yn erbyn dwytroed y llall, ac yna troi fel yr awel nes y byddai pennau'r ddau yn hurt gyda'r bendro.

> [The mischievous couple had nothing but a stick and a broom, and they were not assisted by either harp or crwth/crowd. Pwnsh kept time by striking the floor with his stick, or perhaps across Shiwan's back. Hanging by Pwnsh's clothing a bell rang (...) Pwnsh and Shiwan finished their dance by holding each other's hands or wrists, placing two feet against the other's two feet, and then turning like the breeze until their heads were stunned with dizziness.]

A report from 1883 states that Pwnsh, in the company of the merry dancers, wore 'a cap and mask of some animal's skin, with the hair on (...) a fox's brush, if it can be got, or some other hairy ornament is pendant from behind, and a concealed bell tinkles about his hinder parts'.[40] This bell was the only music. Furthermore, Pwnsh danced a *pas de deux* with 'his wife Judy, who is personated by the tallest man the party are able to procure. He is habited in female attire, the face blacked, and an enormously broad-brimmed slouched beaver hat upon the head.' The dance steps resembled 'a sort of shuffling run, in very short steps, somewhat resembling what in fashionable assemblies, 20 years ago [1799], was known by the name of the "partridge step."'[41]

Were Pwnsh and Siwan part of the Mari Lwyd custom from the outset? Tom Jones suggests that their role developed into a fixed part of the ritual, instead of continuing as an independent form of entertainment. All three – Mari, Pwnsh and Siwan – are unpleasant characters, Pwnsh and Siwan creating havoc in each home they visit, Mari creating terror, neighing and rearing and shaking her head like a wild creature. Many feared her, warning her either to behave or keep her distance:

Os ydyw y Feri
Yn addo i'r Cwmpni
I ymddwyn yn deidi
Heb gnoi na thraflyncu
Caiff ddyfod i'r Cwmpni
Nos heno.[42]

[If Meri | Promises the Company | She will behave [in a] tidy [manner] | Without biting or guzzling | She may join the Company | Tonight.]

The same series of stanzas asks:

Ond beth am y Pwnsh
A'r procar a'r Judi
I ddifa y cysur
A'r tanllwyth i'r Cwmpni (x2)
Nos heno?

[But what of Pwnsh | And the poker and Judy | That spoil the
comfort | And the roaring fire for the Company (x2) | Tonight?]

At the singing of the above song Mari, Pwnsh and Siwan stand together
to convey the sense of a fertility ritual. The prime function of Pwnsh
and Siwan is to promote fertility, with or without Mari's assistance.
The horse is a long-recognised symbol of fecundity and abundance:
'the sexual vigour of the horse endowed it with symbolism associated
with fertility and prosperity.'[43]

Often it was men from the same family who undertook the care
of Mari Lwyd, stabling her for the summer, and preparing her for her
winter visitations. The Pentyrch Mari Lwyd is now housed at St Fagans
National Museum of History (Cardiff), but in her heyday she was led
by two brothers, John Davies who died in 1953 aged 82 and Tom
Davies (c.1880–1945), two of the sons of Cae'r-Wâl, near the village
square. Tom led Mari Lwyd, and John squatted under the sheet. They
visited widely – in Pentyrch, Radyr, St Fagans, St Brides, Peterston-
Super-Ely, Welsh St Donats, Llantrisant, Llantwit Fardre, Coryton, Taff's
Well, Nantgarw, Treforest and as far as Pontypridd.[44] Keepers of Mari
Lwyd were not obliged to be members of the same family. Mr Oak of
Neath[45] notes that during the period 1900–c.1908 his uncle, together
with an unrelated man 'Dai Clwb' (since he had a club foot), led Mari
around the neighbourhood. Mr Oak's uncle carried a tin whistle or a
harp, and his friend carried the horse's head.

It is often assumed that the players were urban people, since
the Mari Lwyd custom is so closely linked to the industrial areas of
south Wales. This, however, was not immutably the case. The iconic
image of Sianco'r Castell (see figure 10) leading Mari Lwyd around
Llangynwyd village c.1904–10 is a case in point. It is often included
in Mari Lwyd studies, but whenever this image is published Sianco's
official name, as registered on a birth certificate, is not provided and
no particulars are offered that might reveal the man's identity other
than his nickname. The sobriquet suggests he had links with a house
or farm in the Llangynwyd area called Castell. The 1911 Census shows
that a family of five lived at Castell Farm: the head of the house-
hold, Edward Rees, a seventy-three-year-old widower; his daughter,
Mary Elizabeth Davies; his son-in-law, David John Davies (possibly
'Sianco'r Castell'?); and their two children, a daughter aged 5 and a
one-year-old son. The Census states that the son-in-law was born in

Llandygwydd, between Newcastle Emlyn and Cardigan in Ceredigion, and was forty years old in 1911; he was Mary Elizabeth's second husband. They had been married for seven years, which suggests that David John Davies had moved into the farmhouse in 1905, a large proportion of the 1904–10 time slot. The 1901 Census records that Castell Farm was home to Edward Rees and his wife; their daughter Mary Elizabeth, categorised as married (presumably to her first husband whose name does not appear on the Census form as living in Castell Farm); and two servants, Edith Davies (eighteen years old) and Samuel Jones (twenty-five years old). In 1911 the family employed a fourteen-year-old live-in domestic servant, Lily Maud Carroll, but no mention is made of a male live-in servant. Castell Farm was not the happiest of homes. The Christmas Day edition of *The Glamorgan Gazette* 1914 reports a hearing at Bridgend Police Court:

> in which David J. Davies, Castell Farm, summoned his wife's father, Edward Rees, living at the same address; Griffith Jones (Rees' nephew), Station Road, Pontrhydycyff, and Stanley Jones, formerly a solicitor's clerk, for having, he alleged, used threats towards him which 'put him in fear'.[46]

The same report states that Rees 'was of drunken habits' and was trying to oust his son-in-law from the farm, threatening to 'hang him by the feet' and calling him 'a — Cardi'. There had been several planned attacks on David John Davies, and at one point he had barricaded himself in his bedroom with his wife, children, and Lily the maid. The case was dismissed. The Chairman and the Bench 'were not quite unanimous with regard to the case', and it was thought that 'the proceedings were discreditable to both sides' and 'ought to have been settled in the proper way in the proper place'. In January 1915 there was a second hearing at Bridgend Police Court involving Castell Farm, when Lily Carroll 'summoned Griffith Jones, collier, for assault'.[47] And there was yet another issue. Edward Rees proposed to sell Castell Farm, and that was the subject of a motion before Mr Justice Neville in the Chancery Division on 21 December 1914; Edward Rees's son-in-law applied to the court to restrain him from selling.

The identity of 'Sianco'r Castell' remains a mystery. Could he have been David John Davies? As a rule, Sianco is a diminutive form of Jenkin, not John. Added to that, the Castell Farm son-in-law is referred to in court as David J. Davies making it improbable that he used his middle name in daily life if he did not use it in an official capacity. It is also improbable that a stranger who had settled in Llangynwyd, as opposed to a native, would have been given the honour of leading Mari Lwyd, considering he would not be as familiar, perhaps, with the ritual as some of the local lads. Could there have been a servant called Sianco at Castell Farm? If so, he remained very much in the background during the various hearings and is not mentioned once, even though other characters played a prominent part in the unhappy proceedings. It is reasonable to suppose that either Edward Rees, the master of Castell Farm, or his son-in-law, would have numbered and named any servants among their supporters. The search continues.

A different man guided Mari Lwyd as she roamed the streets and farms of Llangynwyd c.1910–14 (see figure 12), but the image held at the National Library of Wales provides no identification of either Mari or the Leader.

T. I. Phillips, whose older brother Ifan Bifan Phillips was a member of a Mari Lwyd party, says that in the Blackmill, Glynogwr and Gilfach Goch area most of the players were farmers' sons.[48] They kept their Mari in pubs for the remainder of the year – the Fox and Hounds in Blackmill, the New Inn in Glynogwr, and the Clun Goch between Glynogwr and Gilfach Goch, suggesting that it was farm hands, in this instance, who observed the Mari Lwyd tradition rather than farm owners, or Mari Lwyd would have been stored in farm buildings. Zealous chapelgoers and lay preachers were not excluded from the observance. The Colliers Arms in Llanharry used to be kept by Twm Richards who preached occasionally with the Congregationalists, and who also played a part in the Mari Lwyd ritual.

Sequence of Events

In traditional wassailing style, '[c]odent y teulu i fyny ar bob adeg o'r nos'[49] (they woke the family up at all times of the night), requesting the company of a young woman, a warm fire, a generous piece of 'cacen fras felys' (sweet currant cake), and for the householder to tap the barrel and serve them great quantities of beer. Mari's trip was planned in advance, so that local people knew on which evening they were expected to welcome her. Mari's prowling and the Company's dancing kept the crowds on the streets giving the group an opportunity to collect money for a local charity; inside every home, too, 'coins of the realm would find their way as an offering into the players' bag'.[50]

A great silence enveloped the homes, each family on the alert for Mari's arrival. On hearing her approaching, the women hid inside, every door locked. At the door, Mari 'would commence to prance, but would ultimately be soothed to silence by cries of "Who-o. Who-a, Mari", "Beth sydd arno ti, gaseg fach" (What is the matter with you, little mare).'[51] The Mari Lwyd party hoped to gain access to homes by winning the *pwnco*, a versified battle of wits in which one side answered the other side's challenges, the wassailers fighting to gain access and the householders responding in kind to prevent them. The wassailers hoped to win the homeowners over by appealing to their better natures and listing the obstacles and difficulties encountered on the journey – a ploy to gain admittance:

Ni dorson ein crimpa
Wrth groeshi'r sticila
I ddyfod t(u)ag yma (x3)
    Nos (h)eno.[52]

[We have broken our shins | Crossing the stiles | To come here (x3) | Tonight.]

The *pwnco* continued until one of the two parties failed to respond in impromptu verse. There was a great deal of extempore singing involved, together with the performing of traditional verses. Some were taught to rhyme by an experienced songster. In the upper part of the Vale of Neath a group of young lads learned their *pwnco* skills from 'Shon Tewgoed oedd yn gofalu am beiriant awyr y gwaith glo'[53] (Shon Tewgoed who was in charge of the colliery's ventilation machinery).

Most accounts state that two separate groups took part in the *pwnco*, the Mari retinue and the householders. Evan Bevan explains that all the singers sang in unison up to this point, but that the *pwnco* was sung by a chosen individual from each camp. Another account of the *pwnco* states:

Odd cwmpni yn myn'd a'r 'Feri' rownd trw'r dre ne'r pentra, a chyn bysa nhw yn acto odd un part o'r cwmpni yn mynd miwn i'r ty, a chauad y drws yn erbyn y part arall. Wetin fysa rhai odd mas yn dechra 'pwnc' trw dwll y clo, a'r rhai odd miwn yn 'pwnco' yn u herbyn nhw.[54]

[A company would take 'Meri' around the town or the village, and before they would act, one part of the company would go into the house and close the door against the other part. Then the ones outside would start to 'pwnc' through the keyhole, and the ones inside would 'pwnco' against them.]

And so the *pwnco* continued, conducted according to Tom Jones (Trealaw) in a style that combined singing and chanting.[55] John Evans, touring south Wales at Christmastide 1803, was less generous in his description of a retinue 'of idle people (...) neighing or bellowing in a hideous manner' as they went about accompanied by a man dressed up as a horse or a bull.[56]

Eventually the householders surrendered with good grace and invited Mari and her guard to join the family on the hearth, to frighten away evil spirits and to confer good luck on the household for the coming year. The householder would happily admit defeat and welcome the Mari Lwyd party into the home:

Wel, wir, yr hen Feri,
Rwyt ti wedi fy maeddu;
Dera miwn, ti a dy deulu
    Nos heno![57]

[Well, indeed, old Meri, | You have defeated me; | Come in, you and your family | Tonight!]

D. G. Williams recalls one householder's apparent reluctance to engage with the Mari Lwyd party even though the door of the house was wide open. The women were still in hiding when the Mari Lwyd party entered the kitchen, waited, but no one appeared. When Mari noticed loaves of griddle bread, 'nid hir y bu safnau y ceffyl heb gau am danynt a'u tynu lawr o un i un'[58] (it was not long before the horse's jaws closed over them and pulled them down one by one).

Next, Mari spied a goose being roasted and as she eyed that too, the family came out of hiding to welcome the party.

Infrequently, the householders won the *pwnco* and Mari was forced to continue her journey. Ceinwen H. Thomas tells the tale of her great-grandfather defeating Mari in a robust battle of wits. *c*.1850.[59] A party from Nantgarw, about eight miles from Cardiff, on visiting a particular home had caused confusion there leaving the house in complete disorder. The following year the householders felt it necessary to retaliate. Thomas's great-grandfather was a skilled rhymester and could give a stirring response to any stanzas thrown at him. Persuaded to be present for Mari's visit to Rhiw-dder, he quickly revealed that Mari was not welcome there because she had misbehaved on her previous visit. Mari's friends repeatedly tried to convince him that they were the men of Caerphilly and not the gang who had visited the previous year, but the old man would not be persuaded and they had to move on. A little later he heard that they had gone down to the Royal Oak in Taff's Well where they met the party who had misbehaved, and a fight broke out between the two parties. The old man's son played the part of Pwnsh for the Caerphilly party that night, and for years he delighted in the hiding they gave the Nantgarw men for spoiling their fun.

Although refusing admittance was permitted, John Williams, Bryngwenith Farm in Pen-coed, Glamorgan, did not once see a householder send Mari away even if she was beaten at the *pwnco*, and he had been part of the custom in that area for over fifty years. Others suggest that householders were too generous to Mari and her followers: 'such of those of their neighbours who are not wiser than themselves, give them ale and cake, or money, others that are wiser send them away from their doors with each a flea in his ear.'[60]

More recently the practice in Mallwyd and Dinas Mawddwy is to fashion verses beforehand rather than compose on the spot. Stanzas are often witty and parochial, appropriate for the area and its characters. The wassail singers prepare a dozen or fifteen verses, stand outside the door singing all their verses in succession, and are then answered by the party inside the door singing their stock of verses, with little or no extempore rhyming, a deviation from the *pwnco* norm.

Having gained entrance, ample space would have been cleared for the visitors. In Monmouthshire, Mari and the Ostler entered first:

the [Mari Lwyd] figure would pretend to be restive, bite or run over any that came in its way, till one would seize the rein of the bridle, and another strike the figure on the forehead with a small wooden axe provided for the purpose. The figure would then fall prostrate upon the floor, the leader disappear. This ended the first part of the performance. The concealed would then come from under the sheet, fold it up, and lay the head aside; the disappeared re-enter; one of the party would then produce a violin and play a hornpipe: and the party, with any who choosed to join them, go through a country dance. This concluded the performance.[61]

Mari would nip and neigh, sniff the girls and pretend to bite them, dancing and running around, the Ostler attempting to pacify her:

A dyna lle bu'n dawnsio,
Yn cicio ac yn cnoi,
A'r plant ar draed a dwylo
O dan y byrddau'n ffoi.[62]

[And that is where she danced, | Kicking and biting, | And the children on hands and knees | Fleeing under the tables.]

Having calmed down a little, the Mari costume was removed while the retinue sang, before retiring to the fireside where ale and cakes were served. Pwnsh always poked the fire, sometimes with such vigour he managed to extinguish it. In Nantgarw, Mari's retinue had to promise in song during the rhyming contest that Pwnsh would not interfere with the fire or he would not be admitted. Siwan's task was to extinguish any candles and sweep the hearth with a broom to banish evil spirits that might weaken the attempt to promote fertility. In Nantgarw, Siwan's sweeping was so vigorous one year that ashes were thrown across the floor and crunched underfoot during the merrymaking – she was not permitted to return the following year. As well as sweeping the hearth, Siwan gives the walls and windows a once over – she even sweeps the occasional person who ventures too close. When Pwnsh kisses the women (seen as a desire to procreate) to the accompaniment of music provided by Merryman and possibly another fiddle, Siwan becomes jealous and runs after her husband, beating him with her broom. It has been suggested that their fighting might be indicative of the seasonal battle fought between summer and winter, but neither Pwnsh nor Siwan dies even though the following stanza was sung by the inhabitants of Neath:

Mae Shiwan wedi marw,
A'i chorff hi yn y bedd,
A'i hysbryd yn y wilber
Yn mynd i Gastell Nedd.[63]

[Siwan is dead, | And her corpse is in the grave, | And her spirit in the wheelbarrow | Travelling to Neath.]

Trefor M. Owen suggests that the above is a stanza to be sung on All Hallows' Eve.[64]

After the feast, the singing and dancing ceased and it was time to don the horse's head and collect money and gifts. On departure,

when they got into the porch, and the door had been closed after them, they stopped, to sing a parting stanza, in which they returned thanks for their good cheer, and prayed that prosperity and happiness, long life and health, and a well-stored cellar and plenteous living, might long continue to be the lot of the hospitable dwellers under that roof.[65]

After the departure song, they proceeded to the next home.

Unwritten law declared that a Mari Lwyd from one parish should not trespass on another Mari's area of activity, or the offending Mari would be punished ruthlessly.[66] The following describes a fight that followed the appearance of a foreign Mari:

byddai y ddau eilun fel dau farch porthianus yn gweryru ar eu gilydd; a phan ddeuent i gyffyrddiad, dechreuent gnoi a llarpio y naill y llall. Wedi brwydr galed, bwrid y penglogau i'r llawr, deuai y ddau arwr allan odditan y gorchudd i fyned yn mlaen â'r ymrysonfa gyda dyrnau a thraed; yna dyna y ddwy fintai yn curo eu gilydd; byddai y frwydr yn boeth echryslon erbyn hyn; a chyn terfynu, yr oedd llawer dan eu cleisiau a'u clwyfau, os nad wedi dryllio eu hesgyrn.[67]

[the two figures would be like two spirited horses neighing at one other; and when they came into contact, they would start to bite and maul one another. After a hard battle, the skulls would be thrown to the floor, the two heroes would come out from under the covers to continue the contest with fists and feet; then the two companies would beat one another; by now they were in the heat of the terrible battle; and before it ended many would be bruised and injured, if not suffering broken bones.]

Mari Lwyd Songs

Six types of song might be sung during the course of the evening: the 'waiting' stanza sung inside the house, Mari's arrival and her request song that she might enter, the challenge and reply (*pwnco*), the song/ stanza to conclude the pwnco, Mari's song performed within the home, and her song on departure.[68] Strict adherence to a framework that covered all of the above is unlikely: not all six song functions or types were sung at every Mari Lwyd observance and their perfor-mance (or otherwise) varied within the formal guidelines. Sometimes other kinds of music were on offer: 'the singing of ballads and love songs, such as *The Maid of Cefn Ydfa* and *The Maid of Sker*, dancing to the fiddle and harp and after some hours the Feri would sing her farewell (...) at the door.'[69]

In general, Mari Lwyd tunes seem to be variants of a single air and share the same characteristics:

(a) the opening processional words, '*Wel dyma ni'n dwad* ...'; (b) the octave leaps in the melody at particular points; (c) the syncopated rhythm that derives from the tendency often found in Welsh folk-songs to extend the unaccented syllable; and (d) the general melodic shape that tends to oscillate between major and minor. There is a distinct pentatonic aspect to some of these tunes (...) though none remains strictly in that scale pat-tern throughout.[70]

'Hyd yma bu'n cerdded' (poem 28) is in a major key, and although the customary opening line 'Wel, dyma ni'n dŵad' is missing, 'stepwise motion is prominent' and 'there is no syncopation'; nevertheless, 'from the formal structure, melodic style and nature of the words, it belongs with the others of this group.'[71] Tempo instructions state that 'Hyd yma bu'n cerdded' should be 'GAY' and that 'O dyma enw'r feinwen' should be sung 'VERY SLOW'.[72]

The Mari Lwyd ritual opens with a stanza or song sung by the women who wait for Mari's approach. Not part of the tradition in every area, few examples have been preserved. The following stanza, recorded by T. I. Phillips, was sung by his sisters:

A gloisoch chi drysa?
Ma bois y Cwrseila
Yn siwr o ddod yma (x3)
I gianu.[73]

[Have you locked [the] doors? | The Wassail lads | Are sure to come here (x3) | To sing.]

The waiting stanza is followed by a request (sometimes called the Vigil Chorus,[74] or Vigil lay) by Mari's followers:

Wel, dyma ni'n dwad
Gyfeillion diniwad
I ofyn am gienad (x3)
I gianu.[75]

[Well, here we come | Innocent friends | To ask permission (x3) | To sing.]

Some homeowners requested that all the retinue members be named, but no detailed answers have survived:

Rhowch glwad ych enwa
Ac enw'ch trigfanna
Cyn cewch ddod miwn yma (x3)
    Nos heno.[76]

[Let us hear your names | And the name of your homes | Before you are permitted to come in here (x3) | Tonight.]

The challenge and reply (*punco*) follows, sung to the same melody 'in a combination of traditional and impromptu stanzas'.[77] Each side had sharp words to offer as they discredited the other side for their harsh voices, discordant singing, drunkenness, and unkempt appearance:

Mari Lwyd: Os oes yma ddynion
                 All dorri englynion
                 Yn r(h)wydd r(h)owch atebion (x3)
                     Y Nos (h)eno.

Ateb: Mi ddeuthum o'r beudy
                 Gan wir benderfynu
                 Y gwnawn i dy facddu (x3)
                     Y Nos (h)eno.

Mari Lwyd: Mi saf ar y beili
                 'S bo'r llechi yn pantu
                 Cyn ildiwn i'r teulu (x3)
                     Y Gwyla.

Ateb: Ti sefi am wthnos
                 A phart o bythewnos
                 A mis os bydd achos (x3)
                     Y Nos (h)eno.

Mari Lwyd: Nawr grynda'r gŵr digri,
                 Ma'th anal di'n drewi
                 Trwy ddwylath o dderi'r (x3)
                     Nos (h)eno.

Ateb: Ma'r tecill a'r ffrimpan
                 Yn tampo (a)r y pentan
                 Wrth glywad shwd glerian (x3)
                     Y Nos (h)eno.

Mari Lwyd: Ma mwlsyn gan Siani
                 Ar ben Waun Llanharri
                 A chlansith di i ganu (x3)
                     Y Gwyla.

Ateb: Ma'r cŵn a ma'r catha
               Yn cilio ta'r tylla
               Wrth glywad shwd lisha (x3)
               Y Nos (h)eno.[78]

[Stanza 1: Mari Lwyd: If there are men here | Who can compose stanzas, | Give [us] quick answers (x3) | Tonight.

Stanza 2: Answer: I have come from the cowshed | Fully determined | To defeat you (x3) | Tonight.

Stanza 3: Mari Lwyd: I shall stand on the farmyard | Until the slates sag in the middle | Before I surrender to the family (x3) | At Christmastide.

Stanza 4: Answer: You will stand [there] for a week | And part of a fortnight | And a month if need be (x3) | Tonight.

Stanza 5: Mari Lwyd: Now listen, you crazy man, | Your breath stinks | Through two yards of oak (x3) | Tonight.

Stanza 6: Answer: The kettle and the frying pan | Are bouncing on the hearthstone | On hearing such low-quality rhyming (x3) | Tonight.

Stanza 7: Mari Lwyd: Siani has a mule | Up on Llanharri Heath | That will challenge you to sing (x3) | At Christmastide.

Stanza 8: Answer: The dogs and the cats | Are retreating into holes | On hearing such voices (x3) | Tonight.]

Pwnco stanzas were challengingly robust:

Wel, gwranda'r pen bwldog
A chlustia sgyfarnog
A dannedd hen ddraenog
Y nos heno![79]

[Well, listen, you head of a bulldog | And ears of a hare | And teeth of an old hedgehog | Tonight!]

And:

Pe gen i ddrysïen
Fe'i tynnwn trwy dy gegen
Nos heno, nos heno, nos heno.[80]

[If I had a briar | I would draw it through your mouth | Tonight,
tonight, tonight.]

Reports from Anglesey c.1700–20 note the singing of cumulative
songs as part of the contention at the door during *Gŵyl Fair* festivi-
ties,[81] the most popular of those songs being 'Cyfri'r geifr' (Counting
the goats). In time, contest songs that were part of one observance
sometimes became part of a different custom. Barbara Bailey, a resi-
dent of Monmouthshire, recounts that the retinue attending Mari, fol-
lowing the contest at the door, would ask, in Welsh, 'Oes bwyd yma?'
(Is there food here?). If the answer was 'oes' (yes) they would enter
the house and Mari would ask 'Oes gafr eto?' (Are there any more
goats?) and this cumulative song has now become part of the Mari
Lwyd custom in some areas of Monmouthshire. Everyone present
'would join in the song, whilst the Mari would run wildly around the
house, snapping at any girls present, until it was time to eat'.[82]

When it was felt that the *pwnco* was at an end and could not be
sustained any longer, it terminated officially with a stanza referred to
by Tom Jones as 'Darfod Canu' (Concluding the Singing) sung outside
the door:

Ond yn awr rwy'n darfod canu,
Agorwch y drws i ni!
Mae'n o'r ma's ar y gaseg las,
Mae ei sodlau bron â rhewi.[83]

[But now I shall stop singing, | Open the door to us! | It is
cold outside for the grey mare, | Her heels are nearly frozen.]

William Roberts states clearly that Mari sings a song of many stanzas,
of which the above single stanza recorded by Tom Jones (Trealaw)
is a part, before entering the house, addressing the family and intro-
ducing the retinue:

1. Y tylwyth teg o'r teulu
A ddewch chwi i'r golau heb gelu
I weld y Wasael yn ddi-aeth?
Nid oes ei bath hi'n Nghymru.

2. Mae'n berllan o lydan flodau
O lwyrfryd hardd a lifrai,
Rhubanau gwychion, brithion, braf
A luniwyd yn ddolennau.

3. Mae'n gaseg lwysgedd, wisgi,
Mae miloedd yn ei moli,
Ei phen hi'n gnotog enwog iawn,
O foddion llawn difaeddu.

4. Daw'r *Sergeant* gwych a'i Gwmni
Yn wrol i'n blaenori;
At y gwaith mae eto i'w gael
Wych wastad Gorp'ral gwisgi.

5. Daw'r Osler gyda'i gaseg
A ledia hon yn landeg,
A'i ffrwyn a'i gyfrwy gydag e
I rodio'r lle dan redeg.

6. Daw hefyd Bwnsh a Siwan
Ar unwaith o'r un anian,
Dau filain draw'r un lliw â'r drwg,
Neu'r annedd fwg ei hunan.

7. (Ond) yn awr rwy'n darfod canu,
Rhowch i mi i ymborthi,
Blwyddyn newydd dda i chwi gyd
A phawb o'r byd, serch hynny.[84]

[Stanza 1: The fair family of the household | Will you come into the light, without hiding, | To see the Wassail without fear? | There is none like it in Wales.

Stanza 2: It is an orchard of plentiful flowers, | Exceptionally beautiful [and] in its livery, | Magnificent, delightful [and] splendidly coloured ribbons | Tied into bows.

Stanza 3: She is a beautiful, lively mare, | Thousands praise her, | Her head is [decorated] very splendidly with bunches [of ribbons and flowers], | Perfect [and] unsurpassed in manner.

Stanza 4: The excellent Sergeant and his Company enter | To lead us valiantly; | For this purpose there is yet at hand | [The] excellent, steadfast [and] nimble Corporal.

Stanza 5: The Ostler enters with his mare | And he leads her in a comely manner, | Bringing her bridle and saddle with him | To roam and run about the place.

Stanza 6: Pwnsh and Siwan will also enter | At once [and] are kindred spirits, | Two villains over there of the same colour as sin, | Or hell itself.

Stanza 7: (But) I shall now cease singing, | Give me something with which to feed myself, | A good New Year to you all | And to everyone in the world, for that matter.]

Further stanzas recorded by Gomer M. Roberts include:

A gawn ni drwy eich ffafwr
Eich cegin neu eich parlwr,
Neu eich neuadd, os cawn ddod?
Nid ym i fod ond chwegwr.[85]

[May we, through your favour, | To your kitchen or your parlour | Or your residence, be admitted? | We are only six men.]

This suggests that the singers were not yet inside the house, as does Gomer Roberts's explanation that the retinue sang the song 'wrth bob tŷ', at every house rather than 'in' every house.

Daniel Huws, however, suggests that it is after the dialogue outside the door and 'after gaining admission to the house' that the following stanza, part of the series of stanzas recorded by Gomer

Roberts, was sung; the measure and the tune changed as Mari sang on one of the favourite measures of the Glamorgan poets, *triban*:

> O dyma enw'r feinwen
> Sydd yn codi gyda'r seren
> A hon yw'r Washael fawr ei chlod
> Sy'n caru bod yn llawen.[86]

[O this is the name of the slender and beautiful one | Who rises with the star | And this is the Wassail of great renown | That loves to be merry.]

Having been welcomed inside, they are now 'ar y parth' (on the premises), possibly in the farmhouse kitchen. If the merriment continued and the wassailers were suitably impressed by the food and entertainment on offer, they would sing on departure a stanza or two in gratitude:

> Dymunwn i'ch lawenydd
> I gynnal blwyddyn newydd,
> Tra paro'r gŵr i dincian cloch,
> Well, well y boch chwi beunydd.[87]

[We wish you joy | To uphold a new year, | As long as the fellow continues to ring a bell, | May you prosper more and more each day.]

The 'gŵr' (fellow) referred to above is Pwnsh, who had a bell hanging from his costume. The following rhyme was popular in the parish of Llandybïe should the wassailers have received a hearty welcome:

> Ffarwel i chwi, foneddigion,
> Ni gawsom groeso ddigon;
> A bendith Dduw fo ar eich tai,
> A phob rhyw rai o'ch dynion.[88]

[Fare you well, gentlemen, | We have received ample welcome; | And may God's blessing be upon your homes, | And upon all your people.]

In the Vale of Glamorgan an English-language stanza sung on departure might be:

> God bless the ruler of this house,
> And send him long to reign,
> And many a merry Christmas
> May he live to see again.
>   And God send you a happy new year.[89]

In return for their blessings the retinue demanded gifts: 'o nhw yn doti cap ne het yn ngheg y "Feri" i fyn'd rownd i gasglu at yr achos, ac o nhw yn llwyddo i neid coin piwr cyn cwpla'r Gwila'[90] (they placed a cap or hat in the mouth of the 'Feri' to go about taking a collection for the cause, and they succeeded in making a pretty penny before the end of the Christmas season).

Should they have received a chilly welcome, the Llandybïe wassailers would sing:

> Ffarwel iwch, hen gybyddion,
> Ni chawsom ni ddim rhoddion;
> Eich aur a'ch arian chwi bob rhai
> Fo'n mynd i dai cymdogion.[91]

[Fare you well, old misers, | We did not receive any gifts; | May all your gold and your silver | Go to your neighbours' houses.]

Decline and Revival

Observing the Mari Lwyd custom was common in almost every parish and village in Glamorgan and Gwent until about the mid-nineteenth century (c.1850–75),[92] and was popular to varying degrees until the 1920s. With the decline of the Mari Lwyd custom, the *pwnco* in particular suffered: 'the genuine wits, the ready rhymesters, and the clever leaders and mummers of the Mari Llwyd, are no longer to be found' (1909).[93] In Llantrisant, some twelve miles from Cardiff, the retinue sang their verses upon arrival, followed by a few Christmas carols for good measure. In Llanharry, Cowbridge and the Vale of Glamorgan language skills declined and wassailers sang at each door:

about three verses of the Wassail song (...); upon the fourth they changed from Welsh to English, thus:

We've got a fine Mary,
She's dressed very pretty
With ribbons so plenty
  This Christmas.

This is how it would be managed in the bilingual district comprising the Vale of Glamorgan. In the northern parts of the county the singers continued in Welsh, thus:

Mae Mari Lwyd yma
Mae'n werth i gael gola',
Yn llawn o rhubana,
  Y Gwyla![94]

The Mari Lwyd custom remained widespread in south Wales until the last quarter of the nineteenth century, albeit in decline. In Blaenau Gwent, Mari Lwyd 'was carried around Briery Hill and Beaufort at Christmas time until the middle 1870's and was last seen at some public houses in Rassau about 1880'.[95] A native of Carmarthenshire 'remembers *Mari Lwyd Lawen* visiting a school at Llanfihangel Rhos y Corn about 50 years ago [c.1880]. On that occasion, there was only one man, carrying a horse's skull over his own and singing a doggerel rhyme.'[96] According to a report dated 1895: 'Odd hi yn arfadd bod mewn bri mawr yn amsar Nadolig slawar dydd, ond os fawr o son am deni nawr'[97] (She [Mari Lwyd] used to be very popular at Christmastide a long time ago, but there is little talk of her now). The last appearance of Mari Lwyd in Abercynon in Rhondda Cynon Taf 'was in 1901, although a party from the Rhondda appeared outside the Clarence Hotel, Pontypridd, in 1939'.[98]

Glyn Richards, born in 1909 in Rhossili on the south-western tip of the Gower Peninsula, recalls the last days of the Mari Lwyd custom in his village:

When I was about twenty [c.1929] a few of us decided to revive the old custom of the Mari Lwyd, which was just dying out. I remember now going to look for this horse's head. We knew a horse had been buried in a field at Kimley Moor, years and years before. So we went and dug it up and sure enough, the head was as good as new, the real thing. So we took it over to a fellow by the name of Willie Clement of Porteynon, who was a dab hand at dressing up a horse's head. He used to get the proper stuff, you know, ribbons and all that, and it was a sight to behold what he could make out of it. Then at Christmas, we used to go around with this old thing, the fellow underneath the sheet – usually me – would work the jaw with a piece of wire, very realistic. We'd go to a house, and p'rhaps they'd be having supper, so the old horse would go to the table and catch hold of a piece of cake or something in his jaws and champ away as we went off. Or he'd snap his jaws and try to scare the girls, we really did have fun out of that.

Horse's Head Song

Once I was a young horse
And in my stable gay
I had the best of everything
Of barley oats and hay,
But now I am an old horse
My courage is getting small
I'm 'bliged to eat the sour grass
That grows beneath the wall.

Chorus:

    Poor old horse, let him die,
    Poor old horse, let him die.

I've eaten all my oats and hay
Devoured all my straw,
I can hardly move about
Nor can my carriage draw:
With these poor weary limbs of mine
I've travelled many miles
Over hedges, bramble bushes,
Gates and narrow stiles.

Chorus:
> Poor old horse, let him die,
> Poor old horse, let him die.

People used to give us money, for charity. Some of them would give us a bribe not to come into the house. By gosh they were times, I can tell you.[99]

In 1934 a Mari Lwyd with a retinue of at least twelve singers sang on Christmas Eve at a chemist's shop in Mumbles, Swansea, 'and in the same district, on the same evening, a small boy carol-singer was seen carrying a "toy" *Mari Lwyd* on a stick – a significant deterioration'.[100] By the beginning of World War II the custom had died out in all but a few villages, for example Pentyrch, Pen-coed – and Llangynwyd, where it has continued unbroken.

In Llantrisant the custom was revived, very much in the traditional style, during the 1990s by members of the Llantrisant Folk Club:

> Mr Vernon Rees, a freeman of Llantrisant, remembers that his father, Tom John Rees, was in charge of the Llantrisant Mari. The Llantrisant head was not a real skull but was made of wood, bandaged right down to the snout to make it look like a genuine horse's head. Mr Rees remembers the Mari being kept in the cupboard under the stairs and knows it was still around in 1937, when the family moved house (...) Mr Rees does not know whether his mother gave the Mari Lwyd away or what became of it.[101]

There were four Mari Lwyd parties in Llantrisant until recently: the one owned by Tom John Rees, the Pontyclun Mari Lwyd with Cyril Harvey in attendance, the Castellau Mari Lwyd whose entourage includes chapelgoers singing the traditional 'Cân y Fari' and 'Y Washael' songs, and the Llantrisant Folk Club Mari Lwyd. Nowadays there is only one. 'The "new" Mari is a genuine skull, prepared and mounted in the traditional fashion by Ian Jones of Pencoed, the last thatcher working in South Wales. Ian kindly donated the Mari to Llantrisant Folk Club.'[102]

In Mallwyd and Dinas Mawddwy in Gwynedd, Mari's journey centres around two or three pubs. Mallwyd being located in a rural area, the players are sometimes transported in cars from one place to the next, keeping Mari away from public sight for a short period. Individuals decide early on in the process which role they will play, and high-quality costumes are provided for the occasion. These can be specially made up for the event and kept from year to year, or can be hired from a professional costume hire company. About a month beforehand, the players are called together to enquire about sizes, depending on how much notice local tailors or hire companies require. Other players may choose to wear traditional Welsh costume. On the night of the ritual the retinue meets to dress up and to apply make-up, perhaps in the home of one of the players or in a convenient hall – an excellent excuse for a party – before starting out. At about six in the evening, after dark, is believed to be a good time to start the fun. Each year, in addition to the local enthusiasts, a boisterous folk group or hearty soloist is invited to join in, to get the singing underway. Weather permitting, a folk dance group will perform outside the pub window, or in the bar if the weather is inclement.

The ritual commences at the Brigand's Inn in Mallwyd. After the Mari Lwyd party has won the rhyming contest and been admitted to the pub, the innkeeper provides Mari and her retinue with a finger buffet and a drink, at his own expense. Then local children act out the contest in the inn parlour – rather than under the dripping eaves. They will have learnt the movements and stanzas beforehand, and know how to perform the ritual. The Mari Lwyd ceremony, however, remains a ritual for adults with children playing a small part in the festivities, as was always the case. Children sang (or shouted) after Mari Lwyd and her retinue c.1895:

Ma dy wallt di'n cwrlo
O eishe ca'l i gribo;
Ma dy foche di'n pantu
O achos dy hen ddiogi.[103]

[Your hair is curling | For want of combing it; | Your cheeks are sunken | On account of your long-standing laziness.]

Origins

The three earliest animal masks were those of the horse, the deer and the calf. As early as the fourth century St Augustine declared: 'Si adhuc agnoscatis aliquos illam sordissimam turpitudinem de hinnicula vel cervula exercere, ita durissime castigate'[104] (if you ever hear of anyone pursuing this extremely filthy practice of dressing like a horse or deer, punish him most severely). Rituals involving animal skulls are found throughout the United Kingdom,[105] but the Mari Lwyd ritual is unique to Wales.

Much has been written concerning the origins of the Mari Lwyd custom. Theories include it being a signifier of 'marw llwyd y flwyddyn' (the grey death of the year), an animal support society, and a custom linked to the death of the Saviour of the world and the redemption of sinners.[106] The ritual has been linked to the fairies on the basis that they are called 'the verry volks' in the Gower Peninsula.[107] Another popular theory is that Mari Lwyd is linked to the Festival of the Ass held on 14 January and is based on the flight of the Holy Family into Egypt with the baby Jesus.[108] Most origin theories can be traced back to William Roberts 'Nefydd', who linked it to the mystery plays and interludes,[109] the English mumming plays, the Merry Lude, and an origin in Marian devotions.[110] Nefydd also suggests that the presence of a horse's skull in the *pwnco* implies a relationship with an animal cult associated with marriage and that the custom of 'Rhoddi Penglog' (Skull-giving) observed in north Wales is related. This involves young men obtaining a horse's skull, or preferably that of a donkey, and hanging it on May Day eve above or on the door of the house of a maid or married woman whom they wish to discredit, with the female's name attached to the skull.[111]

Mari Lwyd has been erroneously identified by several as Bwca Llwyd, a horse's head formed of canvas stuffed with hay and led about on All Hallows' Day; and by Marie Trevelyan as 'The Aderyn Pig Llwyd, or the "Bird with the Grey Beak"',[112] possibly on the basis of evidence that a bird may have formed part of the Mari Lwyd ritual:

Mae gyda ni aderyn yn yr allt yn y dyffryn,
A'i big ef mor wynned â'r eira;
O tapwch y faril, mae syched ar Darby,
O tapwch y faril, gollyngwch yn rhigil y Gwyle.[113]

[We have a bird in the forest in the valley, | With its beak as
white as snow; | O tap the barrel, Darby is thirsty, | O tap the
barrel, let [the beer] flow freely at Christmastide.]

The creature incorrectly named 'Y ganfas farch' (canvas horse),[114] later
proved to be 'Y ganfas faich' (the burden/load canvas, used for carry-
ing corn chaff and other small loads),[115] a prowling monster from the
St Davids area of Pembrokeshire. Other records state that the 'curious
custom' of Mari Lwyd 'was not known in Pembrokeshire'.[116] Frances
Hoggan suggests a possible association with the invading, conquer-
ing white horse of King Arthur's legend,[117] and asks whether Mari is
linked to the various white horses carved into chalk hills, such as the
White Horse of Uffington, or connected with the white horse of Death
(Revelation 6:8), and the Erlkönig tale.

Iorwerth C. Peate believes the custom 'is no doubt a survival of a
pre-Christian tradition, an "ecotype" of the many hobby-horse customs
found in Britain, Ireland, Europe and even as far afield as Java'.[118] He
suggests that 'Mari' could be 'a borrowal of the English *mare*, which
was (as in *nightmare*) a female monster supposed to settle upon peo-
ple to pound them to suffocation'.[119] 'Llwyd' in such a context would
have its ordinary meaning of 'grey'. Roy Saer believes that Mari Lwyd 'is
more likely to mean 'grey (or 'pale') mare' than anything else.[120]

T. H. Parry-Williams discusses the possibility that Welsh was-
sail stanzas may be loans from the English tradition, or imitations of
English originals written in parallel with their English counterparts.
Wassail singing occurs in English at an early date, but extant Welsh
examples do not date as far back.[121] Iolo Morganwg lists wassail-
ing and Mari Lwyd as two separate items on his list of Glamorgan
customs, '12. Mari Lwyd – a gwashaela – Ffiol Ddeunaw ddolen'[122]
(12. Mari Lwyd – and wassailing – Cup with eighteen looped han-
dles). David Jones, writing in 1888, describes both customs as being
similar but quite separate. He maintains that the wassailers 'blackened
their faces, wore rough masks, or disguised themselves in any man-
ner, and the rougher the disguise the better', and that they carried a
stick to beat 'each other's sides and backs in a manner which would
have been painful to behold if one had not known that each and
all were pretty well protected by straw under their puffed-out gar-
ments'.[123] They engaged in the *pwnco*, and carried a wassail vessel.
The Ewenny pottery flourished in the late eighteenth and nineteenth

centuries, producing fine-quality wares (see figures 2–4). The wassail bowl would be passed around so that the participants might drink from it, or a mugful of drink might be offered out of it while the householder kept it replenished from his tapped barrel, 'but the "survival" of these articles within the time to which my own memory extends was a common bucket, or even, it might be, a tin can!'[124] There are too many similarities between the Christmastide wassailing and the Mari Lwyd custom, and between the two rituals and English wassailing, for them to be completely separate ideologies – the difficulties of travel, the locked door, *pwnco*, the food and drink, and the emphasis on generosity and an exchange of blessings.

Many wassailing customs that were at one time in the province of adults have now become the preserve of children, the significance of the custom being greatly diminished and the powerful ritual having become a children's game. The Mari Lwyd ceremony, however, remains a ritual primarily for adults, and affords an opportunity for frivolity and colourful pageantry in the bleak midwinter. Its origins, however, must remain a mystery for the present. Following the discovery of a horse's skull in what appeared to be a shaft grave near Epple Bay (Margate), the skull lying on a bed of uncut oysters, at least two contrasting theories concerning its significance were offered. The first suggested that pearls were 'important givers of life' and that 'the horse-cult was brought to Britain by a pre-Celtic people'.[125] The second theory claimed that 'the assorted animal bones (...) do not seem to have been placed there with any kind of arrangement, but rather to have been thrown in anyhow (...) the animal remains simply comprise part of a rubbish dump'.[126] In the absence of hard evidence it is unwise to jump to conclusions regarding either the shaft grave at Epple Bay, or indeed the origins of Mari Lwyd.

Notes

1. Marie Trevelyan, *Folk-Lore and Folk-Stories of Wales* (London: Elliot Stock, 1909), p. 31, available online at *https://archive.org/stream/afl2317.0001.001.umich.edu#page/22/mode/2up* (accessed 17 August 2020).

2. Violet Alford, *Sword Dance and Drama* (London: Merlin Press, 1962), p. 15.

3.   Iorwerth C. Peate, 'Mari Lwyd: A Suggested Explanation', *Man*, 43 (1943), 53.

4.   [Anonymous], 'Daeth Mari Lwyd yn ol dros y Nadolig' [Mari Lwyd has returned over Christmas], *Y Cymro* [The Welshman], 29 December 1950, 1.

5.   Arfon Hughes, 'Canlyn y Fari' [Following Mari], *Canu Gwerin (Folk Song)*, 31 (2008), 88–94.

6.   D. Craionog Lewis, *Hanes Plwyf Defynog* [The History of the Parish of Defynog] (Merthyr Tydfil: H. W. Southey a'i Feibion, Cyf., 1911), pp. 304–5.

7.   Frances Essex Hope, 'Radnorshire Legends and Superstitions: Compiled by Mrs. Essex Hope from MS. left by the Rev. R. F. Kilvert, Curate of Clyro, 1865–72', *The Radnorshire Society Transactions*, 24 (1954), 6–7.

8.   M. M., 'Atgyfodi'r Fari Lwyd' [Resurrecting Mari Lwyd], *Papur Pawb* [A Paper for Everyone], February 2006, 1.

9.   Gomer M. Roberts, *Hanes Plwyf Llandybïe* [The History of the Parish of Llandybïe] (Cardiff: University of Wales Press, 1939), p. 276.

10. Frances Hoggan, 'Notes on Welsh Folk-Lore', *Folklore*, 4 (1893), 122.

11. Information compiled by D. Roy Saer, St Fagans National Museum of History (Cardiff), in conversation with Llewelyn Davies, Pentyrch, 17 November 1965.

12. [Anonymous], 'Daeth Mari Lwyd yn ol dros y Nadolig', 1.

13. William Roberts, *Crefydd yr Oesoedd Tywyll* [The Religion of the Dark Ages] (Caerfyrddin [Carmarthen]: printed by A. Williams, 1852), p. 15.

14. T. C. Evans 'Cadrawd', *History of Llangynwyd Parish* (Llanelly: printed at the Llanelly and County Guardian Office, 1887; facsimile reprint Bridgend: Mid Glamorgan County Libraries, 1992), p. 159.

15. NLW 21414E, 26.

16. David Jones, 'The Mari Lwyd: A Twelfth Night Custom', *Archaeologia Cambrensis* (1888), 389.

17. Tom Jones (Trealaw), 'Llên Gwerin Morgannwg' [Glamorgan Folklore], *Y Darian* [The Shield], 12 August 1926, 1.

18. Note that the song pertaining to 'Mari Lwyd Lawen' [Merry Mari Lwyd] included by Jennie Williams in her collection of folk-songs from Carmarthenshire and submitted to the National Eisteddfod of Wales in 1911, stating it was sung 'gan yr hen bobl trwy eu trwynau' [by the old folks through their noses], was not a Llandybïe song. She had collected it from Thomas Mathews of Llandybïe, who later taught in the Rhymney Valley, which is where he had heard it – not in Llandybïe; this misconception was published by several authors until 2011; see Roy Saer, 'Cân "Mari Lwyd Lawen" o Landybïe: Ei Gwir Leoliad' [The song of 'Mari Lwyd Lawen' from Llandybïe: its true location], in *"Canu at Iws" ac Ysgrifau Eraill* ['Song for use' and other articles] (Talybont: Cymdeithas

Alawon Gwerin Cymru [Welsh Folk Song Society], 2013), pp. 229–31; see also Thomas Mathews (ed.), *Llen Gwerin Blaenau Rhymni: o gasgliad bechgyn Ysgol Lewis, Pengam* [Folklore of Blaenau Rhymni: from the collection of the boys of Lewis School, Pengam] (Pengam: Ysgol Lewis, 1912).

19. T. I. Phillips, Llys Myfyr, 30 Dinas Terrace, Aberystwyth, in a letter to the author dated 12 February 1976; facsimile copy NLW Facs 369/3.

20. Poem 32.17–20.

21. Roberts, *Crefydd yr Oesoedd Tywyll*, p. 15.

22. Thomas Evans, *The Story of Abercynon* (Cardiff: Western Mail, 1944; 3rd edn revised and enlarged, Risca: Starling Press, 1976), p. 26.

23. J. D. Davies, *A History of West Gower, Glamorganshire*, 2 (Swansea: H. W. Williams at 'The Cambrian' office, 1879), p. 84.

24. D. Rhys Phillips, *The History of the Vale of Neath* (Swansea: the author, 1925), pp. 585–6.

25. Evan Powell, *The History of Tredegar* (Cardiff: South Wales Printing Works, 1885; facsimile reprint Tredegar: Blaenau Gwent Heritage Forum, 2008), p. 118; D. Rhys Phillips Papers 136 (NLW), 'Atgofion am Fro Morgannwg, y wlad a'r bobl' [Memories of the Vale of Glamorgan, the land and the people], p. 89 (manuscript created in 1938).

26. Jonathan Ceredig Davies, *Folk-Lore of West and Mid-Wales* (Aberystwyth: Welsh Gazette offices, 1911), p. 61, available online at: *http://www.gutenberg.org/files/53915/53915-h/53915-h.htm#ch4* (accessed 16 July 2020).

27. AWC MS 1723/1, ex inf. Mrs Bowden, 37 Woodville Road, Oystermouth.

28. Phillips, *History of the Vale of Neath*, p. 585.

29. Jones, 'The Mari Lwyd: A Twelfth Night Custom', 391.

30. AWC 560/120; ex inf. Evan Bevan, Tre-bryn, Coety, Bridgend.

31. Jones, 'The Mari Lwyd: A Twelfth Night Custom', 391.

32. Jones, 'The Mari Lwyd: A Twelfth Night Custom', 391–2.

33. Charles Ashton, 'Bywyd Gwledig yng Nghymru' [Rural Life in Wales], *Transactions of the National Eisteddfod of Wales, Bangor, 1890* ([Liverpool]: The National Eisteddfod Association, 1892), p. 71.

34. Ashton, 'Bywyd Gwledig yng Nghymru', p. 71.

35. Essex Hope, 'Radnorshire Legends and Superstitions', p. 6.

36. AWC Tape Archive 3132.

37. E. H., 'Mr. Urban, West Glamorgan', *The Gentleman's Magazine*, 89 (March 1819), 222.

38. AWC MS 1723/1, ex inf. Mrs Bowden, 37 Woodville Road, Oystermouth.

39. Tom Jones, 'Llên Gwerin Morgannwg', *Y Darian* [The Shield], 9 February 1928, 3.

40. E. H., *The Gentleman's Magazine*, 89 (March 1819), 222.

41. E. H., *The Gentleman's Magazine*, 89 (March 1819), 222.

42. Poem 35.13–18, 25–9.

43. Miranda Aldhouse Green, 'The Symbolic Horse in Pagan Celtic Europe: An Archaeological Perspective', in Sioned Davies and Nerys Ann Jones (eds), *The Horse in Celtic Culture: Medieval Welsh Perspectives* (Cardiff: University of Wales Press, 1997), p. 3; for the Mari Lwyd custom see Juliette Wood, 'The Horse in Welsh Folklore: A Boundary Image in Custom and Narrative', in Davies and Jones, *The Horse in Celtic Culture*, pp. 164–8.

44. Information compiled by D. Roy Saer, St Fagans National Museum of History (Cardiff), in conversation with Llewelyn Davies, Pentyrch, son of John Davies, 17 November 1965.

45. Information compiled by D. Roy Saer, St Fagans National Museum of History (Cardiff), in conversation with Mr Oak, 39 Hawthorn Avenue, Cimla, Neath, 21 May 1968.

46. [Anonymous], 'Relatives in Police Court', *The Glamorgan Gazette*, 25 December 1914, 7.

47. 'At Bridgend Police Court on Saturday, there was another echo of the Castell Farm trouble, when Lily Carroll, the domestic servant at the farm at Llangynwyd, summoned Griffith Jones, collier, for assault'; see [Anonymous], 'Another Echo', *The Glamorgan Gazette*, 15 January 1915, 7.

48. T. I. Phillips, in a letter to the author.

49. Ashton, 'Bywyd Gwledig yng Nghymru', 71; poem 28.7–12.

50. D. Rhys Phillips Papers 282 (NLW), 'Welsh New-Year Customs Discussed in the Trenches', p. vi (pre-1952).

51. E. T., 'Letters to the Editor: Mari Lwyd', *The Carmarthen Journal and South Wales Weekly Advertiser*, 9 January 1914, 7.

52. D. Roy Saer (ed.), *Caneuon Llafar Gwlad (Songs From Oral Tradition)*, 1 (Cardiff: National Museum of Wales/Welsh Folk Museum, 1974), p. 16. The song was recorded in October 1953 from the singing of William Morgan Rees (a railway worker, b. 1883), Woodlands, Brynmenyn near Bridgend in Glamorgan. William Morgan Rees saw the Mari Lwyd out and about in villages such as Coety, Bryncethin, etc. to the north-east of Bridgend until *c*.1933.

53. D. Rhys Phillips Papers 188 (NLW), 'Penillion y Ludus Mari a Phriodas' [Mari Lwyd Stanzas and Marriage Stanzas], p. viii (manuscript created pre-1952).

54. [Anonymous], 'Llythyra' Newydd gan Fachan Ifanc: Nadolig wrth y drws' [New Letters by a Young Chap: Christmas at the door], *Tarian y Gweithiwr* [The Worker's Shield], 26 December 1895, 3.

55. Tom Jones, 'Llên Gwerin Morgannwg', *Y Darian*, 12 August 1926, 1.

56. John Evans, *Letters written during a Tour through South Wales, in the year 1803, and at other times* (London: printed for C. and R. Baldwin, New Bridge-Street, 1804), p. 441.

57. Tom Jones, 'Llên Gwerin Morgannwg: Mari Lwyd II', *Y Darian*, 29 July 1926, 3.

58. D. G. Williams, 'Casgliad o Len-Gwerin sir Gaerfyrddin' [A collection of Carmarthenshire folklore], *Transactions of the National Eisteddfod of Wales, Llanelly, 1895* (Cardiff: The National Eisteddfod Association, 1898; Caerfyrddin [Carmarthen]: Cyngor Sir Caerfyrddin [Carmarthen County Council], 1996), p. 19.

59. Information recorded by D. Roy Saer, St Fagans National Museum of History (Cardiff), in conversation with Dr Ceinwen H. Thomas (1911–2008), undated.

60. NLW 21414E, 26.

61. Thomas Young, The New Inn, Risca, 'Mari Lwyd', *The Monmouthshire Merlin and South Wales Advertiser*, 31 December 1864, 8.

62. Thomas Williams 'Brynfab' (1848–1927), littérateur and farmer who retired to Hendre Wen, St Athan in the Vale of Glamorgan; his poem entitled 'Mari' first appeared in the *Western Mail*, 17 January 1925, 6; further see Dafydd Morse, 'Thomas Williams (Brynfab, 1848–1927)', in Hywel Teifi Edwards (ed.), *Cwm Rhondda* (Llandysul: Gomer, 1995), pp. 134–52.

63. Solfen, 'Noswaith o Hwyl gyda'r Fari Lwyd Lawen' [An evening of fun with Merry Mari Lwyd], *Y Ford Gron* [The Round Table] (December 1933), 34.

64. Trefor M. Owen, *Welsh Folk Customs* (Cardiff: National Museum of Wales/Welsh Folk Museum, 1974), p. 134.

65. Charles Redwood, *The Vale of Glamorgan* (London: Saunders and Otley, 1839), pp. 154–5.

66. Jones, 'The Mari Lwyd: A Twelfth Night Custom', 392.

67. William Williams (Hirwaun) and William Williams (Aberdare), *Traethodau Hanesyddol ar Ddyffryn Nedd* [Historical essays on the Vale of Neath] (Aberdare: printed by J. T. Jones, 'Gwron' Offices, 1856), p. 31.

68. For tunes sung during the observance of the Mari Lwyd custom see Phyllis Kinney, *Welsh Traditional Music* (Cardiff: University of Wales Press in association with Cymdeithas Alawon Gwerin Cymru [Welsh Folk Song Society], 2011), pp. 73–7.

69. Margaretta Thomas on the Mari Lwyd custom in Nantgarw near Cardiff (1880–1920), in Peter Kennedy (ed.), *Folksongs of Britain and Ireland* (London: Cassell & Company Ltd, 1975), p. 172.

70. Kinney, *Welsh Traditional Music*, p. 74.

71. Kinney, *Welsh Traditional Music*, p. 75.

72. Maria Jane Williams, *Ancient National Airs of Gwent and Morganwg (...) with introduction and notes on the songs by Daniel Huws* (Llandovery, 1844; facsimile reprint Aberystwyth: Cymdeithas Alawon Gwerin Cymru [Welsh Folk Song Society], 1994), pp. 30–1; see poems 28 and 30.

73. Poem 31.1–4.
74. Owen Morgan 'Morien', *History of Pontypridd and the Rhondda Valleys* (Pontypridd: Glamorgan County Times, 1903), pp. 138–9.
75. Poem 31.5–8.
76. AWC MS 560/120.
77. Saer, *Caneuon Llafar Gwlad*, p. 54.
78. Recorded from the singing of John Williams, Bryngwenith Farm, Pencoed near Bridgend, by D. Roy Saer, St Fagans National Museum of History (Cardiff), 1971, AWC Tape Archive 3119.
79. As in n. 78.
80. Gruffydd Evans, 'Carmarthenshire Gleanings (Kidwelly)', *Y Cymmrodor, the Magazine of the Honourable Society of Cymmrodorion*, 25 (1915), 114.
81. See the chapter entitled '*Gŵyl Fair y Canhwyllau* (Candlemas)'.
82. Mark Lawson-Jones, *Why was the Partridge in the Pear Tree? The History of Christmas Carols* (Stroud: History Press, 2011), available online at: *https://books.google.co.uk/books?hl=en&lr=&id=A1k7AwAAQBAJ&oi=fnd&pg=PT4&dq=a+study+of+wassail+singing&ots=UtSUBFxe26&sig=qLwdmwebD6ioCxpXujYM_c9QCVQ#v=onepage&q&f=false* (accessed 2 April 2020).
83. Tom Jones, 'Llên Gwerin Morgannwg', *Y Darian*, 12 August 1926, 1.
84. Roberts, *Crefydd yr Oesoedd Tywyll*, pp. 16–17; for the tune see 'Y Washael' [The Wassail], p. 183, first published in Williams, *Ancient National Airs of Gwent and Morganwg*, p. 30.
85. Roberts, *Hanes Plwyf Llandybïe*, pp. 273–4; see also poem 30.25–8.
86. Williams, *Ancient National Airs of Gwent and Morganwg*, p. 30, notes by Daniel Huws, p. [16]; see poem 30 for further stanzas and a variant on the first.
87. Williams, *Ancient National Airs of Gwent and Morganwg*, p. 17.
88. Poem 30.29–32.
89. Jones, 'The Mari Lwyd: A Twelfth Night Custom', 392.
90. [Anonymous], 'Llythyra' Newydd gan Fachan Ifanc: Nadolig wrth y drws', 3.
91. Poem 30.33–6.
92. Tom Jones, 'Llên Gwerin Morgannwg: Mari Lwyd II', *Y Darian*, 29 July 1926, 3.
93. Trevelyan, *Folk-Lore and Folk-Stories of Wales*, p. 33.
94. Jones, 'The Mari Lwyd: A Twelfth Night Custom', 392.
95. Arthur Gray-Jones, *A History of Ebbw Vale* (Ebbw Vale: Urban District Council, 1970), p. 157.
96. T. Gwynn Jones, *Welsh Folklore and Folk-Custom* (London: Methuen & Co. Ltd, 1930), pp. 163–4.

97. [Anonymous], 'Llythyra' Newydd gan Fachan Ifanc: Nadolig wrth y drws', 3.
98. Evans, *The Story of Abercynon*, p. 27.
99. J. Mansel Thomas, *Yesterday's Gower* (Llandysul: Gomer, 1982), pp. 197–8.
100. Peate, 'A Welsh Wassail-Bowl: With a Note on the Mari Lwyd', 81.
101. *http://www.folkwales.org.uk/mari.html* (accessed 5 August 2020).
102. *http://www.folkwales.org.uk/mari.html* (accessed 5 August 2020).
103. Williams, 'Casgliad o Len-Gwerin sir Gaerfyrddin', p. 19.
104. Quoted in Alford, *Sword Dance and Drama*, p. 24.
105. E. C. Cawte, *Ritual Animal Disguise: A Historical and Geographical Study of Animal Disguise in the British Isles* (Cambridge: Brewer for the Folklore Society, 1978).
106. [Anonymous], 'Daeth Mari Lwyd yn ol dros y Nadolig', 1.
107. J. D. Davies, [*A History of West Gower, Glamorganshire*] *Historical Notices of the parishes of Penrice, Oxwich and Nicholaston, in the Rural Deanery of West Gower, Glamorganshire*, 4 (Swansea: Cambrian Office, 1894), p. 108.
108. For example Jones, 'The Mari Lwyd: A Twelfth Night Custom', 392–3.
109. As did Henry Howell, 'Mari Lwyd: The Origin and Meaning of the Custom', *The Carmarthen Journal and South Wales Weekly Advertiser*, 2 January 1914, 5.
110. 'Hanes Dechreuad "Mari Lwyd"' [The story of the origin of 'Mari Lwyd'], in Roberts, *Crefydd yr Oesoedd Tywyll*, pp. [1]–18; for a translation by William Eilir Evans of an account by William Roberts of the origin of the Glamorgan Mari Lwyd see NLW 3125C; see also Mary Williams, 'Another Note on the "Mari Lwyd"', *Man*, 39 (1939), 96.
111. Roberts, *Crefydd yr Oesoedd Tywyll*, p. 12.
112. Trevelyan, *Folk-Lore and Folk-Stories of Wales*, p. 31.
113. E. T., 'Mari Lwyd', 7.
114. Peate, 'Mari Lwyd: A Suggested Explanation', 55.
115. Roy Saer, 'The Supposed *Mari Lwyd* of Pembrokeshire', in *'Canu at Iws' ac Ysgrifau Eraill*, pp. 314–27.
116. Davies, *Folk-Lore of West and Mid-Wales*, p. 61.
117. Hoggan, 'Miscellanea – Notes on Welsh Folk-Lore', 122.
118. Iorwerth C. Peate, 'A Welsh Wassail-Bowl: with a Note on the Mari Lwyd', *Man*, 35 (1935), 81.
119. Peate, 'Mari Lwyd: A Suggested Explanation', 53.
120. Saer, 'The Supposed *Mari Lwyd* of Pembrokeshire', p. 315.
121. T. H. Parry-Williams, *Llawysgrif Richard Morris o Gerddi* [Richard Morris's Manuscript of Poems] (Cardiff: University of Wales Press, 1931), p. xliv.

122. G. J. Williams, *Iolo Morganwg, 1747–1826* (Cardiff: University of Wales Press, 1956), p. 39.
123. Jones, 'The Mari Lwyd: A Twelfth Night Custom', 390.
124. Jones, 'The Mari Lwyd: A Twelfth Night Custom', 390.
125. W. H. Corkill, Letter to the Editor, 'Horse Cults in Britain', *Folklore*, 61 (1950), 216–17.
126. Theo Brown, Letter to the Editor, *Folklore*, 63 (1952), 44.

Gŵyl Fair y Canhwyllau (Candlemas)

MARY THE MOTHER OF JESUS was highly venerated in Wales throughout the Middle Ages. Many feast days were celebrated in her honour, among them *Gŵyl Fair y Canhwyllau* (Mary's Festival of the Candles) held on 2 February.[1] Writing poems in praise of Mary was common practice among the medieval professional poets on *Gŵyl Fair Forwyn ddechre gwanwyn* (The Feast of the Virgin Mary at the beginning of spring), another title for the Welsh Candlemas. Such poems are a far cry from the *canu gwirod* (wassail songs) also sung on this last day of winter wassailing, and sometimes referred to as *canu yn drws* (singing at the door), *canu tan bared* (singing beneath the wall), or on occasion *pricsiwn* (prick song) used by John Jones in the song title 'Pricsiwn Gŵyl Fair', and by an anonymous poet in the couplet: 'Doed yn nes er lles 'wyllysiwn | I ateb procsi hyn o bricsiwn'[2] (For the common good, may he come closer | To answer by proxy this pricksong).

Gŵyl Fair carols appear in a collection of poems recorded during the years 1716–18 by the teenager Richard Morris of Anglesey (1703–79).[3] A century earlier Robert Bulkeley noted in his diaries for February 1630–6 instances of wassailing in his native north-west Anglesey. In Caernarfonshire the main song source is 'Llyfr Amruwawg-cerdd Godidogol Waith Prydyddion Cymry o gasgliad Wm. Jones Dydd pured Mair flwyddyn 1767' (A book of various poems from the splendid works of the poets of Wales collected by William Jones, the day of the purification of Mary in the year 1767), the manuscript of a local poet from the Caernarfon area (NLW 9168A). A second source is the collection of William Williams (1738–1817) of Llandygái near Bangor dated 1806 (NLW 821C), in which he states that the custom 'has now ceased'.[4]

Trefor M. Owen suggests the practice may have been observed in Denbighshire and Flintshire. The poem 'Gwyliau'[5] (Festivals/Feast days), to be sung on St Bride's day (1 February) and urging each one to be ready with his liquor, refers to St Asaph, Holywell, Northop, Denbigh, Rhuddlan and Mold.[6] St Bride or Brigid was famed for the beer she brewed, but her feast day may not necessarily have been associated with, or formed part of, the *Gŵyl Fair* celebrations on the following day.

A clear example of *Gŵyl Fair* wassail singing from outside the Anglesey/Caernarfon area is the anonymous song that refers to Corwen (formerly in Merionethshire), Bala (also in Merionethshire), and Denbigh. This humorous, ebullient song is neither subtle nor understated:

> Mae gennym ni ordor dan law ein pen-cyngor
> I beri i bawb agor, pa ddiogi na chwyd?
> Fe'i gwnaed yn Rhydychen, fe'i printiwyd yn Llunden,
> Oddi yno i dre Gorwen fe'i gyrrwyd.
>
> A ninna a'i cadd gynta rhwng Dimbach a'r Bala
> I gadw'r ŵyl yma er gwaetha i bob gwyll;
> Pwy bynnag ni agoro lle canwn ni heno
> Ni fynnwn eu ffinio nhw â phennill.[7]

[Stanza 1: We have authority, given to us by our chief counsellor, | To command everyone to open [his door], what laziness is it that will not arise? | It was composed in Oxford, it was printed in London, | It was sent from there to Corwen town.

Stanza 2: And we first received it between Denbigh and Bala | In order to observe this feast day in spite of all darkness; | Whoever does not open [to us] where we sing tonight | We shall insist on fining them with a verse.]

No *Gŵyl Fair* carols from outside north Wales have survived.

Gŵyl Fair songs are mostly simple, free-verse songs generally sung by local rhymesters and musicians such as William Jones of 'Llyfr Amruwawg-cerdd' fame, and Robert Griffith, Pen-y-cefn, one of Arfon's most notable musicians,[8] who bought the book from Jones for sixpence 'ar ol gwyl fair diwautha 1787' (after last *Gŵyl Fair* 1787). There is evidence, however, of a different social class observing the *Gŵyl Fair* custom, albeit pre-eighteenth century. In some manuscripts the names of William (1579/80–1669/70) and Gruffudd Phylip (d. 1660) of Ardudwy are linked to wassail songs;[9] 'Carol i yrru rhai oddi tan y pared a fyddo yn canu' (A carol to send away those who are singing under the wall) by Huw Llwyd of Cynfal (1568?–1630?) near Maentwrog has survived;[10] and 'Carol Noswyl Fair, yn y Plas Hen, 1649 – yr Hen Don'[11] by Rowland Vaughan (*c*.1590–1667) of Caer-gai near Bala was noted in 1649. William Phylip was a landed gentleman, Gruffudd Phylip a professional poet. Both Huw Llwyd and Rowland Vaughan were landowners; Vaughan was appointed sheriff of Merioneth in 1642/3. The heir of Bylchwyn, four miles north-east of Llangefni in Anglesey, composed a poem[12] to obtain liquor from Edward ap Hugh Gwynn heir of Bodewryd, four miles from Amlwch, also in Anglesey. Edward (by Elin (d. 1589)) was the eldest of six sons. The heir of Bylchwyn 'was probably Thomas Vychan who signed the Heraldic Visitations in 1594 (...) He is dated 1540 in the index by Richard Morris at the end of the volume; probably a guess. Edward ap Hugh Gwyn's wife was a cousin to Thomas Vychan.'[13]

Gŵyl Fair festivities were not limited to 2 February. Huw ab Evan suggests an alternative date:

Ar ddechrau'r mis, rai dilys, da,
Bûm yn eich noddfa anheddfawr
Â chân i chwi, down ni un wedd
Ar ddiwedd iawnwedd Ionawr.[14]

[At the beginning of the month [of January], sincere good people, | I visited your spacious refuge | With a song for you, we come in the same manner, | Fittingly, at the end of January.]

He had previously visited on New Year's Day and had returned some three days prior to *Gŵyl Fair*. The intimation is that the festivities

extended over several days, observing the custom at one house one
evening and moving elsewhere for the next, reaching a climax (and
ending) on 2 February:

Gartre nis bûm er nos dydd Llun
Ac nid â, hyd y gwn, dan nos Sadwrn,
Ond gwirota 'r hyd tai gwyrda.[15]

[I have not been home since Monday night | Nor will I go, as
far as I know, until Saturday night, | But drinking liquor [and
moving] from one gentleman's house to the next.]

The poems are mostly traditional, colloquial pieces, composed
for a communal purpose, often with a complex twist in syntax to
accommodate the metre. Songs were learned by heart and sung from
memory. Richard Morris lists in his manuscript the many carols he
knew by rote. Occasionally, new carols were composed, by named
authors but not always on paper, and were added to the repertoire
often by word of mouth.

Some Anglesey songs use nonsense words to fill out a met-
rical line without adding much to its sense, for example 'clirwm
clarwm',[16] or 'Howtra! Hora! Pwy sy mewn?'[17] (Howtra! Hora! Who
is inside?), used by singers to attract the householder's attention.
Such words were sung on the corresponding musical notes, keeping
as closely as possible to the speech sound half-remembered from
long ago. They do not appear, however, in the *Gŵyl Fair* poetry of
Caernarfonshire.

Wassailing at *Gŵyl Fair* may have evolved from an ancient pagan
drinking ritual becoming linked to the Christian festival of the Purifica-
tion of the Blessed Virgin Mary. It appears, however, that the earliest
surviving Welsh *Gŵyl Fair* carols were religious rather than baccha-
nalian in nature. A carol by John Hughes published in 1670, 'Hymnau
i'w dywedyd bob dyddgwyl Fair fend. ac ar y dyddiau Satwrn, a gellir
eu dywedyd beunydd os bydd defotiwn i hynny'[18] (Hymns to be said
every *Gŵyl Fair* and on Saturdays, and they can be said daily if there
are [family] devotions for that) is in three parts, 'Ar amser y Pylgain'
(during Matins), 'Ar amser y Lawdau' (during Lauds), and 'Ar amser
Gosper' (during Vespers), and incorporates the main points of the
religious *Gŵyl Fair* poems: the perpetual virginity of Mary, and the

fact that Christ was conceived by the power of the Holy Spirit. 'Carol *Gŵyl Fair* o waith Siôn Efan i'w chanu ar "Ffarwel Ned Puw"'[19] (A *Gŵyl Fair* carol composed by John Evans to be sung to 'Ffarwel Ned Puw') dated 1740 serves the same purpose. Even though its emphasis is on Mary's purification in the temple, other scriptural characters appear in the narrative, including Mary's cousin Elizabeth (the mother of John the Baptist); Simeon, who met Mary and her family at the presentation of Jesus at the temple and who sang the 'Nunc Dimittis' (Luke 2:25–35); and Anna the elderly prophetess (Luke 2:36–8). It lists the five sorrows and five joys of Mary, together with the five heavenly gifts she received.

The period between the birth of a child and the mother's purification lasted approximately a fortnight in eighteenth-century Wales, and would end when the mother had attended church to give thanks for her life and for that of her offspring, and had been cleansed. This rite was part of the Mosaic Law and is described in the Book of Leviticus 12:2–7:

> A woman who (...) gives birth to a son will be ceremonially unclean for seven days (...) On the eighth day the boy is to be circumcised. Then the woman must wait thirty-three days to be purified from her bleeding. She must not touch anything sacred or go to the sanctuary until the days of her purification are over (...) When the days of her purification for a son or daughter are over she is to bring to the priest at the entrance to the tent of meeting a year-old lamb for a burnt offering and a young pigeon or a dove for a sin offering. He shall offer them before the Lord to make atonement for her, and then she will be ceremonially clean from her flow of blood.

Both William Phylip and Rowland Vaughan thought it seemly that salvation should come by means of a woman, since it was on account of a woman that the Fall was wrought:

> Trwy ferch yr aeth colledigaeth
> A merch a'n dug yn gadwedig.[20] (William Phylip)

> [It is by means of a woman that we were lost | And it is a woman who has brought us to salvation.]

A poem composed by John Morgan,[21] curate of Llanllechid and Abergwyngregyn in Gwynedd, in 1694 focuses on Christ rather than Mary, emphasising Christ's humility, his obedience and his atonement for sin. Having left the company of cherubs to enter a woman's womb, he humbled himself to the point of being circumcised on the eighth day following his birth. There is an exhortation that mankind should follow Christ's example and live in obedience to God.

Some *Gŵyl Fair* carols outline the history of the world, particularly the Fall and restoration of man. Gabriel's conversation with Mary is narrated, Mary's humility and prayers to God in thanksgiving for his blessing, Christ's birth, the visit of the Magi bearing gifts, the purification of Mary at the altar, and lastly the exhortation to mankind to repent and to receive God's forgiveness. Protestants were keen to declare an interest in this initially Catholic custom:

O daw gofyn pwy a wnaeth hyn
O garol ffraeth ddibabyddiaeth.[22] (Rowland Vaughan (1649))

[If anyone should ask who composed this | Eloquent carol devoid of popery.]

A *Gŵyl Fair* carol by William Evans 'Gwilym o Arfon' (1730–93)[23] in 1768 is an adaptation of 'The Cherry-Tree Carol'.[24] It describes the apocryphal story of Joseph, doubting Mary's faithfulness, refusing to pick fruit from a tree at her request:

Ewch at y gwŷr heini lle cawsoch feichiogi,
Dewisan nhw ai rhoddi ai peidio.[25]

[Go to those nimble men by whom you conceived, | Let them choose whether to give or not.]

But as if to prove Mary's innocence, the bough bowed down (a cherry bough in the English carol, apple in its Welsh counterpart) so that Mary could pick its fruit herself.

Over time, the *Gŵyl Fair* wassail song may have developed from being a carol praising Mary or the events of the *Gŵyl Fair* season, to being a song sung at the door referencing Mary at the beginning and/ or end of the carol but with the emphasis on offering, or more often requesting, drink.[26]

The running order of the wassailing evening would be: the request song sung on the doorstep, followed by an answer from inside the door, and thus the contention at the door would begin – the wassailers hoping to be welcomed into the warmth, the home-owners bent on keeping them outside. The wittier the performance, the better. This contention included feat-singing and riddle songs, but eventually all would join in the festivities of the house, particularly the chair ceremony and the singing and carousing that followed. Four types of song were called for: 'cân yn drws' (a song [to be sung] at the door), response to the 'cân yn drws', 'carol cadair' (chair carol) and a song on departure. Few songs had a chorus; the following (*c*.1760) is a rare exception:

> Sain Hosanna, Haleliwia i'r Alffa, Omega a Mair,
> Gogoniant, moliant ac addoliant rown yn gywrain o'r un gair.[27]

> [Sing Hosanna, Hallclujah to the Alpha, Omega and Mary, |
> Glory, praise and worship let us give expertly, with one accord.]

Richard Morris did not include tunes in his manuscript, but did indicate which to use, suggesting they were tunes well known locally.[28] Where no tune is indicated, wassailers would set the words to a tune of their choice. Familiar metres such as *triban* and *tri thrawiad* were used most commonly, and sung to popular tunes. Other metres were sung to Welsh tunes such as 'Consêt Gwŷr Aberffraw' and 'Sybylltir' (named after a farm in Anglesey), and to English tunes such as 'Peg O'Ramsey' and 'Charity Mistress'. The songs were rehearsed before-hand as singers were often expected to change the tune as often as five times for the singing of one song.[29] According to 'Ystatud Canu *Gŵyl* Fair' (Statute regarding *Gŵyl Fair* singing):

> Tri ar 'Peg O'Ramsey' a rowch,
> Ac yno dowch â thriban,
> A thôn deuair hanner awr,
> A'r 'Fedle Fawr' i'w gorffan.[30]

> [Provide three on 'Peg O'Ramsey', | And thither bring a *triban*,
> | And a *tôn deuair* for half an hour, | And 'Y Fedle Fawr' to
> finish with.]

Wassail songs sung outside the door included a call to attract the householders, stating the number of people gathered outside and why they were there. This was followed by *pwnco*, the question-and-response in verse. The wassailers would complain of the freezing cold and state their desire to sit by the householder's fire in the company of a pretty young woman. They noted the encounters faced, such as deep ditches and rough terrain. A carol dated 1717[31] tells of a company of six who lost four men as they made their dangerous journey: one fell into a ditch, one was injured as he crossed a stile, the burning and itching of his chilblains had made another crazy, and the author himself was bleeding from head to toe after falling on his back into gorse bushes. This, and worse, was the wassailers' lot. They should be admitted into the house to share a meal and a drink:

> Cais di'r goblad fwya yn tŷ
> A llenwch hi yn galonnog,
> Bir a chwrw inni yn sgwâr,
> Mae yma ddarpar medd-dod (...)
>
> Fel y byddo'r bryn yn bant
> A'r pwll yn balmant sycha,
> A'r holl goedydd yn rhoi tro
> A'r tir yn ffo oddi tana.[32]

[Stanza 1: Fetch the largest goblet in the house | And, with enthusiasm, fill it up, | Give us beer and ale squarely, | There is here the beginning of drunkenness (...)

Stanza 2: So that the hill becomes a vale | And the ditch becomes the driest pavement, | And all the trees spin around | And I lose the ground from under my feet.]

Infrequently the wassailers requested money. Richard Morris, however, specifically declares that he is not there for the money, but to embrace a pretty girl who is second only to Venus in looks. All wassailers desire strong ale, good food and lighted candles, and hope that beards, hair and eyelashes may not be singed as they drink from the wassail bowl.[33] There is the occasional warning to avoid misers and churls who begrudge hospitality, but since there might be twenty men outside the door, it is little wonder there was resistance to their plea for provisions. The wassailers claim 'hawl i'r tŷ' (a right to the house), but are mocked for their cackling voices and sent home. Good humour prevailed, however, and all were allowed admittance although the question-and-response verses could last a long while, 'tan y bore' (until morning) if need be.

Taking a different attitude but wishing a similar outcome some householders feigned concern, warning that the wassailers should on entry beware of the dog in case it should bite their ankles, and to avoid tripping in case they should fall flat on their faces where the maid had peed. Householders complained of the lack of heating in their home, no prepared meal, no tobacco, just an empty cellar and used candles. Their visit would be a miserable one – better by far to leave immediately, and to return at a later date when they could be sure of the best beer, a warm fire and good feasting. As things stood, the householder felt much burdened by his numerous children and by high market prices. However:

> Pan deilwy, pan droswy, pan heuwy, pan lyfnwy,
> Pan fedwy, pan rwymwy, pan ddyrnwy ryw dro,
> Pan nithwy, pan burwy, pan silwy, pan falwy,
> Pan bobwy, pan graswy, cewch groeso.[34]

[When I have spread dung, when I have ploughed, when I have planted, when I have harrowed, | When I have harvested, when I have tied, when I have threshed at some time, | When I have winnowed, when I have refined, when I have hulled, when I have ground, | When I have cooked, when I have baked, you will be welcomed.]

Even with plenty of food in the house, some misfortune meant that it was unavailable for use: either the surly maid had damaged the griddle by knocking it against the wall, making it impossible to bake griddle bread, or the pig hanging from the rafters could not be accessed for want of a ladder. There were no pretty young women who would consent to being accompanied at the hearth, just a crabby old woman with a stick. The singers were often mocked for being absent from the hay harvest, at peat-cutting time and at other key events of the agricultural year. Hence the decree that they were forbidden to put even the tip of a fingernail anywhere near the smoke of the peat fire. Astounded at their lack of conscience, swiftly passing by when the rooks were trampling his oats yet making a direct line for his house on this festive evening, all the householder had to offer the visiting company was 'chwart o sucan sur' (a quart of sour flummery). And so the (probably pre-prepared) contention at the door continued until one side surrendered.

Reports from 1700–20 in Anglesey note the singing of cumulative songs at *Gŵyl Fair* festivities. Reports from Caernarfonshire half a century later make no mention of cumulative songs, feat-songs or riddles being part of the contention. Whether this meant a weakening of the tradition in Arfon, or whether it was a custom unique to Anglesey, is unclear. A cumulative song, 'Un o'm brodyr' (One of my brothers), was collected in Chwilog in Caernarfonshire during the nineteenth century, but whether it was a stand-alone song or an estranged *Gŵyl Fair* song is not known. It opens with the words:

Wel, un o fy mrodyr i (...)
Wel, un o fy mrodyr a yrrodd i mi
Un ych, un tarw, un blaidd, un ci.[35]

[Well, one of my brothers (...) | Well, one of my brothers sent to me | One ox, one bull, one wolf, one dog.]

'Un o'm brodyr' has a set answer in the form of 'Un o'm chwiorydd' (One of my sisters); both songs command good breath control, memory and quality of diction to repeat a list of nine objects in quick succession. The challenge was to complete a stanza, particularly the final one with all its added phrases, in one breath. The Chwilog version was collected from a person who half-sang, half-danced his way through his performance of it.[36]

An element of dancing is suggested by some of the words in the jingle: '*un cam, un tro*' (one step, one turn) (...) There are also hints of animal guising in the words of this song: '*un ych, un tarw, un blaidd, un ci*' (an ox, a bull a wolf, a dog), and other songs in the manuscript mention a stag, a bear and a lion, although animal guising may no longer have been part of the wassail procession by Richard Morris's time.[37]

Cumulative songs include 'Un cam i'r ceiliog ac un carw serchog' (One step for the cockerel and one amorous deer) and the response 'Un cam i'r tyrci ac un carw lysti'[38] (One step for the turkey and one lusty deer). Another cumulative song is entitled 'Dechre rhigwm digri i'w ganu ar Wylie gwyl Fair' (The beginning of a humorous rhyme to be sung on the *Gŵyl Fair* holiday)[39] and is an interesting instance of what constitutes Welsh humour in the eighteenth century:

O lun ci, o lun cath, o lun cryman ar un crwth,
O lun iâr yn crafu un halen, o lun pry ar un pren;
Ôl dau gi ac ôl dwy gath, ôl dau gryman ar ddau grwth
Ac ôl y ddwy iâr 'n crafu yr ddau halen, ac ôl y ddau bry ar
fol y ddau bren.

Ac felly ymlaen hyd yn naw fel y canlyn.

[In the form of a dog, in the form of a cat, in the form of a sickle on one *crwth*/crowd, | In the form of a hen scratching one salt, in the form of a fly in one tree; | The marks of two dogs and the marks of two cats, the marks of two sickles on two crowds | And the marks of two hens scratching two salts, and the marks of two flies on the belly of two trees.

And so on as follows until nine is reached.]

The most popular cumulative song of all is 'Cyfri'r geifr' (Counting the goats):

'Oes gafr eto?'
'Oes heb ei godro,
Ar y creigiau geirwon mae'r hen afr yn crwydro.'
'Gafr wen, wen, wen?'
'Ie, finwen, finwen, finwen, foel gynffonwen, foel gynffonwen,
Ystlys wen a chynffon wen, wen, wen.'[40]

['Is there another goat?' 'Yes, not milked, | The old goat wanders the rugged rocks.' | 'A white, white, white goat?' | 'Yes, white-lipped, white-lipped, white-lipped, bald, white-tailed, bald, white-tailed, | White flank and a white, white, white tail.']

The Anglesey version of 'Cyfri'r geifr' is a particularly challenging tongue-twister:

'O, beth yw'r achos fod garw flewyn mân ym mlaen barf gafr?'
'Am fod hi'n pori cyll a chelyn gyda'r cloddiau, clirwm clarwm,
Dyna'r achos fod blewyn garw mân ym mlaen barf gafr.
Gafr goch, burgoch, felan gynffongoch,
Ystlys a chudyn a chynffon goch.'[41]

['O, why are there rough, short hairs at the point of a goat's beard?' | 'Because it grazes among the hazel and holly hedges, *clirwm clarwm*, | That is why there are rough, short hairs at the point of a goat's beard. | Red goat, pure red, tawny red tailed, | Red flank and beard and tail.']

Subsequent verses were sung 'with a change in the colour specified'[42] and sung more and more quickly as the song proceeded. A similar pattern of colour change was first noted in Welsh literature in the elegy composed for Geraint son of Erbin and copied into the Black Book of Carmarthen (*c.*1250). 'The language of the poem gives evidence for a date of composition prior to the year 1100 – perhaps as much as two centuries earlier.'[43] The closing line of the first in a series of *englynion*, 'Rhuddion rhuthr eryron du'[44] (They were ruddy, their sudden attack was like that of black eagles) becomes 'eryron coch' (red eagles), 'eryron gwyn' (white eagles), and 'eryron llwyd' (grey eagles); necessary changes are made in the second line of the *englyn* to accommodate the rhyme.

David Thomas 'Dafydd Ddu Eryri', writing from Amlwch to Edward Jones 'Bardd y Brenin' in April 1799, attests that 'Naw gafr gorniog' (Nine horned goats) was sung in Anglesey at *Gŵyl Fair*:

I humbly apprehend that it is now too late to send anything towards completing your Book, otherwise I might send you some kind of a Copy of Naw Gafr gorniog, which after a long and diligent enquiry I found at Caernarvon, but I do not believe it to be very perfect, neither can I find any great beauty in the same. It appears that it was sung on Noswyl Fair, that is to say during the contest for the house; the Person that could repeat this song, or Rhapsody, whatever you will be pleased to call

it, must have been possessed of a very tenaceous memory,
otherwise, he could not enumerate the nine different colours,
though some of them are in my opinion, rather unnatural. I
mean, no Goat that was ever seen would answer to a certain
colour mentioned in the Rhapsody. Therefore, for my part, I am
willing enough to let it drop into eternal oblivion. (The colours
are forced.)[45]

Riddle songs are a little different in that they require a response.
The earliest Welsh printed riddle song appears in *Eglvryn Phrae-
thineb* (1595),[46] but the genre had been established as a literary
form since the appearance of the 'bibliography of Arabic riddles by
Hajji Khalifa written in the fourteenth century'.[47] Francis Gummere
suggests that the music of riddle poems (and of ballads) was used
as dance accompaniment, and that it was the most popular of all
dance music.[48]

A riddle song in the hand of Richard Morris, dated 1716, sets
challenges for those inside the door to provide answers for, in the
same metre, to the same tune:

Beth sy mor ddyrys a'r naill ben mor giwrus
A'i ddolen yn ddilys, mae yn weddus i waith?
Yn fodrwya mae yn droea, naws dwymyn a'i stumia,
Cig arno bob bora mae bariaeth.

Beth sy mor feinion a'u peisia yn felynion
A'u penna yn o gochion ar gychwyn?
Fy seren siriolwedd a'i thyfiad o edafedd,
Dychymyg, mwyn agwedd, mynegwn.[49]

[Stanza 1: What is it that is so complicated and on one end so
exquisite | And its loop sound, it is suitable for work? | It is
[all] rings and turns, with the disposition of fever and its contor-
tions, | There is meat on it each morning of greed.

Stanza 2: What is it that is so slender and their petticoats yellow
| And their heads quite red and held high? | My star of cheerful
countenance whose growth is [slender] as thread, | We set this
riddle in a courteous manner.]

The solution to the first riddle is a (possibly clockwork) roasting Jack that rotates meat roasting on a spit; the second answer is lighted candles in brass candlesticks. Such stanzas tested the imagination, and creativity of response. The following riddle is more finely wrought (as too is its reply), in the tradition of the quest for the impossible:[50]

Danfoned imi afal heb ynddo yr un dincodyn,
Danfoned imi gapwl heb na phlu nac esgyrn,
Danfoned imi fodrwy heb na thro na chwmpas,
Danfoned imi fabi heb na dig nac anras.

Pa sut y caed yr afal heb ynddo yr un dincodyn?
Pa sut y caed y capwl heb na phlu nac esgyrn?
Pa sut y caed y fodrwy heb na thro na chwmpas?
Pa sut y caed y babi heb na dig nac anras.

Pan oedd yr afal yn ei flode nid oedd ynddo'r un dincodyn;
Pan oedd yr iâr yn eiste nid oedd na phlu nac esgyrn;
Pan oedd y fodrwy yn toddi nid oedd na thro na chwmpas;
Pan oeddem ninne yn caru nid oedd na dig nac anras.[51]

[Stanza 1: Send me an apple without a pip, | Send me a capon without feathers or bones, | Send me a ring without a circle or curve, | Send me a baby without anger or ungraciousness.

Stanza 2: How can there be an apple without a pip? | How can there be a capon without feathers or bones? | How can there be a ring without a circle or curve? | How can there be a baby without anger or ungraciousness?

Stanza 3: When the apple was in blossom it did not have a pip; | When the hen was sitting (i.e. incubating eggs) there were no feathers or bones; | When the ring was being melted down there was no circle or curve; | When we were lovers there was no anger or ungraciousness.]

Guessing riddles was not confined to Welsh *Gŵyl Fair* festivities. Very similar lines to the above were preserved in a fifteenth-century English manuscript in which the narrator speaks of four gifts he received, one from each of his four sisters who live beyond the sea:

The first it was a bird without eer a bone,
The second was a cherry without eer a stone.

The third it was a blanket without eer a thread,
The fourth it was a book which no man could read.

How can there be a bird without eer a bone?
How can there be a cherry without eer a stone?

How can there be a blanket without eer a thread?
How can there be a book which no man can read?

When the bird's in the shell, there is no bone;
When the cherry's in the bud, there is no stone.

When the blanket's in the fleece, there is no thread;
When the book's in the press, no man can read.[52]

The riddle song 'Carol Gŵyl Fair o gwestiwna ar Ffarwel Ned Puw'[53] (A *Gŵyl Fair* carol of questions on 'Ffarwel Ned Puw') written by Richard Parry (?1753) is based on the Scriptures and the Catechism; the answering song is also by Richard Parry and to be sung to the same tune. Questions include:

Pa sawl blwyddyn, cwestiwn yw,
Ar ôl y Dilyw dilys,
Sgrifennodd Moses, yn Hebraeg pur,
Tro cyntaf, Lyfr Genesis?

[How many years, this is the question, | After the undisputed Great Flood, | Had elapsed before Moses, in pure Hebrew, | For the first time, wrote the Book of Genesis?]

The answer: 800 years. How many times was the Jordan River parted (three times) and who was the father of John the Divine (Zebedee)?[54] Each question is answered with unswerving confidence.

When the visiting company had won, or been allowed to win, the contest at the door they sang the entry song.[55] Only one such titled song has survived, although there are stanzas within other songs that serve the same purpose. In this one instance, the singers compare themselves to the Wise Men who travelled from the East to visit Jesus bearing gold, frankincense and myrrh. Generally known as Melchior, Caspar and Balthasar, the Magi are named in this Welsh context as Pope Sergius I (who was responsible, at the end of the seventh century, for introducing the procession to commemorate the Christ Child in the Temple at Candlemas);[56] Cystennin Fendigaid (Emperor Constantine the Great), the first Christian Emperor, son of the Empress Helena, or in Welsh tradition Elen Luyddog, daughter of a chieftain living in Segontium (Caernarfon) and heroine of 'Breuddwyd Macsen Wledig' (The Dream of Macsen Wledig); and Bishop David, the patron saint of Wales who, the poet claims, praised the Virgin Mary and the Alpha (Jesus) to harp accompaniment.

As the wassailers crossed the threshold they requested a chair, placed it in the middle of the floor, and called for a virgin to sit in it. To avoid speculation a young girl would sit in the chair holding a six-week-old baby in her lap. They represented the Virgin and Child. A 'carol gadair' (chair carol) was sung and for this purpose the company chose a brisker tune. The chair ceremony is said to have been instituted and authorised by Mary herself. In a carol dating from 1762 she is said to have been sitting in the Temple 'yni chadar Aur' (in her golden chair) when:

I fo archodd Mair   o'i haur gadair
[R]oddi'r wirod   i forwyndod
[A]c yfed gwen   o'i llaw hirwen.[57]

[Mary requested from her golden chair | That liquor should be given to maidenhood | And that a pretty girl should drink from her slender white hand.]

In remembrance of Mary's ritual purification, 'Mi rown gantro o gwmpas honno'[58] (We shall move around her a hundred times) before receiving the blessing of liquor. During the chair ritual the singers request the wassail cup 'I blejio'r fun dyner sy yna yn ei chader'[59] (In order to pledge the gentle woman who is there in her chair). Ben Jonson's 'Song to Celia' suggests that pledging is done in response to an initial action: 'Drink to me only with thine eyes | And I will pledge with mine.' The young woman is first to drink from the wassail cup and the wassailers respond likewise. Although there may be a little flexibility, there is a preferred order of drinking, as specified in a chair carol written by Robert Prichard 'Robin yr Aber' in 1770:

Y wreigdda fwyn hynod gwrandewch ar ein traethod,
Prysurwch â gwirod wiw hynod i hon;
Gwnaed meinir fwyneidd-dro ei dal rhwng ei dwylo
Tra byddom ni'n deinio gwers union.

Os mynnwch, lliw'r manod, archwaethwch y wirod,
Rhowch hon i'r gŵr hynod awch lewglod o'i law;
Gwnewch chwitha, gŵr gwaredd, roi hon mewn parch puredd
I'r wraig dda, fwyn, haeledd a hylaw.[60]

[Stanza 1: Notable and gentle mistress of the house, listen to our address, | Make haste with a splendid goodly drink for her; | Let the gentle girl hold it in her hands | While we deign to offer an honest stanza of poetry.

Stanza 2: If you please, [one with a complexion] the colour of driven snow, relish the drink, | Place it in the hand of the distinguished gentleman whose mettle deserves mighty praise; | And you, genial gentleman, give it from pure respect | To the good woman who is gentle, generous and obliging.]

A poem by William Evans (1762), however, urges the young woman thus: 'rhowch ddiod i'ch cofled | Er cof am fawr gariad (...) Grist Oen'[61] (give your dear one in your lap a drink | In remembrance of the immense love (...) of Christ the Lamb), before she drinks from the cup herself; it would then be passed on to the householder, his wife, and the wassailers in order, beginning with the company leader.

The leader of the wassail party, according to the William Evans carol, brought a wassail cup with him on his visit; other wassail parties complain that the difficulties they encountered on their journey caused them to spill all the drink they were carrying; an early eighteenth-century poem by Richard Morris provides further evidence that the leader of the wassailers (sometimes but not always) provided the drink:

Mae yma ohonom wyth neu naw, a minna â'r wirod yn fy llaw
A hitha yn chwthu gwynt a glaw yn ddiflas: &c.[62]

[There are eight or nine of us here, and I have the liquor in my
hand | In the driving wind and rain, miserable [weather] &c.]

Even though many wassail parties used a simple jug, bowl or bucket
to carry their drink to the door, the traditional ceremonial *Gŵyl
Fair* wassail cup used within the house is provided by the
householder:

Hir lawenydd fo i'r gwrda
Am byrfeidio'r wirod yma.[63]

[May the good man [be blessed with] joy for a long time to
come | For providing this drink.]

The bowl was splendidly large and well crafted (see figures 2–4),
designed to carry two or three quarts of strong beer with slices of
bread on its surface. It always had lighted candles around its edges:

Sefwch yn eich arfod,   dyma ni yn dŵod
I chwi ag anrheg   hardd ei gweled;
Nid gwaith seiri   dim sydd arni
Na gwaith cerfer   gore yn Lloeger.

Gwaith angylion   sy o amgylch hon;[64]

[Stanza 1: Stand ready, here we come | [Bringing] you a gift [that
is] beautiful to behold; | It is not the work of artisans that [you
see] on it | Or [even] the work of the best carver in England.

Stanza 2: It is the work of angels that is on it all around.]

The lighted cup is carried around the chair, and the family and com-
pany members follow in procession, all singing the chair carol and
sharing the drink. Each person is urged to take the utmost care as
they sip from the cup, particularly the young girl with the baby in her
arms, but men too, to avoid singeing hair and eyebrows:

Fe riwliff yr aelia, mi dynga, rwy'n dallt,
A'r farf bod â blewyn, gwn gwedyn a'r gwallt.[65]

[It will rule [?ruin] the eyebrows, I swear, I realise, | And then
the beard, every hair of it, I know, and the [head] hair.]

Interestingly, this poem by Dafydd Jones is dated 22 January 1768,
eleven days prior to *Gŵyl Fair*.

Following her pledging, the young girl is invited to leave the
room since not one of the wassailers is worthy of her presence, or of
giving her a kiss:

Am hynny 'r fwyn ferch, ewch ar gais llwys hollol o'n llais, allan,
Does yma un mab sy ffit i'w droi i geisio rhoi i chwi gusan.[66]

[Because of that, gentle girl, at the request of our wholly pleas-
ant voice[s], depart, | There is not one young man here who is
fit to be persuaded to try to kiss you.]

Is this synonymous with the 'Holyn ac Ifin' (Holly and Ivy) song in
which the woman must remain outside the hall and the men sit inside
'in chaires of goldc'?

Following the chair ceremony, the feast is sought and when the
evening draws to a close a thanksgiving carol is sung in praise of
good company, food and drink, freely admitting that in their greed
they have drunk 'ddau mwy nag oedd raid'[67] (twice what was neces-
sary). Others profess to be so drunk they cannot find the door:

Ein traed o tanom sydd yn ffoi, mae'n rhy hwyr i ni
Geisio myned allan, ym mhle mae'r drws yrŵan, ŵyr breulan
        eu bri?[68]

[Our feet are fleeing from under us, it is too late for us |
To attempt to go out, where is the door now, men of noble
renown?]

In 1773 John Jones writes that they had almost forgotten to kiss the
young girl in the chair; they then wish her luck, health and good-
ness each day of her life. They wish the family health, fertility and

longevity 'i gofio'r Fareia' (to commemorate Mary), and several children to provide for their parents in old age. Last of all:

> Ond diwedd da a'ch dyco pan ddarffo llafurio
> Ac yno gael huno yn go hen,
> A nef, a gwir foliant i ganu gogoniant,
> A gaffoch mewn mwyniant. Amen.[69]

[But may a good death take you when labour is at an end | And may you die at a ripe old age, | And may heaven, and true praise to sing glory, | Be yours with joy. Amen.]

There would often be a stanza noting the poem's date of composition (1770):

> Oed Iesu dewisol a draethaf i ethol
> Pan luniwyd y garol mwyn moddol, Amen:
> Un mil a saith ganmlwydd, naw chwe deg yn digwydd,
> Ac unflwydd, mawr burffydd heb orffen.[70]

[I elect to declare the age of the chosen Jesus | When the sweet-sounding, seemly carol was composed, Amen: | It was in [the year] one thousand and seven hundred years [and] sixty-nine, | Plus one year, great [and] pure faith without end.]

Gŵyl Fair was observed at the beginning of spring when nature's forces, it was believed, required support. It possibly evolved from an ancient pagan rite to welcome spring. Latterly it is linked to a Church festival: instead of drinking to spring the revellers drink to the Virgin and Child. An early-seventeenth-century poem, Gruffudd Phylip's 'Cân wirod neu *Ŵyl* Fair' (A wassail or *Gŵyl Fair* song), states that:

> Puredigeth Mair yn odieth,
> Pawb a'i wirod i'w chyfarfod.

> Os rhydd Duw Dad inni gennad
> Ni yfwn wirod hyd y gwaelod.

Ni yfwn iechyd haelion hefyd
Heb fod mo'r sôn am gybyddion.[71]

[Stanza 1: [On] the [day of the] wonderful Purification of Mary,
| Each one meets her with his drink.

Stanza 2: If God the Father permits us | We shall drink the
liquor right down to the bottom [of the cup].

Stanza 3: We shall also drink the health of the generous | With
no mention made of misers.]

By the eighteenth century the Virgin and Child were inextricably
linked to the observance of wassailing at *Gŵyl Fair*.

The ritual sets in opposition light and darkness, the lighted can-
dles representing purity and goodness, 'emblems of the divine vitaliz-
ing power of the sun, and were carried in procession at the beginning
of February as a protection against plague, famine, pestilence and
earthquake'.[72] That Simeon spoke of Christ as being 'a light for the
Gentiles'[73] paved the way for the custom to be adopted by the Church:

A phan aned Mab Mair wen
Fe ympiriodd y seren,
A phan aned yr Iesu
Fe ddaeth i'r byd oleuni.[74]

[And when the blessed Son of Mary was born | The star appeared,
| And when Jesus was born | Light came into the world.]

Therefore:

Rhowch yn ole y canhwylle
I gofio Mair, lân uchelgrair.[75]

[Light the candles | To commemorate Mary, cleansed and holy
one.]

St Anselm (1033–1109) described candles as an image of the mys-
tery pertaining to the Presentation of Christ in the Temple, the wax

signifying Christ's flesh, the wick his soul, and the flame his divinity. Tradition has it that candles light themselves at *Gŵyl Fair* to honour Mary's uniqueness, and her superiority over all women:

> Ar gyfan i'r Gwyliau goleuodd canhwyllau
> Eu hunain yn olau o'u pennau heb ball.[76]

> [At a time that corresponds to Christmastide, candles lit | Themselves brightly, ceaselessly.]

Robert Prichard in 1770 attributes their lighting to the hand of God:

> A Mair, pan eisteddodd mewn cadar, hi ganodd
> Gerdd felys o'i gwirfodd pan welodd Ei waith
> Yn ennyn tân golau ar ben y canhwyllau.[77]

> [And Mary, when she sat in a chair, sang | A sweet song of her own accord when she saw His work | Lighting a bright light atop the candles.]

On the day the Church's candles for the year were blessed, many Welsh houses had lighted candles in their windows: one Kidwelly kitchen displayed a candle in each pane of glass. In the same locality the first maid, the highest-ranking maid among the farm servants, was presented with a candle to use in the outhouses, and at *Gŵyl Fair* had to pay back the candle to her mistress because the days had lengthened:

> Some of the younger men entertained a hazy notion that the candle was given to the maid some time in November, and that it had to be returned in April, and yet one of these once reprimanded a shopkeeper in Kidwelly with these significant words – 'Mae Gwyl Fair y Canhwylle wedi dod, Dylech ffeedo'r creduried cyn fod ishe lamp arnoch chi' (Candlemas has come. You ought to feed the animals before a lamp is required).[78]

Marie Trevelyan describes a *Gŵyl Fair* custom as an omen of longevity:

it was customary many years ago for people to light two can-
dles, and place them on a table or high bench. Then each mem-
ber of the family would in turn sit down on a chair between the
candles. They then took a drink out of a horn goblet or beaker,
and afterwards threw the vessel backwards over his head. If it
fell in an upright position, the person who threw it would live
to reach a very old age; if it fell bottom upwards, the person
would die early in life.[79]

E. L. Barnwell notes that a custom similar to the *Gŵyl Fair*
custom, 'the name of which is now lost', was part of the Easter cel-
ebrations in Wales. 'The village belle had on Easter Eve and Easter
Tuesday to carry on her head a curious China article' similar to a
crown, which consisted of three cups full of 'bragawd' (bragget). 'In
the spaces between the cups lighted candles were placed, fixed in
clay.' They were tasked with drinking the liquid from the crown
without burning themselves. 'Her companions sang a stanza, the
last line of which was "Rhag i'r feinwen losgi ei thalcen" meaning,
"Lest the maiden burn her forehead".' The original cup (see fig-
ure 13) was owned by the antiquary Angharad Llwyd (1780–1866),
and Barnwell suggests she may 'in her younger days have seen
it thus used'.[80] However, Angharad Llwyd's father, John Lloyd
(1733–93) rector of Caerwys, had journeyed with Thomas Pennant
(1726–98), the Welsh traveller, and may have come across the cup
elsewhere.[81]

The *Gŵyl Fair* custom had its heyday in the eighteenth cen-
tury and may have survived into the first decade of the nineteenth.
Since then it has been forgotten and ignored by all bar the hardiest
students of Welsh folk-lore – until early January 2020, when Charles
Goring of Eastbourne, East Sussex, contacted me enquiring after
Welsh *Gŵyl Fair* poems. Poem 39 was sent over, partly translated
into English, with the appropriate tune. The carol was subsequently
shared by the Goring family with their 'singing/worship circles in
Sussex'. They met with friends 'in what we might call Candlemas-
tide, and enjoyed singing the carol you kindly sent, as well as oth-
ers. So, thank you! We shall focus more on Candlemas next year,
with yet more carols.'[82] 'Carol Gŵyl Fair' was again sung in Sussex
in 2021, and the clear intention is that they will continue to sing this
old Welsh carol for the foreseeable future.[83]

The singing of *Gŵyl Fair* carols continues, albeit in a different guise and venue.

Notes

1. D. Machreth Ellis notes a weather rhyme that refers to *Gŵyl Fair* adding that the feast was held 'on February 13th before the calendar was revised in 1751; now it falls on February 2nd. But '*Gŵyl Fair*' is still considered to fall on the 13th February in those parts of Wales where the old traditions have persisted', 'A Miscellany of Welsh Weather-Lore', *Montgomeryshire Collections*, 47 (1942), 79.
2. NLW 9168A, f. 80[r].
3. BL Add MS 14992, copied and edited by T. H. Parry-Williams, *Llawysgrif Richard Morris o Gerddi* [Richard Morris's Manuscript of Poems] (Cardiff: University of Wales Press, 1931).
4. NLW 821C, f. 446[v], a survey of Caernarfonshire in 1806 by the land surveyor William Williams of Llandygái; for his account of the *Gŵyl Fair* ceremony see ff. 446[v]–448[v].
5. T. H. Parry-Williams, *Canu Rhydd Cynnar* (Cardiff: University of Wales Press, 1932), pp. 354–6.
6. Trefor M. Owen, 'Canu *Gŵyl Fair* yn Arfon' [*Gŵyl Fair* singing in Arfon], *Transactions of the Caernarvonshire Historical Society*, 25 (1964), 22n5.
7. 'Carol yn y drws ar dri thrawiad' [Carol [to be sung] at the door on *tri thrawiad*], NLW 9168A, f. 53[r].
8. G. T. Roberts, 'Arfon (1759–1822)', *Transactions of the Caernarvonshire Historical Society*, 1 (1939), 61.
9. For example 'Carol Gŵyl Fair wrth Wirota, ar fesur byr' [*Gŵyl Fair* drinking carol, in *mesur byr*] (William Phylip), Bangor 401, 172–3; Cwrtmawr 242B, 231–2; 'Carol i'r Gwylie' [A carol to Christmastide] (Anonymous), NLW 434B, 32; 'Cân Wirod neu Ŵyl Fair' [A wassail or *Gŵyl Fair* song], Peniarth 245, 448 (Gruffudd Phylip).
10. NLW 719B, ff. 40[v]–1[v]; note that *Gŵyl Fair* is not specified.
11. NLW 6499B, 665–6.
12. Poem 43.
13. J. Glyn Davies, 'Two Songs from an Anglesey Ms.', in Osborn Bergin and Carl J. S. Marstrander (eds), *Miscellany Presented to Kuno Meyer by Some of his Friends and Pupils on the Occasion of his Appointment to the Chair of Celtic Philology in the University of Berlin* (Halle a. S.: M. Niemeyer, 1912), p. 128, available online at: *https://archive.org/details/miscellanyprese00berg/page/122/mode/2up* (accessed 23 April

2020). Thomas Vychan signed the Heraldic Visitations on 3 September 1594; see L. Dwnn and S. R. Meyrick (eds), *Heraldic Visitations of Wales and Part of the Marches: Between the Years 1586 and 1613*, 2 (Llandovery: William Rees, 1846), p. 269.

14. Cwrtmawr 128A, 87.

15. Parry-Williams, *Llawysgrif Richard Morris*, pp. 87–8.

16. Grace Gwyneddon Davies, *Alawon Gwerin Môn* [Anglesey Folk Songs] (Caernarfon: The Welsh Publishing Company, 1914), pp. 18–19.

17. 'Carol wirod yn drws ar "Ffading"' [A wassail song [to be sung] outside the door to [the tune] '[With a] Fading'] by Richard Morris; see Parry-Williams, *Llawysgrif Richard Morris*, p. 11. The tune title 'Fadinge' appears in a tune list from Lleweni Hall copied *c*.1590; see Sally Harper, 'An Elizabethan Tune List from Lleweni Hall, North Wales', *Royal Musical Association Research Chronicle*, 38 (2005), 69–70; it is described as 'a fine jig' in Francis Beaumont, *The Knight of the Burning Pestle* (first performed in 1607; published in a quarto in 1613), Act 4, scene 1.

18. John Hughes, *Allwydd neu Agoriad Paradwys i'r Cymru* [The Key of Paradise for the Welsh People] (Lvyck, 1670), pp. 319–20; see further Geraint Bowen, '*Allwydd neu Agoriad Paradwys i'r Cymru*, John Hughes, 1670', *Transactions of the Honourable Society of Cymmrodorion* (1961), part 2, 88–160.

19. NLW 9168A, ff. 4ʳ–8ʳ.

20. 'Carol *Gŵyl Fair* wrth wirota, ar fesur byr' [*Gŵyl Fair* drinking carol, in *mesur byr*], Bangor 401, 172; Cwrtmawr 242B, 232; 'Carol gwirod newydd' [A new wassail carol], NLW 434B, 32; NLW 6499B, 375–6.

21. 'Carol i'w ganu Ŵyl Fair, 1693/4', Bangor 421, 410–11; the double dating 1693/4, arising from the transition from the Julian calendar to the Gregorian, indicates 1694 in the current dating system.

22. NLW 6499B, 665.

23. Known also as William Bifan, he is described as being a 'rhigymwr pert' [a smart rhymester] and a skilful satirist; see W. Gilbert Williams, 'Hen Gymeriadau Llanwnda: William Bifan y Gadlys' [Llanwnda's Old Characters: William Bifan of Gadlys], *Cymru* [Wales], 23 (1902), 138.

24. An English Christmas carol and one of the Child Ballads; see Francis James Child, *The English and Scottish Popular Ballads*, 2 (New York: Dover Publications, Inc., 2003), number 54, pp. 1–6; Hugh Keyte and Andrew Parrott (eds), *The New Oxford Book of Carols* (Oxford: Oxford University Press, 1998), number 129, pp. 446–8.

25. NLW 9168A, ff. 39ᵛ–40ʳ. See further Graham C. G. Thomas, 'Mair a'r Afallen' [Mary and the apple tree], *Bulletin of the Board of Celtic Studies*, 24 (1972), 459–61.

26. Parry-Williams, *Llawysgrif Richard Morris*, p. xci.

27. Poem 39, to be sung beneath the wall at *Gŵyl Fair*, to the tune 'Susannah'.

28. For *Gŵyl Fair* tunes see Phyllis Kinney, *Welsh Traditional Music* (Cardiff: University of Wales Press in association with Cymdeithas Alawon Gwerin Cymru [Welsh Folk Song Society], 2011), pp. 87–97.

29. 'Caniad Gŵyl Fair i'w ganu ar bum mesur: 1. Fedle Fawr yn gynta 2. Bredi Ban 3. Marts 4. Consêt Gŵyr Aberffraw 5. Hobi Horse 6. Fedle Fawr yn ddiwaetha' [A *Gŵyl Fair* song to be sung on five metres: 1. first 'Fedle Fawr' 2. Bredi Ban 3. March 4. 'Consêt Gwŷr Aberffraw' 5. Hobby Horse 6. 'Fedle Fawr' to close], NLW 9168A, ff. 46ʳ–48ʳ. 'Bredi Ban' is perhaps 'a corruption of the eighteenth-century ballad tune-name 'Betty Brown', popular in eighteenth-century Wales, which can be adapted to fit the words; see Kinney, *Welsh Traditional Music*, p. 91.

30. Poem 40.

31. Parry-Williams, *Llawysgrif Richard Morris*, pp. 102–3.

32. Parry-Williams, *Llawysgrif Richard Morris*, pp. 185–6.

33. Parry-Williams, *Llawysgrif Richard Morris*, p. 186.

34. 'Carol Gŵyl Fair yn Tŷ' [A *Gŵyl Fair* carol [sung by those] inside the house], Cwrtmawr 40B, 233.

35. Davies, *Alawon Gwerin Môn*, pp. 16–17.

36. Parry-Williams, *Llawysgrif Richard Morris*, pp. lxxxviii–lxxxix.

37. Kinney, *Welsh Traditional Music*, p. 93.

38. 'Carol wirod yn drws ar y mesur a elwir "I know a t[...]"' [A drinking song [to be sung] at the door in the metre known as 'I know a t[...]'], and 'Ateb' [Response], Parry-Williams, *Llawysgrif Richard Morris*, p. 113.

39. [John Jones] Myrddin Fardd, 'Hen gerddi y Cymry' [Old poems of the Welsh], *Y Traethodydd* [The Essayist], 43 (1888), 427.

40. For the tune 'Cyfri'r Geifr (1)' see p. 176.

41. Davies, Alawon Gwerin Môn, pp. 18–19; for the tune 'Cyfri'r Geifr (2)' see p. 177.

42. J. Lloyd Williams, 'Editor's Notes', *Journal of the Welsh Folk-song Society*, 1 (1909–12), 91.

43. Rachel Bromwich, *Trioedd Ynys Prydain: The Welsh Triads* (Cardiff: University of Wales Press, 1961), p. 356.

44. J. Gwenogvryn Evans (ed.), *The Black Book of Carmarthen* (Pwllheli: issued to subscribers only, 1907), p. 72, line 15.

45. NLW 164C, 73, quoted in Rhiannon Ifans, *Sêrs a Rybana: Astudiaeth o'r Canu Gwasael* [Stars and Ribbons: A Study of Wassail Songs] (Llandysul: Gwasg Gomer, 1983), pp. 164–5.

46. Henri Perri, *Egluryn Ffraethineb* [The Exponent of Wit] (Cardiff: University of Wales Press, 1930), p. 41.

47. D. G. Blaumer, 'The Early Literary Riddle', *Folklore*, 78 (1967), 50. Further see Charles T. Scott, 'On Defining the Riddle: The Problem of a Structural

Unit', in Dan Ben-Amos (ed.), *Folklore Genres* (Austin & London: University of Texas Press, 1976), pp. 77–90; F. H. Whitman, 'Medieval Riddling: Factors Underlying its Development', *Neuphilologische Mitteilungen*, 71 (1970), 177–85; Archer Taylor, *The Literary Riddle before 1600* (Berkley and Los Angeles: University of California Press, 1948); Archer Taylor, 'The Riddle as a Primary Form', in Horace P. Beck (ed.), *Folklore in Action: Essays for Discussion in Honor of MacEdward Leach* (Philadelphia: The American Folklore Society, 1962; New York: Kraus Reprint Co., 1970), pp. 200–7.

48. Francis B. Gummere (ed.), *Old English Ballads* (New York: Russell & Russell, 1967), pp. lxxix–lxxxi.

49. Poem 44:5–12.

50. Reminiscent of the performing of impossible 'anoethau' [wondrous tasks] in the medieval Welsh tale 'Culhwch ac Olwen'; see Rachel Bromwich and D. Simon Evans (eds), *Culhwch and Olwen: An Edition and Study of the Oldest Arthurian Tale* (Cardiff: University of Wales Press, 1992).

51. Parry-Williams, *Llawysgrif Richard Morris*, pp. 37–8.

52. 'I have a young sister far beyond the sea', in Sloane Manuscript 2593 held in the British Library, a manuscript probably owned by a professional minstrel, copied and edited by Thomas Wright (ed.), *Songs and Carols now First Printed, from a Manuscript of the Fifteenth Century* (London: printed by T. Richards for the Warton Club, 1836), carol no. 8; in his Preface, Wright dates the manuscript 'from the character of the writing, to the reign of Henry VI [1422 to 1461]'. The ballad also appears in Francis James Child (ed.), *The English and Scottish Popular Ballads*, 1 (Boston: Houghton Mifflin and Company, 1882–4; unabridged republication New York: Dover Publications, Inc., 2003), p. 415; J. O. Halliwell, *Popular Rhymes and Nursery Tales* (London: John Russell Smith, 1849), p. 150.

53. AWC MS 2, 127–9; for the solution see AWC MS 2, 130–2.

54. Also known as John the Evangelist; he wrote the fourth Canonical Gospel, the three letters of John in the New Testament, and possibly the Book of Revelation.

55. Poem 46.

56. E. O. James, *Seasonal Feasts and Festivals* (London: Thames & Hudson, 1961), p. 233; Trefor M. Owen, 'The Celebration of Candlemas in Wales', *Folklore*, 84 (1973), 248: 'if this is in fact the case, then these eighteenth-century carol-writers were particularly well-versed in this side of church history.'

57. Poem 42.18–20. The significance of the chair of gold is unclear; it would, however, be particularly suggestive in the Caernarfon area. In the medieval Welsh tale 'Breuddwyd Macsen Wledig' (The Dream of Macsen Wledig), Emperor Macsen found the girl of his dream, Elen Luyddog,

in Caernarfon, sitting in a chair of gold. Elen is found a virgin. 'The reputed holiness which Elen derived from her conflation with St. Helena was probably responsible for her appearance in *Bonedd y Saint* as the mother of St. Peblig', Bromwich, *Trioedd Ynys Prydain*, p. 342. Llanbeblig is one mile from Caernarfon.

58. 'Dechrau carol Gŵyl Fair o gwmpas y gadair' (The beginning of a *Gŵyl Fair* carol [sung] around the chair), Cwrtmawr 40B, 230.

59. Poem 48.23.

60. Poem 47.17–24.

61. Poem 48.25–6.

62. 'Carol wirod yn drws ar "Ffading"' [A wassail song [to be sung] at the door to [the tune] '[With a] Fading'], Parry-Williams, *Llawysgrif Richard Morris*, p. 11.

63. 'Dechrau carol Gŵyl Fair o gwmpas y gadair' [The beginning of a *Gŵyl Fair* carol [sung] around the chair], Cwrtmawr 40B, 231.

64. Poem 42.13–17.

65. 'Carol cadair ar nos Ŵyl Fair i'w chanu ar "Lilisfrens"' [A chair carol for *Gŵyl Fair* to be sung to the tune known as 'Lilisfrens'], NLW 9168A, ff. 22ᵛ–25ʳ.

66. William Evans 'Gwilym Arfon', 'Dechrau carol cadair yn tŷ gan Caerwaen' [The beginning of a chair carol by Caerwaen [to be sung] inside the house], NLW 9168A, f. 42ᵛ.

67. NLW 9168A, f. 80ᵛ.

68. Poem 49.12–13.

69. NLW 9168A, f. 82ʳ.

70. Poem 47.25–8 by Robert Prichard 'Robin yr Aber', 1770.

71. Peniarth 245, 448.

72. James, *Seasonal Feasts and Festivals*, p. 233.

73. The Book of Acts 13:47.

74. Mostyn 145, 43.

75. 'Carol Gŵyl Fair wrth Wirota, ar fesur byr' [*Gŵyl Fair* drinking carol, in *mesur byr*] (William Phylip), Bangor 401, 172–3; Cwrtmawr 242B, 231; 'Carol gwirod newydd' [A new wassail carol], NLW 434B, 32.

76. 'Carol Gŵyl Fair tan bared' [*Gŵyl Fair* carol [to be sung] beneath the wall], Cwrtmawr 40B, 233.

77. Poem 47.13–15.

78. Gruffydd Evans, 'Carmarthenshire Gleanings (Kidwelly)', *Y Cymmrodor, the Magazine of the Honourable Society of Cymmrodorion*, 25 (1915), 109–10.

79. Marie Trevelyan, *Folk-Lore and Folk-Stories of Wales* (London: Elliot Stock, 1909), p. 244, available online at: *https://archive.org/stream/afl2317.0001.001.umich.edu#page/22/mode/2up* (accessed 23 April 2020).

80. E. L. Barnwell, 'On some Ancient Welsh Customs and Furniture', *Archaeologia Cambrensis* (1872), 334.
81. Owen, 'Canu Gŵyl Fair yn Arfon', 37.
82. Charles Goring, personal e-mail, 18 February 2020.
83. Charles Goring, personal e-mail, 14 December 2021.

Figure 1: *Wassailing the apple trees at the Gaymers wassail in Stewley Orchard, central Somerset, 2010/2011: the new wassail queen drinks a draught of cider; a piece of toast dipped in cider hangs in the tree in the background; image © Bill Bradshaw.*

Figure 2: *A rare Ewenny wassail bowl and cover, dated 1832–3; image courtesy of Bonhams.*

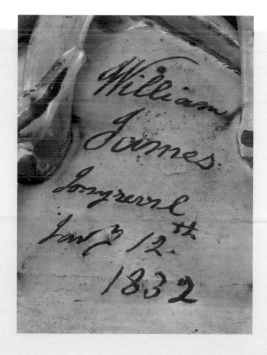

Figure 3 (above): *Ewenny wassail bowl cover, dated 1832; image courtesy of Bonhams.*

Figure 4 (right): *Ewenny wassail bowl inscribed 'William James Tonyrevil January 12th 1832'; image courtesy of Bonhams.*

Figure 5 (above): *Two boys holding a* rhodd galennig, *Llangynwyd c.1905; image © National Museum of Wales.*

Figure 6 (opposite right): *Children singing and collecting* Calennig *(New Year's gifts) in Cwm Gwaun, January 1961; pictured (left to right) are Rita Davies, Ionwy Thomas, Ifor Davies (almost out of sight), Sally Vaughan, Menna James, Eirian Vaughan (Sally's sister), John Morris, and Gwyn Davies (Ifor's brother). The photograph was taken by Geoff Charles (1909–2002) for the Welsh-language newspaper* Y Cymro *outside Tŷ Bach, Cwm Gwaun, where Ionwy Thome's (née Thomas) grandfather lived; image © National Library of Wales.*

Figure 7 (opposite right: *The Bidder's visit; image © National Library of Wales.*

Figure 8: *Two examples of 'Halsing y Dryw' (The wren carol) from 'Melus geingciau Deheubarth Cymru', f. 27ʳ; image © National Library of Wales.*

Figure 9: *Wren-house, Marloes, Pembrokeshire; image © National Museum of Wales.*

Figure 10 (above):
Mari Lwyd and Sianco'r Castell, Llangynwyd; image © National Museum of Wales.

Figure 11 (left):
Mari Lwyd, Llangynwyd, c.1910–14; image © National Library of Wales.

Figure 12 (left): *Sharper, the Swansea Mari Lwyd; image courtesy of Isobel Brown.*

Figure 13 (below): *A cut by J. Blight (possibly J. Slight) from a drawing by Talbot Bury of a cup owned by the antiquary Angharad Llwyd; image* Archaeologia Cambrensis *(1872).*

Tunes

Beth sy mor feinion?

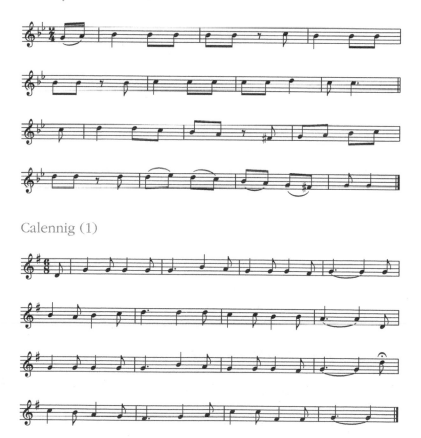

Calennig (1)

Calennig (2)

Cân Hela'r Dryw

Cân y Dryw

Cân y Fari Lwyd

Cerdd Dydd Calan

Consêt Prince Rupert *or* Prince Rupert's Conceit

The Cutty Wren

Cyfri'r Geifr (1)

Cyfri'r Geifr (2)

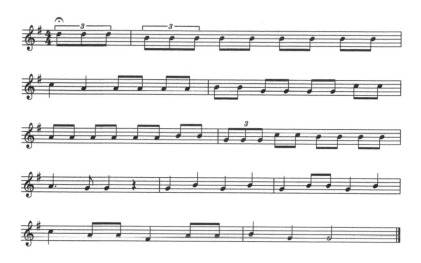

Y cyntaf dydd o'r Gwyliau *or* The first day of Christmas

The 3/4 bar in the last verse accommodates the lines 'Deuddeg (...)' [Twelve (...)] down to 'Pedwar (...)' [Four (...)].

Deffrwch! Benteulu

Dibyn a Dobyn

Y Fedle Fawr

Ffarwel Gwŷr Aberffraw

Hyd yma bu'n cerdded

Joan's Placket

Leave Land *or* Gadael Tir

May Day

Y Mochyn Du

Peg O'Ramsey

Pilgrim

Sosban Fach

Susannah

Tri Thrawiad Gwynedd

Y Washael (Wel, dyma enw'r feinwen)

Ymdaith Gwŷr Harlech *or*
The March of the Men of Harlech

Winter Wassailing Songs and Poems

Christmas Wassail Songs

1   Carol o fawl i Fab Duw, i'w ganu dan bared

Mab Duw a glodforwn, clod lafar cydlefwn,
Da fiwsig dyfeisiwn, cydseiniwn â sant;
Cydgodwch i fyny od aethoch i gysgu,
4   Lân deulu, i ganu gogoniant.

Da y dylem, heb dewi, yn felys ei foli,
Un Mab i'r Goleuni; daioni fu'r dydd
Y ganwyd ail Adda trwy rinwedd, ŵyr Anna,
8   I'n tynnu o blag yna ar blygeinddydd.

Rhown foliant yn llawen o'i blegid ar blygen,
A ganed ar gyfen mae'n gofus ei fod;
Mewn preseb gwael anian y gwelwyd Oen gwiwlan
12   Yn egwan fab bychan dibechod.

Pwy galon na 'styrie, trwy'r dalaith nad wyle,
O ddyn na feddylie pan wele yn ddi-ged
Dyloted fu ym Methlem, am ddialedd a ddylem
16   Yn ninas Caersalem croeshoelied?

Er maint a ddioddefodd nych enwog ni chwynodd,
Tros gamwedd cymerodd a gafodd o gur,
Ond mynd fel Oen gwirion i elyniaeth ei elynion;
20   Pwy galon sy dystion nad ystyr?

O'r bedd lle gorweddodd cof ydyw cyfododd,
Drwy or'chafieth dyrchafodd lle'r ordeiniodd ei Dad,
Eistedd yn Dduw haeledd, wych haul, Fab uchelwedd,
24   Mewn sanctedd a mawredd gymeriad.

1 A carol of praise to the Son of God, to be sung beneath the wall

We praise the Son of God, we unite in our cry of resounding praise,
We devise good music, we harmonize with a saint;
Rise up together if you have gone to sleep,
4   Good family, to sing glory.

It is good that we should praise him sweetly [and] without ceasing,
The only-begotten Son of the Light; it was [a day of] goodness,
    that day on which
The second Adam was born through virtue, Anna's grandson,
8   To pluck us at daybreak from that plague.

Let us merrily give praise at dawn because of him,
And it is kept in remembrance that he was born at a time
    corresponding to this;
The worthy and pure Lamb was seen in a lowly manger
12   As a weak, sinless little child.

What heart is it that does not reflect, throughout the province
    that weeps not,
What man is it that contemplates not when he sees, without reward,
How poor he was in Bethlehem, [and] that as vengeance for
    our wrongdoing
16   He was crucified in the city of Jerusalem?

Despite the magnitude of his sufferings, a severe torment, he did
    not complain,
On account of sin he took upon himself the anguish that was
    bestowed on him,
And faced as an innocent Lamb the hostility of his enemies;
20   What heart that has witnessed [this] does not ponder over [it]?

From the grave where he lay it is recorded that he arose,
In supremacy he ascended to the place his Father had ordained,
Sitting as a generous God, splendid sun, exalted Son,
24   Holy and magnificent of character.

Oddi yno y Duw Iesu, drwy fawr nerth i farnu,
Meddyliwn edifaru, nid yw fore i'r un;
Cawn fynd i'r llawenydd, lu hyfryd, i'r hafddydd
28 I gyd efo'i gilydd i'w ganlyn.

Mab Duw a foliannwn, gogoniant a ganwn,
Clod melys clodforwn, llawenwn ar led;
Cyd-rown o'n geneue fwyn adlais un odle
32 Y bore dydd gole y'i gweled.

Er mwyn y Gogoned daionus ei weithred
Rhowch ddrws yn egored o nodded i ni;
Gollyngwch ni i'ch annedd i ganu gogonedd
36 I rinwedd yr hafedd Dduw heini.

Dienw

Sources
Thomas Jones, *Llyfr Carolau a Dyrïau Duwiol* [A book of carols and devout songs] (Amwythig [Shrewsbury]: Thomas Jones, 1696), pp. 120–1.

Rhiannon Ifans, 'Canu Gwaseila yn y Gymraeg' [Welsh Wassailing] (PhD thesis, University of Wales [Aberystwyth], 1980), 2, 482–3.

Date
Prior to 1696.

Locality
Not noted.

The Lord Jesus, from that place, will in his great power judge,
Let us make it our intention to repent, it is not too early for anyone;
We can enter into the joy [of the Lord], kindly throng, into the
    halcyon days,
28   All of us together, following him.

We praise the Son of God, we sing glory,
We extol sweet praise, we rejoice far and wide;
In unity our lips give a resounding, melodious, combined song
32   On the morning of the bright day on which he appeared.

For the sake of the Lord of glory whose accomplishment
    is beneficent,
Open the door of refuge for us;
Allow us into your house to sing glory
36   To the virtues of the temperate God.

Anonymous

Note
Line 27 cf. 'His lord said to him, "Well done, good and faithful servant; you have been faithful over a few things, I will make you ruler over many things. Enter into the joy of your lord"' (The Gospel according to Saint Matthew 25:23).

Metre
Tri thrawiad sengl; the song can be sung to 'Gadael Tir y ffordd hwyaf'/'Leave Land'; see p. 180; see further Phyllis Kinney, 'The Tunes of the Welsh Christmas Carols (II)', *Canu Gwerin (Folk Song)*, 12 (1989), 11–13; Phyllis Kinney and Meredydd Evans (eds), *Hen Alawon (Carolau a Cherddi)* [Old Tunes (Carols and Poems)] (Welsh Folk Song Society in association with the National Museum of Wales (Welsh Folk Museum), 1993), number 42 and pp. 101–2.

2 Penillion ar fesur 'Joane Blackett' i'w canu dan
y ffenestr ac i ennill y drws yn agored

Pwy ydyw y cacwn sy'n cynnal y byrdwn
Sy'n datsain i'n herbyn bob rhai?
Yn gadael y gwenyn i oeri mewn erwyn,
4 Gwybyddwch fod arnoch chwi fai!
Am hyn, gadewch iddo, cawn amser i dreio,
Od ewch chwi i ymrafaelio â nyni,
In' weled ei warach, wrthnysig wrthnysach,
8 Mo'ch glewach na'ch taerach mewn tŷ.

Cigfranod coegfeiniol sy'n lleisio'n anllesol,
Nid harddol na gweddol mo'r gwaith
Sy'n gadel colomennod i oeri mewn rhyndod,
12 Y mae arnoch chi feie mawr faith;
Chwychwi yn eich c'lomendy a ninne'n ein noethni,
Fel dyna ryfeddod yr oed,
O gollyngwch y golomen i'w hachub drachefen
16 A'r gigfran 'r hyd cangen y coed.

O egorwch, yn rhodd, eich drws, o'ch gwir fodd,
I ennill mae'n anodd i ni,
Ni a ddaethon ar deithiad fel diwyd rai di-wad
20 Trwy gariad a chaniad i chwi;
Trwy gariad, agorwch yn rasol, na ruswch,
Gollyngwch ni i'ch annedd i gyd,
Ne cenwch yn gywir eich miwsig un mesur
24 Ac yno ni awn ymeth o hyd.

Dafydd Humphreys

2   Stanzas on the metre 'Joane Blackett' to be sung
     beneath the window and to win an open door

Who are the wasps sustaining the song
That resounds against us, each one?
Letting the bees grow cold in the pure whiteness,
4   Know that you are in the wrong!
Because of this, let him be, we shall have time to test,
If you will contend with us,
[And] to see whether there is one more genial, a more stubborn
        headstrong [man],
8   More splendid or more ardent in any home than you.

Good-for-nothing authoritative ravens voicing in an unprofitable
        manner,
This act is neither comely nor seemly
That causes doves to grow cold to the point of extreme shivering,
12   You have many enormous faults;
You in your dovecot and we in our exposure [to the weather],
Well, that is the astonishment of the appointed time,
O let the dove [inside] to her rescue once more
16   And let the raven [move] through the bough[s] of the trees.

O open up your door, in blessing, of your own free will,
It is difficult for us to win [this contest in song],
We have come on a journey as diligent people who will not
        be denied,
20   To you in love and song;
In love, open up graciously, do not hesitate,
Let all of us into your house,
Or sing your music sincerely in the same metre
24   And we shall then go away and stay away.

Dafydd Humphreys

Sources
NLW 7191B, f. 237ʳ⁻ᵛ.
Ifans, 'Canu Gwaseila', 2, 538–9.

Date
The manuscript dates from the late seventeenth century.

Locality
Not noted.

3   Penillion eraill ar fesur 'About the Bank' i'r un pwrpas

Gyda'ch cennad, bawb sy'n gwarchod,
Mae yma fagad o'r un teiad
A'n bwriad ni oedd yn barod
4   Gael tân gole a chanhwylle,
Ar eich byrdde chware cardie,
Ac yfed hielth eich diod,
A chael llances o liw'r gwawn
8   Yn llawen iawn i'w llenwi
Nad âi yn sarrug yn y man
Er gofyn cusan iddi,
Yn cellwer, drwy bleser
12 A mwynder, â myfi,
Yn weddol, naturiol,
Yn siriol fwyn heb sorri.

Y mae hi'n rhewi heno o ddifri,
16 Ein h'wllys ni yw cael egori
Cyn inni rynnu ar unwaith;
Yr ŷm ni'n gofyn cael yn gytûn
Ganu i'n herbyn o'r un testun;
20 Y mae yn dostur myned ymaith
Oddi wrth fir a sir, yn siŵr,

Note

Lines 1–4 depict the contention as one between wasps (the household company) and bees (the wassailers); lines 9–12 depict it as one between ravens (the household company) and doves (the wassailers).

Metre

For 'Joane Blackett' see 'Joan's Placket', p. 180.

3   Other stanzas in the metre 'About the Bank' to the same end

With your permission, all those who stand guard,
Out here there is a troop from the same household
And it was our intention that we should have ready [for us]
4   A lighted fire and candles,
To play cards at your tables,
And to drink the health of your liquor,
And to obtain a young woman [with a complexion] the colour
of gossamer
8   To fill it [i.e. our drink] most merrily,
One that would not before long become ill-tempered
On account of having been asked for a kiss,
But exchanging remarks in a good-humoured
12   And pleasant way with me,
In a suitable, natural way,
Cheerful [and] pleasant, without taking offence.

It is freezing hard this evening,
16   It is our desire that [you] open for us
Before we perish with cold here and now;
We ask unanimously that
Someone contends with us in verse the same poetic satire;
20   It is misery to go away
From beer and good cheer, sure enough,

A phurion ŵr cariadus
A'r wraig dda, lân, fonheddig, ffri
24 A welsom ni'n gr'esawus,
A'r tirion gymdeithion,
Rai mwynion eu modded,
Amdanyn, gwawr addf'yn,
28 Mae f'achwyn cyn fynyched.

Eich bir y llynedd yn ddiomedd
Yn eich annedd a wnaeth ddialedd,
A ninne ar ddolydd g'lybion;
32 Cofion eleni, drwy gwrteisi,
Pa le oedd inni gael ein meddwi,
Ac yma dorri yn union,
Ac yno, i gwbi y gŵr da, pêr,
36 A'r wraig dda, dyner, dirion,
A'r holl ferched teg eu gwên,
Mai nyni oedd yr hen gymdeithion;
Egorwch, na rusiwch,
40 Ertolwg, feinir ferch,
Ni fedra i mo'r canu,
Rwyf fi wedi synnu o'i serch.

Dafydd Humphreys

Sources
NLW 7191B, ff. 237ᵛ–8ʳ.

Rhiannon Ifans, *Sêrs a Rybana: Astudiaeth o'r Canu Gwasael* [Stars and Ribbons: A Study of Wassail Songs] (Llandysul: Gwasg Gomer, 1983), p. 75

Date
The manuscript dates from the late seventeenth century.

And from a kind, most perfect man
And the liberal, noble, virtuous good wife
24   Whom we have seen is hospitable,
And the gracious companions
Of amiable disposition,
About whom, gentle dawn,
28   My concern is so frequent.

Last year your free-flowing beer
Wreaked vengeance in your home,
And we were [bogged down] on waterlogged pastures [on our
        way home];
32   This year, with courtesy, we [retain] memories
Of where we were made drunk,
And that we were ruined here straight away,
And it is there, in the home of the agreeable good man
36   And the gentle, tender, good wife,
And all the women with beautiful smiles,
To whom we were long-standing companions;
Open up, do not hesitate,
40   I beseech you, tall and slender young woman,
I am unable to sing
I am so amazed on account of my love for her.

Dafydd Humphreys

Locality
Not noted.

Metre
For 'About the Bank', also known as 'Y Fedle Fawr' [The Great Medley],
see p. 179; see further Phyllis Kinney, 'The Tunes of the Welsh Christmas
Carols (I)', *Canu Gwerin (Folk Song)*, 11 (1988), 37–8; Kinney and Evans,
Hen Alawon, number 29 and p. 98.

4   Carol gwirod ar dri chwarter tôn

Nos dawch, gyda'ch cennad, pwy sy yma'n gwarchod?
Mae 'honom ni fagad mewn bwriad i'ch bir,
Yn fudron ein sgidie, yn gandryll ein sane,
4   Pan ddelo ni i'r gole fe'n gwelir.

Ni adawon ni yn gelfydd na mawnog na mynydd,
Heb gerdded yn ufudd, yn ofer pob un;
Ni welson ni yn unlle na thân na chanhwylle,
8   Na sôn am y Gwylie, na'i ganlyn.

Ond wedi inni lwybro a cherdded a chwilio
Ni ymroesom i gordio fel gwyrda,
A dŵad, o'r diwedd, i wneuthur anhunedd
12   Ar deulu diomedd sydd yma.

Pe gallech chwi agori i'r poenus gwmpeini
Mwyn, llonydd, a llenwi inni ddiod
A'n ledio ni yn hylwydd yn nes i'r cynhesrwydd,
16   Chwi enillech gan f'Arglwydd Dduw fawrglod.

Pan faen ni'n bresennol ar derfyn ein carol
Dôi'r ferch, yn naturiol, ar doriad ei gras
I bawb â chwpaned o'r baril a fratsied,
20   Yn gofus, ac yfed o gwmpas.

Doe i ni â thybaco a thrensiwr i'w friwo
Ac odyn o groeso, a'i grasu ar hon;
Pibell yn oeri ac un arall yn llosgi,
24   A dwy wedi'u llenwi inni'n llawnion.

Ni gawson, yn ddidro, ychwaneg o groeso
Ond eisio gorffwyso a thario mewn tŷ;
I yfed bir caled oedd anos i'w weled
28   Nag aros dan bared i oeri.

4   A wassail song in *tri chwarter tôn*

Good evening, with your permission, who is standing guard here?
There is a troop of us [out here] intent on your beer,
Our boots are dirty, our socks are in tatters,
4   When we come into the light we can be seen.

We have left in good order neither peatbog nor mountain,
Each is worthless if we do not walk with restraint;
We have seen neither fire nor candles anywhere,
8   Nor have we heard mention of Christmastide, nor seen it celebrated.

But once we had covered ground and walked and searched
We devoted ourselves to sounding chords as noblemen do,
And to come, at last, to cause a wakefulness
12   In the generous family that is within.

If you could open [the door] to the aching company
Who are pleasant [and] peaceable [men], and fill us a drink
And lead us speedily nearer to the warmth,
16   You would win yourselves great praise from my Lord God.

When we come to the end of our carol
Naturally the young woman would bring, in her own distinctive
       manner of goodwill,
A cup from the tapped barrel to one and all,
20   Mindful [of us], and drink the health of all around.

She would bring us tobacco and a trencher on which to pound it
And a kiln [pipe] in welcome, and [we would] smoke it in this [pipe];
One pipe cooling and another alight,
24   And two already filled to the brim for us.

Without guile, we were given a greater welcome [than we had
       anticipated],
Merely wanting to rest and to remain inside the house;
To drink hard root beer was more difficult to envisage
28   Than to stand beneath the wall to grow cold.

Ni alla i ond hynny, dan bared, mo'r canu,
Mae 'y ngherddor i'n rhynnu, wych deulu da;
Agorwch yn hafedd ein drws, yn ddiomcdd,
32   Neu'r gwinedd a'r bysedd a basia.

Dienw

Sources
T. H. Parry-Williams, *Llawysgrif Richard Morris o Gerddi* [Richard Morris's
Manuscript of Poems] (Cardiff: University of Wales Press, 1931), pp. 171–2.
Ifans, 'Canu Gwaseila yn y Gymraeg', 2, 502–3.

Variant readings
Line 9 wubro (Parry-Williams, *Llawysgrif Richard Morris*, p. 171).
Line 12 da omedd (Parry-Williams, *Llawysgrif Richard Morris*, p. 171).
Line 19 balir (Parry-Williams, *Llawysgrif Richard Morris*, p. 172).

Date
1718.

5   Yma y dechreuiff carol gwir[od] ar y mesur
     a elwir 'May Day'

Nos dawch, y glân deulu sydd yma'n trigfannu,
Mae 'honom ni fagad mewn bwriad i ganu,
A'n hewyllys diogan, bob un yn ddiwegi,
4   Gael dyfod, cyn tewi, i'r tŷ.

Cydgofiwn yr amser, i gyd yn ddibrudd-der,
Pan ddaeth inni newydd o haeldir uchelder
Y caem ni Waredydd nod ufudd, nid ofer:
8   Yn dyner, gwir fwynder a fu.

Moeswch, nac arbedwch, ddwys 'madrodd os medrwch,
Yn rasol, na rusiwch, ar fesur na fisiwch.

Dienw

I can do no more singing beneath the wall,
My musician is almost frozen to death, excellent good family,
Open the door to us in a temperate manner, without refusal,
32 Or the nails and the fingers will pass away.

Anonymous

Locality
Anglesey/Caernarfonshire.

Note
Line 30 cerddor, player of a musical instrument, especially the harp.

Metre
'Tri chwarter tôn'; stanzas 1–2, 5–8 are in *tri thrawiad sengl* and can be
sung to 'Gadael Tir y ffordd hwyaf'/'Leave Land' see p. 180; see further
Kinney, 'Tunes (II)', 11–13; Kinney and Evans, *Hen Alawon*, number 42
and pp. 101–2. Stanzas 3 and 4 are in *tri thrawiad dwbl* and can be sung
to 'Tri Thrawiad Gwynedd' see p. 183.

5   Here begins a wassail carol in the metre known
     as 'May Day'

Good evening, good family that resides here,
There is a troop of us [out here] intent on singing,
And it is our reproachless desire, each one in a sober manner,
4   To be allowed to enter into the house before we hold our tongue.

We share memories of the time, all of it a delight,
When news came to us from the bountiful land on high
That we would be provided with a Redeemer of obedient
            intention, not futile:
8   With tenderness, a true kindness was brought about.

Give earnest expression, if you are able, do not abstain,
With grace, do not hesitate, do not fail on a metre.

Anonymous

Sources
Parry-Williams, *Llawysgrif Richard Morris o Gerddi*, p. 199.
Ifans, 'Canu Gwaseila', 2, 504.

Date
Early in the eighteenth century.

Locality
Anglesey/Caernarfonshire.

6   Carol tan bared Wyliau'r Nadolig

Cyd-rowch osteg teg, di-dwyll,
Y teulu didwyll, dedwydd,
Er gwrando'n graff, gywreindeg rol,
4   Anniwael garol newydd.

Wedi i Adda 'n gynta i gyd
Ein troi ni i fyd truenus
Mewn gwall a nych o golli ne
8   I fydio i le gofidus,

Ar gyfer hyn, gyfiawna' hwyl,
Daeth inni annwyl Unwr
I dalu Iawn yn gyfiawn gu
12   Dros Adda a fu droseddwr.

Ar Nadolig, ddiddig ddydd,
Yn ufudd, Lywydd nefol,
I'n gwir garu a'n tynnu o'r tân
16   Daeth Iesu glân, dewisol.

Molwn hwn drwy ymlawenhau
Yn nyddiau'r Gwyliau gole
Ar gerdd deg, gywiraidd dôn,
20   A mwynion, dynion danne.

Note

The carol is followed by the note 'John Morris his Book Anno Domini 1726'.

Metre

For 'May Day' see p. 180.

6   A carol [to be sung] beneath the wall at Christmastide

Unite in a call for an amiable, guileless silence,
You honest, blessed family,
In order to listen carefully, [this is a] wise and righteous roll
    of parchment,
4   To an excellent new carol.

After Adam had at the very beginning
Turned us over to a wretched existence
Of destitution and torment for having lost heaven
8   [And forced] to exist in a sorrowful place,

Against this time, most righteous journey,
There came to us a dear Unifier
To atone in a righteous, loving manner
12 For Adam who was a transgressor.

At Christmas, a day of peace,
Obediently, celestial Lord,
In order to love us truly, and to pluck us from the fire,
16 Jesus appeared, [the] pure and chosen one.

Let us praise him by rejoicing
During the bright days of Christmastide
In pleasant song with a fitting tune,
20 And sweet-sounding, taut [harp]strings.

Nid awn at gerlyn dygyn, dig
I gynnig miwsig moesol,
Ond i'r rhai haela, bracia 'n bro
24   A roddo groeso grasol.

Mil saith gant a deugain mlwydd
Ac un i'w gwiwlwydd ganu
Oedd oed ein t'wysog, enwog ŵr,
28   Ein Prynwr, oeswr, Iesu.

Gyrrwch ferch oreuwych fodd
I egori yn rhodd o gariad
O cawn ar cyd, nid gwynfyd gwael,
32   I'ch neuadd ddiwael ddŵad.

Dienw

Sources
Cwrtmawr 128A, 85–6.
Ifans, 'Canu Gwaseila', 2, 486–7.

Date
1741.

We shall not visit crass, bitter churl[s]
To offer high-principled music,
But those who are most generous, most open-handed in
     our neighbourhood,
24   Who offer a gracious welcome.

One thousand seven hundred and forty years
And one, of successful song,
That was the age of our prince, illustrious one,
28   Our Redeemer, one who gives life, Jesus.

Send a young woman of a most excellent disposition
To open [the door] as an offering of affection
So that we can together, it is not a lowly delight,
32   Enter into your fine hall.

Anonymous

Locality
Trawsfynydd, Gwynedd.

Metre
Mesur Salm, 'Psalm Metre,' in Welsh prosody, an iambic stanza of
8.7.8.7. syllables with lines ending in accented and unaccented syllables
alternately.

7   Carol wirod yn drws

Y teulu nod haeledd sydd yma'n dymhoredd,
Ni ganwn dôn beredd dan bared eich llys
Drwy gennad y gwrda sy'n tario'n tŷ yma
4   A'i wraig fwyn, ddiana', ddaionus.

Hyd yma ni ddaethon oherwydd ni glowson
Fod merched glân, tirion yn tario yn eich llys
A chwithau'n rhoi croeso i bawb fel y delo
8   A'ch bir chwi sy'n cwympo rhai campus.

Os cawn ni yma groeso ni fyddwn hy eto
A phrysur ein dwylo yn talu i chwi'n wir:
Pan foch chi'r cynhaea a phawb ar ei ora
12   Ni fedwn eich yda chwi'n chwedir.

Pan oedd ein hen deidiau yn ifanc fel ninnau
Nhwy fydden trwy'r Gwyliau 'n ymganlyn yn llon,
A ninnau sydd eto gyd oll wedi ymrwymo:
16   Ni fedrwn ni fario eu harferion.

Wel, dyma ni'n diwedd, danfonwch yn fwynedd
Eich morwyn deg, iredd i agoryd i ni
A'n ledio fel mwynwr i'ch neuadd neu'ch parlwr:
20   Ni wnawn ni ddim cynnwr' ond canu.

Dienw

Sources
NLW 9168A, ff. 54ᵛ–5ᵛ.
Ifans, *Sêr a Rybana*, p. 74.

Date
Prior to 1767.

7   A wassail song [to be sung] at the door

The family of generous intention that is here at this time,
We sing a sweet song beneath the walls of your court
By permission of the good man who resides at this house
4   And his gentle, faultless, good wife.

We have come this far because we have heard
That there are virtuous, agreeable young women residing at
            your court
And that you welcome all as they come
8   And that your beer topples the valiant.

If we are welcomed here we shall be bold at a later date
And our hands will be busy in true repayment to you:
When you are at the harvest and everyone is at his best
12   We shall reap your crops altogether.

When our forefathers were young as we are [now]
They would follow [the observance] merrily throughout Christmastide,
And all of us have again committed to it:
16   We cannot put a stop to their customs.

Well, we now conclude, send obligingly
Your beautiful, flourishing young woman to open [the door] to us
And lead us like gentlemen into your hall or your parlour:
20   We shall create no disturbance apart from singing.

Anonymous

Locality
Gwynedd.

Metre
Tri thrawiad sengl; the song can be sung to 'Gadael Tir y ffordd
hwyaf'/'Leave Land' see p. 180; see further Kinney, 'Tunes (II)', 11–13;
Kinney and Evans, *Hen Alawon*, number 42 and pp. 101–2.

8   Carol ateb o'r tŷ ar 'Peg O'Ramsey'

Chwi fuoch er llynedd yn rhoi imi glod
A minne heb fod gartre,
Ond eleni teriais i
4   I gadw yn ffri i chwi Wylie.

Mi leddis fuwch oedd hŷn na'm nain
A honno oedd fain ei 'senna:
Chwi gewch ran o gig ei phen
8   I gadw i chwi lawen Wylia.

Ac i sbario cig y fuwch
Mae dan y lluwch ddefeidie:
Mi yrra' i dyrru'r rhain ar led,
12   Fe'u blinged nhw ers dyddie.

Mae yma basta' o aelod march,
Cewch honno o barch, gwmpeini;
Mae hi yn beredd, gwn ei bod,
16   Mae'r llygod gwedi'i phrofi.

Mae yma hwch a haedda glod
Ac ond ei bod yn llodig;
Yn second cwrs cewch bwding hon
20   Os byddwch ddynion diddig.

Mae yma fara o'r ffacbys mân
Gwedi i'r tân ei losgi,
A chacennau o'r pur efrau,
24   Cewch y rhain i'w profi.

Y mae yma ar y tân,
O barch i'r glân gwmpeini,
Gi yn rhostio er hanner dydd
28   A'i berfedd sydd yn berwi.

8   A reply carol from inside the house in 'Peg O'Ramsey'

You have been praising me since last year
[Even though] I was not at home,
But this year I have stayed in
4   To keep Christmastide free for you.

I have slaughtered a cow that was older than my grandmother
And it had sharp ribs:
You can have a little meat from its head
8   To celebrate a merry Christmas.

And to spare the beef
There are sheep under the snowdrift:
I shall send word far and wide to pile these up,
12   They were skinned [several] days ago.

There is a pie here made from a stallion's member,
[Venerable] company, you can have it, out of respect;
It is delicious, I know it is,
16   The mice have tasted it.

There is a sow here that deserves praise
And is probably in heat;
As a second course you can have her entrails
20   If you are good-tempered men.

There is bread here made from fine lentils
That the fire has burned [to ashes],
And cakes made from pure tares,
24   You can have these to taste.

There is on the fire here,
Out of respect for the good company,
A dog roasting since noon
28   And its entrails are on the boil.

Fel bai yr arfer ar ôl bwyd
Gael cosyn llwyd go dene
Ac ynddo o gynrhon fwy na rhi,
32 Mi a'i gwelis i nhw yn chware.

Wel, dyna swper i chwi yn barod,
Nis gwn i am ddiod beth a wna,
Mynna i ddŵr a'i ddrincio yn tŷ –
36 Ni chewch chi mo'r tagu yma.

Dienw

Sources
Parry-Williams, *Llawysgrif Richard Morris o Gerddi*, pp. 114–15.
Ifans, *Sêr a Rybana*, p. 76.

Variant reading
Line 21 phigpus (Parry-Williams, *Llawysgrif Richard Morris*, p. 115).

Date
Early in the eighteenth century.

Locality
Anglesey/Caernarfonshire.

Metre
Triban. The English dance tune 'Peg O'Ramsey', see p. 181, is men-
tioned in a pamphlet written by Thomas Nashe, *Have With You to*

As is the custom after a meal
We shall eat a slim piece of mouldy cheese
That has maggots without number in it,
32   I have seen them at play.

Well, that's supper ready for you,
I don't know what to do for drink,
I shall take some water and drink it in the house –
36   You will not be allowed to die of thirst here.

Anonymous

Saffron-Walden (London: John Danter, 1596; facsimile reprint Menston: Scolar Press, 1971), unpaged (quire T), 'or doo as *Dick Haruey* did, (which information piping hot in the midst of this line was but brought to mee) that hauing preacht and beat downe three pulpits in inueighing against dauncing; one Sunday euening, when hys Wench or Friskin was footing it aloft on the Greene, with foote out and foote in, and as busie as might be at *Rogero, Basilino, Turkelony, All the flowers of the broom, Pepper is black, Greene sleeues, Peggy Ramsey*, he came sneaking behinde a tree and lookt on, and though hee was loth to be seene to countenance the sport, hauing laid Gods word against it so dreadfully, yet to shew his good-will to it in hart, hee sent her 18 pence in hugger mugger [i.e., in secret] to pay the fidlers.' See also W. Chappell, *The Ballad Literature and Popular Music of the Olden Time*, 1 (London: Chappell, 1859), pp. 218–20. In Shakespeare's *Twelfth Night*, Act 2, Scene 3, line 76 (first performed in February 1602), Sir Toby Belch describes Malvolio thus: 'Malvolio's a Peg-a-Ramsey', a busybody, a contemptible person.

9   Ymrafael Holin ac Ifin [   ] ar iddo i'w ganu y Nadolig

[Gwrandewch dda]ngos modd ac achos
[   ] cynnwrf Holin:
Fo aeth ymrafael rhyngddo, yn siŵr,
4   Â *gŵr* a elwid Ifin.

A chymdeithion fuon hwy 'rioed
Ac yn y coed eu trigfa;
Holin ydoedd iôr o ras
8   Yn cadw'r plas yn benna.

Nid oedd Ifin yn ddi-ffael
Ond gŵr gwael i 'mdaro,
Ac ni cherddodd gam erioed
12   Ond wrth y coed ymlusgo.

Mae fo'n feingam ac yn druan
A'i din sy ar ei arre;
Cwlwm gwythi sy ar ei hyd
16   Ne glefyd cryd cymale.

Digon afiach ydyw'r cimach,
Bwbach cilfach coedwig;
Nid da gennyf ddim o'i ryw –
20   Cydymaith yw fo i Eiddig.

Ac mae Ifin, fywyd gafr,
Yn cael ffafr y merched;
Hwy rôn beilliad ar ei len
24   Oni bai mor wen â'r foled.

Y mae Holin yn dwyn nod
Ac arfe parod beunydd;
Gŵr o ryfel ydyw a ga'd
28   I gadw gwlad a chrefydd.

9   The conflict between Holin and Ifin [   ] that he
     should sing it at Christmastide

[Listen to the setting forth] of the how and the why
[   ] Holin's agitation:
Conflict arose between him, for sure,
4   And a man by the name of Ifin.

And they had always been companions
And their dwelling-place was in the woods;
Holin was a gracious lord
8   Chiefly keeping guard over that place.

Ifin was without fail
But a poor fellow to contend with,
And he never walked one step
12   But rather crept around the trees.

He is thin and hunchbacked, and is wretched,
And is at rock bottom;
Spasms spread through him,
16   Or else the disease of muscular rheumatism.

The hunchback is pretty sickly,
A spectre in a secluded spot in [the] forest;
I cannot stand any of his kind –
20   He is a companion of Eiddig.

And Ifin, who lives the life of a goat,
Is favoured by the girls;
They would place white flour on his covering
24   Were it not as white as a wimple.

Holin bears an insignia
And arms readily every day;
He is a man of war who was brought forth
28   To guard country and godliness.

Ac o daw 'morol pwy a wnâi'r carol,
Dyn yn caru Holin,
Ac a gerddodd dref a gwlad
32 [   ] dwaeniad Ifin.

Dienw

Sources
T. H. Parry-Williams, *Canu Rhydd Cynnar* (Cardiff: University of Wales
Press, 1932), pp. 406–7.
Ifans, *Sêr a Rybana*, p. 77.

Variant reading
Line 24 wyn (Parry-Williams, *Canu Rhydd Cynnar*, p. 406).

Date
Sixteenth or seventeenth century, see Brinley Rees, *Dulliau'r Canu
Rhydd, 1500–1650* (Cardiff: University of Wales Press, 1952), pp. 28–31.

10 Carol tan bared y Parchedig Mr William Jones o'r Tŷ Fry

Wel, gyda'ch cennad, fawr a mân,
Y teulu glân, parchedig,
Ni ganwn fawl mewn hawl yn hir
4   Yn deilwng i'r Nadolig.

Nadolig Crist, nid trist mo'r tro,
Gwnawn heno, heb fisio, fiwsig
A rhown o'n genau fawl ar gân,
8   Gu, luniaidd, lân galennig.

Calennig sydd galonnog siŵr,
Deg, lwysedd ŵr eglwysig
Sy â'i glod yn glir ar dir a dŵr,
12   Wych awdwr mwyn, parchedig.

And if the question arises as to who composed the carol,
[It is] one who loves Holin,
And who has walked town and country
32   [   ] aquaintance of Ifin.

Anonymous

Locality
Not noted.

Notes
Line 20 Eiddig, the proverbial jealous husband.
Lines 25–6 may refer to the berries as the insignia and the prickly leaves
to the arms.

Metre
Triban.

10 A carol beneath the wall of the Reverend Mr William Jones of Tŷ Fry

Well, with your permission, great and small,
The good, reverend family,
We shall sing praise[s] for a long while as is our right
4   [And] as is worthy of Christmas.

The Christmas of Christ, this is not a sorrowful time,
Let us this evening, without fail, make music
And let us in song give praise from our lips,
8   A beautiful, well composed, sincere gift.

A New Year's gift is surely cheerful,
Righteous, handsome cleric
Whose praise is evident on land and sea,
12   Excellent author, gentle and revered.

Pob dysg a dawn mewn llawn wellhad
A gadd mewn rhad anrhydedd
A'i annwyl briod o'r un modd,
16 Ond Duw a'i rho'dd mewn rhinwedd.

I'w barchus feibion cyfion, cu,
Swm hynaws sy yma ohonyn,
Yr impia cyfion ar lawr cell,
20 Boed llwyddiant wellwell iddyn.

I Humphrey a John mewn llon wellhad
Boed llwyddiad, dyniad dinam,
Ac Owen sydd mewn cynnydd cu
24 Yn fwyngu heb gelu, ac William.

Un Cathy fwyn, Duw gadwo'r fun
Ac Elin unig eilwaith,
A Margaret gynnes â'r un gair,
28 Daer, geinwych ei dair genaith.

Duw roddo ei ras heb gas i gyd
A lliwus fywyd llawen
A llwydd a chynnydd tra bo chwyth,
32 Da, parchus fyth i'w perchen.

Boed iddyn iechyd, gwyn eu byd,
Dasg hylwydd, hyd ysgolion,
I foddio perchen, lawen lwydd,
36 A'r cofus Arglwydd cyfion.

I ŵr y tŷ, heb gelu ar gân,
A'i gywlaid, lân gywely,
Ein cyfion fugail, araul was,
40 Di-gas weinidog Iesu,

Boed bendith byth i'ch plith a'ch plant
Heb soriant bob amserau,
Hyd lawr Tŷ Fry rhoed Iesu ei ras
44 I ganlyn pas y Gwyliau.

Dafydd Jones o'r Penrhyn (1743–1831)

All learning and talents in total superiority
Were given to him in a gracious accolade
And his dear spouse is of the same manner,
16   But it was God who made him virtuous.

[Blessings] to his esteemed sons, upright [and] beloved,
There is a pleasing number of them here,
The righteous man will cause [them] to grow up on the floor[s]
    of his house,
20   Let them receive progressively more and more successes.

To Humphrey and John in happy improvement
May there be a prospering, faultless men,
And Owen in good progress
24   Is openly obliging and amiable, and William.

The one gentle Cathy, may God keep the young woman
And the only Elin once again,
And warm-hearted Margaret with the same word [of prayer],
28   Ardent, splendid his three daughters.

May God give every blessing without enmity
And may they have a beautiful and happy life [together]
And success and increase while there is breath,
32   To be good [and] to forever respect their owner [i.e. parent].

May they have good health, blessed are they,
Felicitous task, at their schools,
To please [their] owner [i.e. parent], joyous success,
36   And the righteous omniscient Lord.

To the man of the house, openly in song,
And his dear one, virtuous spouse,
Our upright shepherd, bright servant [of the Lord],
40   Gentle minister of Jesus,

May there be blessings forever among you and your children
At all times without anger,
May Jesus give his blessing on the floors of Tŷ Fry
44   To follow the excellence of Christmastide.

Dafydd Jones o'r Penrhyn (1743–1831)

Sources
NLW 6740B, 78–80.

Ifans, 'Canu Gwaseila', 540–2.

Date
1767.

Locality
The poem was written by the bookbinder David Jones 'Dafydd Siôn Siâms' of Llandanwg in the former Merionethshire, who spent most of his life in Penrhyndeudraeth, Gwynedd. The manuscript was compiled *c.*1767–83 in his autograph.

Note
Gwenda Paul, in a report commissioned by The North West Wales Dendrochronology Project in partnership with The Royal Commission on the

11   Carol ddiolch 1767

Hai! 'nglân gymdeithion, dowch ynghyd,
Wel, dyma'r pryd parodol
I roddi diolch ar bob tro
4 Am effro groeso grasol.

Can diolch teg i ŵr y tŷ
A'i lân gywely gwiwlan,
Boed llwydd a ffyniant ar eu byd
8 A lliwus fywyd llawen.

Boed bendith fyth i'ch plith a'ch plant
A ffyniant, haeddiant heddwch;
Sy i'n gwadd gerbron yn llon i'w llys
12 Llais gwyredd w'llysgarwch.

Ancient and Historical Monuments in Wales, writes that Tŷ Fry, Penrhyn-deudraeth, Gwynedd, 'is a stone built sub-medieval house of the Snowdonia type, two storeys with an attic (...) The felling dates for the beams were – winter 1754/5 and 1755/6 and spring 1756 (...) The Rev. William Jones of the Brynhir family married Margaret, the daughter of Humphrey Owen, Lasynys. It is believed that Rev. William Jones drowned crossing Traeth Bach in 1769 on his way down from Llandecwyn Church to take a service at Llanfihangel y Traethau.' [Online]. Available at: *http://discoveringoldwelshhouses.co.uk/library/Hhistory/mer%2009b_HH_30_Ty-Fry.pdf* (accessed 7 September 2020).

Poem 11, 'Carol ddiolch 1767' (A carol of gratitude 1767) composed in the same metre and probably sung on leaving Mr Jones's house on the same evening, follows this carol in the manuscript.

Metre
Triban.

11   A carol of gratitude 1767

Hey! my good companions, assemble together,
Well, this is the appointed time
To give thanks at every opportunity
4   For a keen [and] gracious welcome.

Well-deserved thanks a hundred times over to the master of the house
And his good wife, worthy and pure,
May there be prosperity and good fortune in their life circumstances
8   And may they have a beautiful and happy life [together].

May there be eternal blessing on you and on your children
And success merited by peace;
Inviting us happily into their presence [and] into their court
12   Is the voice that inclines towards goodwill.

Ni gowson yma wyn ein byd
A seigia drud, gwresogol,
A chwrw a bir, wawr rhwyddir rhad,
16   Trwy gariad yn rhagorol.

Boed gras yr Arglwydd, cynnydd cu,
I deulu'r Tŷ Fry yn dryfrith,
Ac am ein croeso mwyn, di-freg
20   Rhown glaerdeg, fwyndeg fendith.

Duw, ffrwytha eu byd i gyd heb gas,
Gwyn, addas ar gynyddiad;
Pob peth a drinioch, deulu gwâr,
24   Mewn gwynfyd ar ei ganfed.

Hir oes ac iechyd i chwi'n siŵr,
Wych odiaeth ŵr parchedig,
A'ch annwyl briod, fawrglod foes,
28   Boed hiroes, einioes unig.

Duw gadwo'n gu eich tŷ a'ch tân
A'ch mawr a'ch mân orchmyniad,
A'ch ŷd a'ch gwair, mewn gair, dan go,
32   Yn filoedd bo'ch 'nifeiliad.

Boed llwydd a chynnydd tra bo chwyth
I goledd fyth y Gwyliau,
A gwir drugaredd mwynedd maith
36   Yn odiaeth i'ch eneidiau.

Rŷm ni'n ddigonol, deud y gwir,
Yn glir o'ch bir a'ch bara,
A phob danteithion, rwyddion rol,
40   O lân, wresogol seigia.

We have received here our fullness of blessings
And warming, expensive feasts,
And beer and ale, in a generous, open-handed way,
16   In love, exceedingly so.

May the grace of the Lord, in precious increase,
Be extensive on the Tŷ Fry family,
And for the kind, unfailing welcome that we received
20   We give a comely, affable blessing.

God, make fruitful their world altogether, [may it be] without
     bitterness,
Blessed [and] deservingly on the increase;
May all that you cultivate, noble family,
24   Prosper a hundredfold.

Long life and health to you, sure enough,
Exceedingly fine reverend man,
And your dear spouse, of esteemed moral principles,
28   May you have a long life, a peerless lifetime.

May God keep with deep affection your house and your hearth
And your command, great and small,
And your corn and your hay grown for harvesting, in a word,
     in remembrance,
32   May your animals be numbered in the thousands.

May there be success and increase while there is breath
To cherish Christmastide for ever,
And true mercy of great gentleness
36   In the extreme for your souls.

We have been well satisfied, truth to tell,
Utterly, with your beer and your bread,
And with all choice foods, generous list,
40   Of good, warming feasts.

Duw, rho i'n calonnau ni mewn hedd
I'ch cyrredd ddiolchgarwch,
Fy mhur gyfeillion o'r un fryd,
44 Odiaethol cydfendithiwch.

Cyfarfod da inni yn nheyrnas ne
Ymysg seintie a gwylie golau;
Mewn modd di-wawd, Ddydd Brawd mewn bri,
48 Amen i chwi a minnau.

Dafydd Jones o'r Penrhyn (1743–1831)

Sources
NLW 6740B, 80–2.
Ifans, *Sêrs a Rybana*, pp. 78–9.

Variant reading
Line 18 Dyfrith (NLW 6740B, 81).

Date
31 December 1767.

Locality
The poem was written by the bookbinder David Jones 'Dafydd Siôn Siâms' of Llandanwg in the former Merionethshire, who spent most of his life in Penrhyndeudraeth, Gwynedd. The manuscript was compiled *c.*1767–83 in his autograph.

Note
The carol is followed by the note: 'Carol ddiolch yn llys Parch. Mr. William Jones o'r Tŷ Fry' (A carol of gratitude at the court of the Revd Mr William Jones of Tŷ Fry). Gwenda Paul, in a report commissioned

God, place in our hearts in [all] peace
A thankfulness that we can extend to you,
My sincere friends with one accord,
44   Together, invoke divine blessing upon them, utterly.

Let us meet happily in the kingdom of heaven
In the presence of saints and at bright festivities;
In a delightful manner, in favour on Judgement Day,
48   Amen to you and me.

Dafydd Jones o'r Penrhyn (1743–1831)

by The North West Wales Dendrochronology Project in partnership with The Royal Commission on the Ancient and Historical Monuments in Wales, writes that Tŷ Fry, Penrhyndeudraeth, Gwynedd, 'is a stone built sub-medieval house of the Snowdonia type, two storeys with an attic (...) The felling dates for the beams were – winter 1754/5 and 1755/6 and spring 1756 (...) The Rev. William Jones of the Brynhir family married Margaret, the daughter of Humphrey Owen, Lasynys. It is believed that Rev. William Jones drowned crossing the Traeth Bach in 1769 on his way down from Llandecwyn Church to take a service at Llanfihangel y Traethau.' [Online]. Available at: *http://discoveringoldwelshhouses.co.uk/library/Hhistory/mer%2009b_HH_30_Ty-Fry.pdf* (accessed 7 September 2020).

    See also poem 10 'Carol tan bared y Parchedig Mr William Jones o'r Tŷ Fry' (A carol beneath the wall of the Reverend Mr William Jones of Tŷ Fry) recorded in NLW 6740B immediately preceding this carol of gratitude, composed in the same metre and probably sung on arriving at Mr Jones's house on the same evening.

Metre
Triban.

New Year Wassail Songs

12 Carol i'w chanu ar nos Galan wrth fynd i'r tŷ a'r ddawns

Cydeiliwn bellach fawl yn bwyllog
O flaen eich cyntedd, annedd enwog;
Y gŵr a'i briod glirfod, glaerfodd,
4   Wiwgu, heddiw a'n gwahoddodd.

Clod i'r Arglwydd, llywydd llawen,
Am ei Wyliau golau gwiwlan;
Ni gawson Geidwad bendigedig,
8   Rhown fawl yn deilwng i'r Nadolig.

Ar gyfer hyn enwaedwyd Iesu
Yn ôl y ffasiwn i'w chyffesu;
Rhown ninna chwedyn fawl barchedig
12   Lawn galonnau, lân galennig.

Nid chwant ar dir eich bir a'ch bara
Mewn detha man y daethom ni yma,
Ond cofio eurglod Wylia yr Arglwydd,
16   A bod yn llawnion mewn llawenydd.

Ni ddown i'ch llawr yn ddynion llariedd,
Mwyn a rhadol mewn anrhydedd;
Wrth ddisgwyliad ar nos Galan
20   Rhown fawl i'n Prynwr, dyddiwr diddan.

Rhown galonnau, lân galennig,
Rhown Gristnogol foesol fiwsig,
Rhown ar ddectant foliant felys,
24   Asiwn eiriau yn soniarus.

Er cofio o febyd Crist yn faban,
Eurnaws gowlad, ar nos Galan,
Yn lle dwy g'lomen lawen, liwus
28   Rhown fawl o'r galon gyfion, gofus.

12 A carol to be sung on New Year's Eve on entering the house and the dance

We are with wisdom composing praise poetry once again
Outside your court, renowned residence;
The gentleman and his pure wife, of a gentle disposition,
4   Worthy and beloved, invited us [here] today.

Praise be to the Lord, joyous ruler,
For his bright Christmastide, worthy and pure;
We have received a glorious Saviour,
8   Let us give praise that is worthy of Christmas.

It was on this day that Jesus was circumcised
As was the custom that must be acknowledged;
Subsequently, let us give reverential praise
12   [From] full hearts, a fine New Year's gift.

It is not on account of a desire for your beer and your bread
At an accessible location that we have come here,
But to call to mind the Lord's Christmastide of golden praise,
16   And to be abounding with joy.

We come to the floor of your hall as genial men,
Noble and gracious in dignity;
As we wait on New Year's Eve
20   We give praise to our Redeemer, blessed mediator.

We give [our] hearts, a sincere New Year's gift,
We give high-principled Christian music,
We give sweet praise on the ten-stringed lyre,
24   Melodiously, we blend words together.

So that we can hold in our thoughts, from his infancy, Christ
    the baby,
The embraced one [who is of] a golden disposition, on New
    Year's Eve,
Rather than [give] two beautiful, joyous doves
28   Let us give praise from an upright, thoughtful heart.

Trwy Adda fe'n rhoed tan golledigaeth,
Trwy Foses wedi deddf a chyfraith,
Trwy Grist a gwiwlan waed ei galon
32 Fe'n gwnaed yn iachus, ddownus ddynion.

Down a lluniwn bob llawenydd
I wawl oreurglod Wylia'r Arglwydd;
Nid cario malais a chenfigen,
36 Ond eilio lliwus Wylia llawen.

Rhad yr Arglwydd, hylwydd haeledd,
Iawn, wych, enwog yn eich annedd;
Rhoed Duw ei odiaethol lân fendithion
40 Ar a drinioch, hyder union.

Ple'r wyt ti'r cerddor ordor eurdeg,
Cain, wych union? Cân ychwaneg!
Ar ddawns y capiwn, fesul cwpwl,
44 Rhannau moddus, o'r un meddwl.

*Dafydd Jones 'Dafydd Siôn Siâms' of Penrhyndeudraeth
(1743–1831)*

Sources
NLW 6740B, 83–4.

Rhiannon Ifans, *Sêrs a Rybana: Astudiaeth o'r Canu Gwasael* [Stars and Ribbons: A Study of Wassailing] (Llandysul: Gwasg Gomer, 1983), pp. 101–2.

Date
1767.

Locality
Penrhyndeudraeth, Gwynedd.

In Adam we were placed under condemnation,
Then in Moses [under the] law and commandments,
In Christ and his heart's blood, worthy and pure,
32 We were made justified, blessed people.

Come, let us bring about every joy
For the exceedingly golden-praised splendour of the Lord's
        Christmastide;
Not bearing malice and jealousy,
36 But creating a richly merry Christmastide.

May the blessing of the Lord, swift generosity,
True, excellent, eminent, be in your dwelling-place;
May God shower his wonderful [and] holy blessings
40 On those with whom you deal, unswerving faith.

Where are you, musician of splendid manner,
Excellent, resolutely correct? Play some more!
In dance we shall cap, in couples/one couplet at a time,
44 Modest parts, with one mind.

Dafydd Jones 'Dafydd Siôn Siâms' of Penrhyndeudraeth
(1743–1831)

Note
Dafydd Jones 'Dafydd Siôn Siâms', bookbinder, Penrhyndeudraeth in
Gwynedd. NLW 6740B is a manuscript of poems composed *c.*1767–83
by Dafydd Jones and in his autograph.

Metre
Hen bennill with a little fluidity in several lines.

13 Cân tan bared i ofyn a diolch am galennig ar
'Royal William'

Mi godais heddiw'n fore
I gerdded at eich tai
I 'mofyn ambell chwechyn,
4   Mi gymraf peth fo lai.

Gobeithio caf fynd adref
Yn llawen er fy lles
A 'nghod yn llawn o arian
8   A bara [a] chaws a phres.

O diolch fyddo ichwi
Am ddim a gefais i,
A bendith fyddo arnoch
12   A phopeth yn eich tŷ.

Boed bendith ar eich gwartheg
A'u llaeth a'u caws fo'n bur
Ac iechyd i'ch ceffylau
16   I droi a thrin eich tir.

Boed llwyddiant ar eich llafur,
Y gwair a'r tatw mawr,
A magu moch a wneloch
20   A'u torrau'n llusgo'r llawr.

Ynghyd â'r cŵn a'r cathod,
Boed llwyddiant ar y rhain
I ladd y wadd a'r llygod,
24   Y piod oll a'r brain.

Cynyddu wnelo'ch defaid
A'r ŵyn fo'n chwarae'n lew
A thyfu wnelon' ['n] burlan
28   I'w cadw rhag y rhew.

Boed llwyddiant ar eich cennin
A'ch wynwyns cochion hardd
A llysiau'r *cabbage* gwynion
32   A phopeth sy'n eich gardd.

13 A song [to be sung] beneath the wall to request and
    give thanks for a New Year's gift on 'Royal William'

This morning I arose early
To walk to your homes
To request the occasional sixpenny piece,
4   I am willing to take a little less.

I hope I can return home
Merrily to my advantage
With my bag full of silver coins
8   And bread and cheese and coppers.

O there will be gratitude to you
For all that I received,
And may you be blessed
12 And everything in your house.

May your cattle prosper
And may their milk and their cheese be pure,
And may your horses be healthy
16 To plough and cultivate your land.

May your wheat [harvest] be successful,
The hay and the large potatoes,
And may you breed pigs
20 With bellies that trail the ground.

Along with the dogs and the cats,
May these prosper,
So that they kill the moles and the rats,
24 All the magpies and the crows.

May your sheep multiply
And the lambs that boldly play,
And may they grow without fault
28 [And be able] to shelter them[selves] from the icy [temperatures].

May your leeks flourish
And your beautiful red onions
And the white cabbage plants
32 And everything that is in your garden.

Coed 'falau a'r coed eirin,
Coed ffebris oll o'r bron
Ynghyd â'r goeden beren,
36   Boed crop go dda ar hon.

Peth penna' wy'n ddymuno
Dywedaf yw marn i,
Cael gras i lywodraethu
40   Pob enaid yn eich tŷ.

Pan byddoch yn cyfrannu
Doed bendith lawr o'r nen
A'ch gwna yn berffaith dduwiol,
44   Yw 'ngweddi byth. Amen.

?Samuel Thomas

Sources
NLW 23925E, f. 60[r].

Cwrtmawr 270B, ff. 26[v]–27[r].

Rhiannon Ifans, 'Canu Gwaseila yn y Gymraeg' [Welsh Wassailing] (PhD thesis, University of Wales [Aberystwyth], 1980), 2, 655–6.

Dafydd Ifans, 'Cerdd Galennig o ardal Trefeglwys' [A New Year's Day Song from the Trefeglwys area], *Canu Gwerin (Folk Song)*, 30 (2007), 83–5.

Variant reading
Title: there is no title in NLW 23925E, f. 60[r].

Date
7 December 1854.

Locality
Trefeglwys, Montgomeryshire.

[The] apple trees and the plum trees,
All the gooseberry bushes in their entirety
Together with the pear tree,
36   May it yield an excellent crop.

The main thing that I wish for
I shall tell you, [this is] my opinion,
Is that you have the grace to rule over
40   Each soul within your house.

When you distribute money
May a heavenly blessing descend
That will make you godly to perfection,
44   This is my eternal prayer. Amen.

?Samuel Thomas

Note

NLW 23925E, f. 60ʳ, is a collection of miscellaneous letters and papers that includes this poem, either composed or copied by Samuel Thomas of Gliniant, Trefeglwys in Montgomeryshire. On the back of this slip of paper is written, possibly in a different hand, 'Samuel Thomas his Paper Gliniant, Trefeglwys, December 7 1854'. According to Daniel Gruffydd Jones, Samuel Thomas would have been thirteen or fourteen years old at the time, 'oedran addas i ofyn calennig hwyrach' (a fitting age to request a New Year's gift possibly); see Dafydd Ifans, 'Cerdd Galennig o ardal Trefeglwys' [A New Year's Day Song from the Trefeglwys area], *Canu Gwerin (Folk Song)*, 30 (2007), 84.

    Cwrtmawr 270B, originally used as an arithmetic exercise book by Jane Richards (1794–1876) in 1807, later includes a variety of transcripts by her sister Mary Richards (1787–1877) of Darowen in Montgomeryshire; Mary has omitted one stanza and misremembered the running order of other stanzas. Both manuscripts originate from Montgomeryshire.

Metre

7.6.7.6.; the tune 'Royal William' has not survived; the words, however, can be sung to 'Calennig (1)'; see p. 173, repeating the second section for the concluding stanza.

14   Tôn 'Ymdaith Gwŷr Harlech'

Blwyddyn Newydd Dda, gyfeillion,
Rown i chwi o eigion calon
Nawr trwy ganu pêr alawon,
4   Blwyddyn Newydd Dda!
Yr hen flwyddyn a aeth heibio,
'R hyn oedd ynddi gas ei guddio,
Blwyddyn newydd wedi gwawrio,
8   Blwyddyn Newydd Dda!

Dienw

Sources

W. J. Davies, *Hanes Plwyf Llandyssul* [The History of Llandysul Parish] (Llandyssul: J. D. Lewis, 1896), p. 259.

David Thomas, OBE, Aberystwyth, Papers (NLW): 'Cardiganshire Schools Folklore Collection', 1918–*c.*1926, B64 Pontsian School, unpaged.

Date
Late nineteenth century, early twentieth century.

14 Tune 'The March of the Men of Harlech'

A Good New Year, friends,
Is what we wish you from the bottom of our hearts
Now as we sing melodious tunes,
4   A Good New Year!
The old year has passed away,
What it held has been concealed,
A new year has dawned,
8   A Good New Year!

Anonymous

Locality
Llandysul and Pontsian, and various areas in Ceredigion.

Measure
For the tune 'Ymdaith Gwŷr Harlech' see p. 183.

15 Calennig

Calennig i mi, calennig i'r ffon,
Calennig i'w fwyta'r noson hon;
Calennig i 'Nhad am glytio fy sgidiau,
4   Calennig i Mam am drwsio fy sanau.

Wel, dyma'r dydd Calan, O cofiwch y dydd,
A rhoddwch galennig o'ch calon yn rhydd;
Dydd cyntaf y flwyddyn, os rhoddwch yn hael
8   Bydd bendith ar bob dydd i chithau'n ddi-ffael.

Calennig i'r mistar, calennig i'r gwas,
Calennig i'r forwyn sy'n byw yn y plas,
Calennig i'r gŵr, calennig i'r wraig,
12   Calennig o arian i bob ysgolhaig.

Dienw

Source
Phyllis Kinney and Meredydd Evans, *Caneuon Gwerin i Blant* [Folk Songs for Children] ([Aberystwyth]: Cymdeithas Alawon Gwerin Cymru [Welsh Folk Song Society], 1981), p. 19.

Date
Not noted.

Locality
Not noted.

15 A New Year's gift

A New Year's gift for me, a New Year's gift for the stick,
A New Year's gift to eat this evening;
A New Year's gift for Father for repairing my shoes,
4   A New Year's gift for Mother for darning my socks.

Well, this is New Year's Day, O remember the day,
And give a New Year's gift freely from [the generosity of] your
       heart;
The first day of the year, if you give generously
8   Every day will be blessed for you without fail.

A New Year's gift for the master, a New Year's gift for the servant,
A New Year's gift for the female servant who lives in the mansion,
A New Year's gift for the husband, a New Year's gift for the wife,
12   A New Year's gift of money for every scholar.

Anonymous

Note
The three stanzas appear as one song in Kinney and Evans, *Caneuon Gwerin i Blant*, p. 19. They appear separately, however, in many sources. Stanza 3 was recorded in the Lampeter area and the mansion mentioned (line 10) may have been Peterwell; see Bethan Phillips, *Peterwell: The History of a Mansion and its Infamous Squire* (Llandysul: Gwasg Gomer, 1983).

Metre
11.11.11.11; see 'Calennig (2)', p. 174.

16   Cerdd Dydd Calan

Codais heddiw'n fore
I ddyfod at y tai
I mofyn am y geiniog
4   A chymryd pres o lai;
Gobeithio cyn mynd adre
O bres caf lawer iawn
Nes bydd fy nghod o arian
8   A bara a chaws yn llawn.
  C'lennig yn gyfan ar fore Dy' Calan,
  Unwaith, dwywaith, tair.

Toc o fara barlys
12   A gaing o'r cosyn coch –
Os hyn a gaf fi gennych
Yn hir yn byw y boch!
Ac os y rhowch galennig
16   Heblaw yr aing a'r toc,
Y penna peth a garwn
Yw ceiniog yn fy mhoc.
  C'lennig yn gyfan ar fore Dy' Calan,
20   Unwaith, dwywaith, tair.

Dienw

Sources
David de Lloyd, 'Forty Welsh Traditional Tunes', *Ceredigion: Journal of the Cardiganshire Antiquarian Society*, 6 (1929), pp. 56–7.

Ifans, *Sêrs a Rybana*, p. 99.

Kinney and Evans, *Caneuon Gwerin i Blant*, p. 21.

Date
Early twentieth century, possibly earlier.

16   A New Year's Day poem

Today I rose early
To visit the houses
To ask for pennies
4   And to accept [even] less money;
I hope before I return home
That I shall have lots of money,
Until my bag, of money
8   And bread and cheese, is full.
>   A New Year's gift in its entirety on the morning of New
>   Year's Day,
>   Once, twice, three [times].

A slice of barley bread
12   And a chunk of the red cheese –
If you give me these
May you live long!
And if you give a New Year's gift
16   In addition to the chunk [of cheese] and the slice [of bread],
The thing I would most love to have
Is a penny in my pocket.
>   A New Year's gift in its entirety on the morning of New
>   Year's Day,
20   >   Once, twice, three [times].

Anonymous

Locality
Ceredigion.

Metre
7.6.7.6.D; chorus: 11.5; see 'Cerdd Dydd Calan', p. 175 and 'Calennig (1)',
p. 173.

17 Deffrowch!

Deffrowch, ben teili, dima flwyddyn newi
Wedi dŵad adre o fiwn ein drwse,
Drwse yng nghâ, ynghlo dros y nos.
4 Drwy'r baw a thrwy'r llaca y daethon ni ima,
Drwy'r eithin weithe dan bigo'n coese,
Dima'n bwriad ninne, mofyn bobo ddime;
Bwriad trwy gariad, rhoddwch heb gennad,
8 Paste nas torrwch, cwrw nas sbariwch,
Plant ifanc i'n ni, gollingwch ni'r tŷ,
Gollingwch ni'n gloi 'te tima ni'n ttoi.

Dienw

Sources
D. Rhys Phillips Papers 143 (NLW), 'Folklore of Dyfed', p. 62.

E. Llwyd Williams, *Crwydro Sir Benfro* [Roaming Pembrokeshire] (Llandybïe: Llyfrau'r Dryw, 1960), 2, p. 74.

Date
Recorded *c*.1910.

17 Awake!

Wake up, head of the household, here is a new year
Come home within our doors,
Doors shut, locked overnight.
4   Through the mire and through mud we have come here,
Sometimes through the gorse and stinging our legs,
This is our intention, to request a halfpenny each;
An intent born of love, give excessively,
8   Don't cut up a pie, don't spare beer,
We are young children, let us into the house,
Let us in quickly or we shall run away.

Anonymous

Locality
Gwaun Valley, Pembrokeshire.

Metre
Tôn deuair, for an example of a *tôn deuair* tune see 'Deffrwch! Ben-teulu', p. 178.

18 [Dideitl]

Good morning, good morning,
Gyfeillion mwyn a llon,
Sut ydych yma'n teimlo
4   Ers blwyddyn gyfan gron?
Mi fues yma llynedd –
Mi gefais docyn braf,
Rwy'n credu'n gryfach 'leni
8   Mai llawer mwy a gaf.

Os gwell yw gennych roddi
Y copor coch ei liw,
Derbyniaf ef yn llawen
12   O law y rhoddwr gwiw.
Dymunaf wrth ymadael
Wir fendith Duw i'ch rhan
A'm calon hael, agored
16   I gofio'r tlawd a'r gwan.

Dienw

Sources
David Thomas, OBE, Aberystwyth, Papers (NLW): 'Cardiganshire Schools
Folklore Collection', 1918–c.1926, B15 Capel Cynon School, unpaged.
Ifans, *Sêr a Rybana*, p. 98.

Date
Early twentieth century, possibly earlier.

18   [Untitled]

Good morning, good morning,
Amiable and merry friends,
How have you been
4   Throughout this whole year in its entirety?
I was here last year –
I was given a substantial slice of bread,
I believe even more strongly this year
8   That I shall be given much more.

If you prefer to give
A copper, red in colour,
I shall receive it merrily
12   From the hand of the worthy giver.
As I leave, I wish
God's true blessing upon you
And my generous, expansive heart
16   To remember the poor and the frail.

Anonymous

Locality
Capel Cynon, south Ceredigion.

Metre
7.6.7.6.D.

19 Calennig

Chwi sy'n meddu aur ac arian
Dedwydd ydych ar Ddydd Calan;
Braint y rhai yw rhoi i'r tlodion
4   A chyfrannu peth o'u moddion.

Mae'r rhew a'r eira yn bur oeredd
A'r awel fain pan ddaw o'r gogledd,
Ond ni goeliwn gyda'n gilydd
8   Mai oerach peth yw calon cybydd.

Â ambell gybydd oddi cartre
Yn lle rhannu ei geinioge,
Llall a lecha yn ei gaban
12   Gan wneud ei gilwg ar Ddydd Calan.

Yr hwn sydd â chyfoeth ac a'i ceidw,
Nid oes lwyddiant i'r dyn hwnnw;
Y neb a gadwo bob rhyw geiniog
16   Sydd yn casglu i'r god dyllog.

Am eich rhoddion trwy'r blynyddau
Rŷm yn diolch o'n calonnau;
Rŷch yn enwog am gyfrannu,
20   Na ddiffygiwch eto eleni.

Dyma'r Calan wedi gwawrio,
Dydd tra hynod, dydd i'w gofio;
Dydd i rannu, dydd i dderbyn
24   Ydyw'r cyntaf yn y flwyddyn.

Dienw

Source
David Thomas, OBE, Aberystwyth, Papers (NLW): 'Cardiganshire Schools
Folklore Collection', 1918–*c*.1926, B72 Talybont School, unpaged.

Date
Early twentieth century, possibly earlier.

19 New Year's gift

You who possess gold and silver
Are happy on New Year's Day;
It is their privilege to give to the poor
4   And to contribute some of their means.

The ice and the snow are quite chilly
And the keen wind when it blows from the north,
But we are in agreement
8   That a miser's heart is a colder matter.

The occasional miser will leave home
Rather than share his pennies,
Another hides in his cabin
12   And scowls on New Year's Day.

He who has riches and retains his hold on them,
There is no prosperity for that man;
The one who retains possession of every penny
16   Gathers into a bag full of holes.

For your gifts throughout the years
We give thanks from our hearts;
You are renowned for your contributions,
20   Do not fall short this year again.

New Year's Day has dawned,
A most remarkable day, a day to remember;
Is is a day to share, a day to receive,
24   The first of the year.

Anonymous

Locality
Tal-y-bont, Ceredigion.

Metre
Hen bennill with a little fluidity in several lines.

20 [Dideitl]

Os oes gennych ddime
O dowch â hi allan,
Mae popeth yn werthfawr
4   I mi bore Calan.
Agorwch, agorwch,
Rwyf yma fy hunan,
Bydd cryn hanner dwsin
8   Yn galw yn fuan;
Rwyf wedi cael falau
A minceg yn barod,
Rhowch rywbeth heb oedi –
12   Mae'r bore bron darfod.

Dienw

Sources
Nansi Hayes, 'Hen Benillion Calan' [Old Verses for New Year's Day], *Y Tincer* [The Tinker] (January 1979), unpaged.
Ifans, *Sêrs a Rybana*, p. 99.

Date
1920s.

20   [Untitled]

If you have a halfpenny
O please bring it out,
Everything is of value
4   To me on New Year's morning.
Open up, open up,
I'm here on my own,
A good half dozen
8   Will call very soon;
I have been given apples
And sweets (lit. mint cake) already,
Give something at once –
12   The morning is almost over.

Anonymous

Locality
South Ceredigion; Nansi Hayes (née Lewis) is originally from the
Llandysul area.

Metre
Tôn deuair.

21 [Dideitl]

Plant bach Cymru ydym ni
Yn canu ein carolau,
Peidiwch chwi â gyrru'r ci
4   I redeg ar ein holau.
Blwyddyn Newydd Dda i chwi
A phawb o'ch teulu serchog,
Dewch, benteulu, atom ni
8   A rhowch inni geiniog.

Dienw

Source
Hayes, 'Hen Benillion Calan', unpaged.

Date
1920s.

Locality
South Ceredigion; Nansi Hayes (née Lewis) is originally from the Llandysul area.

21 [Untitled]

We are the little children of Wales
Singing our carols,
Don't set the dog
4   On us.
A Good New Year to you
And to each one of your genial family,
Come to us, head of the family,
8   And give us a penny.

Anonymous

Metre
7.7.7.7.D, with some fluidity in line 8. On 13 January 2021, as Wales was in lockdown because of the worldwide COVID-19 pandemic, the stanza was sung online by the children of Gwaun Valley to the tune 'Good King Wenceslas'.

22 Cân Calennig: cân 'Y Mochyn Du'

Wele eto flwyddyn newydd
Ar y ddôl ac ar y mynydd,
Blwyddyn lawn o bob bendithion
4 Fyddo hon i chwi gyfeillion.

    Byrdwn: Blwyddyn lon fyddo hon,
              Blwyddyn lon fyddo hon,
              Rhowch galennig inni'n ddiddig
8   A chewch Flwyddyn Newydd lon.

Eich ceffylau fydd yn dewion,
Oll eich gwartheg fydd yn rhadlon,
Fe fydd gwledd o gaws a menyn
12 Ar eich bwrdd o fewn y flwyddyn.

Chwi gewch iechyd a chysuron,
Ni chewch ddannodd na gwynegon,
Ni chewch boen na gofid 'leni
16 Os y rhowch galennig inni.

Chwi gewch dywydd da nodedig
Yn y Gwanwyn i aredig;
Rhwng yr heulwen a'r cawodau
20 Chwi gewch lond y tir o ffrwythau.

Bydd eich geir yn dodwy wyau
Fwy o faint na wyau gwyddau,
Chwi gewch amser bendigedig
24 Os y rhowch galennig inni.

Ni ddaw rhew i rewi'ch tato,
Ni ddaw'r cadno i'ch ysbeilio,
Chwi gewch lonydd gan y llygod,
28 Gan y lladron a'r curyllod.

22 A New Year's Day song: the song 'Y Mochyn Du'

See here once more a new year
On the meadow and on the mountain,
A year full of every blessing
4   May this be for you, [my] friends.

> *Chorus:*   May this be a happy year,
> May this be a happy year,
> Be pleased to give us a New Year's gift
> 8   And you will have a happy New Year.

Your horses will be in good flesh/sturdy,
All your cattle will be docile,
There will be a feast of cheese and butter
12   On your table throughout the year.

You will have good health and comforts,
You will not suffer from toothache or arthritis,
You will have no pain or sorrow this year
16   If you give us a New Year's gift.

You will have exceptionally fine weather
For ploughing in the Spring;
What with the sunshine and the showers
20   You will obtain produce from a land filled to capacity.

Your hens will lay eggs
That are bigger than goose eggs,
You will have a wonderful time
24   If you give us a New Year's gift.

There will be no frost damage to your potatoes,
The fox will not come to rob you,
The mice will leave you alone,
28   So too the thieves and the hawks.

Cewch bris uchel am eich nwyddau,
Am y defaid a'r ceffylau;
Chwi gewch fynd am fis o wyliau
32 I Ben-dein neu Abertawe.

Boed eich llwybrau yn diferi
Gan bob cyfoeth a daioni;
Llechu gafoch dan adenydd
36 Engyl nef drwy'r flwyddyn newydd.

Dienw

Source
D. Roy Saer, personal file.

Date
Not noted.

Locality
Crosswell (near Crymych, Pembrokeshire) or Llanfallteg (Carmarthenshire).

You will receive high prices for your produce,
For the sheep and the horses;
You can go for a month's holiday
32   To Pendine or Swansea.

May your paths be dripping
With all manner of wealth and goodness:
May you be allowed to shelter under the wings
36   Of the angels of heaven throughout the New Year.

Anonymous

Note
The song was recorded from the singing of Mrs Marian James, Tŷ Hen,
Rhos-hill, Cardigan, on 28 September 1971. She was originally from
Crosswell, but it is possible that she learned the song from her mother
who was from Llanfallteg.

Metre
For the popular ballad tune 'Y Mochyn Du' see p. 181.

23 [Dideitl]

Y mae'r eira heno'n oer,
Y mae'r gwynt yn chwythu,
Ninnau'n canu dan y lloer
4   Ydym, bron â sythu.
O rhowch geiniog fach i mi
Sy tu fâs yn canu –
Blwyddyn Newydd Dda i chwi
8   Fydd yn dâl amdani.

Dienw

Sources
Hayes, 'Hen Benillion Calan', unpaged.
Ifans, *Sêrs a Rybana*, p. 100.

Date
1920s.

Locality
South Ceredigion; Nansi Hayes (née Lewis) is originally from the Llandysul area.

23   [Untitled]

The snow is cold tonight,
The wind is blowing,
We are singing beneath the moon,
4   Yes, almost stiff with cold.
O give me a little penny,
I who am singing outside –
A Good New Year to you,
8   That will be your reward for it.

Anonymous

Note
Even though lines 3–4 note the presence of more than one singer, lines
5–6 make a personal plea for a gift.

Metre
7.6.7.6.D.

Wren Hunt Wassail Songs

24 Cân y Wasael

Allan: Gyfeillion mwynion tawel sydd dan yr adail wych,
   Deffrowch, gwrandewch yn dirion ar sain penillion gwych;
   Gerbron y ddôr, gan gywrain gôr, 'nôl i chwi agor draw,
4 Cewch gyda ni newyddion pereiddlon maes o law.

Mewn: Atolwg pwy sydd yna yr amser hyn o'r nos,
   A'r drysau wedi eu bario a'u bolltio fyny'n glòs,
   A minnau yn fy ngwely, chwi hel'soch arnaf aeth,
8 Tua ph'le ry'ch chwi'n trafaelu, y glân gwmpeini ffraeth?

Allan: Mae yma fwyn gyn'lleidfa ddaeth o Sermania draw,
   A chennym beraroglau a llwythau ym mhob llaw;
   Y Wasael bur a hyfryd fir ŷm ni'n ei ddifyr ddwyn,
12 At iechyd cyntaf yfo tu fewn i Frydain fwyn.

Mewn: Arhoswch yma ronyn, 'rwy'n chwennych pledio sias,
   Pa beth yw'r arfer honno? Pwy 'rhoddodd gynta i maes?
   Os dyma'r iechyd hynaf, pa fodd mae'r peth yn bod?
16 Pwy oedd yr un a yfodd y Wasael gynta erio'd?

Allan: Enw'r eneth burwen oedd Rhonwen loyw-wen lân,
   Gynt at Gwrtheyrn pan yfodd hi a'i parchodd yn y bla'n,
   'Nôl arfer gwlad y *Dutchmen* yn gywrain ddiwahân,
20 '*Dutch-Health*' oedd enw'r *Wassail* fwyn araul deg o'r bla'n.

Mewn: Pa beth, wŷr da, a ddygwch, mynegwch yn ddi-o'd,
   Os gennych mae rhialtwch, chwi haeddech barch a chlod;
   Mynegwch im heb amau pa bethau y'ch yn ddwyn,
24 Fel hyn gwnewch fy moddloni, y glân gwmpeini mwyn.

24 Wassail song

Outside: Noble tranquil friends who are under [the roof of] the
          splendid building,
          Wake up, listen kindly to the sound of excellent stanzas;
          In the doorway, [sung] by a skilled choir, after you have
          opened there,
4   We shall give you melodious news in due course.

Inside: I beseech you, who is there at this time of night,
          When the doors are barred and bolted securely
          And I in bed, you sent terror [down my spine],
8   Where are you going, eloquent good company?

Outside: There is here a noble gathering that has come from
          Germany yonder,
          And we bear scents and [full] loads in each hand;
          We bear with pleasure the good Wassail and lovely beer
12   To toast the health of the first person in noble Britain who
          ever drank [it].

Inside: Wait here a while, I wish to debate a challenge,
          What is that custom? Who first established it?
          If this is the oldest toast, how did the matter come about?
16   Who was the one who for the first time ever drank the Wassail?

Outside: The name of the pure and holy maiden was Rowena,
          of a bright white [complexion and] good,
          In times past, when she drank to Vortigen's health, she was
          the first to drink to his health,
          In accordance with the precise, unbroken custom of the land
          of the Dutchmen
20   The Wassail, noble bright and fine, was previously called
          'Dutch-Health'.

Inside: What do you bear, good men, state it without delay,
          If you bring merrymaking you deserve respect and praise;
          Tell me truly what things you bear,
24   In this way you will please me, noble good company.

Allan: Mae gennym elor hynod, a drywod dan y llen,
          A pherllan wych o afalau yn gyplau uwch ei phen;
          A *nutmeg* beth, a *spices* beth, ac ambell eneth wen,
28   Chwi gewch gusanu fynnoch, ni yngan air o'i phen.

Mewn: O braf 'ry'ch chwi yn addo, yn wir mi godaf lawr,
          Mi gadwaf eich cwmpeini o'r awron hyd y wawr;
          Os oes yna ferched ieuainc yng nghwmp'ni'r annwyl ddyn,
32   Mi gymraf un o'r rheini i eistedd ar fy nghlun.

Allan: Mae yma i chwi'ch dewis o ferched hoenus iach,
          'Tifeddesi tirion tawel a breiniol uchel ach,
          Cewch gofleidio a chusanu nes bo ar frig y dydd,
36   A mynd â hi i'r gwely os yn boddloni bydd.

Mewn: O da 'r y'ch chwi'n promeisio, y glân gymdeithion tlws,
          Mi godaf nawr yn fuan, mi dynnaf follt y drws;
          Yr ydych yna ers meitin yn aros ar y twyn,
40   Fe allai yr agorwn ond i chwi fod yn fwyn.

Allan: Ni a fyddwn fwyn a chywir gwmpeini difyr dwys,
          I gynnal yn ddigynnen un noson lawen lwys;
          Gyfeillion glân sy o ddeutu'r tân, anfonwch ŵr y tŷ
44   I agor i ni ar fyrder, onid e dychwelwn ni.

Mewn: Atolwg, na ddychwelwch, ond sefwch yma'n ewn,
          Mae gŵr y tŷ'n cenhadu i chwi gael rhodio i mewn,
          Mae yna'n o'r gerbron y ddôr i'r hyfryd wiwgor gu,
48   Mae i chwi gyflawn roeso i rodio mewn i'r tŷ.

Yna yr agorir y drws, a'r cyfeillion a fyddont yn dwyn y Wassail, pan ddeuant i'r tŷ, a ganant y pennill canlynol:

          Trwy'ch cennad chwi heno, gwmpeini mwyn glân,
          Gadewch in gael tân i ymdwymo,
          A mwgaid o gwrw, na ddywedwch ddim llai,
52   Onid e mi foddlona i fod hebddo;

Outside: We have a remarkable bier, with wrens beneath the sheet,
And an excellent orchard of apples in couples above it;
And some nutmeg, and some spices, and some beautiful girls,
28   You may kiss whomever you wish, she will not speak a word.

Inside: O you promise well, indeed I shall get up and come downstairs,
I shall keep company with you from this hour until dawn;
If there are young girls in the company of the dear man
32   I shall take one of those to sit on my lap.

Outside: There is here your choice of vivacious, carefree girls,
Quiet, tender heiresses and noble high-ranking lineage,
You may hug and kiss until daybreak,
36   And take her to bed if she consents.

Inside: O you promise well, good [and] attractive fellow-travellers,
I shall get up swiftly now, I shall pull open the bolt of the door;
You have been waiting there, out in plain sight, for a good while,
40   It is possible that I shall open [the door] if you would only
be courteous.

Outside: We shall be a courteous and true company, agreeable [and]
solemn,
As we hold a pleasant evening of informal entertainment,
without contention;
Fine friends who are [seated] around the fire, send the master
of the house
44   To open up quickly, otherwise we shall return [home].

Inside: I beseech you, do not return [home] but stay here confidently,
The master of the house permits you to walk inside,
It is cold out there in the doorway for the delightful choir,
excellent and precious,
48   You are most welcome to walk into the house.

Then the door is opened, and the friends who bear the Wassail, when they enter the house, sing the following stanza:

With your permission this evening, noble good company,
Allow us to [come to] the fire to warm ourselves,
And [give us] a mug of beer, do not suggest anything less
52   Or I shall be content to live without it;

Rhowch i mi'n ddi-nag o burion ffrwyth brag,
Pe siawnsiai i mi feddwi a cholli 'Nghymr'ag,
Ac yfed y cwrw a'r faril yn wag
56   A'r gwaddod i'r gwragedd sy'n tendio.

Gwedi treulio y nos mewn llawenydd, yn yfed a bwyta'r Wassail, wrth ymadael, gyda'r dydd, cenir pennill o ffarwél fel y canlyn:

Hir einioes a hir ddyddiau, a hir flynyddau hardd,
A gaffoch i fyw'n ffrwythlon fel pur blanhigion gardd,
Gael gweled plant ac wyrion yn llawnion yn un llu,
60   A dyma ni'n ymadael, ffarwél, yn iach i chi!

Dienw

Sources

Hugh Hughes, *Yr Hynafion Cymreig: neu, Hanes am draddodiadau, defodau, ac ofergoelion yr hen Gymry* [The Antiquities of Wales: or, A history of the traditions, rites, and superstitions of the old Welsh people] (Caerfyrddin [Carmarthen]: J. Evans, 1823), pp. 239–42.

T. H. Parry-Williams, *Llawysgrif Richard Morris o Gerddi* [Richard Morris's Manuscript of Poems] (Cardiff: University of Wales Press, 1931), pp. cvi–cviii.

Rhiannon Ifans, *Sêrs a Rybana: Astudiaeth o'r Canu Gwasael* [Stars and Ribbons: A Study of Wassailing] (Llandysul: Gwasg Gomer, 1983), pp. 145–7.

Date
Pre-1823.

Locality
The dialect suggests south Wales.

Note
The song is preceded by the following note of introduction written by Hugh Hughes:

Hen arferiad yn mhlith y Cymry, ar Nos-Wyl Ystwyll, oedd gwneuthur y WASSAIL, sef teiseni ac afalau gwedi eu pobi, a'u gosod ar

Give me the neat ale without refusal,
Even if perhaps I become drunk and lose my Welsh,
And drink the beer until the barrel is empty
56   And [give] the dregs to the women who tend [us].

After spending the evening in merriment, eating and drinking the Was-
sail, upon departure, at daybreak, a farewell stanza is sung as follows:

Long life and old age, and many beautiful years
May you have to live in fecundity as pure garden plants,
So that you may see children and grandchildren teeming
          in great numbers,
60   And now we depart, farewell, fare you well!

Anonymous

eu gilydd yn rhestri, a sugr rhyngddynt, mewn math o ffiol hardd a
luniesid at yr achos, yr hon a gynnwys ddeuddeg o ddolenau; yna
rhoddent gwrw twym, cymmysgedig â llysiau poethion yr India,
yn y Wassail, y cyfeillion a eisteddent yn gylch crwn gerllaw'r tân,
a chyflwynent ffiol y Wassail o law i law, a phob un a yfai o honi
yn gylchynawl, ac yn olaf rhenid y Wassail (sef y teiseni a'r afalau,
wedi yfed y ddiod oddiarnynt) rhwng yr holl gwmpeini.

Ar Nos-Wyl Ystwyll y dygent y Wassail i dŷ gŵr a gwraig a fyddent
newydd briodi, neu deulu newydd symud o un annedd i'r llall.
Amryw o feibion a merched o'r gymmydogaeth a ddygent y Was-
sail hyd ddrws tŷ y rhagddywededig, ac a ddechreuent ganu y tu
allan i'r drws, yr hwn a fyddai wedi ei gau; yna un neu ychwaneg
o dylwyth y tŷ oddifewn a'u hattebent bob yn ail Bennill, fel y
gwelwch yn y Gân ganlynol.

[An old custom among the Welsh people, on the eve of the feast of
Epiphany, was to fashion the Wassail, that is cakes and baked apples,
and to place them one upon the other in layers, with sugar between
them, in a kind of beautiful cup created for the occasion, which cup
has twelve handles; then they put hot ale, mixed with Indian spices,
into the Wassail, the friends sit in a circle by the fire, and offer the
Wassail cup from hand to hand, each one drinking from it in turn, and

lastly the Wassail was shared (that is the cakes and the apples, having drunk the liquor from them) among the whole company.

On the eve of the feast of Epiphany they carry the Wassail to the house of a man and wife who are recently married, or a family who has recently moved from one dwelling-place to another. Many young men and women from the neighbourhood carry the Wassail to the door of the aforementioned house, and start to sing outside the door, which door would be closed; then one or more of the family inside the house would answer them every other stanza, as you see in the following song.]

This song raises several interesting points. It is unique within the Welsh wren-hunt tradition in that it is the only example of *punco* (the contest

25 Dibyn a Dobyn

'Ddoi di i'r coed?' meddai Dibyn wrth Dobyn,
'Ddoi di i'r coed?' meddai Risiart wrth Robin,
'A ddoi di i'r coed?' meddai John wrth y tri,
4   'A ddoi di i'r coed?' meddai'r cwbwl i gyd.

2. Beth wnawn ni yno?

3. Hela'r Dryw bach.

4. Beth wnawn ni ag eddo?

5. Ei werthu am swllt.

6. Beth wnawn ni â swllt?

7. Ei wario am gwrw.

8. Beth tae ni'n meddwi?

in song to gain access to the home) during the wren ritual; another element not in keeping with the wren hunt is the fact that women form part of the wassailing party outside the door (lines 27–8, 31–6). It raises questions as to whether this is a genuine wren-ritual song, even though line 25 states clearly that the company is escorting a wren (more than one) on a bier. The song in general, however, echoes the Christmastide or *Gŵyl Fair* wassailing songs.

Metre

Stanzas 1, 3, 5, 7, 9, 11, 12:	13.13.14.13.
Stanzas 2, 4, 6, 8, 10:	13.13.13.13.
Lines 49–56:	11.9.11.9.10.11.11.9.
Lines 57–60:	13.13.13.13.

25 Dibyn and Dobyn

'Will you come to the woods?' said Dibyn to Dobyn,
'Will you come to the woods?' said Risiart to Robin,
'Will you come to the woods?' said John to the three,
4   'Will you come to the woods?' said all of them.

2. What shall we do there?

3. Hunt the little Wren.

4. What shall we do with him?

5. Sell him for a shilling.

6. What shall we do with a shilling?

7. Spend it on beer.

8. What if we became drunk?

9. (...)

10. Beth tae ni'n marw?

11. (...)

12. Ple caem ein claddu?

13. Ym mhwll y domen.

Dienw

Source
[Lewis Davies Jones] Llew Tegid, 'Hunting the Wren', *Cylchgrawn Cymdeithas Alawon Gwerin Cymru/Journal of the Welsh Folk-Song Society*, 1 (1911), 107.

Date
Not noted.

Locality
Llanrhaeadr-ym-Mochnant, north Powys.

Metre
For the tune 'Dibyn a Dobyn' see p. 178; the only variant in a minor key 'Cân Hela'r Dryw' (see p. 174) 'was noted from the singing of Mostyn Lewis in 1976; he had learned it from his father's cousin who lived at Ruthin in Denbighshire and sang it often in the early years of the 20th century. There is a strong Welsh flavour about the tune; it has a narrow 5-note compass'; see Phyllis Kinney and Meredydd Evans, *Canu'r Cymry 1 a 2* [Songs of the Welsh People 1 and 2] ([Aberystwyth]: Cymdeithas Alawon Gwerin Cymru [Welsh Folk Song Society], 2014), pp. 112–13. Variant words:

> Ble rwyt ti'n mynd? medda Dibyn wrth Dobyn,
> Ble rwyt ti'n mynd? medda Risiart wrth Robin,
> Ble rwyt ti'n mynd? medda John,
> Ble rwyt ti'n mynd? medda'r Nefar Beyond.

9. (...)

10. What if we die?

11. (...)

12. Where would we be buried?

13. In the dunghill pit.

Anonymous

Rwy'n mynd tua'r coed, medda Dibyn wrth Dobyn (...)

Be wnei di yno? medda Dibyn wrth Dobyn (...)

Lladd y dryw bach, medda Dibyn wrth Dobyn (...)

Hefo be lladdi di o? medda Dibyn wrth Dobyn (...)

Hefo twca a myniawyd, medda Dibyn wrth Dobyn (...)

[Where are you going? said Dibyn to Dobyn,
Where are you going? said Risiart to Robin,
Where are you going? said John,
Where are you going? said the Never Beyond.

I'm going towards the woods, said Dibyn to Dobyn (...)

What will you do there? said Dibyn to Dobyn (...)

Kill the little wren, said Dibyn to Dobyn (...)

What will you kill it with? said Dibyn to Dobyn (...)

With cleaver and awl, said Dibyn to Dobyn (...)]

26 The Cutty Wren

'O! where are you going?' says Milder to Melder,
'O! where are you going?' says the younger to the elder,
'O! I cannot tell you,' says Festel to Fose,
4   'We're going to the woods,' says John the Red Nose.

2. O! what will you do there? | Shoot the Cutty Wren.

3. O! what will you shoot her with? | With bows and with arrows.

4. O! that will not do. | With great guns and cannons.

5. O! what will you bring her home in? | On four strong men's
   shoulders.

6. O! that will not do. | On big carts and wagons.

7. What will you cut her up with? | With knives and with forks.

8. O! that will not do. | With hatchets and cleavers.

9. What will you boil her in? | In pots and in kettles.

10. O! that will not do. | In brass pans and cauldrons.

Anonymous

Sources
G. P. W. Scott, *Tales and Traditions of Tenby* (Tenby: R. Mason,
1858), pp. 13–15.
Llew Tegid, 'Hunting the Wren', 105.

Date
Not noted.

Locality
Tenby, Pembrokeshire.

Note
An English-language wren song sung in Pembrokeshire.

Metre
For the tune see p. 176.

27   The Song of the Wren

Joy, health, love, and peace   be to you in this place.
By your leave we will sing   concerning our king:

Our king is well dressed   in silks of the best;
4   With his ribbons so rare   no king can compare.

In his coach he does ride   with a great deal of pride;
And with four footmen   to wait upon him.

We were four at watch   and all nigh of a match;
8   And with powder and ball   we fired at his hall.

We have travelled many miles   over hedges and stiles
To find you this king   whom we now to you bring.

Now Christmas is past   Twelfth Day is the last.
12   Th' Old Year bids adieu   great joy to the New.

Anonymous

Sources
J. Tombs, 'Twelfth-Day', *Notes and Queries*, Series 3, 5 (1864), 109.
AWC Tape Archive 6508 (song incomplete).

Date
Pre-1864.

Locality
Pembrokeshire.

Note
An English-language wren song sung in Pembrokeshire.

Metre
Tôn deuair.

Mari Lwyd Wassail Songs

28 'Hyd yma bu'n cerdded', Song sung after the Wassail

Hyd yma bu'n cerdded,
Gyfeillion diniwed,
Hyd yma bu'n cerdded,
4   Gyfeillion diniwed,
A phawb yn ymddiried
Cael canu.

Os eithoch yn gynnar
8   I'r gwely'n ddialar,
Os eithoch yn gynnar
I'r gwely'n ddialar,
O codwch i'n hawddgar
12   Roesawi.

Pwy fwstwr, pwy fraban
Sy o gwmpas fy nghaban,
Pwy fwstwr, pwy fraban
16   Sy o gwmpas fy nghaban
'Run llais â dylluan
Ddimennydd?

Rhowch glywed yn ddiau
20   Beth y'ch chwi'n rhoi'ch enwau,
Rhowch glywed yn ddiau
Beth y'ch chwi'n rhoi'ch enwau;
Gadewch ni'n ein teiau
24   Yn llonydd.

Dienw

28 'Hyd yma bu'n cerdded', Song sung after the Wassail

She has travelled this far,
Innocent friends,
She has travelled this far,
4   Innocent friends,
And everyone trusting
That permission will be granted to sing.

If you went early
8   To bed without a care,
If you went early
To bed without a care,
O get up to kindly
12   Welcome us.

What muster, what chatter
Is about my small cottage,
What muster, what chatter
16   Is about my small cottage
Similar to the voice of an owl
Without brains?

Sincerely, let us know
20   Your names,
Sincerely, let us know
Your names;
Leave us alone in our homes
24   In peace.

Anonymous

Source
Maria Jane Williams, *Ancient National Airs of Gwent and Morganwg (...) with Introduction and notes on the songs by Daniel Huws* (Llandovery, 1844; facsimile reprint Aberystwyth: Cymdeithas Alawon Gwerin Cymru [Welsh Folk Song Society], 1994), p. 31, notes by Daniel Huws, pp. [16–17].

Date
Nineteenth century.

Locality
South Wales.

29 Y Pwnco: Y Sialens a'r Ateb

Mari Lwyd: Wel, dyma ni'n dŵad,
                     Gyfeillion diniwed,
                     I 'mofyn am genad – i ganu.

4 Yr Atebydd: Rhowch glywed, wŷr doethion,
                     Pa faint y'ch o ddynion,
                     A pheth yn wych union – yw'ch enwau.

Mari Lwyd: Chwech o wŷr hawddgar,
8   Rhai gorau ar y ddaear,
                     I ganu mewn gwirair – am gwrw.

Yr Atebydd: Rhowch glywed, wŷr difrad,
                     O ble rŷch chwi'n dŵad
12   A pheth yw'ch gofyniad – gaf enwi?

Mari Lwyd: Mae ffasiwn conselau
                     Er's mil o flynyddau
                     A hynny mewn ffurfiau – gwna' brofi.

Note
Stanzas 1–2 were heard by Maria Jane Williams (c.1795–1873); stanzas
3–4 are additional stanzas sent to Maria Jane Williams by Taliesin Wil-
liams 'Taliesin ab Iolo' (1787–1847) 'from imperfect memory'; see Wil-
liams, *Ancient National Airs of Gwent and Morganwg*, p. [17].

Metre
'The metre of these stanzas is based on the *cyhydedd hir*, a metre popular
among the medieval *clêr* (or unofficial poets) and subsequently among
the *cwndidwyr*, composing in free metre, in the sixteenth and seventeenth
centuries', Daniel Huws, in Williams, *Ancient National Airs of Gwent and
Morganwg*, p. [17]; for the tune 'Hyd yma bu'n cerdded' see p. 179.

29 The *Pwnco*: The Challenge and the Reply

Mari Lwyd:	Well, here we come, Innocent friends, To ask permission – to sing.
4 Respondent:	Let us hear, wise men, How many men are [out] there, And what exactly – are your names.
Mari Lwyd: 8	Six amiable men, The best in the world, [Here] to sing in true words – for beer.
Respondent: 12	Let us hear, honest men, Where you come from And what your request is, if I may ask?
Mari Lwyd:	The fashion of wassailing [Has been in existence] for a thousand years And that in [customary] forms – I shall prove [it].

16 Yr Atebydd: Mi gwnnais o'r gwely
                Gan lwyr benderfynu
                Y gwnawn i dy faeddu – di'n foddus.

Mari Lwyd: Cenwch eich gorau,
20   Felly gwnaf finnau,
                A'r sawl a fo orau – gaiff gwrw.

Yr Atebydd: 'Dyw gwiw i chwi'n sgwto
                A chwnnu'r lats heno,
24   Waith prydydd diguro – wyf, gwiriaf.

Mari Lwyd: Mae'm dawn i'n cynhyrfu
                Wrth feddwl am ganu
                Y nos yn y gwely – mi goeliaf.

28 Yr Atebydd: I ffwrdd â chwi'r lladron,
                Ewch ymaith yn union,
                Ni chewch chwi yn hylon – fy ngweled.

Mari Lwyd: Mi ganaf am wythnos,
32   A hefyd am bythefnos,
                A mis, os bydd achos – baidd i chwi.

Yr Atebydd: Mi ganaf am flwyddyn
                Os caf Dduw i'm ca'lyn
36   Heb ofni un gelyn – y Gwyliau.

Mari Lwyd: O tapwch y faril,
                Gollyngwch yn rhugyl,
                Na fyddwch ry gynnil – i ganwyr.

40 Yr Atebydd: Mae Jenkins y 'Ffeiriad
                Yn dyfod, ar f'enaid,
                A gwna fe i chwi fyned – o f'annedd.

Mari Lwyd: Mae Mari Lwyd lawen
44   Am ddod i'ch tŷ'n rhonden
                A chanu yw ei diben – mi dybiaf.

Dienw

16 Respondent: I got out of bed
Fully determined
To defeat you – commendably.

Mari Lwyd: Sing your utmost,
20   I shall do the same,
And whoever is best – shall have beer.

Respondent: You would not dare run to and fro
And lift the latch [of my house] tonight,
24   Because I am an unsurpassable poet – I declare.

Mari Lwyd: My talent is aroused
As I think of singing
At night in bed – I trust.

28 Respondent: Away with you, thieves,
Go away at once,
You shall not with exceeding joy – see me.

Mari Lwyd: I shall sing for a week,
32   And for a fortnight too,
And a month, if need be – a challenge for you.

Respondent: I shall sing for a year
If God is at my side
36   Without fearing one enemy – this Christmastide.

Mari Lwyd: O tap the barrel,
Let [the beer] flow freely,
Do not be ungenerous – to singers.

40 Respondent: Jenkins the clergyman
Is coming, upon my soul,
And he will make you depart – from my home.

Mari Lwyd: Merry Mari Lwyd
44   Wants to come into your house in a heap
And her intention is to sing – I believe.

Anonymous

Sources

William Roberts 'Nefydd', *Crefydd yr Oesoedd Tywyll* [The Religion of the Dark Ages] (Caerfyrddin [Carmarthen]: printed by A. Williams, 1852), p. 16. For variants see Charles Ashton, 'Bywyd Gwledig yng Nghymru' [Rural Life in Wales], *Transactions of the National Eisteddfod of Wales, Bangor, 1890* (Liverpool: The National Eisteddfod Association, 1892), pp. 71–2.

30 Cân y Warsel

Wel, dyma enw'r feinwen
Sy'n codi gyda'r seren,
A dyma'r Warsel ore'i chlod
4   Sy'n canu a bod yn llawen.

Mae'r Warsel wedi'i 'phwyntio
Erioed i gael ei chario;
A'ch ffrind a'ch cyfaill ar eu taith
8   Gael hala'r noswaith heno.

Wel, dyma'r ddysgyl g'redig
A 'bwyntiwyd erbyn N'dolig,
A'i sŵn a'i sain sy'n mynd ymhell,
12   A beth sy'n well na chlennig?

O dewch ymlaen â gole,
A rhancwch beth cadeire
I chwi gael gweld y Warsel lân
16   Sydd yma dan ei lifre.

O dewch ymlaen â diod
A hefyd beth pastïod,
Ac ambell lwnc o gwrw gwych,
20   Waeth stiff a sych yw'r tafod.

Date
Before 1852.

Locality
South Wales.

Metre
For the metre see poem 28; for the tune see 'Cân y Fari Lwyd', p. 175.

30 Wassail song

Well, this is the name of the slender and beautiful one
Who rises with the star,
And this is the Wassail of greatest praise
4   Who sings and is merry.

It is appointed that the Wassail
Should always be carried;
And that your friend[s] and your companion[s] should on
        their travels
8   Spend this evening.

Well, this is the generous bowl
That was appointed for Christmas,
And its sound and its noise travels afar,
12   And what is there that is better than a gift?

O bring some light,
And arrange some chairs in rows
So that you can see the fine Wassail
16   That is here in its livery.

O bring some drink,
And some pasties too,
And some sips of excellent beer,
20   As the tongue is stiff and parched.

O cerwch lawr i'r seler
I dapo'r gasgen borter,
A pheidiwch â bod i ni yn gas,
24   Dewch mas â'r hen ddecanter.

A gawn ni drwy eich ffafwr
Eich cegin neu eich parlwr,
Neu eich neuadd, os cawn ddod?
28   Nid ym i fod ond chwegwr.

Pe digwyddent gael croeso gweddol galonnog aent i ffwrdd dan ganu
fel hyn:

Ffarwel i chwi, foneddigion,
Ni gawsom groeso ddigon;
A bendith Dduw fo ar eich tai,
32   A phob rhyw rai o'ch dynion.

Ond os fel arall y digwyddai, odid nad fel yma y canent:

Ffarwel iwch, hen gybyddion,
Ni chawsom ni ddim rhoddion;
Eich aur a'ch arian chwi bob rhai
36   Fo'n mynd i dai cymdogion.

Dienw

Source
Gomer M. Roberts, *Hanes Plwyf Llandybïe* [The History of the Parish of
Llandybïe] Cardiff: University of Wales Press, 1939), pp. 273–4.

Date
The second half of the nineteenth century.

O go down to the cellar
To tap the barrel of porter ale;
And do not be unkind to us,
24   Bring out the old decanter.

May we, through your favour,
To your kitchen or your parlour
Or your residence, be admitted?
28   We are only six men.

If they happened to receive a fairly hearty welcome they would depart
singing as follows:

Fare you well, gentlemen,
We have received ample welcome;
And may God's blessing be upon your homes,
32   And upon all your people.

If it happened otherwise, it is probable that they sang in this manner:

Fare you well, old misers,
We did not receive any gifts;
May all your gold and your silver
36   Go to your neighbours' houses.

Anonymous

Locality
Llandybïe, Carmarthenshire.

Metre
Triban; for the tune see 'Y Washael', p. 183.

31 Cân y Fari Lwyd

Cyfarchiad y merched

Y merched:	A gloisoch chi drysa?
	Ma bois y Cwrseila
	Yn siwr o ddod yma (x3)
4	I gianu.

Y Gofyniad

Y Cwmni:	Wel, dyma ni'n dŵad
	Gyfeillion diniwad
	I ofyn am gienad (x3)
8	I gianu.

Y merched:	Ma nhw ar y beili,
	Clywch arnyn nhw'n gweiddi,
	Dewch ferchid, mwn diain i, (x3)
12	I gwato.

Y Pwnco

Y Cwmni:	Ma'r Fari Lwyd yma'n
	Llawn sêr a rhubana,
	Mae'n werth i roi gola (x3)
16	I'w gwelad.

Y merched:	Hen Fari Lwyd druan,
	Do's neb am weld rhupan
	Na sêr ar dy dalcan (x3)
20	Nos heno.

Y Cwmni:	Fe dorswn ein crwmpa
	Wrth groesi'r sticila
	Wrth ddwâd tag yma (x3)
24	Nos heno.

Y merched:	Sawl crwmpad a giesoch?
	Sawl sticil a groesoch
	Wrth ddod y ffordd ddethoch (x3)
28	Nos heno?

31   The Mari Lwyd song

The women's greeting

The women: Have you locked [the] doors?
                    The Wassail lads
                    Are sure to come here (x3)
4   To sing.

The Request

The Company: Well, here we come
                    Innocent friends
                    To ask permission (x3)
8   To sing.

The women: They are on the farmyard,
                    Listen to them shout,
                    Come girls, for goodness' sake, (x3)
12   Let's hide.

The *Pwnco*

The Company: Mari Lwyd is here
                    Full of stars and ribbons,
                    It is worth shining a light (x3)
16   To see her.

The women: Poor old Mari Lwyd,
                    No one wants to see a ribbon
                  Or stars on your forehead (x3)
20   Tonight.

The Company: We have injured our buttocks
                    Crossing the stiles
                    As we made our way here (x3)
24   Tonight.

The women: How many buttocks did you have?
                    How many stiles did you cross
                    As you travelled on your way (x3)
28   Tonight?

Y Cwmni: Wel, tapwch y faril,
            Giyllyngwch hi'n rhicil,
            A llanwch y ddishgil (x3)
32   O gwrw.

Y merched: Ma yma farilid
            O gwrw bach sblendid,
            Ond chewch chi'r un llymid (x3)
36   O gwrw.

Y Cwmni: O! tynnwch y bollta,
            Agorwch y drysa,
            I fois y Cwrseila (x3)
40   ⋅ Rhowch greso.

Y merched: Y bollta a dynnwn,
            Y drysa agorwn,
            A'r Fari gresaw-wn (x3)
44   I'n Gwyla.

Y Cwmni – cyn ymadael
            Wel, diolch i chitha
            Am greso i ninna,
            Ag nes Dolig nesa, (x3)
48   Ffarwelwch.

    Dienw

Source
T. I. Phillips, Llys Myfyr, 30 Dinas Terrace, Aberystwyth, in a letter to the author dated 12 February 1976 (NLW Facs 369/3).

Date
Sung during the last quarter of the nineteenth century according to T. I. Phillips.

The Company:	Well, tap the barrel,
	Let it flow freely,
	And fill the bowl (x3)
32	With beer.

The women:	There is here a barrelful
	Of splendid beer,
	But you will not get one drop (x3)
36	Of beer.

The Company:	O! draw back the bolts,
	Open the doors,
	To the Wassail lads (x3)
40	Give [a] welcome.

The women:	We shall draw back the bolts,
	We shall open the doors,
	And we shall welcome Mari (x3)
44	To our Christmas festivities.

The Company – before departing

Well, thank you
For welcoming us,
And until next Christmas, (x3)
48 Farewell.

Anonymous

Locality
The Blackmill area, near Bridgend in Glamorgan.

Metre
For the metre see poem 28; for the tune see 'Cân y Fari Lwyd', p. 175.

32 Tribannau 'Mari Lwyd Lawen' o Ferthyr

Yn dwryn o Bendarran
Daeth lot sy'n caru loetran
Gan whare *tricks* y *Mary* Lwyd
4   I storio bwyd ac arian.

Fe wisgwyd mewn rhybana
Ben ceffyl am y gora,
A chrwth a thelyn yr un pryd
8   I fyw ar hyd tafarna.

Mi fuo'n ffair y bwrli
Yn dawnsio step Wil Benji
Nes cael ffetanaid lawn o fwyd
12   I *Mary* Lwyd y *lady*.

Mae'r gaseg bert ar wanco
A'r asyn bach ar gwympo
O eisiau maeth i'w cadw'n fyw:
16   Rhowch rywbeth i'w cysuro.

Daeth *Mary* Lwyd lawen
I lawr o Bendarren
Gan branco a neidio a thawlu ei thin
20   A Sol Nant-y-ffin yn ei harwain.

Wel, dyma ni'n dŵad
Yn Gwmpni glân diniwad
A Mari Lwyd y ladi wen
24   Yn dal, cewch gennym ganiad.

Wel, dyma ni'n dŵad
Yn burion ein bwriad
I ofyn am gennad
28   I ganu'r hen ganiad.

32 'Merry Mari Lwyd' of Merthyr *Tribannau*

In a crowd from Penydarren
A lot that loves loitering has come down [here],
Playing the tricks of Mary Lwyd
4   To store up food and money.

[It] was dressed in ribbons,
A horse's head in best form,
Along with a *crwth*/crowd and a harp,
8   Moving from one public house to the next.

She was in a frenzy of boisterous activity
Dancing the Wil Benji step
Until a sack full of food was received
12   For Mary Lwyd the lady.

The pretty mare is almost desperate
And the little donkey almost falling down
For want of nourishment to keep them alive:
16   Give something to comfort them.

Merry Mary Lwyd came
Down from Penydarren
Prancing and jumping and wiggling her backside
20   And Sol Nant-y-ffin leading her.

Well, here we come,
A fine, innocent Company,
And Mari Lwyd the lady in white
24   In harness, we shall sing you a song.

Well, here we come,
Honest in our intention,
To ask permission
28   To sing the old song.

Os rhowch i ni gennad
Ni ganwn ni ganiad
Nes bydd y Ladi yn ledo'n y dawns;
32   Os na chawn ni gennad,
      I ganu'r hen ganiad
      A stepo'r un stepad nid oes yr un siawns.

Dienw

Source
NLW 1131B, 18–19.

Date
The manuscript was created early in the twentieth century by Ebenezer
N. Williams 'Gwernyfed' (1843–1913) of Merthyr Tydfil.

Locality
Merthyr Tydfil.

If you give us permission
We shall sing a song
Until the Lady leads the dance;
32 If we are refused permission,
Of [us] singing the old song
And stepping the same dance-steps there is no chance.

Anonymous

Note
Line 14 refers to the use of a skull of a donkey in the absence of a horse's skull, as noted by Roberts, *Crefydd yr Oesoedd Tywyll*, p. 15.

Measure
Triban.

33 Y Pwnco

Tu fas: Agorwch y drysa,
          Gadewch i ni wara,
          Mae'n ôr yn yr eira
4   Y Gwila.

Tu fiwn: Cer odd na'r hen fwnci,
          Ma d'anadl di'n drewi,
          A phaid â baldorddi
8   Y Gwila.

Tu fas: Ma'r gaseg o'r perta,
          Gadewch i ni wara,
          Mae 'phen yn llawn cnota
12   Y Gwila.

Tu fiwn: Yn lle bo chi'n sythu,
          Wel, ledwch y Feri
          I fiwn i'n difyrru'r
16   Nos heno.

Wetin fe fysan yn martsho miwn dan ganu rhw hen lol fel hyn, –

          Ti dy lodl lidl,
          Tym tidl odl idl,
          Tym, tym, tym.

Dienw

Source
[Anonymous], 'Llythyra' Newydd gan Fachan Ifanc: Nadolig wrth y drws' [New Letters by a Young Chap: Christmas at the door], *Tarian y Gweithiwr* [The Worker's Shield], 26 December 1895, 3

Date
The second half of the nineteenth century.

33 The *Pwnco*

Outside: Open the doors,
          Let us perform,
          It is cold in the snow
4   At Christmastide.

Inside: Go away you old monkey,
          Your breath stinks,
          And don't talk nonsense
8   At Christmastide.

Outside: The mare is of the prettiest,
          Let us perform,
          Her head is covered in knots [of ribbons and flowers]
12   At Christmastide.

Inside: Instead of you freezing to death,
          Well, lead the Feri
          Inside to entertain us
16   Tonight.

Then they would march inside singing some silly nonsense like this, –

      Ti dy lodl lidl,
      Tym tidl odl idl,
      Tym, tym, tym.

Anonymous

Locality
Tarian y Gweithiwr was published in Aberdare, Rhondda Cynon Taf.

Metre
Lines 1–16: for the metre see poem 28; for the tune see 'Cân y Fari Lwyd', p. 175.

34 Cân y Fari Lwyd

Wel, dyma ni'n dywad,
Gyfeillion diniwad,
I ofyn (o)s ciawn gannad (x3)
4   I gianu.

Os na chawn ni gannad,
R(h)owch glywad ar ganiad
Pa fodd ma'r 'madawiad (x3)
8   Nos (h)eno.

Ni dorson ein crimpa
Wrth groeshi'r sticila
I ddyfod t(u)ag yma (x3)
12   Nos (h)eno.

Os o(e)s yna ddynion
All dorri anglynion,
R(h)owch glywad yn union (x3)
16   Nos (h)eno.

Os aethoch r(h)y gynnar
I'r gwely'n ddialgar,
O, codwch yn (h)awddgar (x3)
20   Nos (h)eno.

Y dishan fras felys
Â phob sort o sbeisys,
O, torrwch (h)i'n r(h)atus (x3)
24   Y Gwyla.

O, tapwch y baril
A 'llengwch a'n r(h)ugul;
Na rannwch a'n gynnil (x3)
28   Y Gwyla.

Dienw

34 A Mari Lwyd song

Well, here we come,
Innocent friends,
To ask permission (x3)
4   To sing.

If we are not granted permission,
Let us hear from you in song
How the departure should be (x3)
8   Tonight.

We have broken our shins
Crossing the stiles
To come here (x3)
12   Tonight.

If there are men here
Who can compose stanzas,
Let us hear [them] at once (x3)
16   Tonight.

If you went too early
To bed out of vengeance,
O, get up in all good-naturedness (x3)
20   Tonight.

The sweet currant cake
With every sort of spice,
O, slice it generously (x3)
24   Tonight.

O, tap the barrel
And let [the beer] flow freely;
Do not share it frugally (x3)
28   This Christmastide.

Anonymous

Source

D. Roy Saer (ed.), *Caneuon Llafar Gwlad (Songs From Oral Tradition)*, 1 (Cardiff: National Museum of Wales/Welsh Folk Museum, 1974), p. 16.

Date

The song was recorded in October 1953 from the singing of William Morgan Rees (a railway worker, b. 1883), Woodlands, Brynmenyn near Bridgend in Glamorgan. William Morgan Rees saw the Mari Lwyd out and about in villages such as Coety, Bryncethin, etc. to the north-east of Bridgend until *c*.1933.

35 Y Feri Lwyd

Wel, dyma ni'n dŵad,
Gyfeillion diniwad,
I ofyn am gennad (x3)
4   I ganu.

Beth ydyw y twrw,
Y ffustio a'r curo?
A beth yw eich ewyllys (x3)
8   Nos heno?

Y Feri Lwyd lawen
A'i chwt ar i chefan
Sy' yma â'i miri (x3)
12   Nos heno.

Os ydyw y Feri
Yn addo i'r Cwmpni
I ymddwyn yn deidi
16   Heb gnoi na thraflyncu
Caiff ddyfod i'r Cwmpni
Nos heno.

Locality
The Bridgend area in Glamorgan.

Note
This is the most common and best known of the *pwnco* songs associated with the Mari Lwyd custom.

Metre
For the metre see poem 28; for the tune see 'Cân y Fari Lwyd' p. 175.

35 The Feri Lwyd

Well, here we come,
Innocent friends,
To ask permission (x3)
4   To sing.

What is the noise,
The banging and the knocking?
And what do you want (x3)
8   Tonight?

The merry Meri Lwyd
With her tail held high
Is here with her merriment (x3)
12   Tonight.

If Meri
Promises the Company
She will behave [in a] tidy [manner]
16   Without biting or guzzling
She may join the Company
Tonight.

Mae'r Feri yn addo
20 I uno'n y Cwmpni
Heb gnoi na thraflyncu
Ond dyplu y miri
Wrth ganu baleti
24 Nos heno.

Ond beth am y Pwnsh
A'r procar a'r Judi
I ddifa y cysur
28 A'r tanllwyth i'r Cwmpni (x2)
Nos heno?

Mae'r Feri yn addo
Fod Pwnsh a'r hen Judi
32 I sefyll yn llonydd
Ac ymddwyn yn deidi
A gatal y tanllwyth i'r Cwmpni
Nos heno.

36 Mae'r Cwmpni yn fishi
Yn doti y llestri
A'r dishan yn deidi
Cyn acor drws iddi,
40 Cyn acor i'r Feri
Nos heno.

Mae'r Feri yn rhewi
A'i thrad bron â fferru
44 Wrth aros i'r Cwmpni
I acor drws iddi,
I acor i'r Feri
Nos heno.

48 Mae'r Cwmpni yn fishi
Yn doti y llestri
A'r dishan yn deidi
Cyn acor drws iddi,
52 Cyn acor i'r Feri
Nos heno.

Meri promises
20 To join the Company
Without biting or guzzling
But will double the merriment
By singing ballads
24 Tonight.

But what of Pwnsh
And the poker and Judy
That spoil the comfort
28 And the roaring fire for the Company (x2)
Tonight?

Meri promises
That Pwnsh and old Judy
32 Will stand still
And behave [in a] tidy [manner]
And leave the roaring fire alone for the Company
Tonight.

36 The Company is busy
Setting the dishes
And the cake tidily
Before opening [the] door to her,
40 Before opening [the door] to Meri
Tonight.

Meri is freezing cold
And her hooves almost stiff with cold
44 Waiting for the Company
To open [the] door to her,
To open [the door] to Meri
Tonight.

48 The Company is busy
Setting the dishes
And the cake tidily
Before opening [the] door to her,
52 Before opening [the door] to Meri
Tonight.

Fe ddotiff y Feri
Y dishan yn deidi
56 Ym mola y Feri
Yng ngenol y miri
Ond acor drws iddi
Nos heno.

60 Yr ydym yn acor
Y cloeon am noson
O ganu a dawnsio
A'r crwth a'r hen delyn;
64 Pob croeso i'r Feri
Nos heno.

Pob croeso i'r Feri
I ganu faint fyn hi
68 Ynghenol y twrw
Wrth rannu y cwrw;
Pob croeso i'r Feri
Nos heno.

72 Wel, dyma ni'n mynad
Â'n penna i'r gweirad
A Duw wŷr cyn bellad (x3)
Nos heno.

Dienw

Source
Peter Kennedy (ed.), *Folksongs of Britain and Ireland* (London: Cassell & Company Ltd, 1975), pp. 158–9.

Date
The second half of the nineteenth century.

Meri will set
The cake tidily
56 In Meri's belly
In the midst of the merriment
If only [the] door is opened to her
Tonight.

60 We are opening
The locks for an evening
Of singing and dancing
To the *crwth*/crowd and the old harp;
64 A warm welcome to Meri
Tonight.

A warm welcome to Meri
To sing as much as she desires
68 In the midst of the noise
As the beer is shared out;
A warm welcome to Meri
Tonight.

72 Well, here we go
On our heads downhill
And only God knows how far (x3)
Tonight.

Anonymous

Locality
South Wales.

Metre
For the metre see poem 28; for the tune see 'Cân y Fari Lwyd', p. 175.

36   Penillion y Fari Lwyd

Wel, dyma ni'n dŵad
Gyfeillion diniwad,
I ofyn am gennad – i ganu.

4   Deg o griw hawddgar
Rhai gorau ar y ddaear,
I ganu yn deyrngar – am gwrw.

Mae ffasiwn ymrysona
8   Ers mil o flynydda
A hynny y cara – i brofi.

Cenwch eich gorau
Cans felly gwnan ninnau
12   A'r sawl a fo orau – gaiff gwrw.

Mae'n dawn i'ch cynhyrfu
Wrth feddwl am ganu
Y nos yn y gwely – mi goeliaf.

16   Mi ganwn am wythnos
A hefyd bythefnos
A mis os bydd achos – baidd i chwi.

Tapiwch y faril
20   Gollyngwch yn rhugil,
Na fyddwch ry gynnil – i ganwyr.

Mae Mari Lwyd lawen
Yn dod heb genfigen
24   A chanu yw ei diben – mi dybiaf.

'Dyw wiw i chwi'n ffalsio
Na thrio ein swcro
'Ry'm ni yn ddiguro – fel dysgwyr.

36 Mari Lwyd stanzas

Well, here we come,
Innocent friends,
To ask permission – to sing.

4   A gang of ten amiable [people]
The best in the world,
[Here] to sing loyally – for beer.

The fashion of bardic contention
8   [Has been in existence] for a thousand years
And that is what I would love – to prove.

Sing your utmost
For we shall do the same
12   And whoever is best – shall have beer.

Our talent is to arouse you
As [we] think of singing
At night in bed – I trust.

16   We shall sing for a week
And for a fortnight too
And a month if need be – a challenge for you.

Tap the barrel
20   Let [the beer] flow freely,
Do not be too ungenerous – to singers.

Merry Mari Lwyd
Comes without jealousy
24   And her intention is to sing – I believe.

It is useless for you to lavish insincere praise on us
Or to try to succour us
We are unbeatable – as learners [of Welsh].

28 Mae criw Dinas Mawddwy
Yn feirdd sy'n ganadwy
O yma i Gonwy – 'n ddiguro.

Mi ganwn bob blwyddyn
32 Os cawn griw i'n dilyn
Heb ofni 'run gelyn – ond cymorth.

Mae Roland y 'ffeirad
Yn dyfod, ar f'enad,
36 Gwna fe i chwi fynad – i ddysgu.

*(Llinellau 1–24 penillion traddodiadol; llinellau 25–36
Arfon Hughes (1960–))*

Source
Arfon Hughes, 'Canlyn y Fari' [Following the Mari], *Canu Gwerin (Folk
Song)*, 31 (2008), 89–90.

Variant reading
Line 7 ymsona (Hughes, 'Canlyn y Fari', 89).

Date
First sung on 13 January 2007.

28   The Dinas Mawddwy crew
     Are poets who compose songs that can be sung
     From here to Conwy – [and] are unbeatable.

     We shall sing every year
32   If we can find a crew to follow us
     Without fearing any foe – but assistance.

     Roland the clergyman
     Is coming, upon my soul,
36   He will make you go – to learn [Welsh].

(Lines 1–24 traditional stanzas; lines 25–36 Arfon Hughes (1960–))

Locality
Mallwyd and Dinas Mawddwy, Gwynedd.

Note
Lines 25–7: followers of the Mari Lwyd included learners of Welsh. Lines
34–6: the Revd Roland Barnes, serving the Bro Cyfeiliog and Mawddwy
Ministry Area, has learned Welsh and is a fluent speaker.

Metre
For the metre see poem 28; for the tune see 'Cân y Fari Lwyd', p. 175.

37 Cân y Merched

Waeth pa mor ddiniwad y byddwch chi'n dŵad,
Waeth pa mor ddiniwad y byddwch chi'n dŵad
'Sdim croeso i'ch ciwad (x3)
4   Na'ch cennad.

Cer o'ma 'rhen Fari a thaw ar dy weiddi,
Cer o'ma 'rhen Fari a thaw ar dy weiddi
Does dim croeso iti (x3)
8   Waeth tewi.

Chwi ddynion sy'n ubain am swper mewn plygain,
Chwi ddynion sy'n ubain am swper mewn plygain
Cewch chwislo mewn unsain (x3)
12   Am frecwast.

Sawl bwthyn 'sgen Elwyn ysgweiar Nantnodyn?
Sawl bwthyn 'sgen Elwyn ysgweiar Nantnodyn?
Ewch yno i ofyn (x3)
16   Am lety.

Nid baswr mo Arfon ond bas ydi'r afon,
Nid baswr mo Arfon ond bas ydi'r afon
Lle daliwyd eich briwsion (x3)
20   O dalent.

Rhyw denor go dila 'di Arwel Puw ynta',
Rhyw denor go dila 'di Arwel Puw ynta'
Prin iawn ydi donia (x3)
24   Chwi'r dynion.

Pyncio rhyw fymryn wna Robat o'r Boncyn,
Pyncio rhyw fymryn wna Robat o'r Boncyn
Cyn drachtio ei wydryn (x3)
28   I'w waelod.

37 The Women's Song

No matter in how innocent a manner you come,
No matter in how innocent a manner you come
Your rabble is not welcome (x3)
4   Nor is your message.

Go away old Mari and stop your bawling,
Go away old Mari and stop your bawling
You are not welcome (x3)
8   [And] you may as well shut up.

You men who howl for supper at a *plygain*,
You men who howl for supper at a *plygain*
You can whistle in unison (x3)
12   For breakfast.

How many cottages does Elwyn squire of Nantnodyn own?
How many cottages does Elwyn squire of Nantnodyn own?
Go there to ask (x3)
16   For lodgings.

Arfon is not a bass singer but the river is base (i.e. low),
Arfon is not a bass singer but the river is base (i.e. low)
That confined your breadcrumb (x3)
20   Of talent.

Arwel Puw too is a pretty feeble tenor,
Arwel Puw too is a pretty feeble tenor,
Talents are very scarce [among] (x3)
24   You men.

Robat of Boncyn warbles the smallest possible amount,
Robat of Boncyn warbles the smallest possible amount
Before drinking deeply from his glass (x3)
28   To its bottom.

Ma'r Marc 'na'n cyboli a'r England sy'n porthi,
Ma'r Marc 'na'n cyboli a'r England sy'n porthi
Mae 'migraine' ar Mari (x3)
32   O'r mawredd!

Hen fustych go salw o'r Cut Lloi yn fan'cw,
Hen fustych go salw o'r Cut Lloi yn fan'cw
Rhowch daw ar eich twrw (x3)
36   Rai truain.

Mae dawnswyr Llangadfan yn prancio'n go simsan,
Mae dawnswyr Llangadfan yn prancio'n go simsan
'Rôl oriau o botian (x3)
40   O beintiau.

Wnawn ni ddim gwrthod os prynwch chi ddiod,
Wnawn ni ddim gwrthod os prynwch chi ddiod
I bob un o'r genethod (x3)
44   A gana.

Os rhowch i bob lodes rhyw fymryn o anwes,
Os rhowch i bob lodes rhyw fymryn o anwes
Bydd cig yn eich potes (x3)
48   O'r popty.

Ma'r gasgen 'di chrafu a chitha 'di sythu (neu glychu,)
Ma'r gasgen 'di chrafu a chitha 'di sythu (neu glychu)
Dowch mewn a chynhesu (x3)
52   I'n cwmni.

Fe lusgwn y bolltia ac agor y drysa,
Fe lusgwn y bolltia ac agor y drysa
Cewch aros tan bora (x3)
56   A brecwast.

Dienw (o bosibl Rhiain Bebb)

That Marc talks nonsense and England makes supportive
    exclamations,
That Marc talks nonsense and England makes supportive
    exclamations
[And] Mari [now] has a migraine (x3)
32   O goodness!

[You] sorry old bullocks from the Cut Lloi [singing party] over there,
[You] sorry old bullocks from the Cut Lloi [singing party] over there
Put an end to your clamour (x3)
36   Wretched ones.

The Llangadfan dancers are prancing unsteadily,
The Llangadfan dancers are prancing unsteadily
After hours of boozing (x3)
40   From pint pots.

We won't refuse if you buy drinks,
We won't refuse if you buy drinks
For each one of the girls (x3)
44   Who sing.

If you give each young woman a little caress,
If you give each young woman a little caress
There will be meat in your stew (x3)
48   From the oven.

The [bottom of the] barrel has been scraped and you are freezing
    cold (or wet),
The [bottom of the] barrel has been scraped and you are freezing
    cold (or wet),
Come inside to warm up (x3)
52   In our company.

We shall drag open the bolts and open the doors,
We shall drag open the bolts and open the doors,
You can stay until morning (x3)
56   And breakfast.

Anonymous (possibly Rhiain Bebb)

Source
Hughes, 'Canlyn y Fari', 90–2.

Date
13 January 2007 and 12 January 2008.

Locality
Mallwyd and Dinas Mawddwy, Gwynedd.

Note
Line 9 *plygain* refers to the service of traditional carols held at Mallwyd
Church on 13 January, and the supper that follows.

38 Penillion y Fari Lwyd

O'r Parc ger y Bala
Daw'r Hen Lywarch hyna'
A'i feibion ysmala – i drio canu.

4   'Rhen Lywarch a'th deulu
Pa les i chwi frefu?
'Se'n well i chwi ddysgu – chwibanu.

Er clywed sibrydion
8   Eich bod yn brydyddion,
Eich cerddi sy'n gochion – 'rhen Wylliaid.

Rhiain Bebb

Line 13 Elwyn Jones who farms Nant-y-nodyn, Dinas Mawddwy, and lets holiday cottages.
Line 17 Arfon Hughes, organiser of the Mari Lwyd visitation in Mallwyd and Dinas Mawddwy.
6.1 Arwel Puw, leader of the Mawddwy *plygain* party.
7.1 Robat o'r Boncyn: Robert Wyn Jones, Boncyn, Dinas Mawddwy.
8.1 Marc ac England: Marc Lewis, Penegoes, a native Welsh-speaker; and Stuart England of Dinas Mawddwy, a Welsh-learner.

Metre
For the metre see poem 28; for the tune see 'Cân y Fari Lwyd', p. 175.

38   Mari Lwyd stanzas

From Parc near Bala
Come Old Llywarch the elder
And his whimsical sons – to try to sing.

4   Old Llywarch and your family
What good will your braying do?
It would be better for you to learn – to whistle.

Even though [we] heard rumours
8   That you are poets,
Your poems are feeble – old Bandits.

Rhiain Bebb

Source
Hughes, 'Canlyn y Fari', 94.

Date
12 January 2008.

Locality
Mallwyd and Dinas Mawddwy, Gwynedd.

Note
Line 2; Yr Hen Lywarch; Dan Puw, a farmer in Parc, a small rural com
munity near Bala in Gwynedd; conductor and founder of Meibion Lly-
warch, a party of men who sing folk songs and *cerdd dant* (singing

poetry to harp accompaniment) in the traditional style. They had been invited to entertain at the Mari Lwyd evening held in Mallwyd and Dinas Mawddwy in 2008.

Line 9: 'rhen Wylliaid: a reference to the 'Red Bandits of Mawddwy (or Dugoed), a notorious band of robbers or brigands who for several centuries (roughly from 1155 to 1555) infested the wooded fastnesses of that district, striking terror into the hearts of the surrounding country-side by their acts of plunder and violence', *Geiriadur Prifysgol Cymru/ Dictionary of the Welsh Language* (Cardiff: University of Wales Press, 1950–), p. 1765.

Metre
For the metre see poem 28; for the tune see 'Cân y Fari Lwyd', p. 175.

Gŵyl Fair Wassail Songs

39 Carol tan bared i'w chanu nos Ŵyl Fair ar y dôn
    a elwir 'Siwsanna'

Wel, down un fwriad, dawn arferol,
Â sain iawn gywrain seiniwn garol,
Wel, dyma'r noswaith, berffaith burffydd,
4   Mwya oreurglod, mam yr Arglwydd:
Morwyn nefol, lân, ysbrydol, rhagorol ydyw'r gair,
Down, dihunwn dan do heno, er naws, wawr foddio nos Ŵyl Fair
      Sain Hosanna, Haleliwia i'r Alffa, Omega a Mair,
8   Gogoniant, moliant ac addoliant rown yn gywrain o'r un gair.

Mair wen, odiaeth, morwyn ydoedd,
Lwyr iawn afael, lloerwen nefoedd,
O gwmpas hon yn gampus hynod
12 Rhôi angylion puredd foliant parod.
Mair oedd gannwyll mawr ogoniant mewn urddiant, mwyniant
      mawl,
Mair fwyneiddgu a faga yr Iesu i'n gwaredu, hoywgu hawl.
      Sain Hosanna, Haleliwia i'r Alffa, Omega a Mair,
16   Gogoniant, moliant ac addoliant rown yn gywrain o'r un gair.

Pan oeddem ddeillion, ddylion ddelwau,
Mewn baich adwyth o bechodau,
Fe roddodd Duw ei Ysbryd Sanctedd
20 Hefo'i forwyn yn ddioferedd,
A hon feichioga ar aer gorucha nôl gwyrthiau a doniau Duw,
Yn lân wyryfes, ddoniol ddynes, yn ŵyl angyles, addas yw.
      Sain Hosanna, Haleliwia i'r Alffa, Omega a Mair,
24   Gogoniant, moliant ac addoliant rown yn gywrain o'r un gair.

Ymhen y deugain nydd diogel,
Fawr iaith im, âi Mair i'w themel
A'r Oen grasusol, oeswr Iesu,
28 Ar ei breichiau heb frawychu;

39 A carol [to be sung] beneath the wall at *Gŵyl Fair*,
to the tune known as 'Susannah'

Well, come with a single purpose, [it is] a customary blessing,
With a truly expert sound let us sing a carol,
Well, this is the night, perfect true faith,
4   [When we sing] in the most gilded praises [to] the Lord's mother:
Heavenly maiden, pure, spiritual, glorious is the word [spoken of her],
Come, awake with spirit this night, [all who are] indoors, to please
    the [one who is the] dawn of *Gŵyl Fair*.
        Sing Hosanna, Hallelujah to the Alpha, Omega and Mary,
8   Glory, praise and worship let us give expertly, with one accord.

Blessed, excellent Mary was a virgin,
Wholly superior, beautiful woman of heaven,
About her with splendid distinction
12   The holy angels gave unhesitating praise.
Mary was a candle of great glory, held in dignity, [the] delight
    of praise,
Dear gentle Mary raised up Jesus to save us, joyful and precious right.
        Sing Hosanna, Hallelujah to the Alpha, Omega and Mary,
16   Glory, praise and worship let us give expertly, with one accord.

When we were blind, [following after] foolish idols,
Hemmed in by an evil burden of sins,
God provided his Holy Spirit
20   For his virgin, who was without vanity,
And she conceived the supreme heir, according to God's miracles
    and blessings,
A pure virgin, a gifted woman, a lowly angel, it is seemly.
        Sing Hosanna, Hallelujah to the Alpha, Omega and Mary,
24   Glory, praise and worship let us give expertly, with one accord.

Upon the significant fortieth day [of purification],
This is a great word for me, Mary visited her temple
With the gracious Lamb, Jesus, the one who gives life,
28   Contentedly in her arms;

Fe oleuai ei lampau'n wiwlan olau, yn bleidiau yno o'i blaen,
Angylion yno'n llafar leisio, trwy bwyll, air yno i bob lle'r aen.
    Sain Hosanna, Haleliwia i'r Alffa, Omega a Mair,
32   Gogoniant, moliant ac addoliant rown yn gywrain o'r un gair.

O'i blaen daeth Seimon union yno
Dan rasusol lesol leisio:
'Yr awr hon, Arglwydd, caf ollyngdod,
36 Yn olau heno gwela i'n hynod.'
Fe gawsai hysbysrwydd gan yr Arglwydd y câi weld y llywydd
    llawn,
Cyn câi angau y dôi'r Gorucha yn ei freichiau, doniau dawn.
    Sain Hosanna, Haleliwia i'r Alffa, Omega a Mair,
40   Gogoniant, moliant ac addoliant rown yn gywrain o'r un gair.

Fe draetha yn lân ei gân yn gynnes
Yno, i'r awyr, i'r Meseias:
'I'th was y byddo oesau buddiol
44 Yn ôl dy wyrthia a'th eiria gwrol;
I fod yn olau i'th genedlaethau rhoist ger ein bronnau bryd,
Gogoniant dyfal i'th bobl isradd a'u dwyn o wachel, drafel drud.'
    Sain Hosanna, Haleliwia i'r Alffa, Omega a Mair,
48   Gogoniant, moliant ac addoliant rown yn gywrain o'r un gair.

A Hanna hoff, odiaeth, lân broffwydes,
Oedd mewn disgwyliad o'r Meseias;
Pan ddaeth i'w golwg yn ddigelu,
52 Mewn doniau abal hi a'i hadnabu.
Rhoes iddo foliant mewn gogoniant o wir ddilysiant lef:
'Bendigedig wyt, O Geidwad, Iôr da nwyfiad, aer Duw Nef.'
    Sain Hosanna, Haleliwia i'r Alffa, Omega a Mair,
56   Gogoniant, moliant ac addoliant rown yn gywrain o'r un gair.

Fel y proffwydi heini, hoenus,
Yn rhoi gwybodaeth helaeth, hwylus
Am Fair a'i hepil, forwyn hapus,
60 Parch oedd unol, ferch ddaionus,

Her lamps shone brightly, a pure and holy light, in rows before her,
There were angels there voicing resoundingly, with wisdom,
   a salutation wherever they went.
     Sing Hosanna, Hallelujah to the Alpha, Omega and Mary,
32   Glory, praise and worship let us give expertly, with one accord.

Simon, upright of heart, came before her there
Voicing gracious, profitable praise:
'Now, Lord, shall I be released,
36 This evening I see [salvation] clearly, in an exceptional way.'
The Lord had promised him that he would see the all-sufficient
   ruler [i.e. Jesus],
That before he died he would hold the Almighty in his arms,
   blessings [given by] the one of outstanding gifts.
     Sing Hosanna, Hallelujah to the Alpha, Omega and Mary,
40   Glory, praise and worship let us give expertly, with one accord.

He sang his song sincerely and with passion
There, under the firmament, to the Messiah:
'May there be [many] ages of conferring blessings on your servant
44 According to your miracles and your valiant words;
You have given, in our presence, a sight [of one who is] to be a
   light to your generations,
A constant glory to your people of low position, to bring them
   out of their lean, grievous travail.
     Sing Hosanna, Hallelujah to the Alpha, Omega and Mary,
48   Glory, praise and worship let us give expertly, with one accord.

And beloved Anna, excellent, pure prophetess
Who had been awaiting the Messiah;
When she beheld Him clearly,
52 With competent ability she recognised Him.
She praised Him with glory in a true and faultless voice:
'Blessed art Thou, O Saviour, Lord of holy love, the heir of God
   in heaven.'
     Sing Hosanna, Hallelujah to the Alpha, Omega and Mary,
56   Glory, praise and worship let us give expertly, with one accord.

As did the active, spirited prophets
Give extensive, expedient information
Regarding Mary and her offspring, blessed virgin,
60 [Their] respect was in unity, gracious young woman,

A Gabriel eto fu'n proffwydo y caem ni yn gryno Grist,
A'i eni yn buredd inni yn barod i'n dwyn o bechod, trallod trist.
    Sain Hosanna, Haleliwia i'r Alffa, Omega a Mair,
64   Gogoniant, moliant ac addoliant rown yn gywrain o'r un gair.

Llawer prudd-der mawr o'i achos
A gafodd Mair yn ddiymaros;
Ac eto'n awr, mewn mawr lawenydd,
68 Yn y nefoedd mae hi yn ufudd,
Yn wynfydedig, fendigedig, yn gwrando'r miwsig mwyn;
Rhown ninna yn helaeth rhyw ddarluniaeth, ora mwyniaith,
    er ei mwyn.
    Sain Hosanna, Haleliwia i'r Alffa, Omega a Mair,
72   Gogoniant, moliant ac addoliant rown yn gywrain o'r un gair.

Mewn gosteg hy mae'n eista'n gyfion
Uwchlaw, yng ngola y gwych angylion;
Mae yn frenhines gynnes, gannaid,
76 Tan bur forwyndod, hynod enaid.
Ei pherchi a ddylem ninna, ddeiliad, o flaen dim merchad mwy,
Oedd forwyn rasol, wyryf wrol, lân, sancteiddiol, nefol mwy.
    Sain Hosanna, Haleliwia i'r Alffa, Omega a Mair,
80   Gogoniant, moliant ac addoliant rown yn gywrain o'r un gair.

Gogoniant, moliant, haeddiant heddiw,
Fawr a hen, i Fair a'i henw;
Bendigedig yw dy gyflwr,
84 Yn geni a chodi i ni Iachawdwr
'R hwn a ddaw i'n hylaw holi a'n barnu oll yn ben;
Duw a'n par'toa erbyn y delo rwy'n faith ddymuno fyth. Amen.
    Sain Hosanna, Haleliwia i'r Alffa, Omega a Mair,
88   Gogoniant, moliant ac addoliant rown yn gywrain o'r un gair.

Dafydd Jones 'Dafydd Siôn Siâms' (1743–1831)

Gabriel once more prophesied that we would opportunely
    receive Christ,
And that he would be born unto us in purity, ready to bring us out
    of sin, sorrowful tribulation.
      Sing Hosanna, Hallelujah to the Alpha, Omega and Mary,
64   Glory, praise and worship let us give expertly, with one accord.

On account of it many great tribulations
Immediately descended on Mary;
And yet now, in great joy,
68 She is faithful in heaven,
Blessed, glorious, listening to the melodious music;
Let us give generously some portraiture [of Mary], in the sweetest
    words, for her sake.
      Sing Hosanna, Hallelujah to the Alpha, Omega and Mary,
72   Glory, praise and worship let us give expertly, with one accord.

In bold silence she sits in righteousness
Above, in the light of the mighty angels;
She is a loving, radiant queen,
76 In a state of pure virginity, illustrious soul.
We also, citizen[s], should henceforth honour her before all other
    women,
[She] who was a gracious young woman, valiant virgin, pure,
    sanctified, holy from now on.
      Sing Hosanna, Hallelujah to the Alpha, Omega and Mary,
80   Glory, praise and worship let us give expertly, with one accord.

May there be glory, praise [and] credit today,
Great and old, to Mary and to her name;
Blessed is your status,
84 Giving birth and raising for us a Saviour
Who will appear as Lord to interrogate us in righteousness and
    to judge us all;
My great everlasting hope is that God will prepare us for his
    coming. Amen.
      Sing Hosanna, Hallelujah to the Alpha, Omega and Mary,
88   Glory, praise and worship let us give expertly, with one accord.

Dafydd Jones 'Dafydd Siôn Siâms' (1743–1831)

Sources
NLW 9168A, ff. 19ᵛ–22ʳ.

Rhiannon Ifans, 'Canu Gwaseila yn y Gymraeg' [Welsh Wassailing] (PhD thesis, University of Wales [Aberystwyth], 1980), 3, 803–5.

Date
176[0].

Locality
Gwynedd.

40 Ystatud Canu Gŵyl Fair

Tri ar 'Peg O'Ramsey' a rowch,
Ac yno dowch â thriban,
A thôn deuair hanner awr,
4   A'r 'Fedle Fawr' i'w gorffan.

Dienw

Sources
NLW 9168A, f. 43ʳ.

Rhiannon Ifans, *Sêrs a Rybana: Astudiaeth o'r Canu Gwasael* [Stars and Ribbons: A Study of Wassailing] (Llandysul: Gwasg Gomer, 1983), p. 176.

Variant reading
Line 1 Bigyransi (NLW 9168A, f. 43ʳ).

Date
Before 1767.

Locality
Gwynedd.

Note

Dafydd Jones spent most of his life in Penrhyndeudraeth, Gwynedd, but was christened at Llandanwg church and lived for a time in Maentwrog.

Metre

For 'Siwsanna'/'Susannah' see p. 182; see further Phyllis Kinney and Meredydd Evans (eds), *Hen Alawon (Carolau a Cherddi)* [Old Tunes (Carols and Poems)] (Welsh Folk Song Society in association with the National Museum of Wales (Welsh Folk Museum), 1993), number 25 and p. 96.

40   Statute regarding *Gŵyl Fair* Singing

Provide three on 'Peg O'Ramsey',
And thither bring a *triban*,
And a *tôn deuair* for half an hour,
4   And 'Y Fedle Fawr' to finish with.

Anonymous

Note

Line 1: the English dance tune 'Peg O'Ramsey', see p. 181, is mentioned in a pamphlet written by Thomas Nashe, *Have With You to Saffron-Walden* (London: John Danter, 1596; facsimile reprint Menston: Scolar Press, 1971), unpaged (quire T), see poem 8; see also W. Chappell, *The Ballad Literature and Popular Music of the Olden Time*, 1 (London: Chappell, 1859), p. 248.
Line 2: for *triban* see 'Verse Forms' p. 344.
Line 3: for *tôn deuair* see 'Verse Forms' pp. 343–4.
Line 4: for 'Y Fedle Fawr' see p. 179; see further Phyllis Kinney, 'The Tunes of the Welsh Christmas Carols (I)', *Canu Gwerin (Folk Song)*, 11 (1988), 37–8; Kinney and Evans, *Hen Alawon*, number 29 and p. 98.

Metre

Mesur Salm 'Psalm Metre' in Welsh prosody, an iambic stanza of 8.7.8.7. syllables with lines ending in accented and unaccented syllables alternately.

41 Pricsiwn Gŵyl Fair ar dri mesur

'Ffarwel Gwŷr Aberffraw'

Y teulu mwyn foddau, agorwch eich drysau,
Yn lân eich calonnau â hwyl union,
Gadewch i ni ymdwymo, rŷm ni agos â starfio,
4   Fe ellwch ein coelio o'ch gwir galon.
Dowch, dowch y wraig rasol a gwnewch i ni groeso
Â chimin o gwrw ag alloch chwi 'i gario;
O 'wyllys glân eich calon, lliw'r hinon inni rhowch
8   Fir yn weddedd, wreigdda haeledd, yr ŷm ni'n daeredd, dowch!

'Country Bumpkin'

Os oes un cantwr, hwyliwr hy, o fewn eich tŷ neu ped fai lu,
Dowch yma ar gais fel cwmni cu i ganu ag awen gynnes;
I'n dal ni allan dan y rhod mewn union nod, chwi a gewch glod
12   Os gwnewch yn buredd, fwynedd fod i'n hateb, hynod hanes.

'Pilgrim'

Cyneuwch dân gwresog, iawn groeso, down ato fe ar dymer
    i ymdwymo,
Y mae hi yn oer hynod, mi wn, heno i diwnio a baetio mewn baw;
Os byddwch yn fwynedd, ddigyffro, ni ganwn yn iawn i chwi
    heb gwyno,
16   Yn lanweth dôn heleth dan hwylio, yr ydym yn llunio 'mlaen llaw.
Yn brysur rhowch gysur yn gyson, yn weddus, iawn ddawnus
    i ddynion,
Gwnewch fwyd i ni'n barod, gwedd burion, gwŷr haelion,
    gwych union ŷch chwi,
A digon o gwrw, iawn gariad, yn rhwyddedd, wych, buredd
    eich bwriad,
20   Yn fwynedd, heb suredd, oer siarad, da driniad yn wastad i ni.

John Jones, Llanddeiniolen

41 Pricksong at *Gŵyl Fair* in three metres

'Ffarwel Gwŷr Aberffraw'
The gentle-mannered family, open up your doors,
[You who are] sincere of heart and in good form,
Allow us to warm ourselves, we are close to freezing,
4 You can believe us from your truthful hearts.
Come, come gracious lady and welcome us
With as much beer as you can carry;
According to your heart's good desire give us, [one with a
    complexion] the colour of the sunshine,
8 Beer in a fitting manner, generous good woman, we are in earnest,
    come!

'Country Bumpkin'
If there is one singer, bold leader, within your house or if there
    are a great many,
Come here immediately as a dear company to sing with warm
    inspiration;
For keeping us outside under the heavens which is your direct aim,
    you will receive praise
12 If you answer us with honesty and courtesy, excellent tale.

'Pilgrim'
Light a warm fire, a fitting welcome, we shall come to it disposed
    to warm ourselves,
It is very cold this evening, I know, to be singing and baiting in dirt;
If you would be gentle [and] calm we shall sing you, sincerely,
    without complaining,
16 A well wrought, extensive tune, in high spirits, that we have
    devised beforehand.
Swiftly, fittingly [and] with true skill, give men constant comfort,
Prepare food for us in a faultless manner, generous people, you
    are noble [and] just,
And [give us] plenty of beer readily, true affection, excellent [and]
    pure your intent,
20 With gentleness, without tartness [or] cold conversation, always
    treat us well.

John Jones, Llanddeiniolen

Sources
NLW 346B, 134.
Ifans, *Sêr a Rybana*, pp. 176–7.

Date
?1773. John Jones was a schoolteacher in Llanddeiniolen, near Caernarfon in Gwynedd, *fl.* the second half of the eighteenth century. Poems recorded in NLW 346B are dated variously between 1768 and 1786.

Locality
Llanddeiniolen, four miles from Caernarfon in Gwynedd.

42   Carol deuair eto

	Gartre nis bûm	er nos duw Llun
	Ond gwirota	'r hyd tai gwyrda;
	Ni bûm gartre	er nos Difie
4	Ond gwirota	draw ac yma.
	[Ni g]llowson fod	medd a bragod
	[A chw]rw da	yn tŷ yma,
	[A] gwraig lwydwen	a'i rhôi yn llawen
8	A bod y gŵr	yn gwmpnïwr.
	Ac am ei fod,	fo a gaiff wirod;
	Agorwch chi'r drws	fy rhiain feindlws
	A gillwng fi i'r tŷ,	rwy mron rhynnu,
12	Agorwch chi y ffenestri,	dyma Fair wen a'i goleuni.
	Sefwch yn eich arfod,	dyma ni yn dŵod
	I chwi ag anrheg	hardd ei gweled;
	Nid gwaith seiri	dim sydd arni
16	Na gwaith cerfer	gore yn Lloeger.

Metres

For 'Ffarwel Gwŷr Aberffraw' also known as 'Difyrrwch Gwŷr Aberffraw' see p. 179; see further Kinney and Evans, *Hen Alawon*, number 27 and p. 97. The title [The Men of Aberffraw's Farewell] 'may have had connotations of antiquity, since Aberffraw in Anglesey was in ancient times the principal seat of Gwynedd'; see Phyllis Kinney, 'The Tunes of the Welsh Christmas Carols (II)', *Canu Gwerin (Folk Song)*, 12 (1989), 10–11. For 'Country Bumpkin' see John Walsh, *Caledonian Country Dances* (London: J. Walsh, *c*.1745), p. 85, but it is difficult to see how this version of the tune would fit lines 9–12. For 'Pilgrim' see p. 181.

42 Another *carol deuair*

I have not been home		since Monday night
But drinking liquor		[and moving] from one gentleman's house to the next;
I have not been home		since Thursday night
4	But drinking liquor	here and there.
We have heard that there is		mead and bragget
And good ale		in this house,
And a virtuous wife		who will give it gladly
8	And that the good man	is a sociable person.
And because he is,		he shall have liquor;
Open the door,		my slender, pretty young woman
And allow me into the house,		I am almost freezing with cold,
12	Open the windows,	here is blessed Mary and her lights.
Stand ready,		here we come
[Bringing] you a gift		[that is] beautiful to behold;
It is not the work of artisans		that [you see] on it
16	Or [even] the work of the best carver	in England.

	Gwaith angylion	sy o amgylch hon;
	I fo archodd Mair	o'i haur gadair
	[R]oddi'r wirod	i forwyndod
20	[A]c yfed gwen	o'i llaw hirwen.

	[M]inne a barcha	wen os medra,
	Pob bys hirwyn	i liw'r ewyn
	Yn fodrwye	aur chweugeinie.
24	Wasel! Wasel!	forwyn ddiogel.

	Wasel! eto	er mwyn honno
	Ac Wasel! eto	at bawb a'n caro;
	[Y cwmp]ni mwyn,	mi a yfaf atyn
28	[A] g[a]llw glanddyn,	'Holin! Holin!'

Dienw

Sources

J. Glyn Davies, 'Two Songs from an Anglesey Ms.', in Osborn Bergin and Carl J. S. Marstrander (eds), *Miscellany presented to Kuno Meyer by some of his friends and pupils on the occasion of his appointment to the chair of Celtic philology in the University of Berlin* (Halle a. S.: M. Niemeyer, 1912), pp. 123–4, available on-line at *https://archive.org/details/miscellanyprese00berg/page/122/mode/2up* (accessed 23 April 2020).

T. H. Parry-Williams, *Llawysgrif Richard Morris o Gerddi* [Richard Morris' Manuscript of Poems] (Cardiff: University of Wales Press, 1931), pp. lxx–lxxi.

Date
Sixteenth century, after 1544.

Locality
Anglesey.

It is the work of angels   that is on it all around;
Mary requested   from her golden chair
That liquor should be given   to maidenhood
20 And that a pretty girl should   from her slender white hand.
      drink

I shall pay my respects   to the pretty girl, if I am able to,
Each long white finger   that belongs to the [one with
                                        a complexion] the colour
                                        of the crest of a wave

Is [bejewelled] with rings   of golden half sovereigns.
24 Wassail! Wassail!   true young woman.

Wassail! once more   for her sake
And Wassail! again   to all who love us;
The genial company,   I shall drink to them
28 [And] I call a good man,   'Holly! Holly!'

Anonymous

Note

It is plausible that this poem is answered by the poem entitled 'Ateb i
gân wasael' [An answer to a wassail song] that follows it in the Richard
Morris manuscript; see Poem 43 below.
Line 23: *aur chweugeinie*, half sovereigns were first produced in 1544.
Line 28 those outside the door call out to Holin, the householder, to
open up and allow the wassailers entrance; cf. poem 9.7–8. In the folk-
lore of some of the early Welsh free-metre poems Holin (Holly) repre-
sents manhood and Ifin (Ivy) represents womanhood; see Brinley Rees,
Dulliau'r Canu Rhydd 1500–1650 [The Forms of Free-verse Poems
1500–1650] (Cardiff: University of Wales Press, 1952), pp. 28–31.

Metre
Tôn deuair.

43 Ateb i gân wasael

[Erbyn d]arfod i chwi eich cân
[Fe a]eth y tân yn niffod;
[Mae bwyd] a diod yn ein tŷ
4   [Er hyn] nid ydi o'n barod.

Roedd gin y forwyn yn ei dwrn
Gynne swrn o gynhwylle;
Nhw a ddarfuon, bod ac un,
8   Nid oes yr un heb ole.

Ac os ewch chi i'n tŷ ni
'Mogelwch chi rhag llithro:
Torri eich gyddfe a ellwch chi
12   Gin li a defni dano.

Mae yma fwrdd heb ddim o'i draed,
A hwn, fe'i gwnaed o'n isel,
A hen garthen arno fydd –
16   A'i thaflu hi'r dydd i'r gornel.

Mae yma dorth o fara haidd
A hon, o fraidd, heb enllyn,
Gwedi malu hon yn lluwch
20   Â'r gogor rhuwch o'i gogryn.

Mae yma fail o enwyn glas
Ac arno mae blas y fudde;
Hawdd ichwi wybod, erbyn hyn,
24   Mai hwn yw'ch enllyn chwithe.

Mae yma asgwrn lle bu cig,
Nid â mo'th big di ynddo;
Ti gei hwnnw ger dy fron
28   A hoga di ddigon arno.

Mae yma lonaid baril glân
O loywon sucan eisin,
Ac o bydd syched arnoch chi
32   Mi a'i llenwaf i fo yn ddibrin.

43 A reply to a wassail

Now you have finished your song
The fire has gone out;
There is food and drink in our house
4   But it is not ready.

The maid had in her fist,
A moment ago, a number of candles;
They are all burned out, every one,
8   There is not one that is unlit.

And if you come into our house
Be careful in case you slip:
You could break your necks
12   On a flow [of water] and trickles under[foot].

There is a table here with no legs,
And this, it was built low,
Usually has an old blanket over it
16   That is thrown into a corner during the day.

There is a loaf of barley bread here
And this almost without a relish [i.e. dry bread],
This has been ground into dust
20   And sifted through a ranging sieve.

There is here a pail of buttermilk diluted with water
That tastes of the churn;
It is easy for you to know, by now,
24   That it is to be your relish.

There is here a bone where there was once meat,
Your beak will not bite into it;
That will be set before you
28   And you must keep at it with a grindstone.

There is here a completely full barrel
Of shiny flummery,
And if you are thirsty
32   I shall fill it unsparingly.

Mynna ichwi fara gwyn
Ac erbyn y flwyddyn nesa
O'r gwenith sydd yn y llong
36   O'r tu hwnt i Garmon Seia.

Mi fynna eto wella eich ffâr:
Pasteiod adar gwylltion
Sydd yn hedeg [draw] yn stôr
40   O'r tu hwnt i Fôr y Werddon.

Os daw gofyn pwy a'i gwnaeth,
Pa waeth pwy fu'n canu?
Dyn yn enwi i chwi bob saig
44   Rhag codi'r wraig o'i gwely.

Aer Castell Bylchwyn

Sources
Davies, 'Two Songs', pp. 124–8.
Parry-Williams, *Llawysgrif Richard Morris o Gerddi*, pp. lxxi–lxxiii.
Ifans, *Sêrs a Rybana*, pp. 178–9.

Date
Sixteenth century, possibly after 1544.

Locality
Anglesey.

Notes
It is plausible that this poem answers the poem entitled 'Carol deuair eto' [Another *carol deuair*] that precedes it in the Richard Morris manuscript; see Poem 42 above. 'The beginning and end of the song are apparently preserved, the last stanza ending conventionally. The condition of the text points to a defective oral source in the original Ms.'; see Davies, 'Two Songs', p. 128.
Line 36 Garmon Seia, an unknown location, possibly a sea, cf. line 20.
The following note appears immediately following the poem: 'Aer kastell bylchwyn ai kant i dderbun gwirod gun Edward ap Hugh Gwynn aer Bodewrud oedd yn trigo yn llan beder' [The heir of Castell Bylchwyn

I shall insist that you have white bread
For next year
Made from the wheat that is on the ship
36   That is beyond Garmon Seia.

I insist further to improve your fare:
[With] pies [where the main ingredient is] wild birds
That fly [over] in numbers
40   From beyond the Irish Sea.

If anyone asks who composed this,
What does it matter who composed it?
A man who names for you each course of a feast
44   In order to avoid having to call the wife from her bed.

The Heir of Castell Bylchwyn

sang this to receive liquor from Edward ap Hugh Gwynn heir of Bod-
ewryd who was staying in Llanbedr].
Castell Bylchwyn, the home of Thomas Vychan, is situated in the parish of
Llanddyfnan in Anglesey, about four miles north-east of Llangefni. The heir
of Castell Bylchwyn 'was probably Thomas Vychan who signed the Heral-
dic Visitations in 1594. He was a cynghanedd poet, and in Llanstephan MS.
118, there are two poems by him, one (fo. 45b) to Huw Gwyn and his wife
Mary Gruffydd, and the other (fo. 59b) to Sian the wife of Morus Gruffydd.
He is dated 1540 in the index by Richard Morris at the end of the vol-
ume; probably a guess. Edward ap Hugh Gwyn's wife [Jane] was a cousin
to Thomas Vychan, and this fixes his period independently of the other
dates ascertained'; see Davies, 'Two Songs', p. 128. See also L. Dwnn and
S. R. Meyrick (eds), *Heraldic Visitations of Wales and Part of the Marches:
Between the Years 1586 and 1613, Under the Authority of Clarencieux and
Norroy, Two Kings at Arms*, 2 (Llandovery: W. Rees, 1846), p. 269. Thomas
Vychan married Elin daughter of Ieuan Llwyd ap Rhys.
Bodewryd is situated about four miles from Amlwch in Anglesey.
Edward ap Hugh Gwynn of Bodewryd by Elin (d. 1589) was the eldest
of six sons.

Metre
Awdl-gywydd in two verse units, see p. 342.

44   Carol gwirod ar ddychmygion yn drws

Dyma fy hanes a meddwl fy mynwes:
Drwy gariad difales, dyfelwch
Beth ydi'r gornelog, fel dolen ddu, ddeiliog
4   A'i chanol yn holltog, dealltwch?

Beth sy mor ddyrys a'r naill ben mor giwrus
A'i ddolen yn ddilys, mae yn weddus i waith?
Yn fodrwya mae yn droea, naws dwymyn a'i stumia,
8   Cig arno bob bora mae bariaeth.

Beth sy mor feinion a'u peisia yn felynion
A'u penna yn o gochion ar gychwyn?
Fy seren siriolwedd a'i thyfiad o edafedd,
12   Dychymyg, mwyn agwedd, mynegwn.

Beth ydi'r las hirwen sy'n tywallt yn llawen
O'i bol i'r winwydden wineuddu
A'i min yn ddywedog a'i godre yn fodrwyog
16   Yn derbyn yn bwyllog heb ballu?

Beth ydi'r glew, cadarn, di-ŵr a diarian,
Difales, difilen, dyfelwch?
Difater mewn cannyn yw gweled gyferbyn
20   Y priddyn coluddyn, cwilyddiwch!

Mi ddwedis, do, ddigon o'm ofer ddychmygion
Ni cha[e]d mo'r atebion, rwy'n tybied.
Ertolwg, gwawr heini, 'rwy yma ymron sythu,
24   Tyrd yn gwit i agori i mi o gariad.

Richard Morris (1703–79)

44 A wassail song in the form of a riddle song
    [to be sung] at the door

This is my story and the opinions of my heart:
In well-intentioned love, guess
What is it that has corners, like a dark leafy loop,
4   With a cleft centre, you understand?

What is it that is so complicated and on one end so exquisite
And its loop sound, it is suitable for work?
It is [all] rings and turns, with the disposition of fever and
        its contortions,
8   There is meat on it each morning of greed.

What is it that is so slender and their petticoats yellow
And their heads quite red and held high?
My star of cheerful countenance whose growth is [slender]
        as thread,
12   We set this riddle in a courteous manner.

What is the shiny, tall and radiant [vessel] that pours merrily
From its belly to the tawny black vine
And its mouth loquacious and its hem in rings
16   Receiving with patience [and] without ceasing?

What is it that is strong, robust, without husband and without money,
Without malice, is kind, take a guess?
A hundred people would be reluctant to see opposite [them]
20   The bilious wretch, shame on you!

I have said, yes, enough of my foolish riddles,
No answers were found, I presume.
I beseech you, nimble dawn, I am almost stiff with cold here,
24   Come quickly to open up for me out of love.

Richard Morris (1703–79)

Sources
Cwrtmawr 167B, 113–15.
Parry-Williams, *Llawysgrif Richard Morris o Gerddi*, pp. 8–9.
Ifans, *Sêrs a Rybana*, p. 181.

Date
1716.

Locality
Anglesey.

45 Ateb i'r carol dychmygion [*Taw rhag cywilydd*]

Pwy ydi'r gwŷr acw sy'n gweiddi mor arw,
Ein bygwth ni heddiw, yn salw ac yn sur?
I'ch ateb yn gynta, rwy'n tybied mai pastai –
4 Ydyw'r saig ora i segurwyr.

Yn ail, y mae'ch cwestiwn am Jack, mi debygwn,
A bery i wŷr Annwn ymrwymo,
A chaffael, i'w ganlyn, gig y ci melyn,
8 Mae hyn yn rhy erwin i'w wario.

Yn drydydd, dychmygwn eich meddwl a'ch cwestiwn,
Canhwylle cynullwn, mae fi'n rhydrwm rhwth,
A chael canhwyllbren o bres wedi'i loywi,
12 Ewch ymaith am hynny na amheuwch.

Pedwerydd dychymyg i'w dallt yn ddiddiffyg,
Y fflagen arbennig a'i chynnig nid gwiw
I'r gwpan ddu, fechan yn tywallt yn llawen,
16 Mor gymen ei hamdden hi heddiw.

Ateb
I'ch ateb yn union o'ch ofer ddychmygion,
Chwi gawsoch yn union, wŷr hyfion, y rhain,
Y priddyn coluddyn sy i'w weled gyferbyn
20 Yw cwrw mewn corun dyn cywrain.

Dienw

Note
For the answering carol see Poem 45; lines 1–4 refer to a pie; lines 5–8 a
roasting spit; lines 9–12 candles in brass candlesticks; lines 13–16 a wine
flagon or jug, possibly pewter, and a cup; and lines 17–20 refer to beer.

Metres
Verses 1, 3–6 *tri thrawiad dwbl*; see 'Beth sy mor feinion?', p. 173;
verse 2 *tri thrawiad sengl* can be sung to 'Tri Thrawiad Gwynedd',
see p. 183.

45 Answer to the riddle song carol [*Taw rhag cywilydd*]

Who are those men who are shouting in such a rough manner,
Threatening us today, contemptible and bitter?
The first answer, I believe it is a pie –
4   That is the best dish of food for idlers.

Secondly, I believe your question concerns a Jack,
That causes the men of Annwn to prepare themselves,
And to obtain, with that, the meat of the yellow dog,
8   This is too terrible to behold.

Thirdly, we imagine your thoughts and your question,
Let us gather candles, I am portly [and] greedy,
And obtain a polished brass candlestick,
12   So go away, do not doubt that.

The fourth riddle is perfectly understood,
The special flagon and its excellent offering
Pouring merrily into the little black cup,
16   How appropriate is its leisure today.

Answer
To answer you directly regarding your foolish riddles,
You received these [answers] immediately, intrepid men,
The bilious wretch seen opposite
20   Is so [because the] beer went to the good man's head.

Anonymous

Sources
Parry-Williams, *Llawysgrif Richard Morris o Gerddi*, pp. 152–3.
Ifans, 'Canu Gwaseila', 3, 846.

Date
?1716.

Locality
Anglesey.

46   Dyrïau Mynediad ar Ŵyl Fair

Nos dawch! Gyda'ch cennad
Rŷm ni'n dŵad fesul dau
A chwithau mor garedig
4   Heb gynnig mo'n nacáu;
Am agor drws eich annedd,
Roedd hi'n oeredd acw i ni,
Fe ganwn fel y medrwn,
8   Cychwynnwn atoch chi.

A'n lleisiau sydd yn gryglyd
Gan annwyd yn 'r hin oer
Heb gael na thân na chynnyrch
12   Na llewyrch gan y lloer,
A'n traed a'n dwylo yn oerion
A'r galon sydd yn wan,
Gobeithio cawn ni groeso
16   I mendio yn y man.

Nid o chwant i yfed
Eich cwrw a'ch clared clir
Y daethom yma heno,
20   Os gwnewch chi goelio'r gwir;
I deithio fel y Doethion
Y daethon at eich tai,
Dechreuodd yn Jwdea
24   O'r rheini'r hyna' rai.

Notes
A carol in answer to Poem 44.
Line 5: Jack refers to a roasting Jack that rotates meat roasting on a spit,
seen in Welsh kitchens during the seventeenth and eighteenth centuries.
Line 6: Annwn is the Otherworld in Welsh mythology.

Metres
Verses 1, 3–5 *tri thrawiad sengl* can be sung to 'Tri Thrawiad Gwynedd';
see p. 183; verse 2 *tri thrawiad dwbl* can be sung to 'Beth sy mor fein-
ion?' see p. 173.

46 Verses on Entrance at *Gŵyl Fair*

Good evening! With your permission
We come, two at a time,
And you are so kind
4   In not attempting to deny us [entry];
For opening the door to your dwelling-place,
It was cold out there for us,
We shall sing as we can,
8   We begin our way towards you.

And our voices are hoarse
Because of the chill in the cold air
[And for not] having received fire or provisions
12   Or radiance from the moon,
And our feet and our hands are cold
And we are faint-hearted,
I hope we shall be welcomed
16   In order to be restored to health before very long.

It is not because we wish to drink
Your beer and your bright claret
That we have come here this evening,
20   If you will believe the truth;
To travel as did the Magi,
[That is why] we came to your residences,
They started off in Judaea
24   The oldest ones from among those [Magi].

Seredjws oedd y cynta,
Hwn yma penna Pab;
Cystennin, pan y'u gwelodd,
28 A folodd Fair a'i Mab;
A'r Esgob Dewi daiol,
(Rhagorol oedd y gair)
I'r Alffa gyda'r delyn
32 Rhoes glod i'r Forwyn Fair.

Meddyliwch chwithau'r amsar,
Rhowch gadar ger ein bron
I gofio am forwyndod
36 Y forwyn ryfedd hon;
Cyn i ni newid mesur,
Mae'n rhy hwyr i chwi roi,
O'i chwmpas, nôl y ffasiwn,
40 Fe dreiwn ninnau droi.

Dienw

Sources
NLW 9168A, ff. 82ʳ–3ʳ.
Ifans, *Sêrs a Rybana*, p. 182.

Variant reading
Line 25 Feredjws (NLW 9168A, 82ᵛ).

Date
Before 1767.

Locality
North Wales.

Notes
Line 21 mentions the Magi, or Wise Men, who visited Jesus bearing gifts of gold, frankincense and myrrh (see the Gospel according to Saint Matthew 2:1–12). They are generally known as Melchior, Caspar and Balthasar. Lines 25–9, however, name the Magi in this Welsh

The first was Seregius,
This [person] here is the chief Pope;
Constantine, when he saw them,
28 Worshipped Mary and her Son;
And good Bishop David
(Word has it that [he] was excellent)
To the Alpha, on the harp,
32 Praised the Virgin Mary.

You too [must] consider the date,
Set a chair before us
To remember the maidenhood
36 Of this extraordinary young woman;
Before we change the metre,
It is too late for you to give,
About her, according to custom,
40 We shall attempt to turn.

Anonymous

context as Seredjws (Pope Sergius I, whose Papacy began in 687 and ended at his death in 701); see Jeffrey Richards, *The Popes and the Papacy in the Early Middle Ages: 476–752* (London: Routledge Revivals, 2015); Cystennin, Emperor Constantine the Great, the first Christian emperor, son of the Empress Helena, or in Welsh tradition Elen Luyddog, daughter of a chieftain living in Segontium (Caernarfon) and heroine of 'Breuddwyd Macsen Wledig' [The Dream of Macsen Wledig]; and Bishop David, the patron saint of Wales, see S. Baring-Gould and J. Fisher, *The Lives of the British Saints*, 2 (London: The Honourable Society of Cymmrodorion, 1908), pp. 285–322.

Line 23 states that the Magi set out from Judaea on their journey to find the Messiah, whereas the Scriptures state that Judaea was their destination point: 'After Jesus was born in Bethlehem in Judaea, during the time of King Herod, Magi from the east came to Jerusalem' (see the Gospel according to Saint Matthew 2:1).

Metre
7.6.7.6.D.

47 [Carol cadair]

Wel, nos dawch yn ystig y teulu nodedig,
Trwy'ch cennad gwnawn gynnig cerdd fiwsig i Fair;
Er cofio am ei mawrlles cydbynciwn o bwrpas
4   Lân gyffas i'r ddynas ddianair.

Er cofio am ei noson, mewn cadar rhown wenfron,
Peth ffeind cael yn dirion tra ffyddlon a phur,
Cydgerddwn yn weddus, cydleisiwn yn flasus,
8   Côr trefnus, fawl brydus fel brodyr.

Pan oedd Mair wen hyfryd yn ifanc mewn hawddfyd
Dôi angel Duw'r Bywyd i agoryd y gwir;
Fe chwyddai ei chorff hyfryd trwy asbri'r Glân Ysbryd
12   Ac felly danfonwyd i'r feinir.

A Mair, pan eisteddodd mewn cadar, hi ganodd
Gerdd felys o'i gwirfodd pan welodd Ei waith
Yn ennyn tân golau ar ben y canhwyllau,
16   Rhoi gwirod yn olau i Fair eilwaith.

Y wreigdda fwyn hynod gwrandewch ar ein traethod,
Prysurwch â gwirod wiw hynod i hon;
Gwnaed meinir fwyneidd-dro ei dal rhwng ei dwylo
20   Tra byddom ni'n deinio gwers union.

Os mynnwch, lliw'r manod, archwaethwch y wirod,
Rhowch hon i'r gŵr hynod awch lewglod o'i law;
Gwnewch chwitha, gŵr gwaredd, roi hon mewn parch puredd
24   I'r wraig dda, fwyn, haeledd a hylaw.

Oed Iesu dewisol a draethaf i ethol
Pan luniwyd y garol mwyn moddol, Amen:
Un mil a saith ganmlwydd, naw chwe deg yn digwydd,
28   Ac unflwydd, mawr burffydd heb orffen.

Robert Prichard 'Robin yr Aber' o Lŷn

47 [Chair carol]

Well, good night in earnest, notable family,
With your leave we shall offer up to Mary a poem with music;
In memory of her goodness we shall sing purposefully
4   In sincere acknowledgement of the renowned woman.

In order to celebrate her festival night we shall place a
    white-breasted girl in a chair,
It is a fine thing to find [a girl who is] gentle, exceedingly faithful
    and pure,
We shall walk together in a seemly fashion, we shall sing together
    sweetly,
8   An orderly choir, poetic praise as brothers would.

When the holy and delightful Mary was young and carefree
An angel of the God of Life came to open up the truth;
Her lovely body swelled with the life of the Holy Spirit
12   And in that way was it brought about for the young woman.

And Mary, when she sat in a chair, sang
A sweet song of her own accord when she saw His work
Lighting a bright light atop the candles,
16   Giving Mary for the second time a lighted drink.

Notable and gentle mistress of the house, listen to our address,
Make haste with a splendid goodly drink for her;
Let the gentle girl hold it in her hands
20   While we deign to offer an honest stanza of poetry.

If you please, [one with a complexion] the colour of driven snow,
    relish the drink,
Place it in the hand of the distinguished gentleman whose mettle
    deserves mighty praise;
And you, genial gentleman, give it from pure respect
24   To the good woman who is gentle, generous and obliging.

I elect to declare the age of the chosen Jesus
When the sweet-sounding, seemly carol was composed, Amen:
It was in [the year] one thousand and seven hundred years [and]
    sixty-nine,
28   Plus one year, great [and] pure faith without end.

Robert Prichard 'Robin yr Aber' of Llŷn

Sources
NLW 19163A, ff. 34ᵛ–6ʳ.

Ifans, 'Canu Gwaseila', 3, 876–7.

Date
1770.

Locality
North-west Wales.

48 Carol cadair i'w chanu ar un o'r hen fesurau –
'Cynllaiddief Gŵyl Fair, y rhan gyntaf ohono'

Y teulu mwyn, llariedd, am agor eich annedd
Fe leisiwn gynghanedd wych, hoywedd i chwi
O glod i Fair sanctedd, mam Iesu Tangnefedd,
4   A ddaeth o'i nef orsedd i'r groywedd, oer gri.

A hyn oedd ryfeddol i Frenin gwlad nefol
Ymwisgo yn gnawd dynol, mor raddol Mair oedd;
Rhyfeddach ei eni o hon heb iôr iddi,
8   O Dad y goleuni, rhôi ei gweddi iddo yn goedd.

Trwy'ch cennad, y gwrda, fe ddown rhag ein blaena
I'ch hyfryd gynteddfa, deg lawna dŷ glân,
I gofio Mair addas yn magu ei Meseias,
12   Fe ganwn o'i chwmpas, ŵyl gynnes, wael gân.

Rhowch gadair mewn trefnoedd ar ganol eich neuoedd
A merch o'ch gwyryfoedd anhenoedd yn hon,
A bach-fab chwech wythnos o oed, os yw'n agos,
16   Ar liniaiu, yn ddiymaros, wir linos, wawr lon.

Ynghylch deugain nydd, felly, oedd oedran yr Iesu
Nos Ŵyl Fair y darfu, mawr garu, Mair gu,
Sef g'leuo'r canhwylla i hon a'i Mab hyna
20   A wnaeth y Gorucha i'r Meseia er moes hy.

Note
The author is Robert Prichard of Llŷn, as noted in the manuscript NLW 19163A.

Metre
Tri thrawiad sengl; the song can be sung to 'Gadael Tir y ffordd hwyaf'/'Leave Land' see p. 180; see further Kinney, 'Tunes (II)', 11–13; Kinney and Evans (eds), *Hen Alawon*, number 42 and pp. 101–2.

48 Chair carol to be sung in one of the old metres – 'Cynllaiddief Gŵyl Fair, the first part'

Noble, genial family, for having opened up your dwelling-place
We shall sing you an excellent, vivacious harmony
Of praise for holy Mary, the mother of Jesus [the Prince of] Peace
4   Who descended from his throne in heaven into the clear, cold lament.

And this was extraordinary, that the King of a heavenly realm
Should put on human flesh, Mary was so blessed;
It is even more extraordinary that he was born of her who had
        no lord,
8   Of the Father of lights, she prayed to him in the sight of all.

With your permission, good man, we come at once
Into your pleasant court, a fine, bustling, good dwelling,
To remember worthy Mary bringing up the Messiah,
12   Around her we shall sing [on this] happy feast day a humble song.

Place a chair, in an orderly manner, in the middle of your room
And a young woman from the midst of your young virgins [to sit]
        in it,
And a six-week-old baby boy, or thereabouts,
16   Without delay, in the lap of the pure girl, joyous dawn.

Therefore Jesus was about forty days old
On *Gŵyl Fair* when this happened to beloved Mary, immense loving,
Namely that the Almighty lit the candles for her and her firstborn Son,
20   To the Messiah, on account of a steadfast life.

Troi'r mesur yn frisgiach:

Wel, bellach, mewn undod chwenychem gael gwirod
O law y gŵr priod, dda fragod di-freg
I blejio'r fun dyner sy yna yn ei chader
24 Dim 'ato mewn amser, fwyn, dyner fun deg.

Ertolwg, wawr ganned, rhowch ddiod i'ch cofled
Er cof am fawr gariad, gras daenied, Grist Oen:
Fel hyn mewn cyffelybiaeth ar fraich ei fam berffaith
28 O Jwda yn mynd ymaith draw Beniaeth, drwy boen.

Os darfu i chwi yfed, fain, teredd, fun eurad,
Fe gym'wn, trwy'ch cennad, y llestriad o'ch llaw,
Am hynny, wawr hawddgar, awch codwch o'ch cadair
32 Pan weloch eich amser, fwyn tro, ar fynd [draw].

Pennill i'r cantor cyntaf a gaffo'r cwpan â'r wirod i'w law:

Y cwpan â'r wirod, pan welwy' dy waelod,
Pâr hynny i'm pen fedd-dod a syndod i'm sain;
Gan rif y canhwyllau sy o amgylch dy 'mylau
36 Mi losga'r ceg fochau coeg fychain.

Cydsafwn o gwmpas i yfed o gwmpas
Gu rodd y gŵr addas, fawr hanes fir hen;
Bid llwydd i chwi a'ch cerant a'ch gwraig am eich rhoddiant
40 A nefoedd i'ch meddiant a mwyniant. Amen.

Y teulu mwyn, talgrwn, i chwi mae i ni ymostwn,
Fe ddarfu inni'n mosiwn a'n mesur, rŵ, rŵ,
Os byddwch mor weddol â'm harwain i'r gongol
44 Fe ffeiriwn hen garol am gwrw.

William Evans (1730–93)

Change to a brisker tune:

> Well, henceforth, in unity we desire liquor
> From the hand of the married man, a good bragget in continuous
>   supply
> In order to pledge the gentle woman who is there in her chair
24 Without losing time, beautiful, fine gentle woman.

> I beseech you, bright dawn, give your dear one in your lap a drink
> In remembrance of the immense love of Christ the Lamb, who
>   disseminated grace:
> In this way in comparison, in the arms of his perfect mother,
28 The Lord moved away yonder from Judah, in anguish.

> If you have drunk, slender, pure, glorious young woman,
> With your permission we shall take the cup from your hand,
> Consequently, comely dawn, keenly arise from your chair
32 When you see it is time for you to move [yonder], a pleasant
>   occasion.

A stanza for the first person who receives into his hands the cup
containing the liquor:

> The cup containing the liquor, when I see your bottom,
> It will bring a drunkenness to my head and a stupefaction to
>   my voice;
> On account of the number of candles that are about your [i.e. the
>   cup's] edges
36 It will singe the cavities of the cheeks, empty [and] small.

> Let us all stand together in a circle to drink round about
> The kind gift of the worthy man, the splendid story of ancient beer.
> May you, your wife and your loved ones prosper on account of
>   your gift
40 And may heaven and joy be yours. Amen.

> Noble family, complete, we submit ourselves to you,
> We have finished making our requests and our song, rŵ, rŵ.
> If you would be so excellent as to guide us into the corner
44 We shall exchange an old carol for beer.

William Evans (1730–93)

Sources
NLW 9168A, ff. 8ᵛ–11ʳ.

Ifans, *Sêrs a Rybana*, pp. 183–4.

Date
1762.

Locality
North Wales.

Notes
For the author, William Evans/Bifan y Gadlys (1730–93), see W. Gilbert Williams, 'Hen Gymeriadau Llanwnda: William Bifan y Gadlys' [Llanwnda's Old Characters: William Bifan of Gadlys], *Cymru* [Wales], 23 (1902), 138.

49 Carol diolch nos Ŵyl Fair i'w ganu ar 'Consêt Prince Rupert'

Can diolch, wŷr dilys awch hoenus, i chwi,
Eich croeso oedd yn barod iawn nod yma i ni;
Ni gawson wledd wresogol sir
4   A chariad pur a chwrw a bir;
Od y clod a bwyd yn glir, mae'n eirwir fy nod,
Ni gawson ein digonedd, werth punt o helynt haeledd, mae'n
      glirwedd y clod,
Yn helaeth a hylwydd a rhwydd tan y rhod.

8   Ni gawson ein digon, wedd burion, o'r bir,
Rŷm ni wedi meddwi, dowch â g'leuni yma'n glir;
Yr ŷm ni'n gweld y tŷ yn troi,
Mae'n pennau yrŵan wedi ymroi,
12 Ein traed o tanom sydd yn ffoi, mae'n rhy hwyr i ni
Geisio myned allan, ym mhle mae'r drws yrŵan, wŷr breulan
      eu bri?
Nos da, deulu haeledd, wych, hafedd, i chwi.

Line 8 cf. the Epistle of James 1:17 'Every good gift and every perfect gift is from above, coming down from the Father of lights, with whom there is no variation or shadow due to change.'

Line 28 references the flight into Egypt recounted in the Gospel according to Saint Matthew 2:13–23.

Metre

The tune 'Cynllaiddief Gŵyl Fair' has not been preserved. Stanzas 1–8 and 10 (lines 1–32, 37–40 minus the 'Amen') are on *tri thrawiad dwbl* and can be sung to 'Tri Thrawiad Gwynedd' (see p. 183); stanzas 9 and 11 (lines 33–6, 41–4) are on *tri thrawiad sengl* and can be sung to 'Leave Land'/'Gadael Tir y ffordd hwyaf' (see p. 180).

49   A *Gŵyl Fair* carol of thanksgiving to be sung to 'Prince Rupert's Conceit'

Thank you a hundredfold, sincere men of keen spirit,
You have given us a ready welcome here, in true purpose;
We have received a feast of warming cheer
4   And pure love and ale and beer;
Of complete praise and provisions, my objective is sincere,
We have had our fill, a pound's worth of generous conduct,
        the praise is shining,
Abundant and speedy and swift under the sun.

8   In good manner we have had our fill of beer,
We are drunk, bring a bright light here;
We can see the house spinning,
Now our heads have surrendered,
12   Our feet are fleeing from under us, it is too late for us
To attempt to go out, where is the door now, men of noble
        renown?
Good evening to you, generous family, splendid [and] gentle.

O, wrth gofio, dowch lancie da droie, di-drai,
16   Rhowch gusan i'r lodes sy liwdeg, ddi-fai,
        A fu'n y gader ger ein bron
        Ar ddiwedd nos, hardd linos lon,
        Meinir hynod ydyw hon a phurion ei ffydd;
20   Lwc dda a fyddo iddi heb gas, a gras i ymgroesi rhag gwegi yn
                ddi-gudd,
        Ac iechyd yn heini a daioni bob dydd.

        Ffarwél a fo ichwi am eleni yn ddi-lys,
        Mi awn ymaith ar adeg, yr ydym ar frys;
24   Cewch ganddon lonydd, ar fy ngair,
        Y flwyddyn yma, ffeindia ffair,
        Ni ddown ni ond hynny tan Ŵyl Fair i drwblio mo'ch pen,
        A bendith Duw rown eto i'r wraig rasol am ein croeso a'n sirio'n
                ddi-sen;
28   Rhoed Duw i chwi lwyddiant a mwyniant. Amen.

John Jones, Llanddeiniolen

Sources
NLW 346B, 147.
Ifans, *Sêrs a Rybana*, p. 185.

Date
1773.

Locality
Llanddeiniolen, four miles from Caernarfon in Gwynedd.

O, now that I remember, come, young men of unfailing good turns,
16   Give the young woman who is of fair countenance [and] faultless,
       a kiss,
[She] who was in the chair before us
At the close of the evening, beautiful, joyful young woman,
She is an excellent woman and pure of faith;
20   May she have good luck without enmity, and grace to guard
       against open vanity,
And vigorous health and goodness each day.

Fare you well for this year, with certainty,
We shall depart at the proper time, we are in a hurry;
24   Upon my word, we shall leave you in peace
For this year, most pleasant commotion,
We shall not come to trouble your head [with anything] again until
       [next] *Gŵyl Fair*,
And we wish God's blessing once again on the gracious wife for
       welcoming us and cheering us up without rebuke;
28   May God give you prosperity and joy. Amen.

John Jones, Llanddeiniolen

Note
Prince Rupert of the Rhine (1619–82) was a Royalist cavalry commander
who fought in the English Civil War (1642–51).

Metre
For the English Civil War tune 'Consêt Prince Rupert' or 'Prince Rupert's
Conceit' see p. 175.

APPENDIX

Verse Forms

1. Strict-metre Welsh poetry

Cyhydedd hir [long *cyhydedd*]: is 'a metrical double line of 19 sylla-
bles, having four parts of 5, 5, 5, 4 syllables, the first three rhyming
together and the fourth supporting the chief rhyme', see *Geiriadur
Prifysgol Cymru/A Dictionary of the Welsh Language*, available online at
http://geiriadur.ac.uk/gpc/gpc.html s.n. cyhydedd (accessed 26 March
2020).

Englyn unodl union [direct monorhyme *englyn*] (pl. *englynion unodl
union*): it has four lines of 10, 6, 7, 7 syllables, each line in full *cyng-
hanedd* (consonance). The last syllables of lines 2–4 rhyme with the
sixth, seventh, eighth or ninth syllable of line 1. The syllables in line 1
that follow the rhyme alliterate with the first part of line 2.

> Mi dybiais coeliais mai Calan – Ionawr
>   Sydd inni'n Ŵyl weithian;
>   Rhoddwch, wŷr rhwydd, o'ch arian
>   Ddernig o Galennig lân.

[I have judged [and] believed it to be New Year's Day | That is
now our high festival; | Give, generous men, from your wealth
| A small sum as a fine New Year's gift.]

On strict-metre verse forms see further:

R. M. Jones, 'Mesurau Cerdd Dafod' [Metres of Welsh Poetic Art], *Bulletin of the Board of Celtic Studies*, 27 (1978), 533–51.
John Morris-Jones, *Cerdd Dafod* [Welsh Poetic Art] (Oxford: Oxford University Press, 1930).

2. Free-metre Welsh poetry

Awdl-gywydd (pl. *awdl gywyddau*): in Welsh prosody a poem consisting of two lines of seven syllables; the end of the first line rhymes with the caesura of the second line. 'This is the strophe of the various Welsh metrical Psalms, the equivalent of the English model', see J. Glyn Davies, 'Two Songs from an Anglesey Ms.', in Osborn Bergin and Carl J. S. Marstrander (eds), *Miscellany Presented to Kuno Meyer by Some of his Friends and Pupils on the Occasion of his Appointment to the Chair of Celtic Philology in the University of Berlin* (Halle a. S.: M. Niemeyer, 1912), p. 127, available online at: *https://archive.org/ details/miscellanyprese00berg/page/126/mode/2up* (accessed 26 March 2020).

> Roedd gin y forwyn yn ei dwrn
> Gynne swrn o gynhwylle;
> Nhw a ddarfuon, bod ac un,
> Nid oes yr un heb ole. (Poem 43.5–8)

[The maid had in her fist, | A moment ago, a number of candles; | They are all burned out, every one, | There is not one that is unlit.]

Hen bennill [old stanza] (pl. *hen benillion*): a traditional quatrain popularly used to convey folk wit and wisdom: 'cynnyrch celfyddyd ddihyfforddiant, ddiddiwylliant, 'anymwybodol', i raddau helaeth (...) at eu canu, a hynny gan amlaf gyda'r delyn, y cedwid hwy gan rai pobl ar y cof ' [largely the product of an untrained, uncultivated, 'unconscious' art (...) some people knew them by heart so that they could sing them, most often to harp accompaniment', and to such an extent that they were referred to as *penillion telyn* [harp stanzas];

see T. H. Parry-Williams, *Hen Benillion* [Old Stanzas] (Llandysul: Gomer, 1988), p. 9.

> Chwi sy'n meddu aur ac arian
> Dedwydd ydych ar Ddydd Calan,
> Braint y rhai yw rhoi i'r tlodion
> A chyfrannu peth o'u moddion. (Poem 19.1–4)

[You who possess gold and silver | Are happy on New Year's Day, | It is their privilege to give to the poor | And to contribute some of their means.]

Mesur Salm 'Psalm Metre' in Welsh prosody, an iambic stanza of 8, 7, 8, 7 syllables with lines ending in accented and unaccented syllables alternately.

> Nid awn at gerlyn dygyn, dig
> I gynnig miwsig moesol,
> Ond i'r rhai haela, bracia'n bro
> A roddo groeso grasol. (Poem 6.21–4)

[We shall not visit crass, bitter churl[s] | To offer high-principled music, | But those who are most generous, most open-handed in our neighbourhood, | Who offer a gracious welcome.]

Pennill telyn [verse for harp] (pl. *penillion telyn*): see *Hen bennill* [old stanza].

Tôn deuair: This is a 4 + 4 rhyming couplet. 'Its bardic adoption was late, probably 16th century. It was a lower grade tune metre, semi-rhythmical, 4 to 7 syllables, limited only by two accents. It survived in its looser form well into the 18th century'; see J. Glyn Davies, 'Two Songs from an Anglesey Ms.', p. 127.

> Gartre nis bûm   er nos duw Llun
> Ond gwirota   'r hyd tai gwyrda;
> Ni bûm gartre   er nos Difie
> Ond gwirota   draw ac yma. (Poem 42.1–4)

[I have not been home since Monday night | But drinking liquor [and moving] from one gentleman's house to the next; | I have not been home since Thursday night | But drinking liquor here and there.]

Triban [triplet] (pl. *tribannau*): an epigramatic stanza in Welsh folk poetry, 'one of the metres used by the non-professional poets, the minstrels or the *Clêr*. It consists of two seven-syllable lines, followed by a third line of seven or eight syllables which rhymes with the caesura of the fourth line; the fourth line ends with an unaccented syllable rhyming with the first two lines'; see Meic Stephens (ed.), *The New Companion to the Literature of Wales* (Cardiff: University of Wales Press, 1998), p. 735.

Wel, dyma enw'r feinwen
Sy'n codi gyda'r seren,
A dyma'r warsel ore'i chlod
Sy'n canu a bod yn llawen. (Poem 30.1–4)

[Well, this is the name of the slender and beautiful one | Who rises with the star, | And this is the wassail of greatest praise | Who sings and is merry.]

See further Tegwyn Jones, *Tribannau Morgannwg* [Glamorgan *Tribannau*] (Llandysul: Gwasg Gomer, 1976), and the tunes and notes on the tunes by Daniel Huws, pp. 209–15.

Tri thrawiad sengl: [a single three-beat (metre)] 'so called because there are only 3 accents in the last line. It consists of dactyllic half lines of 6. 6. 6. 5.; 6. 6. 6. 3. syllables rhyming *aaab*; *cccb* (or *aaab*), the 4th ending in a masculine and the others in unaccented rhymes. The *a* rhyme is repeated in the middle of the 4th half line'; see Joseph T. Shipley (ed.), *Dictionary of World Literature – Criticism, Forms, Technique* (New York: The Philosophical Library, 1943), s.v.

Mab Duw a glodforwn, clod lafar cydlefwn,
Da fiwsig dyfeisiwn, cydseiniwn â sant;
Cydgodwch i fyny od aethoch i gysgu,
Lân deulu, i ganu gogoniant. (Poem 1.1–4)

[We praise the Son of God, we unite in our cry of resounding praise, | We devise good music, we harmonize with a saint; | Rise up together if you have gone to sleep, | Good family, to sing glory.]

Tri thrawiad dwbl: [three-beat (metre) doubled] because there are three accents in lines two and four:

Ond wedi inni lwybro a cherdded a chwilio
Ni ymroesom i gordio fel gwyrda,
A dŵad, o'r diwedd, i wneuthur anhunedd
Ar deulu diomedd sydd yma. (Poem 4.9–12)

[But once we had covered ground and walked and searched | We devoted ourselves to sounding chords as noblemen do, | And to come, at last, to cause a wakefulness | In the generous family that is within.]

See e-publication R. M. Jones, *Seiliau Beirniadaeth*, 2 (Caerfyrddin [Carmarthen]: Coleg Cymraeg Cenedlaethol, 2014), unpaged.

Bibliography

Primary sources

Aberystwyth, National Library of Wales

Cwrtmawr 40B 'Barddoniaeth' [Poetry].
Cwrtmawr 128A 'Llyfr Ofer Gerddi Margaret Davies 1738' [A book of Frivolous Poems by Margaret Davies 1738].
Cwrtmawr 167B 'Llyfr o hen ganeuon (...) ' [A book of old songs (...)].
Cwrtmawr 171D 'Casgliad o Hen Gerddi' [A collection of Old Poems].
Cwrtmawr 225D 'Llyfr Dafydd Marpole' [The book of Dafydd Marpole].
Cwrtmawr 228A 'Barddoniaeth' [Poetry].
Cwrtmawr 242B 'Llyfr Cywyddau' [A book of *Cywyddau*].
Cwrtmawr 270B 'Transcripts by Mary Richards, etc.'.
Cwrtmawr 294B 'Llyfr John Morris' [The book of John Morris].
Cwrtmawr 398B 'Barddoniaeth' [Poetry].
Llanstephan 118 'Poetry'.
NLW 164C 'Sir John Williams Manuscripts: Edward Jones: Poetry, music, etc.'
NLW 346B 'Welsh Poetry by John Jones, Thomas Edwards, and Others'.
NLW 431B 'Welsh and English Poetry'.
NLW 434B 'Sir John Williams Manuscripts: Barddoniaeth' [Poetry].
NLW 527A 'Carwr y Cymru' [Lover of the Welsh people].
NLW 566B 'Celynog Manuscripts: "Llyfr Cedewain"' [The book of Cedewain].

NLW 719B 'Plas Power Manuscripts: Barddoniaeth' [Poetry].

NLW 788B 'Barddoniaeth, etc.' [Poetry, etc.].

NLW 821C 'A Survey of the Ancient and Present State of the County of Caernarvon by a Land surveyor, 1806'.

NLW 1131B 'Fforest Legionis Manuscripts Barddoniaeth' [Poetry].

NLW 1578B part of the 'Kinmel Manuscripts' collection.

NLW 1940A, i 'Melus-seiniau Cymru' (1817–25) available online, digitised by the National Library of Wales.

NLW 1940A, ii 'Per-seiniau Cymru' (1824–5) available online, digitised by the National Library of Wales.

NLW 3048D (Mostyn 145) 'Llyvyr Gwyn Cors y Gedol' [The White Book of Corsygedol].

NLW 3125C 'Arlunydd Penygarn Manuscripts: Mari Lwyd'.

NLW 4550B 'Transcripts of Poetry and Correspondence'.

NLW 5261A 'Dingestow Court Manuscripts: Barddoniaeth' [Poetry].

NLW 6499B 'Barddoniaeth, &c.' [Poetry, &c.].

NLW 6740B 'David Jones ('Dafydd Sion Siams'): Barddoniaeth, etc.' [Poetry, etc.].

NLW 7191B 'Llyfr Ystrad Alun' [The book of Ystrad Alun].

NLW 9168A 'Llyfr Amruwawg-cerdd Godidogol Waith Prydyddion Cymry o gasgliad Wm. Jones Dydd pured Mair flwyddyn 1767' [A book of various poems from the splendid works of the poets of Wales collected by William Jones, the day of the purification of Mary in the year 1767].

NLW MSS 10551–10554 'Pantyclochydd Manuscripts'.

NLW 11991A 'J. T. Evans Manuscripts: Barddoniaeth' [Poetry].

NLW 13148A 'Llanover Manuscripts: Barddoniaeth, etc.' [Poetry, etc.].

NLW 19163A 'Carolau gan Robert Prichard ('Robin R'Aber o Lyn')' [Carols by Robert Prichard ('Robin R'Aber of Llŷn)].

NLW 21414E 'Iolo Morganwg and Taliesin ab Iolo manuscripts and papers: Miscellaneous papers (prose)'.

NLW 23925E 'Miscellaneous letters and papers, 1804–2005'.

NLW Facs 369/3.

NLW Photo Album 929A.

Peniarth 245 'Casgliad o Farddoniaeth' [An anthology of Poetry].

D. Rhys Phillips Papers 136, 'Atgofion am Fro Morgannwg, y wlad a'r bobl' [Memories of the Vale of Glamorgan, the countryside and the people].

D. Rhys Phillips Papers 143, 'Folklore of Dyfed'.

D. Rhys Phillips Papers 188, 'Penillion y Ludus Mari a Phriodas' [*Ludus Mari* and wedding stanzas].

D. Rhys Phillips Papers 282, 'Welsh New-Year Customs discussed in the Trenches'.

David Thomas, OBE, Aberystwyth, Papers: 'Cardiganshire Schools Folklore Collection', 1918–*c*.1926.

Dr J. Lloyd Williams Music MSS and Papers AH1/34 'Melus geingciau Deheubarth Cymru'.

Bangor, Bangor University

Bangor 401 'Cerddi' [Poems].

Bangor 421 'Llyfr John Morgan, 1695–1700' [The book of John Morgan, 1695–1700].

Brussels, Bibliothèque Royale de Belgique

MSS 4190–4200.

Cardiff, Central Library

Cardiff 2.63 'Fenton: Pembrokeshire notes'.

Cardiff 2.137 'Barddoniaeth Edward Morris' [The Poetry of Edward Morris].

Cardiff, St Fagans National Museum of History

AWC MS 2.

AWC MS 560.

AWC MS 1723.

AWC MS 1737.

AWC MS 2186.

AWC Tape Archive 3119.

AWC Tape Archive 3132.

AWC Tape Archive 3396.

AWC Tape Archive 6508.

London, British Library

BL Add MS 5665 'Ritson Manuscript'.

BL Add MS 14968.

BL Add MS 14992 'Llawysgrif Richard Morris o Gerddi, &c.' [Richard Morris' Manuscript of Poems, &c.].

BL Add MS 14993.

BL Sloane Manuscript 2593.

Oxford, Bodleian Library
Arch. Selden B. 26 'Selden Carol Book'.
Bodley Welsh f 6.
Jesus College MS. 111 'The Red Book of Hergest'.

Secondary sources

Alford, Violet, *Sword Dance and Drama* (London: Merlin Press, 1962).
—— 'The Hobby Horse and Other Animal Masks', *Folklore*, 79 (1968), 122–34.
[Anonymous], 'A Quaint Pembrokeshire Custom', *The Pembroke County Guardian and Cardigan Reporter*, 4 January 1907, 4.
—— 'Another Echo', *The Glamorgan Gazette*, 15 January 1915, 7.
—— 'County Notes', *The Pembroke County Guardian and Cardigan Reporter*, 11 January 1907, 4.
—— 'Daeth Mari Lwyd yn ol dros y Nadolig', *Y Cymro*, 29 December 1950, 1.
—— 'Hunting the Wren' [Online]. Available at: *https://dingle-peninsula. ie/what-s-happening/item/december-26-wren-s-day.html*.
—— 'Llythyra' Newydd gan Fachan Ifanc: Nadolig wrth y drws', *Tarian y Gweithiwr*, 26 December 1895, 3.
—— 'Mari Lwyd: Llangynwyd' [Online]. Available at: *http://www. folkwales.org.uk/mari.html*.
—— 'Relatives in Police Court', *The Glamorgan Gazette*, 25 December 1914, 7.
Armstrong, Edward A., *The Folklore of Birds: An Enquiry into the Origin and Distribution of some Magico-Religious Traditions* (London: Collins, 1958).
—— 'The Triple-Furrowed Field', *The Classical Review*, 57 (1943), 3–5.
—— 'The Wren-Boys Ritual', *Country Life*, 122 (26 December 1957), 1417.
Ashton, Charles, 'Bywyd Gwledig yng Nghymru', *Transactions of the National Eisteddfod of Wales Bangor, 1890* ([Liverpool]: The National Eisteddfod Association, 1892), 36–92.
Aubrey, John, *Miscellanies upon Various Subjects* (London: printed for Edward Castle, 1696; London: Reeves and Turner, 1890).
Baring-Gould, S., and J. Fisher, *The Lives of the British Saints*, 4 vols (London: The Honourable Society of Cymmrodorion, 1907–13).

Barnaschone, L. P., 'Manners and Customs of the People of Tenby in the Eighteenth Century', *The Cambrian Journal*, 4 (1857), 177–97.

Barnwell, E. L., 'On some Ancient Welsh Customs and Furniture', *Archaeologia Cambrensis* (1872), 329–38.

Beaumont, Francis, *The Knight of the Burning Pestle* (first performed 1607; published in a quarto 1613).

The Bible: The Book of Genesis, The Book of Leviticus, The Gospel according to Saint Matthew, The Gospel according to Saint Luke, The Book of Acts, The Epistle of James, The Book of Revelation.

Blackburn, B., and L. Holford-Strevens, T*he Oxford Companion to the Year* (Oxford: Oxford University Press, 2003, repr. with corrections).

Blaumer, D. G., 'The Early Literary Riddle', *Folklore*, 78 (1967), 49–58.

Canu Gwerin (Folk Song) (Cymdeithas Alawon Gwerin Cymru/The Welsh Folk-Song Society, 1978–).

Bowen, Geraint, *'Allwydd neu Agoriad Paradwys i'r Cymru*, John Hughes, 1670', *Transactions of the Honourable Society of Cymmrodorion* (1961), 88–160.

Brand, John, *Observations on the Popular Antiquities of Great Britain* (London: Henry G. Bohn, 1849; first edition 1777).

Breeze, Andrew, 'Two English Carols in a Radnorshire Deed of 1471 at Bridgwater, Somerset', *National Library of Wales Journal*, 31 (Winter 1999), 117–19.

Bromwich, Rachel, *Trioedd Ynys Prydain: The Welsh Triads* (Cardiff: University of Wales Press, 1961).

—— and D. Simon Evans (eds), *Culhwch and Olwen: An Edition and Study of the Oldest Arthurian Tale* (Cardiff: University of Wales Press, 1992).

Brown, Theo, Letter to the Editor, *Folklore*, 63 (1952), 44.

Bruford, Alan, 'Festivities and Customs, Seasonal', in David Daiches (ed.), *A Companion to Scottish Culture* (London: Edward Arnold, 1981), pp. 118–25.

Byrne, Hugh James, 'All Hallows Eve and other festivals in Connaught', *Folklore*, 18 (1907), 437–9.

Cardi, 'Cardiganshire Customs and Superstitions', *Bye-gones: Relating to Wales and the Border Counties* (29 September 1897), 206–9.

Cawte, E. C., *Ritual Animal Disguise: A Historical and Geographical Study of Animal Disguise in the British Isles* (Cambridge: Brewer for the Folklore Society, 1978).

Chappell, William, *The Ballad Literature and Popular Music of the Olden Time*, 1 (London: Chappell, 1859).

Child, Francis James (ed.), *The English and Scottish Popular Ballads*, 1 (Boston: Houghton Mifflin and Company, 1882–4; unabridged republication New York: Dover Publications, Inc., 2003).

—— (ed.), *The English and Scottish Popular Ballads*, 2 (Boston: Houghton Mifflin and Company, 1885–6; unabridged republication New York: Dover Publications, Inc., 2003).

Clague, John, *Cooinaghtyn Manninagh/Manx Reminiscences* (Castletown: M. J. Backwell, 1911), available online at *http://www. isle-of-man.com/manxnotebook/fulltext/mr1911/index.htm*.

Cockell, John. and Ann Holmes, *Ewenny Pottery: The Cockell Collection* (no imprint; 2007).

Corkill, W. H., Letter to the Editor, 'Horse Cults in Britain', *Folklore*, 61 (1950), 216–17.

Costigan, N. G. (Bosco), R. Iestyn Daniel and Dafydd Johnston (eds), *Gwaith Gruffudd ap Dafydd ap Tudur, Gwilym Ddu o Arfon, Trahaearn Brydydd Mawr ac Iorwerth Beli* (Aberystwyth: Centre for Advanced Welsh and Celtic Studies, University of Wales, 1995).

Curtis, Mary, *The Antiquities of Laugharne and Pendine and their Neighbourhoods: Carmarthenshire, Amroth, Saundersfoot, Cilgetty, Pembrokeshire, South Wales* (London: printed for the author by R. Clay, Sons & Taylor, 1880).

Dass, John, 'Hunting the Wren' (SA 1971/265/A1) [Online]. Available at School of Scottish Studies Archives, The University of Edinburgh, PEARL server: *http://www.pearl.celtscot.ed.ac.uk/ Samples/08-233/08-233.html*.

Davidson, Thomas, 'Plough Rituals in England and Scotland', *The Agricultural History Review*, 7 (1959), 27–37.

Davies, Grace Gwyneddon, *Alawon Gwerin Môn* (Caernarfon: The Welsh Publishing Company, 1914).

Davies, J. D., *A History of West Gower, Glamorganshire*, 2 (Swansea: H. W. Williams at 'The Cambrian' office, 1879).

Davies, J. Glyn, 'Two Songs from an Anglesey Ms.', in Osborn Bergin and Carl J. S. Marstrander (eds), *Miscellany Presented to Kuno Meyer by Some of his Friends and Pupils on the Occasion of his Appointment to the Chair of Celtic Philology in the University of Berlin* (Halle a. S.: M. Niemeyer, 1912), available online at *https:// archive.org/details/miscellanyprese00berg/page/128/mode/2up*.

Davies, J. H., *A Bibliography of Welsh Ballads printed in the Eighteenth Century* (London: The Honourable Society of Cymmrodorion, 1908–11).

Davies, Jonathan Ceredig, *Folk-lore of West and Mid-Wales* (Aberystwyth: Welsh Gazette offices, 1911; reprint Felinfach: Llanerch Press, 1992), available online at *http://www.gutenberg.org/files/53915/53915-h/53915-h.htm#ch4*.

Davies, W. J., *Hanes Plwyf Llandyssul* (Llandyssul: J. D. Lewis, 1896; facsimile reprint Llandysul: Gomer, 1992).

de Lloyd, David, 'Forty Welsh Traditional Tunes', *Ceredigion: Journal of the Cardiganshire Antiquarian Society*, 6 (1929).

Dictionary of Welsh Biography down to 1940 (London: The Honourable Society of Cymmrodorion, 1959), available online at *http://yba.llgc.org.uk/en*.

Dwnn, L., and S. R. Meyrick (eds), *Heraldic Visitations of Wales and Part of the Marches: Between the Years 1586 and 1632* (Llandovery: W. Rees, 1846).

Earwaker, J. P., 'The Ancient Parish Books of the Church of St. Mary-on-the-Hill, Chester', *Journal of the Chester Archaeological and Historic Society* (1888), 132–48.

Edwards, Huw M., 'Rhodiwr fydd clerwr': sylwadau ar gerdd ymffrost o'r bedwaredd ganrif ar ddeg', *Y Traethodydd*, 149 (1994), 50–5.

Ellis, D. Machreth, 'A Miscellany of Welsh Weather-Lore', *Montgomeryshire Collections*, 47 (1942), 68–90.

Ellis, Peter Berresford, *A Brief History of the Druids* (London: Robinson, 2002).

Essex Hope, Frances, 'Radnorshire Legends and Superstitions: Compiled by Mrs. Essex Hope from MS. left by the Rev. R. F. Kilvert, Curate of Clyro, 1865–72', *The Radnorshire Society Transactions*, 24 (1954), 4–12.

Evans, D. Silvan, 'Hunting of the Wren', *Bye-Gones: relating to Wales and the Border Counties* (April 1885), 206.

Evans, Gruffydd, 'Carmarthenshire Gleanings (Kidwelly)', *Y Cymmrodor, the Magazine of the Honourable Society of Cymmrodorion*, 25 (1915), 92–160.

Evans, Gwyneth, and Ieuan R. Evans, *Ewenny – Potteries, Potters and Pots* (Abertillery: Old Bakehouse Publications, 2001).

Evans, J. Gwenogvryn (ed.), *The Poetry in the Red Book of Hergest* (Llanbedrog: the author, 1911).

Evans, John, *Letters written during a Tour through South Wales, in the year 1803, and at other times* (London: printed for C. and R. Baldwin, New Bridge-Street, 1804).

Evans, T. C. 'Cadrawd', *History of Llangynwyd Parish* (Llanelly: printed at the Llanelly and County Guardian Office, 1887; facsimile reprint Bridgend: Mid Glamorgan County Libraries, 1992).

Evans, Thomas, *The Story of Abercynon* (Cardiff: Western Mail, 1944; 3rd edn revised and enlarged, Risca: Starling Press, 1976).

Feeney, D., *Caesar's Calendar: Ancient Time and the Beginnings of History* (Berkeley and London: University of California Press, c.2007).

Frazer, J. G., *The Golden Bough: A Study in Comparative Religion* (London: Macmillan and Co., 1890; Edinburgh: Canongate Books Ltd, 2004).

—— *The Golden Bough: A Study in Magic and Religion* (London: Macmillan and Co., 1922).

Gardner-Medwin, Alisoun, 'The Wren Hunt Song', *Folklore*, 81 (1970), 215–18.

Geiriadur Prifysgol Cymru/Dictionary of the Welsh Language [Online]. Available at *http://geiriadur.ac.uk/gpc/gpc.html*.

Gill, W. Walter, *A Second Manx Scrapbook* (London: Arrowsmith, 1932).

Glen, John, *Early Scottish Melodies* (Edinburgh: J. & R. Glen, 1900).

Gray-Jones, Arthur, *A History of Ebbw Vale* (Ebbw Vale: Urban District Council, 1970).

Green, Miranda Aldhouse, 'The Symbolic Horse in Pagan Celtic Europe: An Archaeological Perspective', in Sioned Davies and Nerys Ann Jones (eds), *The Horse in Celtic Culture: Medieval Welsh Perspectives* (Cardiff: University of Wales Press, 1997), pp. 3–22.

Gruffydd, Eirlys, and Ken Lloyd Gruffydd, *Ffynhonnau Cymru*, 2 (Llanrwst: Gwasg Carreg Gwalch, 1999).

Gummere, Francis B., *Old English Ballads* (New York: Russell & Russell, 1967).

H., E., 'Mr. Urban, West Glamorgan', *The Gentleman's Magazine*, 89 (March 1819), 222–3.

Halliwell-Phillipps, J. O. (ed.), *The Debate and Stryfe Betwene Somer and Wynter: A Poetical Dialogue* (London: printed for the editor by Whittingham & Wilkins, 1860).

Harper, Sally, 'An Elizabethan Tune List from Lleweni Hall, North Wales', *Royal Musical Association Research Chronicle*, 38 (2005), 45–98.

—— *Music in Welsh Culture Before 1650: A Study of the Principal Sources* (Abingdon: Routledge, 2007).

Harris, Mary Corbett, *Crafts, Customs, and Legends of Wales* (London: David & Charles, 1980).

Harris, W. C., 'Hunting the Wren in Pembrokeshire. – An Old Twelfth Night Custom', *The Carmarthenshire Miscellany* (May–June 1892), 46–8.

Hayes, Nansi, 'Hen Benillion Calan', *Y Tincer* (January 1979), unpaged.

Herd, David, *Ancient and Modern Scottish Songs, Heroic Ballads, etc.*, 2 (Edinburgh: John Wotherspoon, 1776).

Hoggan, Frances, 'Notes on Welsh Folk-Lore', *Folklore*, 4 (1893), 122–3.

Hopkin-James, L. J., and T. C. Evans, *Hen Gwndidau, Carolau a Chywyddau, Being Sermons in Song in the Gwentian Dialect* (Bangor: Jarvis & Foster, 1910).

Howell, Henry, 'Mari Lwyd: the Origin and Meaning of the Custom', *The Carmarthen Journal and South Wales Weekly Advertiser*, 2 January 1914, 5.

Hughes, Arfon, 'Canlyn y Fari', *Canu Gwerin (Folk Song)*, 31 (2008), 88–94.

Hughes, Hugh, *Yr Hynafion Cymreig: neu, Hanes am draddodiadau, defodau, ac ofergoelion yr hen Gymry* (Caerfyrddin: J. Evans, 1823).

Hughes, John, *Alluydd neu Agoriad Paradwys i'r Cymru* (Lvyck, 1670).

Hughes, John Ceiriog, *Oriau'r Haf* (Wrecsam: R. Hughes and Son, 1870).

Hughes, Jonathan, *Bardd, a Byrddau* (Amwythig: Stafford Prys, 1778; facsimile reprint Whitefish (Montana): Kessinger Publishing, 2010).

Humphreys, Jennett, *Old Welsh Knee Songs, lullabies, frolic rhymes, and other pastime verse: now first collected and issued in English form/ the English by Jennett Humphreys* (Caernarvon: Welsh National Press Company, 1894).

Husk, William Henry, *Songs of the Nativity* (London: John Camden Hotten, 1868).

Ifans, Dafydd, 'Cerdd Galennig o ardal Trefeglwys', *Canu Gwerin (Folk Song)*, 30 (2007), 83–5.

—— 'Lewis Morris ac Arferion Priodi yng Ngheredigion', *Ceredigion: Journal of the Cardiganshire Antiquarian Society*, 8 (1977), 193–203.

Ifans, Rhiannon, 'Canu Gwaseila yn y Gymraeg', 3 vols (PhD thesis, University of Wales [Aberystwyth], 1980).

—— *Mari Lwyd* (Cardiff: trac: Traddodiadau Cerdd Cymru/Music Traditions Wales, 2013).

—— *Sêrs a Rybana: Astudiaeth o'r Canu Gwasael* (Llandysul: Gomer, 1983).

—— 'Y canu gwasael a barddoniaeth rydd', *Ysgrifau Beirniadol XVIII* (1992), pp. 189–222.

—— 'Y canu gwaseilia a'r gyfundrefn farddol', *Ysgrifau Beirniadol XV* (1988), pp. 142–73.

Isaac, Evan, *Coelion Cymru* (Aberystwyth: Gwasg Aberystwyth, 1938).

James, Allan, 'Astudiaeth o'r geiriau a genir ar alawon Gwent a Morgannwg' (unpublished MA thesis, University of Wales [Swansea], 1968).

James, E. O., *Seasonal Feasts and Festivals* (London: Thames and Hudson, 1961).

James, E. Wyn, 'Hen Garol o'r Gororau', *Canu Gwerin* (Folk Song), 14 (1991), 40–4.

Johnston, Dafydd (ed.), *Canu Maswedd yr Oesoedd Canol* (revised edn, Bridgend: Seren, 1998).

Jones, Bryan J., 'Wren Boys', *Folklore*, 19 (1908), 234–5.

Jones, Dafydd, *Blodeu-Gerdd y Cymry* (Amwythig: Stafford Prys, 1779; first edn 1759).

Jones, David, 'The Mari Lwyd: A Twelfth Night Custom', *Archaeologia Cambrensis* (1888), 389–94.

Jones, Francis, *The Holy Wells of Wales* (Cardiff: University of Wales Press, 1992; first published 1954).

Jones, Gwenllian, 'Bywyd a Gwaith Edward Morris Perthi Llwydion' (unpublished MA thesis, University of Wales [Aberystwyth], 1941).

Jones, Heledd Maldwyn (ed.), *Blas ar Fwynder Maldwyn* (Llanrwst: Gwasg Carreg Gwalch, 2003).

Jones, J. Islan, *Yr Hen Amser Gynt* (Aberystwyth: Cymdeithas Lyfrau Ceredigion, 1958).

Jones, John 'Myrddin Fardd', 'Hen gerddi y Cymry', *Y Traethodydd*, 43 (1888), 427–34.

—— *Llên Gwerin Sir Gaernarfon* (Caernarfon: Cwmni y Cyhoeddwyr Cymreig, Swyddfa Cymru, [1908]).

Jones, Lewis Davies 'Llew Tegid', 'Hunting the Wren', *Journal of the Welsh Folk Song Society*, 1 (1911), 99–113.

Jones, R. M., 'Mesurau Cerdd Dafod', *Bulletin of the Board of Celtic Studies*, 27/4 (1978), 533–51.

—— *Seiliau Beirniadaeth*, 2 (Coleg Cymraeg Cenedlaethol, e-publication, 2014).

Jones, R. W., *Bywyd Cymdeithasol Cymru yn y Ddeunawfed Ganrif* (Llundain: Gwasg Gymraeg Foyle, 1931).

Jones, Tecwyn Vaughan, '"Calennig a Chalennig a Blwyddyn Newydd Dda": Y Plentyn ar Ddydd Calan yng Nghymru', in Robert M. Morris (ed.), *Ar Lafar ei Wlad: Cyfrol Deyrnged John Owen Huws* (Llanrwst: Gwasg Carreg Gwalch, 2002), pp. 219–32.

Jones, Tegwyn, *Ar Dafod Gwerin: Penillion Bob Dydd* (Aberystwyth: Cymdeithas Lyfrau Ceredigion Gyf., 2004).

—— *Tribannau Morgannwg* (Llandysul: Gwasg Gomer, 1976).

Jones, Thomas, *Llyfr Carolau a Dyrïau Duwiol* (Amwythig: Thomas Jones, 1696).

Jones, Thomas Gwynn, *Welsh Folklore and Folk-Customs* (London: Methuen & Co. Ltd, 1930).

Jones, Tom (Trealaw), 'Llên Gwerin Morgannwg', *Y Darian*, 29 July 1926, 3.

—— 'Llên Gwerin Morgannwg', *Y Darian*, 12 August 1926, 1.

—— 'Llên Gwerin Morgannwg', *Y Darian*, 9 February 1928, 3.

Journal of the Welsh Folk-Song Society (Bangor: Welsh Folk-Song Society, 1909–77), vols 1–5.

Kennedy, Peter (ed.), *Folksongs of Britain and Ireland* (London: Cassell, 1975).

Keyte, Hugh, and Andrew Parrott (eds), *The New Oxford Book of Carols* (Oxford: Oxford University Press, 1998).

Kinney, Phyllis, 'The Tunes of the Welsh Christmas Carols (I)', *Canu Gwerin (Folk Song)*, 11 (1988), 28–57.

—— 'The Tunes of the Welsh Christmas Carols (II)', *Canu Gwerin (Folk Song)*, 12 (1989), 5–29.

—— *Welsh Traditional Music* (Cardiff: University of Wales Press in association with Cymdeithas Alawon Gwerin Cymru, 2011).

—— and Meredydd Evans, *Caneuon Gwerin i Blant* ([Aberystwyth]: Cymdeithas Alawon Gwerin Cymru, 1981).

—— *Canu'r Cymry 1 a 2* ([Aberystwyth]: Cymdeithas Alawon Gwerin Cymru, 2014).

—— *Hen Alawon (Carolau a Cherddi)* (Welsh Folk Song Society in association with the National Museum of Wales (Welsh Folk Museum), 1993).

Krappe, Alexander Haggerty, *The Science of Folklore* (London: Methuen and Co., 1930).

Kyffin, Edward, *Rhann o Psalmae Dafydd Brophwyd* (London: Simon Stafford for T[homas] S[alisbury], 1603).

Lawrence, Elizabeth Atwood, *Hunting the Wren: Transformation of Bird to Symbol: A Study in Human–Animal Relationships* (Knoxville: The University of Tennessee Press, 1997).

Laws, Edward, *A History of Little England beyond Wales, and the Non-Kymric Colony Settled in Pembrokeshire* (London: George Bell and Sons, 1888).

Lawson-Jones, Mark, *Why was the Partridge in the Pear Tree? The History of Christmas Carols* (Stroud: History Press, 2011), available online at *https://books.google.co.uk/books?hl=en&lr=&id=A1k7AwAAQBAJ&oi=fnd&pg=PT4&dq=a\study+of+wussail+singing&ots=UtSUBFxe26&sig=qLwdmwehD6ioCxpXujYM_c9QCVQ#v=onepage&q&f=false*.

Lewis, Barry J. (ed.), *Gwaith Madog Benfras ac eraill o feirdd y bedwaredd ganrif ar ddeg* (Aberystwyth: Centre for Advanced Welsh and Celtic Studies, University of Wales, 2007).

Lewis, Ceri W., 'The Literary History of Glamorgan from 1550 to 1770', in Glanmor Williams (ed.), *Glamorgan County History*, 4 (Cardiff: University of Wales Press, 1974), pp. 535–639.

Lewis, Charles Bertram, 'The "Agilaneuf" and "Trimazo" Begging Songs and their Origin', in Mary Williams and James A. de Rothschild (eds), *A Miscellany of Studies in Romance Languages & Literatures presented to Leon E. Kastner* (Cambridge: W. Heffer & Sons Ltd., 1932), pp. 308–41.

Lewis, D. Craionog, *Hanes Plwyf Defynog* (Merthyr Tydfil: H. W. Southey a'i Feibion, Cyf., 1911).

Lewis, J. M., *The Ewenny Potteries* (Cardiff: National Museum of Wales, 1982).

Lhuyd, Edward, *Parochialia: being a summary of answers to 'Parochial queries' in order to a geographical dictionary, etc., of Wales* (1696), ed. Rupert H. Morris (London: Clark, for the Cambrian Archaeological Association, 1909–11).

Lloyd, Bertram, 'Notes on Pembrokeshire Folk-Lore, Superstitions, Dialect Words, Etc.', *Folklore*, 56 (1945), 307–20.

Lloyd, Nesta (ed.), *Cerddi'r Ficer* ([Swansea]: Cyhoeddiadau Barddas, 1994).

M. M., 'Atgyfodi'r Fari Lwyd', *Papur Pawb* (February 2006), 1.

Mac Coitir, Niall, *Ireland's Birds: Myths, Legends and Folklore* (Cork: The Collins Press, 2015).

Mathews, Thomas (ed.), *Llen Gwerin Blaenau Rhymni: o gasgliad bechgyn Ysgol Lewis, Pengam* (Pengam: Ysgol Lewis, 1912).

Matthews, E. Gwynn, 'Denbighshire's Democratic Druids', *Denbigh and its Past*, 8 (1994), 21–4.

Mee, Arthur, Editor's note, *The Carmarthenshire Miscellany* (May–June 1892), 48.

—— (ed.), 'New Year's Customs in South-West Wales', *The Caermarthenshire Miscellany*, 1 (London: Elliot Stock, 1892), 1–3.

Mirehouse, Mary Beatrice, *South Pembrokeshire: Some of its History and Records* (London: David Nutt, 1910).

Moore, A. W., *The Folk-Lore of the Isle of Man* (London: D. Nutt, 1891; facsimile reprint Felinfach: Llanerch Press, 1994).

Morgan, Owen 'Morien', *History of Pontypridd and the Rhondda Valleys* (Pontypridd: Glamorgan County Times, 1903).

Morgan, Prys, 'Jonathan Williams (1752–1829) a derwyddon Sir Faesyfed', *Taliesin*, 82 (1993), 89–94.

Morris-Jones, John, *Cerdd Dafod* (Oxford: Oxford University Press, 1930).

Morse, Dafydd, 'Thomas Williams (Brynfab, 1848–1927)', in Hywel Teifi Edwards (ed.), *Cwm Rhondda* (Llandysul: Gomer, 1995), pp. 134–52.

Nashe, Thomas, *Have With You to Saffron-Walden* (London: John Danter, 1596; facsimile reprint Menston: Scolar Press, 1971).

'North West Wales Dendrochronology Project: Dating Old Welsh Houses – Gwynedd' [Online]. Available at *http://discoveringoldwelshhouses. co.uk/library/Hhistory/mer%2009b_HH_30_'Iy-Fry.pdf*.

Ó Cuív, Brian, 'Some Gaelic Traditions about the Wren', *Éigse*, 18 (1980–1), 43–66.

O'Leary, Seán C., *Christmas Wonder* (Dublin: O'Brien Press, 1988).

Opie, Iona and Peter Opie, *The Oxford Dictionary of Nursery Rhymes* (Oxford: Clarendon Press, 1951).

Owen, A. L., *The Famous Druids: A Survey of Three Centuries of English Literature on the Druids* (Oxford: Clarendon Press, 1962).

Owen, Trefor M., 'Canu Gŵyl Fair yn Arfon', *Transactions of the Caernarvonshire Historical Society*, 25 (1964), 22–41.

—— 'Some Aspects of the Bidding in Cardiganshire', *Ceredigion: Journal of the Cardiganshire Antiquarian Society*, 4 (1960–3), 36–46.

—— 'The Celebration of Candlemas in Wales', *Folklore*, 84 (1973), 238–51.

—— *Welsh Folk Customs* (Cardiff: National Museum of Wales/Welsh Folk Museum, 1974).

Oxford English Dictionary, available online at: *https://www.oed.com* (accessed 7 November 2020).

Palmer, K., and R. W. Patten, 'Some Notes on Wassailing and Ashen Faggots in South and West Somerset', *Folklore*, 82 (1971), 281–91.

Parry-Williams, T. H., *Canu Rhydd Cynnar* (Cardiff: University of Wales Press, 1932).

—— (ed.), *Carolau Richard White* (Cardiff: University of Wales Press, 1931).

—— *Hen Benillion* (Llandysul: Gomer, 1988).

—— *Llawysgrif Richard Morris o Gerddi* (Cardiff: University of Wales Press, 1931).

—— *The English Element in Welsh: A Study of English Loan-Words in Welsh* (London: The Honourable Society of Cymmrodorion, 1923).

Paton, C. I., 'Manx Calendar Customs', *Folklore*, 51 (1940), 179–94.

Peate, Iorwerth C., 'A Welsh Wassail-Bowl: with a Note on the Mari Lwyd', *Man*, 35 (1935), 81–2.

—— 'Mari Lwyd', *Man*, 39 (1939), 136.

—— 'Mari Lwyd: A Suggested Explanation', *Man*, 43 (1943), 53–8.

—— 'The Wren in Welsh Folklore', *Man*, 36 (January 1936), 1–3.

Perri, Henri, *Egluryn Ffraethineb* (London: printed by Ioan Danter, 1595; reprint Cardiff: University of Wales Press, 1930).

Phillips, Bethan, *Peterwell: The History of a Mansion and its Infamous Squire* (Llandysul: Gwasg Gomer, 1983).

Phillips, D. Rhys, *The History of the Vale of Neath* (Swansea: the author, 1925).

Pilato, Anastasia S., 'The carols of the Ritson Manuscript, BL Add. 5665, at Exeter Cathedral: repertory and context' (Senior Honors Thesis, University of Connecticut, 2013) [Online]. Available at *https://opencommons.uconn.edu/cgi/viewcontent.cgi?article=1506&context=srhonors_theses*.

Playford, Henry, *Dancing-master, or, Directions for dancing country dances* (London, printed by W. Pearson, 1709).

Powell, Evan, *The History of Tredegar* (Tredegar: Eisteddfod Gadeiriol Cymrodorion Tredegar, 1884; facsimile reprint Tredegar: Blaenau Gwent Heritage Forum, 2008).

Prichard, Rhys, *Canwyll y Cymry* (London: printed in Shrewsbury by Thomas Durston, 1696).

Rattue, James, *The Living Stream: Holy Wells in Historical Context* (Woodbridge: The Boydell Press, 1995).

Redwood, Charles, *The Vale of Glamorgan* (London: Saunders and Otley, 1839).

Rees, Brinley, *Dulliau'r Canu Rhydd, 1500–1650* (Cardiff: University of Wales Press, 1952).

Reeve, Michael D. (ed.), and Neil Wright (trans.), *The History of the Kings of Britain: An Edition and Translation of* De gestis Britonum [Historia regum Britanniae]/*Geoffrey of Monmouth* (Woodbridge: The Boydell Press, 2007).

Rhys, Ann Gruffydd, 'Gwell crefft na golud: Caitlin Jenkins a phriddlestri Ewenni', *Barn* (July/August 2012), 66–8.

Rhys, John, 'Folk-lore Miscellanea', *Folklore*, 3 (1892), 375–86.

Rhŷs, John, and J. Gwenogvryn Evans (eds), *The Text of the Bruts from the Red Book of Hergest* (Oxford: J. G. Evans, 1890).

Richards, Gwynfryn, 'Y Plygain', *Journal of the Historical Society of the Church in Wales*, 1 (1947), 53–71.

Richards, Jeffrey, *The Popes and the Papacy in the Early Middle Ages: 476–752* (London: Routledge Revivals, 2015).

Roberts, Brynley F., 'Edward Lhwyd (c.1660–1709): Folklorist', *Folklore*, 120 (2009), 36–56.

Roberts, Enid P., 'Hen Garolau Plygain', *Transactions of the Honourable Society of Cymmrodorion* (1952), 51–70.

Roberts, G. T., 'Arfon (1759–1822)', *Transactions of the Caernarvonshire Historical Society*, 1 (1939), 55–67.

Roberts, Gomer M., *Hanes Plwyf Llandybïe* (Cardiff: University of Wales Press, 1939).

Roberts, William, *Crefydd yr Oesoedd Tywyll* (Carmarthen: printed by A. Williams, 1852).

Rosser, Siwan M. (ed.), *Bardd Pengwern* ([Swansea]: Cyhoeddiadau Barddas, 2007).

Saer, D. Roy (ed.), *Caneuon Llafar Gwlad (Songs from Oral Tradition)*, 1 (Cardiff: National Museum of Wales/Welsh Folk Museum, 1974).

—— 'The Christmas Carol-Singing Tradition in the Tanad Valley', *Folk Life*, 7 (1969), 15–42.

Saer, Roy, 'A Midnight Plygain at Llanymawddwy Church', in *'"Canu at Iws" ac Ysgrifau Eraill* (Talybont: Cymdeithas Alawon Gwerin Cymru, 2013), pp. 81–9.

—— 'Cân "Mari Lwyd Lawen" o Landybïe: Ei Gwir Leoliad', in *"Canu at Iws" ac Ysgrifau Eraill* (Talybont: Cymdeithas Alawon Gwerin Cymru, 2013), pp. 229–31.

—— 'The Supposed *Mari Lwyd* of Pembrokeshire', in *"Canu at Iws" ac Ysgrifau Eraill* (Talybont: Cymdeithas Alawon Gwerin Cymru, 2013), pp. 314–27.

Scott, Charles T., 'On defining the riddle: the problem of a structural unit', in Dan Ben-Amos (ed.), *Folklore Genres* (Austin: University of Texas Press, *c.*1976), pp. 77–90.

Scott, G. P. W., *Tales and Traditions of Tenby* (Tenby: R. Mason, 1858).

Scourfield, Elfyn, 'Astudiaeth o Ddiwylliant Lleol a Thraddodiadau Llafar Ardal Tre-Lech' (unpublished MA thesis, University of Wales [Swansea], 1969).

Sharp, Cecil J., A. G. Gilchrist and Lucy E. Broadwood, 'Forfeit Songs; Cumulative Songs; Songs of Marvels and of Magical Animals', *Journal of the Folk-Song Society*, 5 (1916), 277–96.

Sharp, Cecil J., Ralph Vaughan Williams, Frank Kidson, Lucy E. Broadwood and A. G. Gilchrist, 'Ballads and Songs', *Journal of the Folk-Song Society*, 5 (1914), 61–94.

Shipley, Joseph T. (ed.), *Dictionary of World Literature – Criticism, Forms, Technique* (New York; The Philosophical Library, 1943).

Sokolov, Y. M., *Russian Folklore*, translated by Catherine Ruth Smith (New York: Macmillan, 1950).

Solfen, 'Noswaith o Hwyl gyda'r Fari Lwyd Lawen', *Y Ford Gron* (December 1933), 34.

Sonnini, C. S. (translation by Henry Hunter), *Travels in Upper and Lower Egypt* (London: printed for J. Debrett, 1800).

Stephens, Meic (ed.), *The New Companion to the Literature of Wales* (Cardiff: University of Wales Press, 1998).

Stern, S., *Calendars in Antiquity: Empires, States and Societies* (Oxford: Oxford University Press, 2012).

Stokes, Whitley (ed.), 'The Birth and Life of St. Moling', *Revue Celtique*, 27 (1906), 257–312.

Stukeley, W., '"Much Greater, than Commonly Imagined": Celtic Druids and the Universal Religion', in David Boyd Haycock, *William Stukeley: Science, Religion and Archaeology in Eighteenth-Century England* (Woodbridge: Boydell, 2002), pp. 160–88.

Swainson, Charles, *The Folk Lore and Provincial Names of British Birds* (London: Folk Lore Society, 1886), pp. 35–43.

T., E., 'Letters to the Editor: Mari Lwyd', *The Carmarthen Journal and South Wales Weekly Advertiser*, 9 January 1914, 7.

Taylor, Archer, *The Literary Riddle before 1600* (Berkley and Los Angeles: University of California Press, 1948).

—— 'The riddle as a primary form', in Horace Palmer Beck (ed.), *Folklore in Action: Essays for Discussion in Honor of MacEdward Leach* (Philadelphia: American Folklore Society, 1962), pp. 200–7.

Thomas, Graham C. G., 'Mair a'r Afallen', *Bulletin of the Board of Celtic Studies*, 24 (1972), 459–61.

Thomas, Gwyn, 'Derwyddon a Siamaniaid', in Robert M. Morris et al. (eds), *Ar lafar ei wlad – cyfrol deyrnged John Owen Hughes* (Llanrwst: Gwasg Carreg Gwalch, 2002), pp. 261–72.

Thomas, J., *Cofiant y Parch. T. Rees, D.D. Abertawy* (Dolgellau: William Hughes, 1888).

Thomas, J. Mansel, *Yesterday's Gower* (Llandysul: Gomer, 1982).

Thomas, N. W., 'The Scape-Goat in European Folklore', *Folklore*, 17 (1906), 258–87.

Tombs, J., 'Twelfth-Day', *Notes and Queries*, Series 3, 5 (1864), 109–10.

Train, Joseph, *Historical and Statistical Account of the Isle of Man*, 2 (Douglas: Mary Quiggin, North Quay, 1845).

Trevelyan, Marie, *Folk-Lore and Folk-Stories of Wales* (London: Elliot Stock, 1909), available online at: *https://archive.org/stream/afl2317. 0001.001.umich.edu#page/22/mode/2up*.

Vaughan, Herbert M., *The South Wales Squires* (Carmarthen: The Golden Grove Book Company Limited, 1988; first published in 1926 by Methuen & Co. Ltd).

Vaughan, Richard (ed.), *The Illustrated Chronicles of Matthew Paris* (Stroud: Alan Sutton Publishing, 1993).

Waldron, George, *The History and Description of the Isle of Man* (Dublin: printed for E. Rider in George's-Lane, and J. Torbuck at the Bear in Skinner-Row, [1742?]; Gale ECCO, Print Editions, 2010).

Walsh, John, *Caledonian Country Dances* (London: J. Walsh, *c*.1745).

Walters, Huw, 'Pontypridd a'r Cylch: Gwlad Beirdd a Derwyddon', in Huw Walters, *Cynnwrf Canrif: agweddau ar ddiwylliant gwerin* ([Abertawe]: Cyhoeddiadau Barddas, 2004), pp. 184–274.

Wentersdorf, Karl P., 'The Folkloristic Significance of the Wren', *The Journal of American Folklore*, 90 (April–June 1977), 192–8.

Westropp, Thomas J., 'Collectanea: A Folklore Survey of County Clare', *Folklore*, 22 (1911), 203–13.

Whiffen, T. W., 'A Short Account of the Indians of the Issá-Japurá District (South America)', *Folklore*, 24 (1913), 41–62.

Whitman, F. H., 'Medieval Riddling: Factors Underlying its Development', *Neuphilologische Mitteilungen*, 71 (1970), 177–85.

Williams, D. G., 'Casgliad o Lên Gwerin Sir Gaerfyrddin', in *Transactions of the National Eisteddfod of Wales Llanelly, 1895* (London: The National Eisteddfod Association, 1898).

Williams, E. Emrys, 'Arferion Priodasol yn yr hen ddyddiau', *Y Casglwr* (August 1983), 18.

Williams, E. Llwyd, *Crwydro Sir Benfro*, 2 vols (Llandybïe: Llyfrau'r Dryw, 1958, 1960).

Williams, G. J., *Iolo Morganwg, 1747–1826* (Cardiff: University of Wales Press, 1956).

Williams, H. W., *Pembrokeshire Antiquities: Reprints from 'Amsang ein tadau', the Antiquaries' Column in the 'Pembroke County Guardian'* (Solva: H. W. Williams, 1897).

Williams, Ifor, 'Lexicographical Notes', *Bulletin of the Board of Celtic Studies*, 3 (1926), 126–36.

Williams, J. Lloyd, 'Editor's Notes', *Journal of the Welsh Folk-song Society*, 1 and 2 (1910).

Williams, Maria Jane, *Ancient National Airs of Gwent and Morganwg (...) with Introduction and Notes on the Songs by Daniel Huws* (Llandovery, 1844; facsimile reprint Aberystwyth: Cymdeithas Alawon Gwerin Cymru, 1994).

Williams, Mary, 'Another Note on the "Mari Lwyd"', *Man*, 39 (1939), 96.

Williams, Thomas 'Brynfab', 'Mari', *Western Mail*, 17 January 1925, 6.

Williams, W. Crwys, *Cerddi Newydd Crwys* (Wrecsam: Hughes a'i Fab, 1924).

Williams, W. Gilbert, 'Hen Gymeriadau Llanwnda: William Bifan y Gadlys', *Cymru*, 23 (1902), 138–40.

Williams, William (Hirwaun) and William Williams (Aberdare), *Traethodau Hanesyddol ar Ddyffryn Nedd* (Aberdare: printed by J. T. Jones, 1856).

Wood, Juliette, 'The Horse in Welsh Folklore: A Boundary Image in Custom and Narrative', in Sioned Davies and Nerys Ann Jones (eds), *The Horse in Celtic Culture: Medieval Welsh Perspectives* (Cardiff: University of Wales Press, 1997), pp. 162–82.

Wright, A. R., and T. E. Lones, *British Calendar Customs: England* (London: W. Glaisher for The Folk-Lore Society, 1936–40).

Wright, Thomas (ed.), *Songs and Carols now First Printed, from a Manuscript of the Fifteenth Century* (London: printed by T. Richards for the Warton Club, 1856).

Young, Thomas, The New Inn, Risca, 'Mari Lwyd', *The Monmouthshire Merlin and South Wales Advertiser*, 31 December 1864, 8.

Film

Dauna. Lo que lleva el río (Gone with the River), 2015.

Indexes

Index to first lines

A gloisoch chi drysa?	poem 31
Agorwch y drysa	poem 33
Blwyddyn Newydd Dda, gyfeillion	poem 14
Calennig i mi, calennig i'r ffon	poem 15
Can diolch, wŷr dilys awch hoenus, i chwi	poem 49
Chwi fuoch er llynedd yn rhoi imi glod	poem 8
Chwi sy'n meddu aur ac arian	poem 19
Codais heddiw'n fore	poem 16
Cydeiliwn bellach fawl yn bwyllog	poem 12
Cyd-rowch osteg teg, di-dwyll	poem 6
Deffrowch, ben teili	poem 17
Dyma fy hanes a meddwl fy mynwes:	poem 44
'Ddoi di i'r coed?' meddai Dibyn wrth Dobyn	poem 25
[Erbyn d]arfod i chwi eich cân	poem 43
Gartre nis bûm er nos duw Llun	poem 42
Good morning, good morning	poem 18
[Gwrandewch dda]ngos modd ac achos	poem 9
Gyda'ch cennad, bawb sy'n gwarchod	poem 3

Gyfeillion mwynion tawel sydd dan yr adail wych   poem 24

Hai! 'nglân gymdeithion, dowch ynghyd   poem 11

Hyd yma bu'n cerdded   poem 28

Joy, health, love, and peace be to you in this place   poem 27

Mab Duw a glodforwn, clod lafar cydlefwn   poem 1

Mi godais heddiw'n fore   poem 13

Nos dawch! Gyda'ch cennad   poem 46

Nos dawch, gyda'ch cennad, pwy sy yma'n gwarchod?   poem 4

Nos dawch, y glân deulu sydd yma'n trigfannu   poem 5

'O! where are you going?' says Milder to Melder   poem 26

O'r Parc gcr y Bala   poem 38

Os oes gennych ddime   poem 20

Plant bach Cymru ydym ni   poem 21

Pwy ydi'r gwŷr acw sy'n gweiddi mor arw   poem 45

Pwy ydyw y cacwn sy'n cynnal y byrdwn   poem 2

Tri ar 'Peg O'Ramsey' a rowch   poem 40

Waeth pa mor ddiniwad y byddwch chi'n dŵad   poem 37

Wel, down un fwriad, dawn arferol   poem 39

Wel, dyma enw'r feinwen   poem 30

Wel, dyma ni'n dŵad   poems 29, 35, 36

Wel, dyma ni'n dywad   poem 34

Wel, gyda'ch cennad, fawr a mân   poem 10

Wel, nos dawch yn ystig y teulu nodedig   poem 47

Wele eto flwyddyn newydd   poem 22

Y mae'r eira heno'n oer   poem 23

Y teulu mwyn foddau, agorwch eich drysau   poem 41

Y teulu mwyn, llariedd, am agor eich annedd   poem 48

Y teulu nod haeledd sydd yma'n dymhoredd   poem 7

Yn dwryn o Bendarran   poem 32

Index to poets

Aer Castell Bylchwyn (possibly Thomas Vychan)   poem 43

Anonymous   poems 1, 4–9, 14–35,
36.1–24, 37 (possibly
Rhiain Bebb), 40, 42, 45, 46

Bebb, Rhiain   poem 37 (possibly), 38

Evans, William (1730–93)   poem 48

Hughes, Arfon (1960–)   poem 36.25–36

Humphreys, Dafydd   poems 2, 3

Jones, Dafydd, 'Dafydd Siôn Siâms',
    of Penrhyndeudraeth (1743–1831)   poems 10–12, 39

Jones, John, of Llanddeiniolen   poems 41, 49

Morris, Richard (1703–79)   poem 44

Prichard, Robert 'Robin yr Aber' o Lŷn   poem 47

Thomas, Samuel   poem 13 (possibly)

Thomas Vychan *see* Aer Castell Bylchwyn

Index to tunes

About the Bank *see* Y Fedle Fawr

Beth sy mor feinion?   poems 44 (stanzas 1, 3–6),
45 (stanza 2)

Calennig (1)   poem 16

Calennig (2)   poem 15

Cân Hela'r Dryw   poem 25

Cân y Dryw   page 174

Cân y Fari Lwyd   poems 28, 31, 33–8

Cerdd Dydd Calan   poem 16

Consêt Prince Rupert
    or Prince Rupert's Conceit   poem 49

Country Bumpkin   poem 41 (stanza 2)

The Cutty Wren   poem 26

Cyfri'r Geifr (1)   page 176

Cyfri'r Geifr (2)   page 177

Cynllaiddief Gŵyl Fair   poem 48

Y cyntaf dydd o'r Gwyliau

    or The first day of Christmas   page 177

Deffrwch! Benteulu   poem 17

Dibyn a Dobyn   poem 25

Y Fedle Fawr or About the Bank   poem 3

Ffarwel Gwŷr Aberffraw

    or Difyrrwch Gwŷr Aberffraw   poem 41 (stanza 1)

Gadael Tir see Leave Land

Hyd yma bu'n cerdded   poem 28

Joan's Placket   poem 2

Leave Land or Gadael Tir   poems 1, 4 (stanzas 1–2,

    5–8), 7, 47

May Day   poem 5

Y Mochyn Du   poem 22

Peg O'Ramsey   poem 8

Pilgrim   poem 41 (stanza 3)

Prince Rupert's Conceit see Consêt Prince Rupert

Royal William   poem 13

Sosban Fach   page 182

Susannah or Siwsanna   poem 39

Tri Thrawiad Gwynedd   poems 4 (stanzas 3–4),

    44 (stanza 2), 45

    (stanzas 1, 3–5)

Y Washael (Wel, dyma enw'r feinwen)   poem 30

Ymdaith Gwŷr Harlech

    or The March of the Men of Harlech   poem 14

General index

A

Abercastell, 29
Abercynon, 129
Aberdare, 283
Aberffraw, 315
   see also 'Ffarwel Gwŷr Aberffraw'
Abergwili, 46
Abergwyngregyn, 148
'About the Bank', 192–3
   see also 'Fedle Fawr, Y'
Abram, 92–3
Abram, Richard, 'Dic y Dawns', 36–7
accordion, 89
Achilles, 5–6
Adam, 55, 201, 225
   'second Adam' (Jesus Christ), 187
   see also Eden, Garden of
Adderbury West, Oxfordshire, 80
'Aderyn Pig Llwyd', 133
admittance, 15–16, 17
Adpar, 61
Alcuin of York, 32
ale, 34, 86, 117, 118, 150, 219, 257,
   273, 315, 337
Alford, Violet, 11, 105
All Hallows' Day, 106, 133
All Hallows' Eve, 7, 119
All Souls' Day, 64
All Souls' Eve, 86
'All the flowers of the broom', 209
Allt y Saint, 17
alms, 98
almoner, 46
America, 80
   see also Nebraska
          South Carolina
          Texas
Amlwch, 10, 79, 92, 94, 95, 99, 145,
   154, 321
ancestry, 18–19
angels, 160, 249, 305, 307, 309, 317, 331
   see also Gabriel

Anglesey, 11, 18, 36, 53, 99, 124, 143,
   144, 145, 146, 149, 152, 154, 199,
   200, 208, 315, 320, 326
   see also Aberffraw
       Amlwch
       Bodeinial
       Bodewryd
       Bulkeley, Robert
       Bylchwyn
       'Consêt Gwŷr Aberffraw'
       'Ffarwel Gwŷr Aberffraw'
       Hughes, Robert
       Llanddyfnan
       Llangefni
       Morris, Lewis
       Morris, Richard
       Penmon
       Presaddfed
       Rhoscolyn
       St Seiriol's Well
       'Sybylltir'
Anglican Church, 8, 59, 163, 164
Anglo-Norman control, 98
Anglo-Saxon, 1
animals, 133, 164, 219
   animal guising, 152
   animal mask, 133
   animal skin, 111
   animal skull, 133
   animal support society, 133
   dressing up as, 133
Anna, grandmother of Jesus, 187
Anna, prophetess, 147, 187, 307
Annwn, 325
anoethau, 169
anonymous poem, 186–9, 196–9,
   204–5, 206–9, 210–12, 230–51,
   252–63, 264–291, 296–9, 314–17,
   324–9
apple, 18, 47–9, 50, 54–5, 65, 82, 156,
   243, 255, 257–8
apple trees, 2–4, 47–9, 229, fig. 1

apprentice (-s), 46
'Ar gyfer heddiw'r bore', 56
'ar y parth', 127
Arabic riddles, 155
Aristotle, 87
Armstrong, Edward A., 85, 89, 97, 98
Arthur, King, 134
Arthur, Thomas, Ewenny Pottery, 3–4
artisans, 160, 315
Ashmolean Museum, 78
Ashton, Charles, 109
Asia, 20
Atlas, 84
Aubrey, John, 80–1
awdl-gywydd (awdl gywyddau), 321, 342
awl, 95, 261
axe, 118

B
baby, 156, 158, 160, 223, 333
bags, 54, 60, 109, 115, 235, 241
Bailey, Barbara, 124
Bala, 144, 301–2
ballads, 120, 148, 155, 167, 168, 169, 289
Balthasar, 158, 328
Bangor, 144
bara can (white bread), 18
barley, 31, 34, 36, 54, 66, 130
barley bread, 235, 319
barleycorn, 66
Barmouth, 105, 107
barn, 34, 63
Barnaschone, L. P., 90
Barnes, Revd Roland, 295
Barnwell, E. L., 165
barrels, 31, 66, 114, 134, 135, 197, 257, 269, 273, 277, 285, 293, 299, 319
'Basilino', 209
bass voice, 297
bastide towns, 98
bawling, 297

bear, 152
beard (-s), 150, 161
    goat's beard, 154
Beaufort, 129
beaver hat, 111
Bebb, Rhiain, 298–301
bed (-room), 56, 85, 113, 253, 255, 265, 269, 285, 293, 321
Bedwellty, 53
beef, 207
beer, 16, 18, 20, 21, 22, 25, 30, 31, 34, 35, 47–9, 57, 65, 66, 79, 86, 95, 108, 109, 114, 134, 144, 150, 151, 160, 193, 195, 197, 205, 219, 223, 237, 253, 255, 257, 259, 267, 269, 271, 277, 285, 291, 293, 313, 325, 327, 335, 337
bees, 191, 193
beggars, 49, 77
Belch, Sir Toby, 209
bells, 108, 110–11, 127
beneath the wall, 186–9, 199, 201, 205, 213, 227–9, 304–9
    beneath the window, 191
    see also canu tan bared
Berllan, Y *see* Orchard, The, ritual
Berriew, 78
berries, 55, 213
'Beth sy mor feinion?', 173
Bethlehem, 187, 329
'Betty Brown', 168
Bevan, Evan, 115
Bible (Word of God), 30, 46, 157, 329
    see also Genesis, Book of
                James, Epistle of
                Leviticus, Book of
                Matthew, Gospel
                    according to
                Revelation, Book of
                Romans, Epistle to
Bidder, 64, fig. 7
bier, 77–104 *passim*, 255
    see also Hunting the Wren
                wren

birds, 18, 30, 47, 87, 157, 321
'Aderyn Pig Llwyd', 133
see also crow
cuckoo
eagle
hawk
heron
house sparrow
magpie
owl
rook
swallow
swan
woodcock
wren
Black Book of Carmarthen, 154
blackened faces, 89, 110–11, 134
Blackmill, 107, 108, 114, 277
Fox and Hounds, 114
Blaen-y-coed, 56
Blaenau Ffestiniog, 67
Blaenau Gwent, 129
blessing, 3, 79, 127, 128, 135, 217,
221, 225, 233, 239, 247, 273, 305,
307, 309
blind, 93, 305
blood (bleeding), 51, 150
Bodeinial, 31
Bodewryd, 145, 321
bodhrán, 89
Bodleian Library see Oxford, city
'Body and Soul', dispute, 32
bones, 81, 93, 135, 156–7, 319
Bonhams, 4, figs 2–4
bookbinder, 55
Boro Manioc-gathering Dance, 6
Bowden, Mrs, Oystermouth, 110
bows, 125–6
bows and arrows, 90, 262
Bowen, H. Glyn, Brynberian, 75
bowl see wassail bowl (cup/vessel)
boxwood, 53, 54, 55
bragget, 165, 315, 335
brambles (briars), 60, 64, 124, 130

brass pans, 91, 262
brawn, 18
bread, 51, 57, 86, 116, 151, 160, 207,
219, 223, 227, 235, 239, 319, 321
'breadcrumb of talent', 297
see also bara can
barley bread
breakfast, 52, 297, 299
breath, 18, 122–3, 219
Brecknock, county
see Brecon Beacons National Park
Defynnog
Ystradfellte
Brecon Beacons National Park, 105
'Bredi Ban' 168
Bregyn fab Heidden (John
Barleycorn), 9–10, 34
'Breuddwyd Macsen Wledig', 158,
170, 329
brewing, 30, 35
Briary Hill, 129
bribe, 131
Bridgend, 3, 107, 108, 277, 286
Police Court, 113, 138
Bridgwater, 33
bridle, 106, 118, 125–6
bridle bells, 108
Britain, 97, 98, 134, 135, 253
see also Festival of Britain (1951)
British Library see London
Brittany, 98
Bro Cyfeiliog, 295
Broadwood, Lucy E., 102
Bronze Age, 97
broom, 110, 118–19
broth, 18, 94
'Brut y Brenhinedd', 1–2
Bryn Iwan, 56
Bryn Myrddin, Abergwili, 46
Brynberian, 69, 75
see also Bowen, H. Glyn
Bryncethin, 138, 286
Brynmenyn, 138, 286
bugles, 52

Bulkeley, Robert, 143
bulldog, 123
bulls/bullocks, 116, 152, 299
burden, 81
Burford, Alan, 81
burials *see* funerals
burlesque, 93
burning, caution to avoid, 160–1, 165
Burray, Orkney, 81
bushes, 83, 84
butter, 86, 247
buttermilk, 65, 319
'Bwca Llwyd', 133
Bylchwyn, 145, 320–1
Byrne, Hugh James, 89

C
Cae-môr, 16–17
Caerddinen, 18
Caerffawydd *see* Hereford
Caernarfon, county, 143, 144, 146,
    152, 199, 200, 208
    see also Abergwyngregyn
            Bangor
            Caernarfon, town
            Chwilog
            Llanddeiniolen
            Llandygái
            Llanllechid
Caernarfon, town, 144, 154, 158, 170,
    314, 329, 338
Caerphilly, 117
Caerwaen, 170
Caerwys, 165
cakes, 55, 57, 64–5, 86, 114, 117, 118,
    130, 207, 257–8, 285, 289
    see also cwkau
calamities, 16–17
calendars, 10, 59, 82
    see also Gregorian calendar
            Julian calendar
calends, 54
calends gift, 54, 57, fig. 5
caleniga, 55

calennig, 45–75 *passim*, 222–51
    passim, figs 5–6
    rhodd galennig, fig. 5
'Calennig (1)', 173, 235
'Calennig (2)', 174, 233
calf (calves), 11, 35
    calf mask, 133
'Cân Hela'r Dryw', 103, 174, 260
'Cân y Berllan', 48–9
'Cân y Dryw', 174
'Cân y Fari', 131
'Cân y Fari Lwyd', 175, 271, 277, 283,
    287, 291, 301, 303
'Cân y Merched', 296–9
candles, 32, 38, 118, 150, 151, 156,
    160, 163–5, 193, 197, 305, 319,
    325, 331, 333, 335, 342
    blessed by Church for the year
        ahead, 164
    chief maid returns, at *Gŵyl Fair*,
        164
    Easter tradition using, 165
    light themselves at *Gŵyl Fair*, 164
    sitting between two, 165
    tallow, 38
Candlemas *see* *Gŵyl Fair y*
    Canhwyllau
Candlemas Eve *see* *Noswyl Fair*
Candlemastide, 165
candlesticks, 156, 325
cannons, 90, 262
Canton *see* Cardiff
canu gwirod, 9, 15, 143
canu Gwylie, 37
canu tan bared, 9, 15, 24, 26–7, 143,
    145
    see also beneath the wall
canu yn drws, 9, 15, 143, 149, 205
canvas horse/burden, 134
Canwyll y Cymry, 22
cap, animal skin, 111
Capel Cynon, 52, 67, 238
capon, 18, 55, 156
cards, play, 193

Cardi, 113
Cardiff
    Canton, 82–3
    Coryton, 112
    Llanishen, 53
    Radyr, 112
    see also Pentyrch
        St Fagans
Cardigan, county see Ceredigion
Cardigan, town, 51, 79, 82, 113, 249
Carmarthen, county, 21, 40, 51, 53, 54,
    59, 79, 105, 107, 129, 136
    see also Abergwili
        Blaen-y-coed
        Bryn Iwan
        Cross Hands
        Cynwyl Elfed
        Hermon
        Kidwelly
        Laugharne
        Llandybïe
        Llandyfaelog
        Llanelli
        Llanfallteg
        Llanfihangel Rhos-y-corn
        Llangathen
        Llanybydder
        Newcastle Emlyn
        Pendine
        Tre-lech
Carmarthen, town see Black Book of
    Carmarthen
carols, 78–9, 128, 186–339 passim
carol cadair, 149, 158
carol deuair, 314–17, 320
carol gwirod see canu gwirod
carol of thanks on leaving, 217–21
carol tan hared see canu tan bared
carol yn drws see canu yn drws
carols in reply from within, 28
carols requesting admittance, 15–16
carpenters, 31, 46
Carroll, Lily Maud, 113
carts, 90, 262

Casnewydd-bach (Little Newcastle),
    86, 102
Casnodyn, 77
Caspar, 158, 328,
Castell Bylchwyn, 320–1
Castellau, 131
cats, 123, 153, 227
catechism, 157
cattle, 28–9, 51, 108, 207, 227, 247
cauldrons, 91, 262
cellar, 34, 56, 86, 119, 151, 273
Celtic/Celts, 98
    pre-Celtic, 135
Cemmaes, Montgomeryshire, 78
'Cerdd Dydd Calan', 175, 235
cerdd dant, 302–3
Ceredigion 51, 52, 54, 57, 60, 235
    see also Adpar
        Capel Cynon
        Cwm-cou
        Dre-wen
        Ffair-rhos
        Lampeter
        Llandygwydd
        Llandysul
        Llangoedmor
        Llanwenog
        Penrhyn-coch
        Pontsian
        Pren-gwyn
        Tal-y-bont
        Tregaron
chair carols, 11, 149, 158, 160, 330–1,
    332–5
chair ceremony, 149, 158–61, 329,
    331, 333
    chair of gold, 158, 170, 317
    instituted by Mary, 158
    kissing young girl, 339
    procession with wassail cup, 160
Chancery Division, 113
chant/chanting, 80, 93, 116
chapelgoers, 114, 131
'Charity Mistress', 149

Charlemagne, 32
charms, 88, 102
cheeks, 132, 335
cheese, 18, 29, 50, 57, 63, 65, 86, 209,
  227, 235, 247
chemist shop, 131
cherry, 148, 157
'Cherry-Tree Carol, The', 148
Chester, 32, 78
chilblains, 150
'Child Ballads', 148, 167
childless couples, 49
children, 10, 12, 28, 36, 53, 56, 58–61,
  64–5, 70, 78, 80, 81, 82, 84, 85,
  86, 96, 99, 112, 118, 132, 135, 151,
  162, 165, 217, 237, 245, 257
chimney stack, 66
china crown, 165
chorus, rare exception, 149
Christianity, 7–8, 15, 21–5, 34, 46,
  146–8, 158, 186–221 passim, 223
  see also Jesus Christ
         God
Christmas (Christmastide), 1, 2, 7–8,
  9–10, 15–43 passim, 46, 49, 50,
  58, 66, 69, 77, 81, 82, 83, 86, 88,
  97, 106, 107, 116, 122–3, 128, 129,
  130, 131, 134, 135, 191, 201, 205,
  207, 213, 215, 219, 223, 225, 263,
  269, 271, 277, 283, 285
  see also Christmas Wassail Songs,
         186–221
         distyll y Gwyliau (ebb
         of Christmastide)
churls, 150, 203, 343
churn, 319
Chwilog, 152
cider, 3, 47, fig. 1
circumcision, 46–7, 55, 147–8, 223
  Mosaic Law, 147
Clare, county, 97
claret, 327
Claypits Pottery, Ewenny, 4–5
cleaver, 91, 95, 261, 262

Clement, Willie, 130
clêr, 267
clirwm clarwm, 146, 154
cloak, mottled, 108
cloth/clothing, 59–60, 108, 197
cloves, 55
Clwyd, Vale of, 78
Clydach (Swansea Valley), 38
Clyro, 106
coach, 95, 263
coal, 11, 108
Coety, 138, 286
coffin (wren house), 84
collier, 113
colliery, 115
colour, in cumulative song, 153–5
condemnation, 55
conductus (motet), 22
conflictus (contention), 32
'conflictus Veris et Hiemis', 32
Connacht, 89
'Consêt Gwŷr Aberffraw', 149, 168
'Consêt Prince Rupert', 175, 337
Constantine the Great, 158, 329
contest songs, 124
conundrums, 11, 30
Conwy, 295
corn, 36, 134, 219
Coronavirus (Covid-19), 70, 245
Corporal, 109, 125–6
Corwen, 17, 144
Coryton see Cardiff
Costigan (Bosco), N. G., 77
'Country Bumpkin' ('Cyntri Boncyn'),
  16, 312–13, 315
Cowbridge, 128
cows see cattle
cowshed, 122–3
Craig-cefn-parc, 38
crêpe paper, 82, 84, 109
Crespo, Mario, 13
Croatia, 5
crooked aunt, 63
Cross Hands, 56

Crosswell, 248–9
crow, 34, 227
crown, 165
   see also china crown
Crucifixion, 24
cruth (crowd/crowther), 27, 109, 110,
   153, 279, 291
Crymych, 52, 248
cuckoo, 97
cudgel, 54, 64
'Culhwch ac Olwen', 30
cumulative songs, 9, 15, 29, 124, 152–3
   see also 'Cyfri'r geifr'
         'Dechre rhigwm digri'
         'Un cam i'r ceiliog ac un
           carw serchog'
         'Un cam i'r tyrci ac un
           carw lysti'
         'Un o'm brodyr'
         'Un o'm chwiorydd'
cup *see* wassail bowl (cup/vessel)
currants, 86, 285
custard, 18
customs
   continuity of, 19, 37, 70, 205,
      267, 293
   preserving Welsh identity, 37
   upholding folk custom, 70
Cut Lloi, 299
'Cutty Wran' (Cutty Wren, The), 79,
   90, 176, 262
cwkau, 82, 86
Cwm-cou, 61
Cwm Gwaun, 58–9, 237, 245, fig. 6
   Caersalem, 58
   Tŷ Bach, fig. 6
cwndidau, 22
cwndidwyr, 267
cwnseila, 107
cwrseila, 107, 121
'Cyfri'r geifr', 124, 153–4
'Cyfri'r geifr (1)', 176
'Cyfri'r geifr (2)', 177
cyhydedd hir, 267, 341

'Cynllaiddief Gŵyl Fair', 332–3, 337
'Cyntaf dydd o'r Gwyliau, Y', 29, 41,
   177
'Cyntri Boncyn' *see* 'Country Bumpkin'
Cynwyl Elfed, 56

D
'Dai Clwb', Neath, 112
dancing, 5, 6, 11, 21, 55, 89, 95, 105,
   110–11, 115, 118, 119, 120, 132,
   152, 155, 208, 209, 225, 279, 281,
   291
   see also Abram, Richard, 'Dic y
        Dawns'
        'All the flowers of the
          broom'
        'Basilino'
        'Greensleeves'
        hilt-and-point Sword
          Dance
        hoen ddawnswyr
        hornpipe
        Llangadfan dancers
        New Year's Eve dance
        partridge step (dance)
        pas de deux
        'Peg O'Ramsey'
        'Pepper is black'
        'Rogero'
        'Turkelony'
        Wil Benji step
Darby (horse), 134
'Darfod Canu', 124
Darowen, 229
Dass, John, Burray, Orkney, 81
dated poems, 27, 47, 55, 69–70, 92,
   162, 331
Dauna. Lo que lleva el río (2015 film),
   13
Davies, David John, 112–14
Davies, Edith, Castell Farm,
   Llangynwyd, 113
Davies, John, Cae'r Wâl, Pentyrch,
   107, 112

Davies, Llewelyn, Pen-tyrch, son of John Davies, 136
Davies, Mary Elizabeth, Castell Farm, Llangynwyd, 112–13
Davies, Revd T. A., Llanishen, 53
Davies, Tom, Cae'r Wâl, Pentyrch, 112
Davis, T. R., Newport, Pembs., 99
dawn, 187, 255, 257, 299, 305, 335
death, 67–8, 134, 261
  good death, 162
'Dechre rhigwm digri', 153
deer, 5, 11
  deer mask, 133
defamation
  defamatory stanzas, 20
  of misers, 19–20
'Deffrwch! Benteulu', 178, 237
Defynnog, 105
Denbigh, county, 144
  see also Denbigh, town
    Llanferres
    Llanrhaeadr-ym-Mochnant
    Lleweni
    Marchwiel
    Morris, Edward
    Ruthin
    Wrexham
Denbigh, town, 10, 79, 144
dendrochronology, 216–17, 221
departure songs, 119, 128, 161–2
Derby, earls of, 98
Devil, the, 24
'Devil's servants' (wrens), 80
Dibyn (Dibin), 92–5, 258–61
'Dibyn a Dobyn', 103, 178, 260
  variant in minor key, 103
'Difyrrwch Gwŷr Aberffraw'
  see 'Ffarwel Gwŷr Aberffraw'
Dinas, near Fishguard, 58
Dinas Mawddwy, 105, 107, 117, 131, 295, 300, 303
  see also Jones, Elwyn, Nantynodyn
    Jones, Robert Wyn, Boncyn
    Puw, Arwel

Dionysian practices, 6
distyll y Gwyliau (ebb of Christmas-tide), 87
ditches, 35, 88, 150
'Diwarnod Rhana' see Sharing day
Dobin, 92–5, 258–61
dogs, 28, 29, 123, 151, 152, 153, 207, 227, 245, 325
donkeys, 106, 133, 279, 281
door cheeks, 93
doors, 58–9, 93, 95, 106, 109, 115–17, 119, 121, 124, 133, 135, 144, 150, 161, 191, 197, 203, 205, 237, 253, 255, 258, 275, 277, 283, 289, 299, 315, 323, 327, 337
Douglas, 95
doves, 30, 191, 193, 223
dream song, 32
Dre-wen, 61
drink (drinking), 28, 31, 34, 36, 48–9, 57–8, 86, 109, 132, 135, 146, 148, 149, 150, 158, 159, 160, 161, 162–3, 165, 193, 197, 257, 271, 297, 299, 317, 319, 327, 335, 344
  see also ale
    barrel
    beer
    cider
    claret
    liquor
    spirits
    whisky
'Drink to me only with thine eyes', 158
Druids, 10, 53, 79
drunkenness, 35, 48–9, 64, 109, 113, 122, 150, 161, 195, 257, 259, 335, 337
'Dryw bach yn dedwi pedwar ar ddeg', 96
Dublin, 31
ducks, 28, 33
dumplings, 29–30
dung, 151, 261
Durham, County, 80

'Dutch-Health', 253
Dutchmen, 253
Dwnn, James, 46
'Dychan i Gasnodyn', 77
Dyffryn, 31

E
eagle, 87, 98, 154
Eastbourne, 165
Easter, 165
Easter Eve, 165
Easter Tuesday, 165
Edward I, 98
Edward VI, 55
Edward ap Hugh Gwynn, Bodewryd,
    145, 321
Edwards, Huw M., 78
Edwards, John, Cae-môr, 16–17
Eden, Garden of, 37
eggs, 55, 88, 96, 156, 247
Eglvryn Phraethineb (1595), 155
Fgypt, flight into, 133, 337
Eiddig, 211
elbury, 3
elder (wood), 12
elegy, 154
Elen Luyddog see Helena, Empress
Elizabeth, mother of John the Baptist,
    147
Elizabeth I, 55
England, 2, 10, 29, 47, 80, 81, 98, 160,
    315
    West Country, 2
    see also Somerset
        Suffolk
        Sussex
England, Stuart, Dinas Mawddwy,
    299, 301
English Christmas carol, 148, 167
English emigrants, 80
English-language songs, 128, 262–3
English riddle poem, 156–7
englyn (-ion) unodl union, 3, 57, 65,
    154, 341

entry songs, 157–8, 199, 327
Epiphany, 82, 87, 107
Epiphany Eve, 257–8
Epple Bay, 135
Erlkönig tale, 134
Eros, 83
Europe, 20, 83, 97, 134
Evan, Davy, Bryn Myrddin, Abergwili,
    46
Evan, Robert, Rhedyn Cochion,
    Trawsfynydd, 28
Evans, D. Silvan, 88
Evans, Gwennan, Fferm Parc-y-
    mynydd, 56
Evans, H. W., Solva, 98
Evans, Ifan, Fferm Parc-y-mynydd, 56
Evans, John, 116
Evans, T. C., 'Cadrawd', 107, 108
Evans, Thomas, Abercynon, 108
Evans, William (1762), 159
Evans, William, 'Gwilym o Arfon',
    'William Bifan', 148, 167, 170,
    332–6
evil spirits, 3, 7, 66, 116, 118
cvil wishes, 66
Ewenny Pottery, 3–4, 134, figs 2–4
    see also Claypits Pottery
eyebrows, 160–1
eyelashes, 150
eyes, 35, 93, 108–9

F
fairies, 133
    'the verry volks', 133
Fall of Man, 24, 34, 147, 148
farewell, 48–9
farewell carols, 9, 15, 34
'Fari Lwyd Lawen, Y', 107
farms, 57, 63, 83, 85, 86, 98, 112–14,
    122–3, 127, 275
Feast of Fools, 98
fcat-singing, 149, 152
feathers, 87, 88, 89, 92, 94, 99, 156
February, 163

'Fedle, Fawr, Y', 149, 168, 195, 311
  see also 'About the Bank'
felt, 108
female company, 16, 18, 24, 25, 36,
  86, 114, 118, 150
  see also woman (women)
'Feri Lwyd, Y', 107
fertility (land, animals, humans), 1, 3,
  5–6, 8, 9, 11, 36, 47, 49, 53, 54,
  83, 87, 88, 118, 161, 219, 227, 257
Festel, 90–2, 262
Festival of Britain (1951), 105
Festival of the Ass (14 January), 133
'Ffading', 167, 170
Ffair-rhos, 56
'Ffarwel Gwŷr Aberffraw', 179,
  312–13, 315
'Ffarwel Ned Puw', 147, 157
Fferi, Y (unknown location), 78
fiddle, 27, 109, 118, 120
  see also violin
Fiddledefoze, 91–2
fiddler, 209
fingernails, 60, 152, 199
fire, 59, 114, 118, 151, 193, 197, 207,
  255, 257, 289, 313, 319, 327
firebrand, 31
fireside, 118
'First day of Christmas, The', 29, 177
Fishguard, 58, 86
flagon, 325
flame, 164
Flint, county, 144
  see also Caerwys
            Holywell
            Mold
            Nannerch
            Northop
            Rhuddlan
            St Asaph
Flood (Noah), 157
Flotta, Orkney, 81
flour, 50, 54, 82, 86, 211
flowers, 126, 283

flummery, 152, 319
flute, 106, 109
food, 15, 22, 28, 30, 50, 57, 124,
  125–6, 127, 132, 135, 150, 151,
  161, 219, 233, 257, 279, 313, 319,
  325
foot, 30, 38, 80, 106, 209
footman, 95, 263
forfeits game, 29
forks, 91, 93, 95, 262
Fose, 90–2, 262
fox (-es), 4, 111, 247
France, 5, 81, 97, 98
  see also Brittany
            Gulf of Lion (Lyons)
            La Ciotat, near Marseille
            Lascaux, Dordogne
frankincense, 158, 328
Frazer, James, 97
free-metre poetry, 342–5
freezing conditions, effects of, 60,
  199, 247, 283, 289, 299, 313, 315,
  323, 327
frying pan, 123
fruit, 55, 148
funeral (-s), 32, 97, 261

G
Gabriel, Angel, 148, 309
'Gadael Tir', 180, 189, 199, 205, 333,
  337
  see also 'Leave Land'
'ganfas farch, Y' 134
gardens, 46, 227, 257
Garmon Seia, 320
Gaymers wassail, fig. 1
gemstones, 55
generosity, 135, 163, 203, 205, 233,
  241, 269, 285, 293, 313, 343, 345
Genesis, Book of, 157
gentleman, 55, 63, 315, 331, 344
Geoffrey of Monmouth, 1
George II, 59
Geraint son of Erbin, 154

Germany, 253
gifts *see* bread
 monetary gifts
Gilfach Goch, 114
 Clun Goch, public house, 114
Gill, W. Walter, 80, 91–2, 94
girls *see* woman (women)
Glamorgan (-shire), 3–4, 22, 38, 49,
 54, 77, 105, 107, 108, 127, 128,
 134
 Vale of, 107, 128–9, 139
 see also Abercynon
  Blackmill
  Bridgend
  Bryncethin
  Brynmenyn
  Caerphilly
  Cardiff
  Castellau
  Clydach
  Coety
  Coryton
  Cowbridge
  Gilfach Goch
  Glamorgan Gazette, The
  Glynogwr
  Gower
  Kimley Moor
  Llangynwyd
  Llanharry
  Llantrisant
  Llantwit Fardre
  Mari Lwyd
  Merthyr Tydfil
  Mumbles
  Nantgarw
  Neath
  Neath, Vale of
  Oystermouth
  Pen-coed
  Pentyrch
  Penydarren Ironworks
  Peterston-super-Ely
  Pontrhydycyff
  Pontyclun
  Pontypridd
  Porteynon
  Radyr
  Resolven
  Rhondda Valley
  Rhossili
  St Athan
  St Brides
  St Fagans
  Swansea
  Taff's Well
  Tonyrefail
  Trealaw
  Treforest
  Welsh St Donats
Glamorgan Gazette, The, 113
glass wren house, 84
gloves, 55
Glynogwr, 114
 New Inn, 114
goats, 124, 153–5, 211
 goat meat, 18
 milking goats, 153
 see also 'Cyfri'r geifr'
  'Naw gafr gorniog'
goblet, 4, 150, 165
God, 22–6, 30, 34, 37, 52, 55, 68, 88,
 127, 148, 163, 164, 187, 189, 197,
 215, 219, 221, 225, 239, 269, 273,
 291, 304–8, 330–1
 Father of Lights, 23, 333, 337
 Father of the Destitute, 61
gold, 158, 161, 328, 343
gold wires, 52, 72
golden knives, 10, 53
'Good King Wenceslas', 245
goose, 18, 30, 117, 247
gooseberry bushes, 229
Goring, Charles, 72, 165, 171
Goring, Jeremy, 72
Goring, Rosemary, 72
gorse, 60, 150, 237
gossamer, 193

Gower, 3, 108, 129–31, 133
  'the verry volks' in, 133
  see also Kimley Moor
    Porteynon
    Rhossili
grain, mixed-crop (*siprys*), 66
grave (-s), 55, 68, 119, 135, 187
Greece, 6, 97
'Greensleeves', 209
Gregorian calendar, 59
Griffith, Robert, Pen-y-cefn, 145
Griffiths, Selina, Garn, 58
grindstone, 319
Gruffydd, William, 24
Gulf of Lion (Lyons), 97, 98
Gummere, Francis, 155
guns, 90, 262
gwasael, 1
'gwashaela', 134
Gwaun Valley *see* Cwm Gwaun
Gwent, 105, 107, 128
  see also Blaenau Gwent
Gwreiddiau, Y, Llanwddyn, 78
Gwrtheyrn (Vortigern), 1–2, 253
Gŵyl Fair ddechre gwanwyn, 143
Gŵyl Fair y Canhwyllau (Candlemas),
  8, 11–12, 54, 124, 143–71, 304–39
  passim
  alternative date for, 145
  'Carol Gŵyl Fair o gwestiwna', 157
  'Carol Noswyl Fair', 145
  carols and songs for, 143–71
    passim, 304–39 *passim*
  confined to N. Wales, 145
  'custom has now ceased' (1806),
    144, 165
  goblet thrown over head to
    foretell longevity, 165
  religious early carols for, 146
  revived in Sussex (2020), 165–6
  self-lighting candles at, 164
  Virgin and Child linked with,
    162–3
  Wassail songs for, 304–39

'Ystatud Canu Gŵyl Fair', 149,
  310–11
Gwylliaid Cochion Mawddwy, 300, 303
Gwyn, Richard, martyr, 22

H

hair, 51, 132, 150, 160–1
Hajji Khalifa, 155
Halloween, 7
'Halsing y Dryw', 79, fig. 8
hare, 122–3
Harlech *see* 'March of the Men of
  Harlech, The'
  'Ymdaith Gwŷr Harlech'
harness, 279
harp, 26–7, 110, 112, 120, 199, 201,
  279, 291, 303, 329, 342
  harper, 26–7
Harris, J. Rendel, 47
harvest, 28, 36, 47, 59, 65, 66, 151,
  205, 219, 227
Harvey, Cyril, 131
hat, 109, 111, 128
hatchet, 91, 262
Haverfordwest, 86, 99
hawk, 247
Hawkins, Mr, shepherd, 80
'hawl i'r tŷ', 151
Haxey, Lincolnshire, 6
hay, 130, 133, 151, 219, 227
Hay-on-Wye, 106
Hayes, Nansi, 242–4, 250
hazel, 154
hazelnuts, 54
health, 1–2, 36, 48–9, 54, 65, 66, 88,
  119, 161, 215, 219, 247, 253, 263,
  339
hearth, 59, 116, 118, 151, 219
hearthstone, 122–3
heating, lack of, 151
heaven, 37, 68, 162, 189, 201, 221,
  249, 305, 309
hedge, 83, 87, 88, 130, 263
hedgehog, 123

Helena, Empress, 'Elen Luyddog', 158, 170, 329
  see also St Helena
hell, 125–6
hens, 30, 153, 156, 247
hen bennill (hen benillion), 225, 342–3
'Hen Dôn, Yr', 145
hen gostwm (old custom), 19
'Hen Lywarch, Yr', *see* Puw, Dan
Hengist, 1
Henry III, 10, 55
Henry VIII, 55
Heraldic Visitations (1594), 145, 321
Hereford, 78
Hermon, Carms, 56
Herod, 329
heron, 87–8
herring, 65, 88–9, 102
hilt-and-point Sword Dance, 11, 105
Historia Regum Britanniae, 1
hobby horse, 85, 134
'Hobby Horse', 168
hoen ddawnswyr, 110
hoof (hooves), 289
Hoggan, Frances, 107, 134
Holin (Holly), 32–4, 161, 211–13, 316–17
holly (celyn), 51, 52, 54–5, 82–3, 154, 213
  see also Whipo'r Celyn
Holly and Ivy, conflict, 32–4, 161, 211–13
'Holvyr and Heyvy Made a Grete Party', 32
Holy Communion, 15
Holy Family, 133
Holy Spirit, The, 147, 305, 331
Holywell, 144
home, threat to return, 255
honesty, 279, 313
horn lantern, 38
hornpipe, 118
horse, 11, 28, 30, 35, 124, 129–31, 134, 227, 247, 249, 279

buried skulls of, 108
horse and carriage, 130
horse and cart, 93
horse cult, 135
horse mask, 133
horse's head, 279
horse's jaw, 130
horse's skull, 105–42 *passim*, 264–303 *passim*
pantomime-type horse, 85
white horses, 134
  see also hobby horse
    'Horse's Head Song'
    Mari Lwyd
    Sharper
    stallion
    White Horse of Uffington
'Horse's Head Song', 130–1
house, on entering, 55, 126, 223, 225, 255, 319
house sparrow, 83–4
household, 125, 193, 237
  recently moved family, 258
householder (-s), 15–16, 17, 18, 20–1, 24, 26, 27, 28, 30, 34, 48–9, 56, 58–9, 61, 62, 63, 66, 85, 86, 114, 115, 116–17, 121, 128, 135, 146, 149, 150–2, 159, 160, 191, 195, 205, 207, 217, 223, 237, 245, 253, 255, 313, 315, 321, 331, 335
householder's reply, 28, 207–9
householder's wife, 34–5, 48–9, 58–9, 64, 85, 86, 159, 195, 205, 217, 223, 313, 315, 321, 331, 335, 339
'Howtra! Hora!', 146
hugger mugger, 209
Hugh, 94
Hughes, Arfon, 294, 297, 301
Hughes, John (1670), 146
Hughes, Jonathan, Llangollen, 10, 37, 46
Hughes, Robert, 'Robin Ddu yr Ail o Fôn', 57
Humphrey, William (1690–1), 24

Humphreys, Dafydd, 190–5
hunchback, 33, 211
Hunting the Wren, 8, 10–11, 34,
    77–104 *passim*, 252–63 *passim*
    close to coast, 98
    demise of, 98–9
    dialogue song, 89–90
    disapproval of cruelty, 99
    English-language songs, 90–2
    origins of custom, 97
    use of replica wren, 99
    Welsh-language songs, 92–5
    wren house procession, 89–90
    wren hunt, 89–90
    wren-hunt songs, 90–5, 104,
        252–63
Huw ab (Evan) Ifan, 54, 145
Huws, Andreas, 45
Huws, Daniel, 126, 344
Hwch Ddu Gwta, 7
'Hyd yma bu'n cerdded', 179, 267
hymn, 98–9
Hywel Dda, laws of, 27

I
'I have a young sister far beyond the
    sea', 169
'iach wythoes' (eight ages of health),
    36
Ifin (Ivy), 32–4, 161, 211–13, 317
    womanhood, 317
Iliad, The, 5
immortality of the soul, 55
impossible tasks, 30
India, 20, 257
interlude, 133
Iocyn Ddu ab Ithel Goch, 77–8, 82
Ireland, 34, 80–1, 82, 84, 89, 94, 95,
    98, 99, 134
    see also Clare
            Connacht
            Kerry
            Louth
            Roscommon

Irish youths, 82–3
Irish Sea, 319
irony, 28–9
Isle of Man, 80, 81, 88–9, 94, 95, 97, 98
    see also Derby, earls of
            Douglas
            Stanley family
Issá, of South America, 6
itinerant poet (-s), 77–8
Ivy *see* Ifin

J
J. J., Ystrad Alun, 34
James, Epistle of, 23, 337
James, Marian, Tŷ Hen, Rhos-hill, 249
James, William, Tonyrefail, 4, fig. 4
January, 54, 133, 145
Japurá, of South America, 6
Java, 134
jelly, 65
Jenkin, 113
Jenkins, John, 'Ifor Ceri', 79, 82
Jenkins the clergyman, 269
Jerusalem, 187
jesting, 28–9
Jesus Christ, 8, 10, 24, 27, 46–7, 55,
    69, 133, 147, 148, 158, 159, 162,
    163–4, 187, 189, 201, 203 , 215,
    219, 223, 225, 304–8, 328, 331,
    333, 335
    'Alpha, Omega', 149, 304–8
    'Alpha' praised by St David, 158
    'Carol of praise to the Son of
        God', 186–9
    Christ Child in the Temple, 158
    Lamb, 159, 187, 305
    light for the Gentiles, 163
    Lord of glory, 189
    Man who walked on water, the, 68
    Presentation of, in the Temple,
        8, 163–4
    'Saviour of the world', death of,
        133
    second Adam, 187

Son of God, 24, 187, 189, 345
Son of the Light, 187
Unifier, 201
see also Christmas (-tide)
    Mary, mother of Jesus
    Messiah
'Joan's Placket' ('Joane Blackett'), 180,
    191, 193
John (Dibyn a Dobyn), 258–61
John the Divine, 157
John, Sir W. Goscombe, 82–3
John Barleycorn, Sir see Bregyn fab
    Heidden
    tooling for, 86
John the Red Nose, 90–2, 262
Johnnie Bach, Stafell-wen, 61
Johnnie Red-hosie, 81
Jones, Mr, of Cardiff, 83
Jones, Mr and Mrs, Llandybïe, 62
Jones, Dafydd (1768), 161
Jones, Dafydd, 'Dafydd Siôn Siâms',
    42, 47, 55, 212–25, 304–8
Jones, Daniel Gruffydd, 229
Jones, David (1888), 107, 134
Jones, Edward, 'Bardd y Brenin', 154
Jones, Elwyn, Nantynodyn, Dinas
    Mawddwy, 297, 301
Jones, Francis, 53
Jones, Griffith, collier, Pontrhydycyff,
    113
Jones, Gwion, Fferm y Lan, 56
Jones, Ian, Pen-coed, 131
Jones, Revd J. S., St Davids, 82
Jones, John, 143
Jones, John (1773), 161
Jones, John, and Son, 94
Jones, John, Llanddeiniolen, 312–14,
    336–9
Jones, Lewis Davies, 'Llew Tegid', 10,
    79–80, 96–7
Jones, Manon, Fferm y Lan, 56
Jones, Mrs Margaret, Tŷ Fry,
    Penrhyndeudraeth, 215, 217, 219,
    221

Jones, Robert Wyn, Boncyn, Dinas
    Mawddwy, 297, 301
Jones, Samuel, Castell Farm,
    Llangynwyd, 113
Jones, Stanley, 113
Jones, Tom, Trealaw, 110–11, 116,
    124
Jones, William, Caernarfon (1767),
    143, 145
Jones, Revd William, Tŷ Fry,
    Penrhyndeudraeth, 42, 213–21
    drowning of, 217, 221
    family of (sons Humphrey, John,
      Owen and William; daughters
      Cathy, Elin and Margaret),
      215, 219
Jonson, Ben, 158
Jordan, river, 157
Joseph, husband of Mary, 148
joy, 127, 162, 223, 225, 263, 269, 309,
    335, 339
Judaea (Judah), 327, 329, 335
Judgement Day, 37, 221, 309
Judy see Siwan
Julian calendar, 59

K
'Kenmure's on and awa', 81
Kerry, county, 85
kettle, 52, 91, 122–3, 262
Khonds of Bengal, 7
Kidwelly, 47, 53, 64, 82, 164
    Lady Street, 53
kiln, 31
Kilvert, Revd Francis, 106
Kimley Moor, 130
'King and Queen', 93
'King of the Birds' see wren
kiss, 2, 18, 30, 36, 161, 193, 255, 339
kissing-bush, 86
Knell, 97
knife, 10, 53, 91, 93, 95, 262
knife and fork, 91, 93, 95, 262
Knighton, 33

Krappe, A. H., 9
Kyffin, Edward, 22

L
La Ciotat, near Marseille, 81
'Ladi Wen heb ddim pen', 7
Lampeter, 59, 233
    see also Peterwell mansion
            Peterwell school
lamps, 164, 307
lantern, 84
Lascaux, Dordogne, 5
latch, 269
Laugharne, 46, 53
'Leave Land', 180, 189, 199, 205, 333, 337
leeks, 89, 227
lentils, 207
Leviticus, Book of, 147
Lewis, Marc, Penegoes, 299, 301
Lewis, Mostyn, 103, 260
Lhuyd, Edward, 78, 82, 88
light, 97, 108, 125, 163, 271, 275, 305, 309, 315, 331, 333, 337, 342
lignum vitae, 3
'Lilisfrens', 170
lime, to prevent yellowing, 108
liquor, 30, 34, 144, 145, 146, 158, 160, 163, 193, 258, 315, 317, 321, 335, 344
liquorice, 57
Little Newcastle see Casnewydd-bach
Llanbeblig see Caernarfon, town
Llandanwg, 216, 311
Llanddeiniolen, 312–14, 338–9
Llanddewibrefi, 51
Llanddyfnan, 321
Llandecwyn, 217, 221
Llandeilo Fawr, 50
Llandrygarn, 31
Llandybïe, 62, 68, 106–7, 127, 128, 136, 273
Llandyfaelog, 64
Llandygái, 144

Llandygwydd, 113
Llandysul (Ceredigion), 45, 60, 62, 63, 70, 231, 243, 245, 250
Llanelli (Carms), 63
Llanerfyl, 56
Llanfallteg, 248–9
Llanferres, 78
Llanfihangel Rhos-y-corn, 129
Llanfihangel y Traethau, 217, 221
Llanfyrnach, 52
Llangadfan dancers, 299
Llan-gan (Glam.), 4
Llangathen, 50
Llangefni, 31, 145, 321
Llangoedmor, 79
Llangollen, 10, 37, 46
Llangunllo (Rad.), 33
Llangyfelach, 38
Llangynwyd, 112–14, 131, figs 5, 10–11
Llanhaearn, 31
Llanharry, 114, 122–3
    Colliers Arms, The, 114
    Llanharri Heath, 122–3
Llanishen see Cardiff
Llanllechid, 148,
Llanrhaeadr-ym-Mochnant, 10, 79–80, 95, 260
    Cwm-du, 80
Llansilin, 31
Llantrisant (Glam.), 112, 128, 131
    Folk Club, 131
Llantwit Fardre, 112
Llanwddyn, 78
Llanwenog, 60. 62
Llanybydder, 63
Lleweni, 167
Llidiart Fawr, 17
Lloyd, Bertram, 98, 99
Lloyd, Revd John, Caerwys, 165
Lloyd, Revd Ll., Nannerch, 65
Llwyd, Angharad, 165
    Wassail cup owned by, fig. 13
Llwyd, Huw, Cynfal, Maentwrog, 145
Llwyd, Morgan (1729), 20

Llwyn Ynn, Vale of Clwyd, 18
Llwyngwril, 10, 79, 95
'Llyfr Coch Hergest' (Red Book of
    Hergest), 77, 99
Llŷn peninsula, 10, 79, 94–5
    see also Prichard, Robert, 'Robin
        yr Aber' of Llŷn
locks, 291
London, 10, 144
    British Library, 33
longevity, 55, 65, 66, 68, 165, 219, 257
Louth, county, 84
love, 120, 156, 263
luck, 65, 116, 161
lyre, 223
lyric poetry, 67–8

M
Mac Coitir, Niall, 98
macaronic carol, 32
Macsen Wledig, the Dream of, 158,
    170, 329
Maentwrog, 311
    see also Llwyd, Huw, Cynfal
maggots, 29, 209
Magi, the, 24, 148, 157, 327
magpies, 227
Maid of Cefn Ydfa, The, 120
Maid of Sker, The, 120
maidenhood, 158, 317, 329
    see also virgin
maids, 164, 233, 319
make-up, use of, 132
Maldon (Essex), 6
Mallwyd, 105, 107, 117, 131–2, 295,
    299, 303
    Brigand's Inn, 132
    Plygain at Mallwyd Church, 300
malt, 34
Malvolio, 209
mane, 108
manioc, 6
Manx language, 97
Manx wren song, 93

'March of the Men of Harlech, The',
    183, 230–1
Marchwiel, 78
Margate, 135
Mari Lwyd, 8, 11, 12, 85, 105–42
    passim, 264–303 passim, figs 10–12
    antics of, 107, 109, 110, 115
    biting, snapping by, 108, 111, 118,
        124, 130, 287–9
    disorder and confusion caused
        by, 117
    fighting between rival groups,
        117, 119–20
    'grey mare', 134
    hat placed in mouth of, 128
    neighing and bellowing, 116
    origin theories, 133–4
    pre-written verses for, 117
    promise to behave well, 287–9
    revival of, at Llantrisant, 131
    ritual for adults, 135
    six types of songs, 120–31
    stabling of, 110, 112, 114, 131
    toy version on a stick, 131
    tunes used for, 120–1
    use of cars as transport for, 132
    various names for, 107
'Mari Lwyd Lawen', 136
Marloes, 95, fig. 9
Marseille, 81
'Marts', 168
'marw llwyd y flwyddyn', 133
Mary, mother of Jesus, 8, 11–12,
    304–39 passim
    'Cherry-Tree Carol', relating to, 148
    conversation of Gabriel with, 148
    drinking to Virgin and Child, 162–3
    five sorrows, joys and heavenly
        gifts of, 147
    institutes chair ceremony, 158
    light candles to commemorate, 163
    Marian devotions, 133
    medieval poems praising, 143
    perpetual virginity of, 146

praised by St David, 158
purification of, 143–4, 146, 147,
  148, 305
'radiant queen', 309
sings sweet song as God lights
  candles, 164
Solemnity of, The, 47
veneration in Wales during Middle
  Ages, 143
Virgin and Child, representation
  of, 158
well-wishing to commemorate, 162
see also Holy Family
mash tun, 31
masks, 11, 133, 134
masons, 46
Mathews, Thomas, Llandybïe, 136
Mathri, 29
Matthew, Gospel of, 189, 329, 337
Matthew Paris, 55
Maurice, John (1729), 20
May carols, 8
May Day, 8, 9, 133
'May Day', 180, 199
May Eve, 8
maypole, 8
mead, 315
meat, 18, 29, 34, 36, 86, 92, 155, 207,
  299, 319, 323, 325
  see also goat meat
    venison
Mediterranean region, 97, 98
  see also France
    Greece
    Gulf of Lion (Lyons)
Mee, Arthur, 98
Meibion Llywarch, 302
melancholic poetry, 67–8
Melchior, 158, 328
Melder, 90–2, 262
'Melus geingciau Deheubarth Cymru',
  fig. 8
memory game, 29
merging two customs, 85

Merioneth, county
  see Bala
    Barmouth
    Blaenau Ffestiniog
    Corwen
    Dinas Mawddwy
    Harlech
    Llandanwg
    Llandecwyn
    Llanfihangel y Traethau
    Llwyd, Huw, Cynfal,
      Maentwrog
    Llwyngwril
    Mallwyd
    Maentwrog
    Penrhyndeudraeth
    Phylip, Gruffudd, of Ardudwy
    Phylip, William, of
      Ardudwy
    Traeth Bach
    Trawsfynydd
    Vaughan, Rowland, Caer-gai
Merthyr Tydfil, 107, 279–81
  see also Penydarren
'Merry Lude, The', 133
merriment, 287–9, 291
Merryman, 109, 118
Messiah, 22, 46, 307, 329, 333
mesur byr, 170
mesur salm, 203, 311, 343
metrical psalms, 22, 40
Middle Ages, 53, 78, 83, 143
midnight, 55–6
midwinter see winter solstice
Milder, 90–2, 262
milk, 36, 108, 227
mill, 31
miller, 16, 31
minstrel, 78, 169
mint cake, 243
Mirehouse, Mary Beatrice, 99
misers, 19–20, 61–2, 128, 150, 163,
  241, 273
mistletoe, 10, 52, 53–5

'Mochyn Du, Y', 181, 247–9
Mold, 144
moles, 77, 227
money/monetary gifts, 29–30, 46, 50, 51–3, 55–7, 63, 70, 86, 88, 89, 95, 97, 106, 109, 115, 117, 119, 128, 131, 150, 227–8, 233, 235, 237, 239, 241, 243, 245, 250, 279, 343
    donated to local causes, 110
    golden half sovereigns, 317
money boxes, 46
Monmouth, county, 53, 54, 117–18, 124
    see also Beaufort
        Bedwellty
        Blaenau Gwent
        Briery Hill
        Gwent
        Mari Lwyd
        Rassau
        Rhymney
        Rhymney Valley
Montgomery, county, 46, 56, 67, 229
    see also Berriew
        Cemmaes
        Darowen
        Llanrhaeadr-ym-Mochnant
        Llanwddyn
        Penegoes
        Trefeglwys
moon, 32, 250, 327
Morgan, 94
Morgan, John, (1694), 148
Morris, Mr, Llanwenog, 62
Morris, Edward, Perthillwydion, 39
Morris, Lewis, of Anglesey, 21–2
Morris, Richard, of Anglesey, 11, 143, 145, 146, 149, 150, 152, 155, 159, 320–1, 322–3
Morys, Huw, 34
Mosaic Law, 46, 55, 147, 225
Moses, 55, 157, 225
mouse, 4, 21, 207, 247
mouth organ, 89
mud, 60, 237

mule, 122–3
Mumbles, 110, 131
mummers, 128
mumming plays, 110, 133
music, 118, 191, 203, 213, 223, 309, 331, 343, 345
musician, 55, 89, 145, 199, 225
    see also crowther (under crwth)
        harper
musical instruments, 85, 109, 111
    see also accordion
        bodhrán
        crwth
        fiddle
        flute
        harp
        lyre
        mouth organ
        tin whistle
        violin
mustard, 18
Mycenaean influence, 97
myrrh, 158, 328
mystery plays, 133

N
names demanded, 121
Nannerch, 65
Nant y Fallog, 17
Nantgarw, 112, 117, 118
nasal singing, 136
National Eisteddfod of Wales (1911), 136
National Library of Wales, 114
National Museum of History
    see St Fagans
Nativity, 21, 24, 32
'Naw gafr gorniog', 154
Neath, 112, 119
Neath, Vale of, 65, 107, 108, 115
Nebraska, 80
Never Beyond, 261
Neville, Sir Ralph, judge, Chancery Divison, 113

'new water', 53
New Year, 2, 8, 10, 45–75 *passim*, 82,
    83, 85, 97, 106–7, 127, 222–51
    passim
    Celtic, 7
    religious carols at, 46–7
    wassail songs at, 222–51
New Year's Day, 10, 45–75 *passim*, 85,
    145, 222–51 *passim*, 343, figs 5–6
    avoid giving, 61
    children to sing rising-time to
        mid-day, 56
    Covid-19 (2021), 70–1
    email greeting (2021), 70–1
    first person sighted on, 51
    fortunate men's names on, 51
    gifts not distributed after mid-day
        on, 55
    lucky and unlucky initials for
        callers on, 52
    male visitor ushered upstairs
        on, 51
    midnight to daylight, correct time
        to sing, 55–6
    punishing girls with holly on, 51
    ritualistic significance of, missing
        today, 69
    seeing man named Twm first on,
        51
    seeing man with red hair first
        on, 51
    seeing woman first on, 51–2
    strict-metre poetry on, 57
    throw money down from
        bedrooms, 56
    unremembered, 69
    see also caleniga
            calennig
            Old New Year's Day
New Year's Eve, 53, 55, 223
New Year's Eve dance, 55, 223
New Year's gifts, 45–75 *passim*, 213,
    222–51 *passim*
    gifts to royalty, 55

see also *calennig*
        monetary gifts
New Year's Water, 52, 56
Newcastle Emlyn, 113
Newport (Pembs), 58, 63, 99
Newtown, 31
Nivose, 81
nonsense songs and words, 80–1, 146,
    283, 335
Norman influence, 98
Northop, 144
nosebleed, 17
Noswyl Fair, 154
    'Carol Noswyl Fair', 145
November, 106–7
'Nunc Dimittis', 147
Nugarth, Y, 78
nursery rhyme, 99
nutmeg, 255
nuts, 54–5

O
oak (door), 122–3
Oak, Mr, Neath, 112
oatmeal, 31
oats, 50, 54–5, 66, 130, 152
'Oes gafr eto?' *see* 'Cyfri'r geifr'
Offa's Dyke, 78
old age, 162, 257
'Old Llywarch' *see* Puw, Dan
Old New Year's Day, 53, 59, 107
Old Norse, 1
Old Year, Th', 263
onions, 227
oranges, 54, 55, 65
Orchard, The, ritual, (*perllan, 'Y*
        Berllan'), 4, 47–50, 82
    see also Stewley Orchard, Somerset
orchards, 47–50, 82, 125–6, 255
    orchard boards, 50
    see also apple trees
Orkney Isles, 81
    see also Flotta
            South Ronaldsay

Orinoco Delta, Venezuela, 9
orphans, 61
Ostler Smart, 109, 117, 118, 125–6
Owen, 94
Owen, Humphrey, Lasynys, 217,
    221
Owen, Phillip, 58
Owen, Trefor M., 4, 54, 119, 144
owls, 28, 265
ox, 152
Oxford, city, 144
    Ashmolean Museum, 78
    Bodleian Library, 33
Oxford, county, 80
oyster, 135
Oystermouth, 108, 110

P

Palaeolithic period, 5
Parc (Bala), 301–2
parlour, 126, 132, 273
Parochialia, 78, 88
parody, 98
parrot, 29–30
Parry, Richard (?1753), 157
Parry-Williams, T. H., 134
parting song, 119
partridge, 29
partridge step (dance), 111
pas de deux, 111
pasties and pies, 18, 207, 237, 271,
    321, 325
Paul, Gwenda, 216, 220
peacock, 28
peace, 70, 263
pear tree, 29–30, 229
pearls, 135
peat, 28, 151, 152, 197
Peate, Iorwerth Cyfeiliog, 3–4, 105, 134
peed (urinated), 151
'Peg O'Ramsey', 149, 181, 207, 208–9,
    310–11
*Pembroke County Guardian and
    Cardigan Reporter*, 84

Pembrokeshire, 10, 29, 52, 58–60,
    67, 69, 78–9, 82, 84, 85, 90, 96–7,
    98–9, 134, 262–3
    'little England beyond Wales', 98
    see also Brynberian
        Casnewydd-bach
        Crosswell
        Crymych
        Cwm Gwaun
        Dinas
        Fishguard
        Gwaun Valley
        Haverfordwest
        Little Newcastle
        Llanfrynach
        Marloes
        Newport
        Redberth
        Rhos-hill
        Rhydberth
        St Davids
        Solva
        Tenby
Pen Ceffyl, 107
Pen-coed, 109, 117, 131
    see also Williams, John,
        Bryngwenith
Pendine, 53, 249
Penegoes, 56
    see also Lewis, Marc
Penmon, 53
Pennant, Thomas, 165
pennill telyn (penillion telyn)
    see hen bennill
Penrhyn-coch, 71
Penrhyndeudraeth, 42, 47, 55, 213–21,
    222–4, 311
    see also Jones, Dafydd, 'Dafydd
        Siôn Siâms'
Pentyrch, 107, 112, 131
    Cae'r-wâl, 112
    see also Davies, John
        Davies, Llewelyn
        Davies, Tom

Penydarren, 107–8, 278–81
'Pepper is black', 209
perdrix, 29
perllan (-nau) see orchards
Perot ar y Pren Pêr, Y, 29–30
pertriz, 29
pestilence, 163
Peterston-super-Ely, 112
Peterwell mansion, Lampeter, 233
Peterwell school, Lampeter, 59
petticoats, 155, 323
pewter, 325
Phillips, Dorothy, 82
Phillips, Elizabeth, 82
Phillips, Ifan Bifan, 114
Phillips, T. I., Aberystwyth, 114, 121,
    276
Phylip, Gruffudd, 145, 162–3
Phylip, William, 23–4, 26, 145, 147
Pice Rhana, 65
piddle pot, 18
pies see pasties
pigs, 28, 151, 227
    sow, 207
'Pilgrim', 181, 312–13, 315
pinslab, 30–1
pipes, kiln, 197
pistols, 81
pitchfork, 51
plague, 163, 187
Plas Hen, 145
Pliny, 87
plough, 5–6, 36, 151, 227, 247
    triple-furrowed plough, 6
Plough Monday, 6
plum pudding, 65
plum trees, 229
plygain, 15, 56, 146, 297, 300
poker (fire), 111–12, 289
Pontrhydycyff, 113
Pontsian, 63, 69, 231
Pontyclun, 131
Pontypridd, 112, 129
Porteynon, 130

Portugal, 97
possum, 80
poor, 28, 46, 59–61, 93, 187, 239, 241,
    343
Poor of the Parish, 91–2
potatoes, 66, 99, 227, 247
pots, 91, 262, 299
powder and ball, 263
prayer, 229, 333
prehistoric times, 97
Pren-gwyn (Ceredigion), 45
Presaddfed, 31
Prichard, Rhys ('The Old Vicar'), 22, 40
Prichard, Robert, 'Robin yr Aber', of
    Llŷn, 159, 164, 330–3
Prince Rupert of the Rhine, 339
'Prince Rupert's Conceit', 175, 337
pricsiwn (pricksong), 15, 16, 143,
    312–13
'Pricsiwn Gŵyl Fair', 143
procession, 95–6, 97, 163
processional songs, 94, 95–6
prosperity, 51–5, 62, 65, 69, 119, 127,
    339
Protestants, 148
Prys, Edmwnd, 22
Psalms
    Psalm metre, 25, 203
    see also metrical psalms
            Salmau Cân
public houses, 114, 131, 132, 279
Pugh, 94
    see also Puw
pulli cantus, 15
purification, following childbirth
    in Mosaic Law, 147
    in Wales (18th cent.), 147
    see also Mary the mother of Jesus
purity, 163, 309, 313
purse, 89
Puw, Arwel, Dinas Mawddwy, 297,
    301
Puw, Dan, Parc, Bala, 301–2
puzzles, 11

pwnco (bardic contention/contest for the house), 9, 15–16, 28–9, 106, 115–17, 120, 121, 124, 128, 133, 134, 135, 148, 150–2, 154, 191, 193, 253–8, 266–9, 274–7, 282–3, 284–7, 293
  householders winning, 117
Pwnsh (Punch), 110–12, 117, 118–19, 125–6, 127, 289

Q
Quakers, 20
question-and-answer, 9, 89–95, 150–1
questions, carol of, 157
quête (begging rhyme), 58

R
raccoons, 80
Radnor, county, 33
  see also Clyro
          Hay-on-Wye
          Llangunllo
Radyr *see* Cardiff
ragged clothes, 110
rags, 108
raisins, 54–5
Randell, Francis, Kidwelly, 47
Rassau, 129
rats, 80, 227
ravens, 191, 193
Re di siepe, 87
red, 108, 323
  scarlet braid, 109
Red Bandits of Mawddwy (Dugoed), 303
Red Book of Hergest *see* 'Llyfr Coch Hergest'
Redberth, 91–2
Redeemer, 27, 55, 199, 203, 223
Rees, Edward, Castell Farm, Llangyn-wyd, 112–13
Rees, Brinley, 32
Rees, John, 131
Rees, Revd Thomas, Llangathen, 50

Rees, Tom, 131
Rees, Vernon, 131
Rees, William Morgan, Brynmenyn, 138, 286
Regulus, 87
rein, 109, 118
relish, 319
Renaissance period, 83
renewal, 97
repentance, 37, 148, 189
request (Vigil Chorus or Vigil lay), 121
Resolven, 65
resurrection of the soul, 55
Revelation, Book of, 72, 134
Rhiw-dder, 117
'rhodd galennig', fig. 5
'rhoddi Penglog', 133
Rhondda Valley, 110, 129
Rhonwen (Rowena), 1, 253
Rhoscolyn, 31
Rhos-hill, 249
Rhossili, 129–31
Rhuddlan, 144
Rhydberth, 91–2
Rhymney, 107
Rhymney Valley, 136
rhymes and rhymesters, 109, 115, 117, 118, 122–3, 127, 128, 129, 132, 145, 167
ribbons, 5, 10, 11, 78–9, 82–4, 88, 89, 96, 105–42 *passim*, 263, 275, 279, 283
rice, 65
Richards, Glyn, 129–31
Richards, Jane, Darowen, 229
Richards, Mary, Darowen, 229
Richards, Twm, Colliers Arms, Llanharry, 114
riddles, 9, 15, 30, 149, 152, 155–7, 323, 325
  answers to riddles, 325
  gifts from four sisters beyond the sea, 156–7
  riddle song, 323

rings, 156, 317
Risiart, 92–5, 258–61
roads, muddy, 60
roast meat, 207
roasting Jack (spit), 156, 325
Roberts, Gomer Morgan, 126–7
Roberts, John, 65
Roberts, William, 'Nefydd', 107, 108, 124, 133
Robin (Robyn), 92–5, 258–61
Roi des oiseaux, 87
Roman Catholicism, 22, 148
    see also Sergius I, Pope
Romans, Epistle to, 46
roof *see* thatched roofs
'Rogero', 209
rooks, 152
Roscommon, county, 85
rosette, 109
Rowena *see* Rhonwen
'Royal William', 227, 229
rope, 32, 108
rosemary, 54–5
rowan berries, 50
rubbish dump, 135
Russia, 9
Ruthin, 103, 260
rye, 66

S
sacrificial death, 6, 7, 87, 94, 95, 97
saddle, 125–6
Saer, D. Roy, 29, 55–6, 58, 99, 102, 134
saint, 221, 345
St Anselm, 163–4
St Asaph, 144
St Athan, 139
    Hendre Wen, 139
St Augustine, 11, 133
St Bride (Brigid), 144
St Bride's Day, 144
St Brides-super-Ely, 112
St David, patron saint, 158, 329
St Davids, 58, 82, 98, 134

Cathedral, 33
    Lower Clegyr Farm, 98
St Fagans, 112
    Castle, 3
    Welsh Folk Museum/National Museum of History, 3, 112
St Helena, 170
St John the Evangelist, 98, 169
St Mary-on-the-Hill, Chester, 32
St Moling, 78
St Peblig, 170
St Sannan's Well, Bedwellty, 53
St Seiriol's Well, Penmon, 53
St Stephen's Day, 34, 81, 82–3, 89
St Valentine's Day, 83
Salic Law, 80
Salmau Cân, 22
salvation, 147, 307
Sames, Mr, 30
Sankey and Moody, hymns of, 98–9
satirical poems. 77, 167, 193, 207–9
Saturnalia, 7–8
Saturnus, 7
scaffold, 32
Scandinavia, 98
scarves, 89
Scotland, 81, 93, 98
    see also Flotta
            Orkney
            Shetland
            South Ronaldsay
            University of Edinburgh
sea *see* Garmon Seia
        Irish Sea
Second World War *see* World War II
Segontium (Caernarfon), 158, 329
Sergeant, 109, 125–6
'sergeants', 89
Sergius I, Pope, 158, 329
servants (female) *see* maids
Sharing Day, 64
Sharper, Oystermouth horse, 108, fig. 12
shawl, 108

sheep, 207, 227, 249
    sheep shearing, 28
shepherds, 24, 80
sheet, 108, 118, 130, 255
Shetland Isles, 81
shilling, 95, 259
shins, 115, 285
ship, 321
shit, 67
shoes, 29–30, 233
Shon Tewgoed, 115
shopkeeper, 57
shoulder, 77, 90, 262
Shrewsbury, 38
shroud, 96
Sianco'r Castell, 112–14, fig. 10
Siani, 122–3
sickle, 153
sieve, 319
silks, 263
silver, 241, 343
Simeon (Simon), 'Nunc Dimittis', 147,
    163, 307
sin 46, 125–6, 187, 305, 309
singing *see* songs
Siôn, 95
Siôn Efan, 147
Siôn pen y stryd, 94
Siôn Prys (d. 1640) of Caerddinen
    and Llwyn Ynn, 18
siprys, 66
Siwan (Judy), 85, 110–12, 118–19,
    125–6, 289
    tallest man plays, 111
skull *see* horse's skull
            Skull-giving
Skull-giving, 133
slater's carol, 15, 30
slates, 122–3
smoke, 66–7
snow (-drift), 134, 159, 207, 250–1,
    283, 331
social unrest, 18–19
socks, 64, 233

Sol Nant-y-ffin, 107–8, 279
Solva, 60, 95–6, 98
'Somer and Wynter', dispute, 32
Somerset, 2, 33
'Song of the Wren, The', 263
'Song to Celia', 158
songs (singers/singing), 5, 9, 21, 22,
    24, 25, 26–7, 28, 29, 64, 79, 81, 85,
    106, 115, 118, 119, 120–31, 132,
    149, 150–66, 189, 191, 195, 199,
    201, 205, 213, 231, 253, 255, 258,
    265, 267, 269, 275, 279, 281, 285,
    287, 289, 291, 293, 295, 297, 313,
    319, 331, 333, 342, 345
    bluff to sing for days, weeks,
        months, 269, 293
    see also cumulative songs
            feat-singing
            nasal singing
            riddle songs
            'Song to Celia'
            tunes
sorrow, 247
'Sospan Fach', 67, 182
soul cakes, 86
souling (song), 86
South American natives, 6, 9
South Carolina, 80
South Ronaldsay, Orkney, 81
sowens, 50
Spain, 31
Spanish Witch, 17
spectres, 17
spices, 48–9, 255, 257, 285
spirits, 57, 83
spiritual gifts, 25
Spring, 162, 247
    figure of, 4
    rite to welcome, 12
springs *see* wells
sprinkling water, 52–3, 85
stable lantern, 84
stable loft, 80
stabling *see* Mari Lwyd

stag, 152
stallion, 207
Stanley family, 98
stars, 32, 108–9, 127, 163, 271, 275, 344
stew, 95, 299
Stewley Orchard, Somerset, fig. 1
sticks, 63–4, 67, 80, 89, 95, 109, 110,
    131, 134, 151, 233
stiles, 115, 130, 150, 263, 275, 285
straw, 31, 89, 108, 130
    dressed in, 85, 134
strict-metre poetry, 57, 341–2
Suffolk, 83
sugar, 18, 86, 257
sun, 55, 163, 337
    solar magico-religious beliefs, 97
Sunday best, 109
supper, 209, 297, 300
'Susannah', 168, 182, 304–5, 311
Sussex, 2, 165
swallow (bird), 97
swan, 33
Swansea, 38, 110, 131, 249, fig. 12
sweethearts, 78–9, 88, 108
sweets, 243
swords, 81
    sword dancing, 11, 105
'Sybylltir', 149
Symonds, James, 102

T
T., R., 35–6,
table, 118, 319
Taff's Well, 112, 117
    Royal Oak, 117
tail, 108–9, 287
Tal-y-bont (Ceredigion), 62, 106, 241
tallow see candles
Tarian y Gweithiwr, 283
Taw rhag cywilydd, 324–5
tea, 52, 53, 56
Teifi Valley, 77
Ten Commandments, 55
    see also Mosaic Law

Tenby, 53, 85, 90–2, 98, 262
tenor voice, 297
Texas, 80
thanksgiving carol, 161
thatched roofs, 83, 131
thieves, 247, 269
Thomas, Ceinwen H., 117
Thomas, David, 'Dafydd Ddu Eryri',
    154–5
Thomas, Eliza, 84, 86, 89, 102
Thomas, John, Abercastell, 29–30
Thomas, Samuel, Gliniant, Trefeglwys,
    226–8
Thomas, T. H., Cardiff, 80, 84
Thomas, William, 'Brynfab', 139
threatening behaviour, 113
tin can, 135
tin whistle, 89, 112
Tir y Glyn, 17
toast, fig. 1
tobacco, 18, 151, 197
Tombs, J., 86, 95, 263
tôn deuair, 25, 149, 237, 243, 263,
    311, 343–4
tongue-twister, 154
Tonyrefail, 4
tooling see John Barleycorn
tooth, 28, 108, 123, 247
Tozie Mozie, 81
Traeth Bach, 217, 221
Trahaearn Brydydd Mawr, 77
Train, Joseph, 81
travel difficulties, 16–17, 35, 38, 60,
    115, 135, 150, 195, 237, 285, 319
    see also weather
Trawsfynydd, 28, 43, 203
Trealaw, 110–11, 116
Treberfedd, 31
Trecastell, 31
Trecefel, 57
tree (-s), 2–4, 47–9, 148, 150, 153,
    191, 211
Trefeglwys, 63, 228
Treforest, 112

Tregaron, 51, 57
Tre-lech, 56, 63
trencher, 197
Trevelyan, Marie, 133, 164–5
tri chwarter tôn, 197, 199
tri thrawiad, 149
tri thrawiad dwbl, 199, 325, 337, 345
'Tri Thrawiad Gwynedd', 183, 199,
    325, 337
tri thrawiad sengl, 189, 199, 205, 325,
    333, 337, 344–5
triban (-nau), 127, 149, 208, 273,
    279–81, 311, 344
Tripolos, 6
trivet, 31
tunes, 173–83
'Turkelony', 209
turnpike roads, 38
'twca a mynawyd', 95
Twelfth Day, 29, 89, 263
Twelfth Night, 1, 29, 78–9, 83, 106, 107
Twelfth Night (Shakespeare), 209
Twelfth-tide, 82
Tŷ Fry, Penrhyndeudraeth, 213–21
Tŷ yn y Bryn, 17

U
Ulster, 98
'Un cam i'r ceiliog ac un carw
    serchog', 153
'Un cam i'r tyrci ac un carw lysti', 153
'Un o'm brodyr', 152
'Un o'm chwiorydd', 152
unison, 297
University of Edinburgh, 81
    School of Scottish Studies
        Archives, 81
United States *see* America

V
Vaughan, Rowland, Caer-gai, 145, 147
vegetables, 108, 227
    see also potatoes
Venezuela, 9

venison, 18
Venus, 150
verse forms, 341–5
Vigil Chorus (Vigil lay), 121
village stores, 57
villains, 125–6
vineyard, 94
vintner, 32
violin, 118
    see also fiddle
virgin (virginity), 158–61, 170, 309, 333
    see also Mary, mother of Jesus
Vortigern *see* Gwrtheyrn
Vychan, Thomas, heir of Bylchwyn,
    145, 321

W
wagon, 90, 262
waiting stanzas, 121
Waldron, George, 81
wall, 118, 130
war, 8, 24, 38, 70
Warao language, 13
warmth, 197, 299, 313
'Warsel, Y', 107
'Washael, Y', 131, 183, 273
wasps, 191, 193
wassail bowl (cup/vessel), 3–5, 11–12,
    16, 36, 48–50, 134–5, 150, 158–60,
    165, 257, 271, 335, figs 2–4, 13
wassail procession, 152
wassail queen, fig. 1
wassailers, 2–3, 17, 19–20, 30
    anger of, 86, 273
    as learners of Welsh, 293
    attitudes of, 19–20
    blackened faces of, 89, 110–11, 134
    blessings bestowed by, 36
    bringers of gossip and news, 37–8
    by invitation, 55, 85
    contest for the house by, 274–7
    difficulties encountered by,
        see travel difficulties
        weather

evil wishes bestowed by, 66–7
gifts desired by, 24
girls hiding from, 275
give thanks and praise, 65, 127,
 273, 277
leader of, brings wassail cup and
 provides drink, 159
promises made by, 65
tunes expected/used by, 149
unappreciated visits by, 38
unworthy of wassail queen, 161
water sprinkled by, 52–3, 85
water, 52–3, 85, 209, 319
'Water and Wine', dispute, 32
wax, 163–4
weather
 fine, 247
 inclement, 17, 24, 26, 28, 59, 124,
  132, 150, 160, 166, 191, 193,
  227, 241, 251, 283, 289, 299,
  313, 315, 327
wedding, 8–9, 64
 recently married, 258
welcome, 197, 203, 205, 217, 273, 277,
 291, 337, 343
Welsh Folk Museum see St Fagans
Welsh Government, 70
Welsh learners, 293, 295, 301
Welsh St Donats, 112
Welsh traditional costumes, 132
wells, 52–3
 crop of the well, 53
Wentersdorf, Karl P., 83, 97
West Kerry, 85
wheat, 66, 227, 321
wheat flour, 50
wheeelbarrow, 119
Whiffen, T. W., 6
whip, 109
Whipo'r Celyn (Whipping the Holly),
 51, 72
whisky, 65, 83
whistle, 297, 301
White Horse of Uffington, 134

wick, 164
Wil Benji step, 279
Williams, D. G., 116
Williams, Ebenezer N., 'Gwernyfed',
 280
Williams, Edward, 'Iolo Morganwg',
 40, 49, 134
Williams, Jennie, 136
Williams, John, Bryngwenith,
 Pen-coed, 117, 140
Williams, Maria Jane, 267
Williams, Taliesin, 'Taliesin ab Iolo',
 267
Williams, William, Claypits Pottery, 5
Williams, William, 'Crwys', 38
Williams, William, Llandygái, 144
wimple, 211
windows, 118, 164, 315
 of wren house, 84
wine flagon, 325
winnow, 151
winter solstice, 7, 135
Wise Men see Magi, the
Wise Willee, 81
wits, 128, 149
'Wits o'r Sbaen' (Spanish Witch), 17
wolf, 152
woman (women), 64, 67, 84, 92, 94,
 109, 115, 118, 121, 147, 151, 159,
 164, 193, 195, 197, 203, 205, 211,
 257, 299, 305, 307, 309
 attempt to discredit, 133
 Fall and salvation by means of,
  147
 men dressed in clothes of, 85, 89,
  94, 111
 pretty girls, 255, 317
 women's responses to the Mari
  Lwyd, 274–7
 young girl in chair ceremony,
  158–61, 330–1, 332–3
 see also Ifin (Ivy)
   Mary, mother of Jesus
woodcocks, 30

wood, 90, 92–3, 108, 131, 211, 259, 261, 303
World War II, 70, 131
wren, 48–9, 77–104 *passim*, 252–63 *passim*
  as King, 263
  as Queen, 80
  as symbol of eros, 83
  bier (box/cage/coffin/house) for, 77–9, 82, 84, 255, fig. 9
  body parts and feathers of, distributed, 88–9, 94
  boiling and eating, 94, 95
  bones of, causing shipwrecks, 81
  burial of, in churchyard, 97
  collecting money to bury, 97
  exhausting and killing of, 83
  extent of wren cult, 98
  hunt song (-s), 34, 82, 83, 85, 252–63
  Irish wren parade, 95
  king of the birds, 87
  laying fourteen eggs, 96
  mock funeral for, 97
  multicoloured bier for, 96
  processional song of, 95–6
  protected status of, 87–8
  scarcity of, 96
  'Song of the Wren', 85, 86
  thirteen brothers of, 95–6
  visiting newly married couples with, 88
  wren-house, Marloes, fig. 9
  see also Hunting the Wren
    ribbons
    wrenboys
wrenboys, 85, 89, 94, 99
Wrexham, 38, 78

Y
yeast, 31
'Ymdaith Gwŷr Harlech', 183, 230–1
'Yn tŷ' (tune), 30
Ystrad Alun, 34
Ystradfellte, 56

Z
Zaunkönig, 87
Zebedee, 157